THE MEL
AND
THE ROSE

I must leave this bustling city to the busy city men —
Leave behind its feverish madness,
Its scenes of sordid sadness;
And drink the unpolluted air of Melrose once again!

— Roger Quinn

THE MEL
and
THE ROSE

VINCENT A. YZERMANS

THE MELROSE HISTORICAL SOCIETY
MELROSE   MINNESOTA

Library of Congress Catalog Number: 72-85819

Printed by Sentinel Publishing Company, St. Cloud, Minnesota in the
United States of America. Copyright © 1972 by Vincent A. Yzermans.
Nihil Obstat: Raymond H. Lang, *Censor Deputatus*.
Imprimatur: ✠ George H. Speltz, D.D., Bishop of St. Cloud,
June 9, 1972.

To The Memory Of

CATHERINE FRANCES FAHEY YZERMANS

17 December 1890 — 14 May 1971

Mater Amabilis

— A Daughter of Dakota County Who Gave A Son To Stearns County —

CENTENNIAL BOOK COMMITTEE

Reverend Raymond H. Lang, chairman

Rev. Monsignor Vincent A. Yzermans

Reverend Ralph Keller

Mr. Ernest Bergeron

Mrs. Marson Duerr

Mrs. Herman Hellermann, Jr.

Mr. Peter Jung

Mrs. Russell Lambert

Mr. Joseph Leach

Mr. Jesse Lovelace

Mr. Henry Loxtercamp

Mr. Craig Melville

Mr. Henry Moser

Mr. James Matchinsky

Mr. Bernard Schad

Mr. Lawrence VanHavermaet

Ms. Lucille Vincent

Mr. Norbert Weiss

INTRODUCTION

It is my privilege to introduce this volume to the citizens of Melrose. This volume tells of the outstanding achievements of this community's past pioneers and present residents who have created a culture and way of life that is both unique and enviable. The citizens of Melrose have created a way of life in the Sauk River Valley that has endured and developed into a shining symbol of the fruits of friendship among neighbors, hard work, determination.

The history of Melrose is not simply the story of a smaller community in central Minnesota. It is a story of people who created a community out of a wilderness. Every citizen of Melrose is rightly proud to be part of such a noble heritage.

I take special pride in drawing attention to four outstanding members of the Melrose community who represent Melrose in the finest tradition: Sister Celsa, Captain James Gallagher, Donald Otte, and Father Francis Julig.

In addition, I would like to pay tribute to this volume's author, Monsignor Vincent A. Yzermans. Through long hours of work and loyalty, this dedicated Minnesotan has made this his special project throughout the past year.

Finally, I would like to add one personal note. I have visited Melrose many times in past years. It is a wonderful community whose citizens are as warm and friendly as any I have had the honor of knowing.

WALTER F. MONDALE
U.S. Senate - Minnesota

May 25, 1972

GREETINGS

It was a distinct pleasure for me to be asked to send a message to the good people of Melrose upon the publication of *The Mel and the Rose*. I have quickly examined its contents and discover that it will be a work worthy of the city and the community of Melrose.

In our age when so many values are being questioned, so many traditions being scorned and so many of our institutions being ridiculed, it is heartening to find a city and a church join hands in producing a work of this nature. Someone has once said that we will not know where we are going until we know where we have been. Another person remarked that a rootless people is a godless people and a stable people is a wholesome people. Both sayings apply to this book. It reflects not only the genuine interest a community has in its past, and thus assures its future; it also reflects the wholesomeness of the people of Melrose because they are a stable people.

As a farmer now, and the son of a farmer in the past, I was pleased to see how much attention the author has given to the importance of agriculture in the history of Melrose. As a staunch advocate of rural living and a strong rural economy in our state and nation, I was further pleased to see how through the pages and experiences of the past one hundred years the balance between the farm and the city worked for the benefit of both. Melrose typified in the past what can be accomplished by business and agriculture joining hands as partners. This book is, in part, a record of that accomplishment.

As one who thinks of himself as a Christian man, I was delighted to see a good section of this book deal with the role of religion in the rural society. Those who read this book who are citizens of Melrose, and even those who are not of Melrose, will find in this section on religion the opportunity to recall fondly the many joys and blessings made available to us through the ministry of the Church. The young people who read this volume may laugh at some of the incidents recorded in this section; they may laugh as those of us of an older generation laughed in our younger days. And they, too, will have their turn to laugh at their present experiences when they grow older. Laughter is a religious experience, as the author points out throughout these pages.

My congratulations to the author of this book, Monsignor Vincent A. Yzermans as well as to his collaborators. He has the distinct gift to be at one and the same time both a rural pastor and a journalist. He has used his gifts well in producing a book of this caliber.

My wish is that all who read these pages will find in them gratitude to God for the past and resolution in the future "to make the best better."

JOHN M. ZWACH
Member of Congress

PREFACE

This is the story of a city, not a great city but a good city. On further thought, it is not the story of a city; rather, a story about people who lived in the city and the surrounding area. It tries to tell the story of people who formed a community in and around the banks of the Sauk River in central Minnesota. It is not a history of that city since its author lays no claim to being a historian. Nor is it a mere chronicle of events. The author would prefer to call it an interpretive story, similar in style to the chronicles of the Middle Ages. It is not fiction, although some of the incidents recorded may seem stranger than fiction. The facts are true and the events were real; the comments are simply the author's (no doubt sometimes unintentionally prejudicial) observations.

The title of this story is *The Mel and the Rose* which deserves a few words of explanation. Melrose was named after the ancient city and abbey of Melrose, Scotland. The coat-of-arms of the abbey was a mallet superimposed on the Cistercian rose, since the Cistercian monks were especially dedicated to the Virgin Mary. The city of Melrose, thus, is not only linked to an ancient city of Scotland but also to the honorable Benedictine tradition of prayer and work. The mallet represents the industry and commerce not only of the ancient abbey but also of the city of Melrose, Minnesota. The rose represents religion and culture, developed not only by the monks of Melrose Abbey but also promoted by religion and education in the new city of Melrose, Minnesota by priests, religious, educators and civic leaders in the course of the past one hundred years.

To some readers it may seem strange to have a centennial history of Melrose at this time. Some will recall that Melrose celebrated its centennial in 1958 with appropriate parades, dances and newspaper items. Others will rightly ask why there should be a centennial history at this time? The question demands a reply.

In July, 1970 Reverend Raymond Lang, pastor of St. Mary's Church, asked this writer to author a history of the parish. Since St. Mary's parish was an amalgamation of two previous parishes, St. Patrick's which was founded in 1872 and St. Boniface's which was founded in 1878, he felt it would be most appropriate to mark the centennial of the amalgamated parish of St. Mary's at this time. It was also noted that during the summer of 1972 that Melrose Senior High School was sponsoring a "homecoming" for all former graduates. It was this writer's conviction, that a history of a parish cannot be written apart from the history of a community. This writer further felt that a centennial history of Melrose could not be marked merely by the fact that Moses Adley appeared in the locality in 1857 and then disappeared for another year. If any event would signal the beginning of this community it would be the advent of the railroad which made its appearance in Melrose in 1872. Thus we determined that the centennial story of the Melrose Catholic parish should include a history of the community and the people who settled, developed and presently live in the community.

We then approached Mr. Bernard Schad, president of the Chamber of Commerce, with this idea. He agreed with our idea and shortly after an *ad hoc* committee was formed. Throughout the autumn of 1971 this committee met several times to discuss the nature, contents and progress of a centennial book. From week to week enthusiasm grew and more and more people became involved in the production of this work. As weeks grew into months more and more people became involved, filling out questionnaires, sending in old photographs, supplying information about "the good, old days." Before it was even realized this centennial book became a community enterprise, with neighbor calling neighbor to check out facts, with meetings of senior citizens to recall the early days, with individuals supplying information about families and business establishments. All in all, this book is a product of the love and concern of the citizens of Melrose and the surrounding area.

It was this writer's privilege to gather together this information and organize it as a unit. Needless to say, this book is inadequate in many ways. There are many events that should be recalled that are not recorded; there are many names of prominent people that should be mentioned who are not even suggested. There are, too, many historical items that should be included that are omitted. The writer pleads the reader's forebearance for three reasons. This book was conceived, discussed, researched and written in the comparatively short time of ten months by the writer and his collaborators, all of whom carried out a regular routine of work. Secondly, historians can only record information that is supplied by sources and in many cases there were many stories but few facts. If some names, events or business establishments are absent in these pages the omission is due to the lack of information supplied by the parties concerned. Finally, there is a vast chasm between historic facts and folklore. Many things that the writer has heard in the past ten months were most amusing and appealing. Lack of historical evidence, however, prevented him from including these incidents in this volume.

It is the sincere hope of this writer that present and future citizens of Melrose will take great pride in their heritage, both civic and religious. It is his further hope that those who read these pages will grow to appreciate not only what has been done but also what can be done. We have tried to present every facet of life along the banks of the Sauk River from the beginning to the present, including education, athletics, business, organizations, family life and customs, religious life and growth, agriculture and commerce. All such activities touch upon the life of every man and we hope this story will reveal the best of what has been, what is and what will be.

The final pages of this volume list the names of many people who have cooperated in the production of this volume. Unfortunately, some one or the other will be overlooked and for this human frailty the author apologizes. However, there are several collaborators who assisted more than others in the writing of this book. They deserve to be mentioned at this point for without their collaboraton this book could not have been written. They are Henry Moser, who is the chief author of the section on banking in Melrose; Norbert Weiss, who researched and wrote the chapter on education; Peter Jung, who researched most of the chapter on athletics; Gerald Klassen, who contributed the pages on prohibition; Joseph Leach, who researched the chapter on Indians; Mrs. Lambert Russell, who secured most of the research on organizations and whose previous history of Melrose was a great aid to the present writer. Father Raymond Lang and Mr. Bernard Schad were two guardian angels watching over the writer's shoulders all along the way. Last but by far the least, my father, my brother and my sisters and their families who surely must have despaired of me many times in the failure of performing the virtue of piety in order that this book would meet the deadline set last August.

Three other men who are most responsible for this volume must also be acknowledged at this point. A book of this nature is not possible without the assistance and support of local businessmen. Three men who secured that assistance are Bernard Schad, James Matchinsky and Henry Loxtercamp. When all is said and done they were not only the promoters but also the creators of this volume. The city and area will be indebted to them for their initiative and interest.

Times change. People come and go. Some values, however, remain. The faith, the industry, the creativity, the initiative that once created the community of Melrose remains. *The Mel and the Rose* is a worthy symbol of the good people who formed a people of God on the banks of the Sauk river a hundred years ago and their descendants who have enjoyed God's good earth for more than a hundred years.

VINCENT A. YZERMANS

May 1, 1972
St. Rosa, Minnesota

CONTENTS

BEFORE THE WHITE MAN'S BEGINNINGS

Lo, the poor Indian! whose untutored mind
Sees God in clouds, or hears him in the wind;
His soul proud science never taught to stray
Far as the solar wold or milky way;
Yet simple nature to his hope has giv'n,
Behind the cloud-topped hill, an humbler heav'n.

Alexander Pope, *An Essay on Criticism*

It is difficult to determine a specific date at which to start a history, but a point must be determined. It would probably be most logical to begin with a description of the origin of the terrain in the area and then turn to the inhabitants of that terrain.

During the many glacier or Ice Ages of the North American continent, it seemed that Minnesota was generally on the southern edge of each glacier that penetrated into the United States from the polar ice cap. Each time a glacier advanced and receded, it left its effect on the surface geography of Minnesota. Each particular glacier's effect on the land would probably hold interest only for the expert, so it is sufficient to say that the last ice age, called the Wisconsin glacier (about twelve to fourteen thousand years ago), left Minnesota with its present topography.

The river drainage system in Minnesota runs in three directions. The north-western part of the state drains toward Hudson's Bay through the Red River. The northeastern part of the state drains toward the Atlantic ocean through the Great Lakes and the St. Lawrence River. The southern two-thirds of Minnesota drain through the Minnesota and Mississippi rivers to the Gulf of Mexico. Among these three watershed areas are scattered the many lakes, which are simply depressions left by the last retreating glacier.

As far as present knowledge can determine, the first inhabitants of this area formed a culture known as the Paleo-Indian or Big Game culture. Specific dates are hard to pinpoint at this distance, but it is estimated that this culture existed up to about 6000 B.C. These people seem to have been in appearance somewhat like the modern Eskimo of the far North, who are most probably directly descended from the Paleo-Indians. They were most likely pushed out of the area by more aggressive and technically advanced peoples and migrated to the north.

Although the evidence is rather scanty, a few things can be known about the life of the Paleo-Indians. They were a nomadic hunting people living in small social groups, probably no larger than family units. The tools and weapons they used were of stone. The game that they hunted was the now extinct mammoth and giant bison. Although mammoth bones have been found in Minnesota, no spearpoints have yet been found with them, but it can be assumed from other evidence that they were hunted here. Giant bison bones were found in 1967 east of Melrose.

The Paleo-Indians did not use a bow and arrows for hunting, but used a device called an "atl-atl." This was simply a notched stick which gave greater power and accuracy to a thrown spear. Most of the projectile points found seem to be spear points. Besides these points, knives, scrapers and punches, all of stone, have been found in this area. The only human remains ever found from this time period in central Minnesota is a skeleton found in 1935 in the upper Sauk Valley. This "Sauk Valley Man" dates from the Paleo-Indian age.

The next definite step in the human history is called the Eastern Archaic period and dates from about 5000 B.C. to 1000 B.C. Generally speaking, this age is a continuation of the Paleo-Indian culture but with some definite advances in the exploitation of local resources. For example, during this era, the gathering of wild rice and the preparation of maple syrup seem to have been practiced. With less reliance on game alone, the Archaic peoples, were probably less nomadic than their Paleo-Indian ancestors. Also since they tended to localize themselves, the beginnings of cultural and tribal variations began to appear.

Marked advances in the manufacture of tools were made in the Archaic period. The stone implements found from this age show a greater degree of skill in workmanship. For example, rounded and smoothed shapes for hammers and mauls were common. The process of chipping a stone to a rough outline and then polishing it to its final shape began to make its appearance. Archaic cultures also show an introduction of woodworking tools such as axes, adzes, and scrapers.

Also during this period, the preparation and preservation of food became much more refined. The evidence for this is found in the presence of milling tools for the preparation of flour and pits for the storage of food. Although no pottery has yet been found from the Archaic period, certain rather advanced methods of cooking could still be accomplished: for example, stone boiling, the dropping of a hot stone into a bark or skin container of the food to be prepared.

Perhaps the greatest advance of the Archaic period was the use of copper. Nearly pure copper nuggets were taken from deposits around the northern Great Lakes and pounded and annealed into the desired shapes. This was not a true metallurgical process, since it did not require the smelting of ore, but it was a very significant advance. Copper did not completely replace stone as a raw material, since copper was not always available.

The technical advances of the Archaic age were obviously helpful to the people of the time in their daily lives, but they also had far greater consequences. The invention and refinement of tools and methods of food gathering also made daily living less demanding. This gave each "tribe" a chance to develop more intricate and complex methods of dealing between themselves and with their environment. For instance, it gave them a chance to develop a more elaborate system of burial which today provides the archaeologist with a useful way of piecing tribal information together. A burial site from the Archaic period is located at Brooten, Minnesota, so it is safe to assume that the Melrose area was also occupied by Archaic peoples.

The next stage in the early history of central Minnesota is called the Early Woodland Period and extended from about 1000 B.C. to 300 B.C. A very important feature of the Early Woodland age was the introduction of agriculture and the subsequent establishment of semi-permanent village sites. Agriculture was not too important a part of the Early Woodland pattern in Minnesota. The inhabitants, especially in northern Minnesota, continued to be hunters and gatherers. One important exception to this was the cultivation of tobacco. Artifacts from this period often include clay or stone pipes.

The most important advance at this time was the widespread use of pottery. The many varieties in shape, sizes and decoration have greatly helped archaeologists in pinpointing the date of any particular site. In general, the pottery of the Early Woodland period consisted of cone shaped vessels with a wide mouth and a curved lip. The pointed bottom was intended to be placed directly in a hearth, supported by stones, and a fire built around it.

Five general types of surface decoration are found on Woodland pottery: 1) the cord-wrapped stick, which was applied by rolling or dragging a short stick wrapped with a fiber cord across the surface of the vessel in various patterns; 2) the dentate stamp, which was produced by stamping the wet surface of a new clay vessel with the end of a stick carved with tooth-like patterns; 3) Punctate stamping was applied by simply using the plain end of a stick or cord to make small impressions in the outer surface of a vessel; 4) bosses were produced by pushing a rod or stick into the side of a vessel from the inside, causing small raised areas on the outside surface; 5) incised or trailed lines were simply scratched designs on the outer surface of a vessel.

Two general patterns of surface preparation are also found on the pottery of this period. These indicate in what manner the vessel was formed. First, a smooth surface shows that as the vessel was being made, it was shaped from the wet clay by hand. The second method, called the cord wrapped paddle, indicates that the final shape of the vessel was achieved by slapping the outside with a small paddle wrapped with fiber cords. The cords then left an impression on the entire surface of the vessel.

The Middle Woodland Period generally covered the years 300 B.C. to 1000 A.D. In Minnesota there is not a sharp distinction between the Early and Middle Woodland ages. However, in the Ohio valley, a brilliant civilization flourished at this time. This was called the Hopewell Phase and, even though Minnesota was a great distance from its centers in Ohio and Illinois, its advances still influenced the people here.

The most outstanding feature of Hopewell culture and the one most widely practiced in Minnesota was the detailed attention to burial practices. Up to this time, burial had been rather careless, due possibly to a rather hazy belief in an afterlife. With the growing influence of the Hopewell phase, much meticulous care was given to the burial of the dead. Generally speaking, the actual disposition of a body was accomplished in two ways. "Primary burial" meant that the body was buried whole soon after death. Most primary burials discovered have the body placed in an extended horizontal position with the entire body present. Quite often though the body is found in a flexed position with the knees drawn up under the chin. In either case, primary burials were intended to be the final resting place for the deceased.

On the other hand, "secondary burials" were the partial reburial of only certain portions of the body. In a secondary burial, certain parts of the body, usually the long bones of the arms and legs and the skull, were buried a considerable time after death. This seems to be the beginning of a practice of Algonkian peoples in historical times of holding a regular "Feast of the Dead" in which the remains of all who had died during a specified time were reburied in a common grave.

Whether primary or secondary burial was practiced, the graves were now more carefully constructed in mounds, due to the Hopewell influence. Burial mounds, of which there are an estimated 10,000 in Minnesota, varied in design and elaboration. Some were mounds of earth placed over a pit grave; some were constructed by piling earth over a crude structure of logs in which the body was placed. Some were simple and small, and others were intricately designed into the shape of animals.

The inhabitants of Minnesota remaining at this time were basically Woodland people with the additional practice of mound building. In the Melrose area lived a subculture called the Malmo focus which included roughly the middle third of the state. Malmo pottery found as grave goods show all of the five rim decorations, but generally have plain surfaces. Most of burials in the Malmo focus are secondary burials with the remains wrapped in a sort of bundle along with offerings of food, weapons and ornaments to accompany the dead in the afterlife. Malmo burials are generally mounds built over a body or bodies placed on the surface or in a shallow pit with earth piled above.

Technologically, the atl-atl (throwing stick) was gradually replaced by the bow and arrow as a weapon during this time. Most projectile points found from this time seem to be designed for an arrow tip rather than a spear point.

For the residents of the Melrose area today, an excellent example of Middle Woodland culture was discovered in October, 1963, on the northeast tip of Middle Birch Lake. During the construction of a trench silo on the Arnold Berscheid farm, a shallow pit burial was discovered. The contents of the pit consisted of six skulls, three sets of long bones, three decomposed mussel shells, and a complete pottery vessel (an unusually rare discovery). After confiscating the artifacts, the St. Paul Science Museum conjectured that this was a secondary burial bundle dating from about 900 A.D.

The three sets of long bones and three of the skulls were apparently the remains of three individuals who were intended to receive funeral honors. This is corroborated by the three mussel shells, probably intended as ornaments or eating utensils in the afterlife. The three remaining skulls were possibly trophies, the heads of defeated enemies, meant to enhance the glory of these three warriors in the hereafter.

The pottery vessel belongs to a particular type known as Onamia dentate and is a very good example of Middle Woodland pottery. The fact that it is unbroken suggests that it was made specifically to be a food container for a grave. Also its relatively small size indicates that it was a funerary piece rather than a practical household item.

The artifacts from the Berscheid burial now rest in relative obscurity in the St. Paul Museum of Science and Arts. The pot is displayed on a shelf with very little explanatory material to accompany it.

The Late Woodland Period covered the years from 1000 A.D. to 1700 A.D. During this time period, the Indians of northern Minnesota did not radically change their pattern of living. In the southern part of the state, however, a culture known as Mississippian predominated. The Mississippian culture is best characterized by its extensive use of agriculture and, consequently, the establishment of permanent villages. The usual native crops were grown: squash, beans, corn, and of course, tobacco. Toward the end of this period, the Mississippian culture was almost completely replaced by the Woodland patterns of hunting and gathering. Minnesota at this point was beginning to feel the first influences of the white man.

THE EUROPEAN INFLUENCE

At this time, it would be well to consider in more specific detail the climate, vegetation and animal life of central Minnesota with the arrival of the white man. Central Minnesota lies at the confluence of three types of habitat: pine forest to the north, hardwood forest to the south and east, and prairie to the west and south. Each type supports its own particular vegetation and game and in turn these each support a particular type of culture.

The southeast portion of Minnesota was originally an oak and maple forest gradually thinning toward the west into open prairie. This type of terrain developed a combination hunting-farming type of culture with more or less permanent village sites. The amount of time spent on either hunting or farming varied considerably depending on climate and other conditions from year to year. The arrival of the white man also greatly influenced the patterns of life. Whenever agriculture was practiced, the usual crops of corn, squash, beans and tobacco were planted. This was supplemented by fishing and hunting, usually small game and deer.

In the north, the typical woodland pattern prevailed: wild rice harvesting, fishing and hunting, impermanent village sites. Toward the west, the hunting pattern prevailed also, modified by the differences in terrain and animal life. The Plains people were much more nomadic.

The cultural patterns changed considerably after the arrival of the Europeans on the North American continent. Even though direct contact with whites was not frequent in Minnesota until after 1700, the European influence was felt before that time. Trade goods from the French outposts on the upper Great Lakes began filtering westward. Such items as iron kettles, arrowheads and axes, woven blankets, and glass beads quickly replaced pottery, stone weapons, skins and porcupine quills.

Three great innovations brought by the white men effected vast, relatively swift change in the way of life of the Indians of central Minnesota, and since this area was at the junction point of three different types of habitat, the changes brought about in the various peoples focused in conflict at this point.

The first in time of the three major changes brought by white men was the effect of the fur trade. As the demand in Europe for beaver fur grew, many Indian tribes (in Minnesota, the Chippewa) immigrated from their original territories into new more profitable hunting grounds. Since these new grounds were in most cases already occupied and the intrusion of the newcomers resented, warfare generally resulted. As was the case with Chippewa, these intruders were generally better armed with more modern weapons and therefore pushed the original residents out of their homeland.

The second great influence was the introduction of guns to the Indians. Aggressive hunting tribes were quick to take advantage of the new weapon for both meat-hunting and war. Different European nations vying for control of the rich fur trade country also were quick to capitalize on traditional tribal enmities and each armed the tribes who would best serve their respective national interests.

The third major change brought to the Indians by white men was the introduction of the horse. Originally brought to the Americas by the Spaniards in Mexico early in the sixteenth century, by 1700 the horse had multiplied fantastically in the wild state and populated much of the plains areas. The Indian saw the advantage of horses to a nomadic hunting existence and soon adapted it to their way of life.

These three influences all came to bear on the history of central Minnesota. In a capsule, the years from about 1700 to 1860 progressed in this fashion: the French fur traders on the northern Great Lakes engaged the Chippewa to expand from their original homeland north of Lake Huron toward the north and west around Lake Superior and to penetrate into the rich fur country of northern Minnesota. The Chippewa were armed with guns and powder by the French and steadily drove the native Dakota (Sioux) toward the west and south. In the meantime the use of horses was introduced from the west and south. Between the pressure of the Chippewa and the attraction of expanding their territories into the plains, the Dakota changed from Woodland culture into a High Plains buffalo hunting society.

THE DAKOTA

No treatment of the history of America west of the Mississippi river can be complete without some mention of the Dakota nation. In all the great Indian wars of the nineteenth century, the Dakota were the first to fight and the last to surrender. They bore the gradual encroachment on their homelands with patience and diplomacy until they would be pushed no farther, and yet they fought as fiercely and as honorably as possible until there was no more energy or land left to them.

To the average twentieth century white American, the mention of the Dakota nation summons up images of Sitting Bull and the Battle of the Little Big Horn. This is not an untrue or mistaken impression, but it is really only a small part of the Dakota people's relationship with the white man.

The Dakota originally occupied all of what is now Minnesota, eastern North and South Dakota, northern Iowa, and southwestern Wisconsin. Most of this area was almost exclusively Dakota, but a few smaller groups did occupy some areas within the present state boundaries, at least in the late seventeenth and early eighteenth centuries. According to the anthropoligist N. H. Winchell, the Cheyenne tribe once occupied the upper Minnesota and Red Rivers. The Iowas occupied the lower Minnesota river valley, the Omahas occupied the Mississippi valley below the mouth of the Minnesota river, and the Otoe lived in south central Minnesota. Apparently, these tribes all coexisted peacefully enough, either because the non-Dakota tribes were never large enough to cause trouble, or because the land could support them all. The Cheyenne, Omaha, Iowa, and Otoe all migrated from Minnesota in the eighteenth century.

The name Dakota means "The Allies" in their own language. The more common name "Sioux" is a French adaptation of the Chippewa "Nadowessiu," which means "The Snakes," a contemptuous term applied to the Dakota by their ancient Chippewa enemies. The Dakota refer to themselves as 'The People of the Seven Council Fires" because of their customary organization of the entire tribe into groups of seven. The seven major divisions of the Dakota all lived in Minnesota at the time of the first contact with the white man. They did not all follow the same pattern of life since the vast area they occupied varied greatly in the types of habitat it supported. The northern divisions followed the Woodland pattern as previously described; the southern divisions followed the woodland-agricultural existence and the western and southern divisions followed a plains type culture.

The seven divisions of the Dakota are the Mdewakanton, Wahpeton, Sisseton, Wahpekute, Yankton, Yanktonai, and Teton. Another tribe speaking the Dakota language but completely separate from the rest of the Dakota was the Assiniboin, who occupied the area north of Lake of the Woods. The Assiniboin were originally part of the Yanktonai Dakota, but legend says that early in the seventeenth century, a quarrel over a woman occurred and part of the tribe separated and moved north. Since that time the Assiniboin have been the enemies of the rest of the Dakota and usually allied themselves with the Cree and Chippewa of the north and east.

The Dakota language is divided into four main dialects. The Santee dialect was spoken by the Mdewakanton, Wahpeton, Sisseton, and Wahpekute. The Yankton dialect was spoken by the Yankton and Yanktonai. The Assiniboin spoke their own dialect related to the Yankton, and the Teton division, the largest in terms of both territory and population, spoke the western or Teton dialect. The differences in these dialects were not great enough to prevent understanding from division to division, but it has caused confusion among whites. The dialectal pronunciation differences can be seen by the variances in pronouncing the common tribal name: Santee – "Dakota"; Yankton – "Nakota"; Teton – "Lakota".

To turn to more specific matters, who were the inhabitants of the area where Melrose now stands? In all probability, it was one of the eastern bands of the Dakota. In 1679, Daniel Greysolon, Sieur Du Luth, an unlicensed French trader and adventurer, traveled southwest from a point on Lake Superior where the city of Duluth now stands. He visited a great village on Mille Lacs called "Izatys." This name seems to be a version of "Santee," or eastern Dakota. The people at Izatys called themselves Mdewakanton, which in the Dakota language means "People of the Holy Lake." Mille Lacs lake was considered by all bands of the Dakota to be a place of great religious significance, possibly the center of the world. Du Luth also mentioned visiting the Sissetons and Wahpetons twenty-six leagues (eighty-nine miles) from Izatys.

The following year (1680), Du Luth returned to Izatys and found Father Louis Hennepin, a Franciscan friar, a loosely-guarded prisoner of the Mdewakanton. Hennepin's reports confirm much of Du Luth's information and further adds that the location of the Yankton was to the north and the Teton to the west. Hennepin indicated that the Sisseton

MINNESOTA INDIAN TRIBES
IN CA. 1680

ASSINIBOIN

KILISTINO

(CREE)

YANKTONAI

CHEYENNE

SISSETON

YANKTON

MDEWAKANTON

TETON

WAHPETON

CHEYENNE

WAHPEKUTE

IOWA

OMAHA

YANKTON

OTO

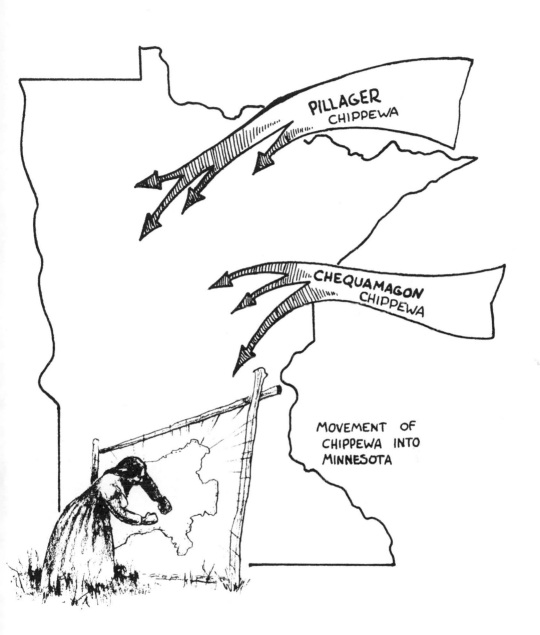

PILLAGER CHIPPEWA

CHEQUAMAGON CHIPPEWA

MOVEMENT OF CHIPPEWA INTO MINNESOTA

LAND CESSIONS IN MINNESOTA

1863 OLD CROSSING

RESERVATION

1854

1858

WINNABAGO RESERVATION

1847

1837

1825 TREATY LINE

1898

1863

Bison Antiquus.

Jerry Breth holding skeleton of Bison Antiquus.

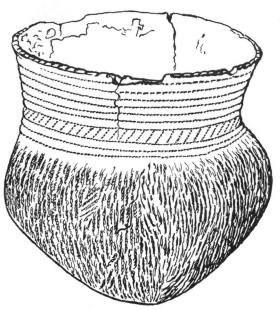

The Onamia dentate pottery found in a burial site on the Arnold Berscheid farm on the shores of Little Birch Lake.

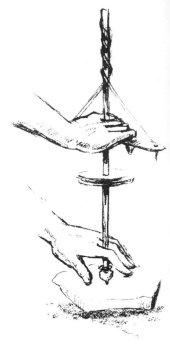

Fire-making with bow and arrow.

Indian artefacts: Drill point found in Melrose area by Lawrence Van Haevermaet.

Jean Kerfeld making an Onamia dentate pot at Melrose High School.

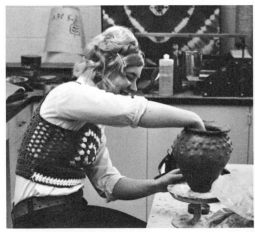

*An Indian peace pipe given by an Indian chief to
Rev. Victor Ronnellenfinsch, O.S.B.*

*Pottery shards found in the
Melrose area by Lawrence
Van Haevermaet, Kevin Blommel
and Ralph Petermeier.*

*Percussion method of
chipping arrowheads.*

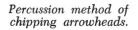

Chief Little Crow, leader of the Sioux uprising in 1862.

Fire-making with bow and arrow.

Arrowheads found in Melrose and the surrounding area.

The "big squeek" of the Red River Ox Cart train as it passed near Melrose about 1860.

A Red River ox cart as reproduced in 1887 in the NORTHWEST MAGAZINE.

Ox cart drivers pausing for a rest along the trail in 1858.

band lived north of Mille Lacs and the Wahpeton to the southwest. Adding up the information of both Hennepin and Du Luth, we can conclude that the immediate area of Melrose was occupied by the Wahpeton Dakota in the seventeenth century.

To summarize, the first part of the historic period in Minnesota (1634-1736) found Minnesota being occupied by the seven bands of the Dakota who gradually expanded to the west and southwest until they were virtually the only Indian tribe in the state. The reports of Du Luth, Perrot, Verendreye, Hennepin, and other French explorers distribute the Dakota bands in this way: the Sisseton in the northeast and north central lake areas, the Yankton and Yanktonai in the northwest, the Mdewakanton around Lake Mille Lacs, the Wahpeton along the upper Mississippi river between the Minnesota and Crow Wing rivers, the Wahpekute along the Minnesota river, and the Tetons in the Lake Traverse area.

THE CHIPPEWA AND THE NINETY YEARS' WAR

As stated previously, the Chippewa (Ojibway, Otchipwe) are relative newcomers to Minnesota. In the very early historic times, the tribe was simply small groups of hunters and gatherers who apparently led a limited migratory existence by traveling seasonally from the northern reaches of Ontario to an area north and west of Lake Huron. It is difficult to determine much about the Chippewa at this early date except that they were of the Algonkian language group and counted as close relatives the Potawatomies, Menominees, and Ottawas, and were more distantly related to the Cree (Kilistino), and Sauk and Foxes (these latter were considered to be one tribe).

After the first contacts with the French traders and explorers, the Chippewa moved toward the west around both the north and south shores of Lake Superior. The reasons for the expansion are many, but probably the most important are these: first, at least chronologically, was the pressure of the powerful Iroquois Confederation of the lower Great Lakes. This vigorous and well-organized coalition of tribes had rapidly taken control of the St. Lawrence valley by 1650. The Confederation represented one of the few times an alliance of Indian tribes worked successfully for a common goal for any great length of time. At the height of their power, the Iroquois exterminated, by conquest or assimilation, entire tribes of people (the Hurons, for example). It is quite possible that to avoid the same fate, the Chippewa moved out of the range of the Iroquois war parties.

A second important and more far-reaching reason for the westward expansion of the Chippewa was the inducement of the fur trade. Most of the remainder of the Chippewa's history is influenced by the development and decline of the fur trade.

The French were the first Europeans to come in contact with the Chippewa in their search for sources of fur. The explorers Nicolas Perrot, Pierre Radisson, and Medart Chouart des Groseillers report that in the period 1640-1670 the Chippewa were living in the region of Sault Ste. Marie and were known to the French as Saulteurs (People of the Sault). The Chippewa were quick to realize the advantage of their position and were soon acting as both direct fur suppliers to the French and as middlemen in trading with the tribes west of the Great Lakes. The material rewards offered to the Chippewa increased their wealth tremendously. With better weapons, tools, and utensils, it was a great deal easier for the Chippewa to expand into new territory than for those who did not deal directly with the traders.

In the later years of the seventeenth century, the Chippewa expansion consisted of establishing villages around Lake Superior. Since their original homeland is about equally distant from the Minnesota shore of Lake Superior no matter which route is taken, this expansion took two general directions: through what is now southern Ontario and through northern Wisconsin. In later years these two groups became important in the conflict with the Dakota.

From 1680 to 1736, the increasing contacts of Dakota and Chippewa were generally peaceful. Since the French traders had not yet penetrated far enough into northern Minnesota to deal directly with the Dakota, the Chippewa acted as middlemen. The southern group of Chippewa had their headquarters at Chequamegon and Keweenaw Bays on Wisconsin's Lake Superior shore. This group dealt with the Dakota to the southwest of Lake Superior. The northern Chippewa group, an aggressive people who became known in later years as Pillagers, used the Rainy River canoe route to reach the areas west of Lake Superior. While it lasted, this was an ideal arrangement for all concerned. The Dakota received French trade goods in return for furs; the Chippewa took a profit from transporting these furs to the French; the French had a nearly inexhaustible supply of fur, the price of which on the European market allowed a fantastic profit over the cost of the furs in trade goods.

In 1736 an event occurred that profoundly influenced the history of northern Minnesota. A French adventurer, La Verendreye, had started in 1731 to establish a direct route to the Dakota fur country. He had used the Rainy River route among the Pillager Chippewa, Assiniboin and Cree, and succeeded in placing outposts all the way west to Lake of the Woods. In 1736, a group of La Verendreye's men were ambushed and massacred on an island in Lake of the Woods. It is unclear as to who the attackers were, although it is believed that the war party consisted of both Dakota and Chippewa. (These tribes were at peace at the time.) At any rate, the French preferred to believe that the attackers were exclusively Dakota. This was a long awaited excuse for the French to "pacify" the area. The French then armed the Chippewa and induced them into a war with the Dakota that did not really end until the Dakota left Minnesota in 1862.

It was not only the intentional play of one tribe against the other that precipitated the long Chippewa-Dakota war, but it was one of a series of related causes. Even if La Verendreye's men had not been massacred, the war most likely would still have happened. The French were trying to establish direct contact with western tribes in order to increase the volume of the fur trade. This would eliminate the position of the Chippewa as middlemen. The Chippewa therefore reacted to place themselves at the richest source of fur, namely northern Minnesota. An alliance of Chippewa, Cree, and Assiniboin was formed and gradually the Dakota were pushed to the west and south. The ironic result of all this is that the fur trade suffered, and all concerned received less from it than previously.

As the Chippewa pushed into Minnesota, a general pattern developed: as the invaders advanced and the natives retreated, a large area of land was left between them, into which neither party could expect to enter peacefully. Since this all occurred slowly from about 1740 to 1830, this unoccupied "debatable zone" (the term used by historians) would become rich in game, and the stronger tribe would move into the area and the debatable zone would shift. Since during most of this time, the Chippewa were stronger, the debatable zone generally moved south.

To chronicle the entire story of the Chippewa-Dakota war would be impossible here. The war followed a pattern of Chippewa victories, periods of uneasy truce, and many ineffectual attempts by various white governments to establish a permanent peace. The advance of the Chippewa through Minnesota took two general directions, just as their original migration did into this new area. The Wisconsin Chippewa moved from their established bases at Chequamagon and Keweenaw into the area east of the Mississippi river. The Pillager bands, who had originally come into Minnesota from the north, now moved southward in the area west of the Mississippi river. This two-pronged movement caught the Dakota in a two front war which gave them no other choice but to retreat to the southwest.

The Wisconsin Chippewa established a village at Fond du Lac on the southwest tip of Lake Superior very soon after 1736. Fond du Lac then served as an important base for further forays into Dakota territory. One of the greatest victories the Chippewa attained was an attack on the three Mdewakanton villages at Lake Mille Lacs. Since the Chippewa were so well armed with French equipment, the Dakota were no match for them. According to Chippewa legend, the attackers crept up on the earth lodges of the Dakota and dropped bags of gunpowder into the fireplaces through the smokeholes in the roof. The Mdewakanton villages were completely destroyed, and the Dakota left their sacred lake forever. This event, called the Battle of Kathio, occurred about 1745 and was the most decisive battle of the war.

About four years later, another war party set out from Fond Du Lac and attacked a Sisseton and Wahpeton village at Sandy Lake, north of modern Aitkin. The attack was successful and formed a base for further Chippewa operations. Most importantly, since Sandy Lake is almost on the Mississippi river, the Chippewa controlled the main north-south route for transportation in hunting, trading and war.

The Dakota were not easily pushed from northern Minnesota. Several counterattacks were made but only a few were successful, and these only temporarily. In 1760, a large war party of Yanktonai assembled at Leech Lake to drive back the Chippewa. Unfortunately for the Dakota, they over-estimated their own strength and tried to attack three different Chippewa bases at the same time: Pembina, Rainy Lake, and Sandy Lake. The Yanktonai were defeated at all three locations and subsequently withdrew toward the River River valley and beyond.

After the withdrawal of the Yanktonai to the west, the Sisseton and Wahpeton moved south toward the Minnesota river, following the Mdewakanton and Wahpekute, who had left the north before them. The retreat of the Yanktonai seemed to cause an accelerated movement of the Dakota to the south. The Yanktonai then must have been a powerful bulwark against the Chippewa and when finally defeated opened the door to great advances by the Chippewa.

The retreat of the Dakota was not actually a panicky route. The desire for revenge by previously defeated Dakota bands led to sporadic warfare for a number of years after the Kathio and Sandy Lake disasters. In 1756 the French and Indian War broke out and somewhat altered the previous French policy on giving arms to the Indians. Since the French were now fighting the English for possession of North America, they attempted to arm any tribe who professed to offer their support. Consequently, the Dakota were now supplied with French guns. It is not difficult to see that Minnesota was a great distance from the main battles of the French and Indian War, and that the Dakota were about to use the new arms against the very available Chippewa and not against the distant British. This equalization in armament slowed down the rapid Chippewa advances.

The Mdewakanton had not forgotten the defeat at Kathio and in 1765 a revenge raid was dispatched up the Mississippi river from the mouth of the Minnesota river. The Dakota warriors were defeated in a fierce battle at the point where the Crow Wing river flows into the Mississippi river. The Mdewakanton and Wahpekute bands thereafter moved to the area south of the Minnesota river. One village, under Chief Wabasha, was established on the site of the present city of Winona.

A last attempt against the Chippewa by the Mdewakanton was made in 1773. The aid of the Sauk and Fox tribe of Wisconsin was obtained and the war party this time moved up the St. Croix river. The Chippewa were waiting at St. Croix Falls and defeated them, although reportedly not as badly as in previous battles.

At the outbreak of the American Revolution, a new phase in the Dakota-Chippewa war began. Both Dakota and Chippewa were allied with the British against the Americans and Spanish. This was a period of relative peace between the tribes, although the debatable zone remained between them. This debatable zone was a sort of no man's land that acted as a buffer between the Dakota and Chippewa. The period of spectacular Chippewa victories was over now and the debatable zone remained fairly stable in location and area for the next twenty-five years. At this time the debatable zone in Minnesota was approximately bounded on the north by a line that would connect the following locations: Taylors' Falls on the St. Croix river, Princeton, Milaca, the mouth of the Crow Wing river, Motley, Wadena, Detroit Lakes, and Georgetown on the North Dakota border. On the south the zone was bounded by a line that would connect the following: Afton on the St. Croix river, Anoka, Buffalo, Litchfield, New London, Morris, Graceville, and Brown's Valley. This places Melrose in the very center of the battlefield when there was war and in an unoccupied territory when there was peace.

The periods of truce were often quite incomprehensible to the white-men. A general truce did not mean that every village on the opposing sides would honor it, nor did a general state of war mean that everyone on either side took part in it. In periods of both peace and war, neutral tribes were often given safe conduct to hunt and trap in the debatable zone. Thus there are reports of hunting parties of Menominee, Winnebago, Sauk and Fox, and even the distant (southern Michigan) Potowatomies and Ottawa. Another factor in making the Chippewa-Dakota war a sporadic thing was the growing interest of the western Dakota in horses. The Teton Dakota had already left Minnesota by the middle of the eighteenth century and were being followed onto the plains by the Sisseton, Wahpeton, Yankton and Yanktonai. This movement to the west was also slow and irregular so that most of the remaining battles with the Chippewa involved the Mdewakanton, Sisseton and Wahpeton. (These last named lived in west-central Minnesota.)

This period of uneasy equilibrium was broken in 1797 when a band of Sisseton and Wahpeton (probably still smarting from the defeat at Sandy Lake fifty years before) attacked a band of Sandy Lake and Mille Lacs Chippewa who had been hunting on the Long Prairie river. This attack occurred somewhere near Cross Lake and was one of the few major Dakota victories. The Wahpeton and Sisseton killed at least forty and possibly up to sixty-five Chippewa and lost only five of their own. The Chippewa decided to permanently seize this section of the debatable zone and organized a settlement at Gull Lake under Chief Curly Head. The inhabitants of this settlement, for all practical purposes a Chippewa military outpost, were drawn from the bravest hunters and warriors of the area. In 1805, this band attacked and decisively defeated a Wahpeton and Sisseton camp on the Long Prairie river, capturing thirty-six Dakota horses. The area around present-day Little Falls and west to Long Prairie became undisputed Chippewa territory.

The debatable zone from 1805 to 1825 remained fairly stable and few real gains were made by the Chippewa except a gradual encroachment toward the west near the Red River south of Pembina, and southwest toward Ottertail Lake. The period was marked by raids from both sides of the debatable zone. No notable battles were reported and Dakota-Chippewa relations settled down to a fitful state of mutual but cautious hostility, occasionally flaring into actual battle.

The Sauk river lies at the heart of the debatable zone and is large enough to float a canoe any time it is not frozen. Its location and size make it highly probable that the Sauk was a main "war-road" between the Chippewa and Dakota. A rather vaguely documented battle occurred at Battle Point on Lake Osakis in the 1830's and another on the present site of St. Michael's hospital in Sauk Centre (date unknown). It is more than likely that other skirmishes occurred along the Sauk, possibly quite close to Melrose.

THE 1825 TREATY AND LAND CESSIONS

Up to this point in this narrative, it would seem that land occupancy in Minnesota was primarily a matter of conflict between the Dakota and Chippewa. There were other interested parties, however, particularly after the War of 1812. This unnecessary war permanently set the area of Minnesota as American territory. In the years following the War of 1812, white interest in the rich northern land grew steadily. Fort Snelling was established in 1819 as part of a vast plan to contain the Indian population, and although neither the Dakota or Chippewa knew it, their ownership of the land was being undermined.

The history of Indian treaties in this country makes disturbing but repetitious reading. Each treaty stated what seemed to be the best of intentions, but had within it the seeds of future trouble. The land cessions in Minnesota have the same insidious pattern.

The first formal treaty affecting the Indian nations of Minnesota was the treaty of Prairie du Chien in 1825. This treaty was ostensibly designed to prevent inter-tribal war in all of the northwest territories. The Dakota and Chippewa were only two of many tribes affected by it. The 1825 treaty attempted to halt inter-tribal wars by setting up boundaries between the warring tribes. This would probably have been sensible for European nations, but the idea of boundaries and land ownership was completely alien to the Indians' way of life. For this reason, the treaty was doomed before it was signed.

Upon retrospect, it can be seen that the writers of the 1825 treaty, knowingly or not, paved the way for future land-stealing. By setting up boundaries, the land is then divided into parcels which are much easier to deal with, especially since the owners of various parcels could then be more easily set at rivalry. "Divide and Conquer" may be an old trick, but it is effective.

The dividing line between the Dakota and Chippewa in Minnesota as set down by the Prairie du Chien treaty runs as follows: the line crosses the St. Croix river about ten miles south of Taylors Falls, extends west to the Mississippi river at Sartell, then runs west northwest to Lake Carlos near Alexandria, then nearly north to Ottertail Lake, and almost straight northwest to the mouth of the Buffalo river north of Moorhead. The line was surveyed in the 1830's, but the survey never reached its conclusion. The Army survey team gave up somewhere in west central Minnesota, claiming fear of Indian attack. Both the Dakota and the Chippewa were contemptuous of the line and each claimed that the other was violating it. There is considerable doubt that the majority of Indians even understood what the line's purpose was, much less approved of it. The real reason, of course, was that the line would establish nominal ownership of the land for future treaties.

Additional land cessions began in 1837 and continued rapidly for the next thirty years. In 1837, the land east of the Mississippi river was ceded as far north as an east-west line from the mouth of the Crow Wing river to the Wisconsin border. The portion north of the 1825 treaty line was ceded by the Chippewa, the southern portion by the Dakota.

In 1847, the Chippewa ceded a tract of land bounded by the Mississippi river on the east, a line from Ottertail Lake to the Crow Wing river on the north and the 1825 treaty line on the south and west. This area includes Melrose on its extreme southern edge and was intended to be used as a reservation for the Winnebago of Wisconsin. The establishment of this Eastern Woodland people in a marginal woods-prairie region was intended to act as a buffer zone between the warring Dakota and Chippewa. It was also an admission that the Prairie du Chien treaty had been a failure from the start.

The Winnebago are a member of the Siouan language family whose original homeland was in central Wisconsin. They were woodland hunters and never caused any real trouble to the American government. As pressure for the rich farm and timberland of Wisconsin increased, the Winnebago were moved to an area of northeast Iowa and southeast Minnesota. When it became apparent that the 1825 treaty line was not fulfilling its purpose of keeping peace between the Chippewa and Dakota, the Winnebago were removed again to the area ceded by the Chippewa in the 1847 cession. This was to become known as the Long Prairie Reservation. The actual reservation boundaries as stated in the treaty were as follows: from the mouth of the Crow Wing river up the Crow Wing to the mouth of the Long Prairie river, up the Long Prairie river to the 1825 treaty line, along this line in a southerly direction to the head of the Long Prairie river, then directly overland to the source of the Watab river, down the Watab to the Mississippi river and then up the Mississippi river to the mouth of the Crow Wing river. This places Melrose just within the southern border of the reservation area.

The seven years during which the Winnebago occupied the Long Prairie Reservation were filled with discontent and turmoil. The agents responsible for the move of the Winnebago, H. M. Rice and E. J. Fletcher, were at a loss as to why the Winnebago were dissatisfied. As far as they could see, the Indians should have been profoundly grateful for the gift of valuable agricultural land. Apparently the agents thought that removal from their "perpetual" homelands three times in twenty years should win the Winnebago's undying friendship for the government. The difficulty was mainly a complete and nearly deliberate ignorance on the part of the government of the Winnebago viewpoint.

Their culture was not an agricultural one, but a semi-nomadic hunting type in which women were expected to do any agricultural work and men were expected to hunt and trap.

When the Winnebago arrived at Long Prairie, one chief is said to have commented, "This place is good for only frogs and mosquitoes." Fletcher and Rice, however, doggedly continued to try to "civilize" the Winnebago and fill them with their own Victorian attitude toward work and reward. Farming is what the land was intended for and farmers the Winnebago would be, whether they wanted it or not. Constant dissatisfaction with the government's plans for them led the Winnebago to a drifting type of existence. Several bands stayed at Long Prairie and made a half-hearted attempt to become farmers. A few bands moved to the west bank of the Mississippi near Sartell, in order to be near a trading post. The agent stubbornly followed them and set up model farms on the Watab Prairie, much to the amusement of the Indians. A third group managed to travel from Minnesota to Iowa and Wisconsin and were constantly being apprehended by the military and returned to the reservation.

The Winnebago were peaceful people and never caused any trouble except to embarrass Governor Ramsey. They did not act as he had predicted and diminished his reputation for intimate knowledge of Indians. His explanation for the failure of the Winnebago to prosper in Minnesota was to blame traders in Wisconsin for selling liquor to the Winnebago. This excuse is a little lame, considering the distance from Long Prairie to Wisconsin.

The Winnebago stayed at Long Prairie for seven years (1848-1855). They petitioned in 1852 to be moved to an area north of Crow River in Wright County. There was some objection to this since this land was recently ceded by the Dakota and most likely some speculators had an eye on it. Nevertheless, some of the Winnebago were moved there, but it was not considered a permanent move. In 1855, the Winnebago were again moved to a reservation at Blue Earth, Minnesota, which was to be their "permanent" home. The official reports of the time all indicate that each move was met with complete satisfaction on the part of the Indians. It is difficult to explain then the constant desertions and petitions for satisfaction that accompanied each move.

The final chapter in the story of the Winnebago in Minnesota ends with the Uprising of 1862. The Winnebago were accused of complicity with the Dakota and their lands were taken from them. There was no proof of Winnebago participation but a condescending government thought it best to remove them from the hostility of their white neighbors. The Winnebago were moved to Fort Randall, Dakota Territory, and then again to Nebraska. About half of them eventually did find a permanent home; they managed to drift back in small groups to their ancestral land in Wisconsin.

After the 1847 cession establishing the Winnebago reservation, the Chippewa made several more land cessions in the next several years. In 1854 a large section of northeast Minnesota was ceded, and a year later a tract in the north central area was ceded. The last Chippewa cession was the extreme north west corner of the state ceded over in 1863 by a treaty called the Old Crossing Treaty which was signed at Red Lake Falls. An area between the Old Crossing Treaty cession and the 1855 cession was left for the Red Lake Reservation.

The cessions made by the Dakota were not piecemeal grants but rather cessions of huge tracts of land. With the formation of Minnesota territory in 1849, the demand for land, particularly agricultural land, rose spectacularly, and pressure was brought to bear on Alexander Ramsey, the first territorial governor, to obtain land for white settlement. With his reputation at stake, Ramsey induced the Santee bands of the Dakota to sign away most of their land south of the 1825 treaty line. The Dakota chiefs were reluctant to sell their land, but Ramsey convinced them that they needed the money. The price for the treaty did not at first seem unreasonable ($1,665,000 to be split between the Sisseton and Wahpeton, $1,410,000 to be divided between the Mdewakanton and Wahpekute) and Ramsey impressed on them that they had run up a huge debt to various traders. The Dakota had no way of checking the accuracy of the traders' claims, so of course many of them were highly padded. Besides, Ramsey had also promised huge commissions to various agents who helped persuade the Dakota to sign the treaty.

Ramsey's political game was obvious. Being the first territorial governor meant that a long successful political career could lay ahead of him. The amount of money offered to the Dakota was huge in comparison to the other land cession treaties, but most of it was intended for white men's pockets.

In July of 1851, the Sisseton and Wahpeton bands signed the treaty at Traverse des Sioux on the Minnesota River, and a month later the Mdewakanton and Wahpekute signed a similar one at Mendota at the mouth of the Minnesota River. The terms of the treaty allowed appropriations for education, agricultural equipment, and some cash payments. The balance was to be put in trust with the United States government, the interest to be paid at five percent annually, with the principal to be paid off in fifty years. The terms sound generous but two stipulations in the treaty made the whole thing a farce: first, the payments due to traders' accounts would be deducted from the total due the Indians; secondly, all terms of the treaty could be abrogated at any time at the discretion of Congress or the President.

What was left to the Indians was a strip of land twenty miles wide on either side of the Minnesota River from New Ulm to Lake Traverse. The portion below the mouth of the Yellow Medicine River was assigned to the Mdewakanton and Wahpekute, the upper portion to the Sisseton and Wahpeton. For thus relinquishing half the state to the government, the Indians were actually paid practically nothing.

The Dakota were very unhappy with the terms of the treaty once they understood its implications. Nonetheless, most of them made a sincere effort to adapt from their old buffalo hunting culture to a white agricultural society. Many began to learn English, became Christians, and adopted the white man's manner of dress. It was not too long, however, before even the narrow strip of reservation began to be eroded away by white squatters. A delegation of Dakota went to Washington in 1858 to obtain justice but the result of their efforts was that the northern half of their reservation was taken from them. They were allowed thirty cents per acre for the confiscated land, but after the payment of the usual traders' claims, there was nothing left.

The result of all this shameful thievery was the famous Sioux Uprising of 1862. The details are fairly well known and do not have to be recounted here. Most of the action of the 1862 Uprising occurred in southern Minnesota. However, whites in all relatively isolated areas lived in mortal terror of Indian attack. A military post was established at Sauk Centre in the winter of 1862-63 not so much for the actual protection it offered, but more for the confidence it inspired. The uneasiness of the settlers in the Stearns County area was compounded by fear of attack by the Chippewa from the north. Although the Chippewa were long-standing enemies of the Dakota, the warlike Chippewa chief Hole-in-the-Day (one of many Chippewa chiefs by that name; in Chippewa—*Bugonaygeshig*) managed to gain enough followers to cause much worry along the northern frontier. Although he could not induce his followers to attack the agency at Gull Lake, his band did enough plundering around the area of Fort Ripley and Crow Wing to cause the settlers in the area to flock to the fort for protection. Hole-in-the-Day's war was short-lived and a council of Chippewa chiefs settled all difficulties. Eventually Hole-in-the-Day was killed by his own men.

The immediate result of the 1862 Uprising was the expulsion of all the Dakota from Minnesota. The active participants fled west to join their Teton and Yankton relatives or escaped to Canada where many of their descendants still reside. The many Dakota who took no part in the war were moved to a reservation in Nebraska. Some of the leaders paid for their actions with their lives. Thirty-eight Santee were hanged at Mankato after a doubtful trial. Shakopi (Little Six) was kidnaped from his refuge in Canada and brought to Fort Snelling for execution. Ta-Oyate-Duta (Little Crow) was shot near Hutchinson after returning from Canada to obtain horses. Wamditanka (Big Eagle) spent several years in a military prison in Davenport, Iowa.

Although the 1862 Uprising marked the end of the Dakota in Minnesota, it was in other ways a beginning. For the next twenty-eight years, the Plains Indians fought with desperation to keep from being swallowed in the flood of white settlers. It did not finally end until the murder of Big Foot's band of Dakota in December, 1890 at Wounded Knee, South Dakota.

SOURCES

Bray, Edmund C. *A Million Years in Minnesota*. St. Paul, The Science Museum, 1962.

Brings, Lawrence M. *Minnesota Heritage*. Minneapolis, T. S. Denison and Company, Inc., 1960.

Brown, Dee. *Bury My Heart at Wounded Knee*. New York, Holt, Rinehart and Winston, Inc., 1971.

Heilbron, Bertha L. *A Pictorial History of Minnesota*. St. Paul, Minnesota Historical Society, 1958.

Hickerson, Harold. *The Chippewa and Their Neighbors: A Study in Ethnohistory*. New York, Holt, Rinehart and Winston, Inc., 1970.

Johnson, Eldon. *The Prehistoric Peoples of Minnesota*. St. Paul, Minnesota Historical Society, 1969.

Lettermann, Edward J. *From Whole Log to No Log*. Minneapolis, Dillon Press, 1969.

Mitchell, William Bell. *History of Stearns County, Minnesota*. Chicago, H. C. Cooper, Jr. and Co., 1915.

Pierce, Parker I. *Antelope Bill*. Minneapolis, Ross and Haines, 1962.

Sandoz, Mari. *Crazy Horse, the Strange Man of the Oglalas*. New York, Knopf, 1945.

Schmitt, Martin F. and Dee Brown. *Fighting Indians of the West*. New York, Scribner's, 1948.

Winchell, N. H. *Aborigines of Minnesota*. St. Paul, Minnesota Historical Society, 1911.

 THE MEL
AND
THE ROSE

CHAPTER ONE

BY A CREEK CALLED ADLEY

The wheels of progress have passed on;
The silent pioneer is gone.
His ghost is moving down the trees,
And now we push the memories
Of bluff, bold men who dared and died
In foremost battle, quite aside.
—Author Unknown

This story, as all good stories, must have a beginning and it begins with a man named Moses. Not the Moses of biblical times who led his people from bondage to freedom, but a latter Moses who was also in search of freedom and wealth. His name was Moses Adley and he came, like the biblical Melchisadech, out of nowhere and cast his eyes upon a richly wooded valley along a river that a later generation would call the Sauk. He came on a wintry day, January 10, 1857, and may have viewed the valley from the hillside that crowns the present city of Melrose from that point on County Road 13, approaching from the south and the already budding settlement of Meirc Grove. Or he may have come from the east, through the industrious village then called Oak and now named New Munich, following the ox cart trail from St. Cloud, already a supply depot for the upper midwest area of the new nation.

We really do not know how or why Moses Adley came to this then unknown and undesired part of a territory created by an act of the Congress of the United States in 1848. This new territory was called Minnesota by its inhabitants, the land of sky-blue-waters. We only know that Moses Adley viewed this spot on a cold day in January, 1857 and then went his way, not to return for another year.

In 1857, after a decade of revolution in Europe, there were few citizens in the nation and the world who did not feel that the world was

3

turning upside down. Karl Marx had published his *Communist Manifesto* a decade before and it was still the talk of the intellectuals on the continent. A brilliant, young politician, Otto von Bismarck, was beginning to flex his muscles in Germany and was already beginning to be the dread of many solid German citizens. Pio Nono in Rome, who first wooed the liberals, was now coming to fear them and well he knew that the fate of the papal states hung in the balance. England, in spite of Charles Dickens' novels of social protest, was engaged in an industrial revolution that would ultimately transform both the face of the nation and ultimately the world. The ugliness of the cities was showing its face in the industrialization of the continent. It would be only a matter of time when the same industrialization would produce for later generations a world unfit for human life.

Russia, too, was having its internal troubles. Nobody thought much about this "holy mother" in those days of daring and do; most people felt that the Romanov's had everything tightly under control. The seeds of dissent were already sown and it was only a matter of time before rebellion would raise its clenched fist. The neighbors of the United States to the South were in no better condition. Rumors of war and real wars in fact were being carried out by Latin American generals, each of whom thought he was the great liberator of his nation. And the Orient? Who at this time ever thought of that vast closed world, populated by yellow people who even then made up at least a third of the human race? Admiral Perry had not as yet appeared at the ports of Japan.

If conditions abroad appeared uneasy, the situation in the nation held no brighter promise. There was talk about the Lincoln-Douglas debates—but few, if any of the local gentry in Central Minnesota were too concerned. They knew about the free-state and the slave-state national conflict, for this had been a crucial factor in admitting the Minnesota territory into the union. The Missouri Compromise would leave the Minnesota pioneers cold, for it had no bearing—as they saw it—on their life. What the settlers chiefly wanted was a good price for their produce and a better and more economical means of getting that produce to market.

Of course, this frontiersman heard about the national slavery debate as he visited the local market or saloon, but the question did not involve him personally so he was not too much concerned. He did not, however, accept the institution of slavery, for he was an enlightened Yankee and had heard about, if not read or seen, *Uncle Tom's Cabin*. He was very interested in the Indian treaties because he was a part of the wholesale land-grab that the United States government was engaged in at the expense of the Indian people. With most of his contemporaries he was elated when he heard of the various government treaties that drove the redman further into oblivion, as depicted on the seal of the state of Minnesota, for it meant more cheap land for the white man. Even the effects of the economic depression of 1857 escaped him because as a frontiersman he was concerned chiefly with clearing the land and providing for the needs of his family.

If we return to Moses Adley we might better understand the frontier situation. He returned to the Melrose area in 1858, the same year that Minnesota was admitted as the thirty-second state of the Union, and settled on section thirty-six, the present site of the city of Melrose. With him came his brother, Warren, and two friends from the state of Maine, Robert and E. C. Wheeler. Contrary to present opinion, they did not settle in section thirty-four (near Adley Creek) but inhabited the area that now comprises the city of Melrose.

The Adley brothers and the Wheelers began clearing the land, building rugged log houses and engaged in farming. They were among the first citizens of the newly-created state of Minnesota as well as of the new county of Stearns. The present area of Stearns County was originally a part of Dakotah and Wahnahta counties, two of the original nine counties created by the territorial legislature on October 27, 1849. In 1850 the area of Stearns county was apportioned to the new county of Cass.

It was merely nine years from territorial status to statehood when the new county of Stearns and the community of Melrose would fulfill the prophecy of Governor Alexander Ramsey when he spoke of the rapid changes taking place throughout the area as "this shorter probation between the bud and the green tree of empire." Along with twenty-five other counties, Stearns county was created by an act of the territorial legislature on February 20, 1855. Originally the county was intended to be named Stevens, in honor of Governor Isaac I. Stevens of the Washington territory, who had conducted the railroad survey that ultimately brought the Great Northern Railroad through the center of the county. However, when the bill creating the county was finally presented to the state legislature the name of Stevens had inadvertently been replaced by Stearns and in such a form the bill was passed.

Charles T. Stearns, for whom the county was named, at the time resided-in St. Anthony Falls and was a member of the territorial council. Subsequently another county in the state, with Morris as its center, would be named to honor Governor Stevens. A year after the creation of the county Charles Stearns moved to St. Cloud, founded the Stearns House, and for many years was actively engaged in the development of the county. In spite of an attempt years later to move the county seat to Albany, St. Cloud continued to be the seat of local government and the largest of the three cities in the county, the other two being Sauk Centre and Melrose.

When Moses Adley and his associates settled on the banks of the Sauk River he found himself a member of a newly-created county which comprised 26,880 acres with an average elevation of 1,275 feet above sea level, and within an area that was almost the highest elevation in the county. He saw a river bank covered with timber, oak, pine, maple and elm, through which the Sauk River entered from the southwestern part of the future township and, flowing through his land, left the future township site in a southeasterly direction. He noted, too, that the soil was chiefly a light, sandy composition and rich for agricultural development. He further noted a creek flowing into the Sauk River from its source at Lake Sylvia and which today is called Adley Creek—the only remembrance we have today of the city's founder. When he surveyed the area he noted a prairie covered with timber and brush with out-croppings of rock. The drainage of the surrounding land, as well as its altitude, gave the area about one and a half times longer growing season than that of the latitude of St. Louis. The dryness of the climate was also attractive, for it would prevent the lassitude that sultry southern climate would produce among its inhabitants. Finally, even on that cold day in January, 1857, he would take notice that the coldness was dry and not a debilitating damp, chilling coldness that one suffers in a more temperate zone.

Moses Adley, however, was not the first white man to view the Melrose area. It seems that as early as 1838 the famed French explorer, J. N. Nicollet, listed the Melrose area on his maps of the Sauk River valley. He recounted that on an exploration expedition with the Sioux Indians he crossed the "second rapids" of the Sauk River which could well be the present dam in Melrose. The Sauk River, although but a small stream on a map of the world, was most significant in the development of the city. Rising out of Lake Osakis and flowing into the Mississippi near Sartell, Minnesota, it recalls the Indian origins of this area. Before a meeting of the Stearns County Old Settlers Association in 1897, Judge L. W. Collins gave this explanation for the name of the river:

"Among the Sioux the tradition is that both river and lake were called O-sa-te, which in their language means the fork of a stream or road. Although this tradition is not very well authenticated, its truth may rest on a solid foundation, as you will discover when you compare the pronunciation of this word with that by which the lake and river have always been known to the Chippewas. Assisted by the late H. P. Beaulieu, one of the best Chippewa interpreters, I learned from Kay-she-aush, Key-she-aush and Zhe-bing-o-goon, patriarchs among the Leach lake band, that the river was never known to the Chippewas by any other name than the O-sau-gee, while the lake was O-sau-gee lake, the fact being that after the Sioux were compelled to remove their habitation from that part of the Mississippi valley north of the Rum river, and while the country was still debatable territory between the Sioux and the Chippewas and the scene of many a conflict, five Sacs, refugees from their own tribe on account of murder which they had committed, made their way up to the lake and settled near the outlet upon the east side. . . . The Sacs Indians were known to the Chippewas as O-sau-kees. . . ."

But even before the white man came, the present area of Melrose was but a dot on the map of European powers. At one time the present area of Melrose was under the dominion of the Spanish kings (1492-1682); under the kings of France (1682-1762) again under the kings of Spain (1762-1801) and, by secret treaty returned to the king of France for one day. On March 10, 1804 Melrose became part of Louisiana territory and came under the flag of the United States. In 1835 the Melrose area became part of Crawford county, Michigan, and the following year was annexed to the newly created Wisconsin territory. Three years later, in 1838, Melrose became part of Iowa territory and only in 1849 did it become a part of the new territory of Minnesota.

In 1853 the United States government authorized a survey to be taken for the building of a railroad that would reach to the Pacific Ocean. Major Isaac I. Stevens, the same man for whom the county should have been named, led his men westward from St. Paul, passing through the present area of Melrose where one of his men noted that the area was infested with mosquitoes and was nothing but an abominable wasteland. Another survey party passed through the area at about the same time the Adleys and Wheelers arrived. The territorial legislature appointed three commissioners, L. M. Ball, William Kinkead and J. T. H. Barrett to survey a wagon road that would begin at St. Cloud (running thereby the most direct and feasible route. . .to Breckenridge, on the Red River of the North.) This road followed old U. S. highway fifty-two. For their services the commissioners each received three dollars a day. A member of this party wrote in later life:

"The surveying party left St. Cloud May 13, 1858, spending the first night at the Nathan Lamb farm, on Sauk river. After leaving St. Joseph they plunged into woods which were an interminable succession of windfalls, making progress so difficult that on some days but little more than a mile of the proposed road was located. No means for the transportation of supplies had been provided, each member of the party carrying not only the tools or instruments his duties rendered necessary, but 'packed' a part of the cooking and sleeping equipment. Both were of the very simplest character. There was no tent, and when the rains fell and the floods came there was neither escape nor protection from the down-pour. Camp fires were built, around which the tired party gathered for the night's rest, the howls of the wolves, which infested the woods, being the lullaby for their slumbers."

Long before the territorial survey party undertook its task, however, the area of Melrose was along the route of one of the most fascinating roads of international commerce. For some thirty years the Red River ox carts, originating in Pembina, North Dakota, had been carrying precious cargo of furs from the great northwest to the thriving commercial centers of St. Paul and St. Anthony Falls. Shortly after the establishment of Fort Snelling in 1819 three ox cart trails were developed. One trail followed the Red River of the North south to the Minnesota River and along that route to Mendota, then called St. Peter. Another trail, called the Woods Trail, followed a route from present-day Crookston to Crow Wing on the Mississippi, to Sauk Rapids and then on to St. Paul. The third trail followed the Red River to present day Breckenridge and then across the prairie, following the Sauk River south of the present site of Melrose toward Richmond, through the forest openings near Jacobs Prairie, St. Joseph, St. Cloud and down to St. Paul on the east bank of the Mississippi.

The Red River ox carts were heavy, cumbersome, two-wheeled carts made entirely of wood. Wooden pegs and rawhide thongs held the carts together. One writer has described them as follows: "The two wheels on which the body of the cart rested were solid disks of wood, five feet across and three inches thick. They were of wide tread to prevent the heavily loaded cart from cutting too deeply into the ground or sinking when crossing the streams. . . . The body of the cart was simply a platform laid upon a crosspiece with stakes standing up at the sides—in a sort of hay rack style."

Early historians have described the drivers of those ox cart expeditions. They were half-French and half-Indian in ancestry, wise in the ways of the forest and ignorant in the ways of the white man, superstitious and happy-go-lucky natives of the Pembina region. They were men with flashing eyes, vivid smiles and a native grace that made the observer aware that they belonged to a special, chosen race of international enterpreneurs whose simplicity belied their native intelligence. They traveled in ox carts trains of from fifty to a hundred and fifty carts camping along the way as the spirit and the time of day dictated. When and where they camped they frequently put on a show for the local citizenry, for they were by nature exhibitionists. The Rev. Elgy V. Campbell of St. Cloud, writing in 1864, observed, "On a pleasant evening the young men on ponies gave free exhibitions of their horsemanship, on the prairies back of town, and did some wonderful tricks from the backs of their horses."

Although the Red River ox cart trains did not pass through Melrose, they passed close enough to make the local citizens of that time refer to their passage, as citizens of other villages did, as "the time of the big squeek." This referred to the exceptionally loud and startling noise that the ox carts would make because they had no lubricants and the turning of their wheels could be heard for miles around as they passed through the vicinity. Writing about the Red River trail, William Bell Mitchell makes the following observations:

"Two made the journey from Pembina to Mendota, 448 miles, in 1842, being in the employ of Morman W. Ittson, who later acquired much wealth and became one of the leading citizens of Minnesota. The enterprise began with six of these carts, the number increasing in the next seven years to one hundred two and in 1858 there were six hundred. They created the thoroughfare known as the "Red River Trail," which passed through St. Cloud and in the early days was one of the main arteries of travel. . . As no lubricant was used, the screechings emitted by the slowly-moving vehicles were ear-piercing and most unearthly and proclaimed for long distances the coming of the caravan. They brought consignments of valuable furs, often sent through in bond to London. At that time a buffalo skin, now almost never to be seen, could be bought for a few dollars, and there was scarcely a man engaged in winter out-door work who did not have a buffalo overcoat, and a buffalo robe could be a part of almost any man's possessions."

When Moses Adley and his associates settled on the banks of the Sauk the neighboring community of Oak, which is now named New Munich, was already established. Answering the call of the West, six miles southeast on the same Sauk river, a handful of German immigrants were busy clearing the wilderness. These early settlers, forerunners of even greater numbers of German immigrants that would follow in the coming decades, had read with joy and wonderment the appeals made by that veteran missionary, Father Francis Xavier Pierz. A brochure which Pierz wrote entitled *Eine kurze Beschreibung des Minnesota-Territoriums,* was widely distributed throughout Germany and the immigrant centers such as Cincinnati, Buffalo, New York and Baltimore. He wrote:

"I do wish, however, that the choicest pieces of land in this delightful Territory would become the property of thrifty Catholics who would make an earthly paradise of this Minnesota which heaven has so richly blessed, and who would bear out the opinion that Germans prove to be the best farmers and the best Christians in America. I am sure that you will likewise do credit to your faith here in Minnesota; but to prove yourselves good Catholics do not bring with you any freethinkers, red republicans, atheists or agitators."

The first settler in the neighboring community was Henry Hoppe. Within a few years a large number of Father Pierz' "dear German Catholics" found their way to Oak and such names as Moritz, Gerard, Woeste, Schwieters, Uhlenkott, Thielen, Back, Marthaler and Wehrmann were among the pioneer families of Oak. As early as 1857 a "good Benedictine" priest visited the settlers in New Munich. The pastor of the already thriving settlement of St. Joseph wrote that year that Father Clement Staub, O.S.B., "visited the small stations of St. James and Richmond, to which were added St. Martin, then known as Ley's Settlement, and New Munich."

Before the Adleys began their work another group of German settlers were already clearing the land five miles to the southwest of Melrose. These settlers had also read with amazement the writings of Father Pierz and began to dream visions when they read such sentences as this: "More than half the open meadows in Minnesota have an excellent black loamy soil, with splendid mixture of sand and clay and a rich top soil formed by the plant decay of thousands of years, so that it would be hard to find anywhere in the world a soil better suited to agriculture and gardening, more likely to yield a rich return for the farmer's toil."

In 1857 Henry and Xavier Shaefer left Iowa for this new settlement. The following year the three Meyers and August Illies found their way to the same area that soon came to be called Meire Grove. Many of these "dear German Catholics" had no doubt also read about the marvellous sign Father Pierz described as follows:

"On the feast of the Epiphany, the sixth of January, of this year, 1855, there was seen here in Minnesota (whether in other places also I do not know) a remarkable apparition of the holy cross in the sky. As the full moon arose at 8:00 o'clock in the evening the holy cross appeared in yellowish hue and most heavenly brilliance upon the rising moon. . . . The cross was surrounded by a bright nimbus of the rarest and loveliest colors. The whole phenomenon was entrancingly beautiful and bright."

The missionary interpreted the sign as an assurance that the territory and future state would soon be populated by Christians and chiefly by

Germans. The immigration of the following decades would fulfill his prophetic words.

More settlers arrived to take up homesteads in the Melrose area, especially after the Civil War. Melrose was not a thriving village nor did it grow as rapidly as the neighboring settlements. Slowly the settlement grew and finally on January 22, 1866, the township of Melrose was organized. The first township supervisors were William Chambers, chairman; Charles W. Taylor and Charles G. Lamb, members; and August Lindbergh, clerk. Strangely, Moses Adley was not elected to the first township board. Even more strangely a decade after his coming he would sell his 160 acres to Edwin and William H. Clark and, for reasons unknown, would move to a farm in Getty township. There he remained until 1880 and after that time no further record is found concerning him. He settled in Melrose and attracted others to settle near him. He did, however, leave the original settlement, the township and the future city a heritage. He called it Melrose.

A story that first appeared at the time of the city's golden jubilee in 1907 claims that the city was named after two girls, one named Melissa (or Melvina) and Rose. Even then no one knew if the girls were Adley's daughters, relatives or friends of the family. No one knew the girls and the girls themselves never laid claim to the area being named in their honor.

It seems more plausible to assume that Adley named his settlement after the city of Melrose in Scotland which is located thirty-five miles from Edinburgh. Melrose, Scotland, would have been well known to the Adley's for their ancestors came to the United States from that area of Scotland. The novels of Sir Walter Scott, who lived near Melrose, Scotland, were at the height of their popularity at the time of settlement. Nor was Melrose an unusual name. There is a city in Massachusetts, as well as villages and townships in seventeen other states, named after the city in Scotland. It is a name rich in history and a Scottish community that justly deserved to be memorialized in the heartland of the newborn state of Minnesota.

Melrose, Scotland, dates back to the second-half of the seventh century when a young shepherd by the name of Cuthbert was received as a novice into a community of monks who lived on the "bare promontory" called Mailros in the ancient Scottish tongue. In time Cuthbert became a missionary to the people of Northumbria and prior of the monastic community. He also established the ancient bishopric of Durham and served as bishop of Lindisfarne before retiring to spend his last few years as a hermit on the island of Farne. In the course of time people gathered about the walls of the ancient monastery and a village called Melrose came into existence.

By the eleventh century the old monastery had disappeared but within a hundred years, in 1136 King David I of Scotland founded Melrose Abbey. Cistercian monks from Rievaulx, Yorkshire assumed charge of the abbey which was dedicated to the Virgin Mary. The monks were engaged in many activities such as farming, sheep-rearing, building, education and the study and writing of books. The abbey and the church were built according to the simple architecture demanded by the Cistercian rule and were most probably whitewashed both inside and outside with roofs of lead and red tile. The abbey was built along the ancient road which had been built by the Romans in the time of the Caesars. The abbey lay in the path of marauding forces who crossed the Scottish border during the centuries of conflict between England and Scotland. One of its claims of glory, which made it a popular pilgrimage center for many centuries, was the fact that the heart of Robert the Bruce, the great Scot hero, was preserved and kept within the abbey church.

Today the abbey lies in ruins. Its death knell was sounded in the mid-sixteenth century when the Earl of Hertford and his forces plundered the venerable structure. The devastation was completed when the Scottish reformers expelled the monks and stripped the buildings of its possessions. Ironically, even after such havoc, a local religious zealot went about the ruins, a hammer in hand, knocking the images from their ornate niches and reducing the scared images to shapeless stumps.

The city of Melrose, Scotland, today is centered around its Market Cross which bears the date 1662. The summit of the shaft in the city square is surmounted by a time-worn figure of the Unicorn and the Royal Arms of Scotland. The city is situated on the historic Tweed River and its main thoroughfare is called High Cross Avenue. The present population of Melrose, Scotland, is 2,100, about the same as its namesake on the Sauk River. Melrose, Scotland, is the locale of three of Sir Walter Scott's works, namely, *The Abbot, The Monastery* and *The Lady of the Lake*. The poet, Roger Quinn, wrote the following verse about this historic city:

> From the moorland and the meadows
> To this city of the shadows,
> Where I wander old and lonely, comes the call I understand;
> In clear, soft notes enthralling.
> It is calling, calling, calling —
> 'Tis the Spirit of the Open from the dear old Borderland.
> Ah, that call who can gainsay it?
> To hear is to obey it;

I must leave this bustling city to the busy city men —
Leave behind its feverish madness,
Its scenes of sordid sadness;
And drink the unpolluted air of Melrose once again!

Well did the Adley brothers name their settlement after so distinguished a city in Scotland, for in so many ways the water and woods, the prairie and hills they saw around them recalled what they heard from their ancestors and read in the works of Sir Walter Scott.

Moses Adley was a Yankee, that is, a person from the New England states who heard the call of the West in the early nineteenth century and went forth as a fortune-seeker. The Yankee was an opportunist, intent on settling a local area in order to acquire wealth for himself and his family. The economic power of these early communities, such as Melrose, was controlled by the Yankees and it would remain in their hands until after the turn of the century. They were shrewd businessmen and though some called them unjust, they were not according to the standards they helped to establish for the frontier. They were, according to their lights, religious men and by that, they meant religion had its place and business had its place and—never the two should meet. By and large, they opened the area of central Minnesota for colonization, encouraged immigration, and established most of the business and financial institutions by which we live today.

The Yankee pioneer was a thrifty fellow, and he encouraged thrift as a virtue among those whom he served as his clients. Generally he inhabited the largest and most handsome dwelling in the village, joined the most fashionable and exclusive clubs and sent his children "back East" for their education. His name might have been Gilman, West, Mitchell, Miller or Adley but that really did not matter too much. They were all of the same group and followed the same Puritan ethic that they inherited from their New England ancestry.

William Bell Mitchell, the first historian of Stearns County who produced a monumental two volume history of the area in 1915, was himself of Yankee stock. Describing the Yankees who pioneered in the county he wrote as follows:

"The sturdy New Englanders have been the subject of song and story, and there are few histories of the subduing of the wilderness in any part of the globe that do not contain the names of the sons of the descendants of the Puritans. The type of old school New England is rapidly passing, but the worth of these men will never be forgotten. Courteous of manner, considerate in bearing, widely informed, and masters of conversational powers, they left their impress on the lives of whatever community they bettered with their presence. Born to the advantages which a community of substantial, educated, God fearing people affords, many of them risked

The only reminder of the founder of Melrose, Adley creek.

*The ruins of
Melrose Abbey, Scotland.*

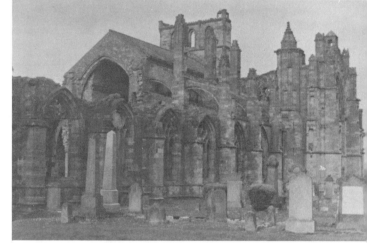

The United States Land Office in St. Cloud about 1860.

Melrose's neighbor, Sauk Centre, as it appeared in 1869.

Charles A. Lindbergh, Sr.
about 1885.

The August Lindbergh family as pioneers
in Melrose in the decade of 1860.

August Lindbergh, seated at left, in the Melrose bank in the 1880's.

Clark's mill as it appeared in 1870. The mill was built in 1867 and the sawmill (marked by "x") was built in 1868. In front of the mill are Mrs. Edwin Clark and daughter, Mabelle (1), Mrs. William H. Clark and son, Levin (2) and Edwin Clark (3).

Edwin Clark, "Father of Melrose" as he appeared on his eighty-seventh birthday in February, 1921.

Melrose as it appeared in 1872 showing Clark's mill, Edwin Clark's residence (1), the warehouse (2), the coopershop (3) and Edwin Clark and son Walter (4).

The coopershop where barrels were made for flour shipped from Clark's mill.

The fourteen employees of the coopershop as they appeared about 1872.

Clark's mill with both the old wagons and the "iron horse" as it appeared in 1887.

"The Modern Ship of the Plains," a drawing by R. F. Zogruk for HARPER'S WEEKLY, showing the interior of a railroad car that brought the immigrants to the West.

The railroad depot in Melrose in 1872. Prominent citizens gathered in front of the depot were, left to right, August Lindbergh, Robert Wheeler, Solomon R. Foot, Benjamin Doe, Cyrus Francis, Stillman Ayers, L. Hultz, Charles Stewart, Joseph Moritz, Charles McPennison, Henry W. VanReneselaer. The occasion was the first train service to Melrose.

St. Paul & Pacific R.R. cars on display in St. Cloud.

Engine "163" which made many trips between Melrose and the Twin Cities.

The foot bridge which was 576 feet long.

The Great Northern yards in Melrose at the turn of the century.

Riverside Avenue, at one time called "the richest street between St. Paul and Seattle."

The Lyric theatre, social hub of Melrose in the "gay nineties."

The Melrose hotel and bridge,
built by John Hoeschen in 1896.

In the early 1890's the fire chief
was important as he is today.
Mr. G. Kukosovitz dressed in his
fire chief's uniform.

The mill dam burst on April 3,
1907. Repair work was begun
immediately.

Melrose Main Street as it appeared at the turn of the century.

On Sunday afternoon in 1910 with Mr. McCarthy, Joseph and Wally Wellenstein and Frank Zitur in front of the Joseph Kraker store.

their lives, their fortunes, their health and their peace of mind in the interests of civilization. Some, pressing gradually westward with the mind in the interests of civilization. Some, pressing gradually westward with the "Star of Empire," found their way to Minnesota, and the influence of their coming has moulded the thought of the more recent influx of population from the countries of Europe."

A striking exception to the Yankee settlers in the Melrose area as well as the subsequent German immigration to the area, was the name and family of an exceptional pioneer. His name was August Lindbergh and he fathered a family that would become famous in our state and national history. At the age of fifty August Lindbergh, then called Ola Mansson, left his native Sweden and chose to settle in the community of Melrose on the site now occupied by Chick's Supper Club. His political activity, as a member of the Rikesdag, the Swedish parliament, as well as financial difficulties in business, forced him to leave his native land in 1859 with his second wife, Louisa, thirty years his junior, and their new son, Charles August, who was born on January 20, 1859. Leaving his homeland, he left behind his former name and came to be called August Lindbergh as he arrived at his new home.

August sold a gold medal given him by the Swedish government to purchase a plow and his wife sold a gold watch in exchange for a cow. Life was hard and labor was the condition of existence as they cleared the land for agriculture, not acre by acre but literally foot by foot. No sooner had they settled in their log cabin with its earthen floor than another tragedy befell the Swedish immigrants. According to the St. Cloud Democrat, on August 2, 1861, "Mr. Lindbergh. . .fell and was caught by the saw, horribly mangling his left arm and side." Twenty-four hours passed before a doctor arrived from St. Cloud, yet August lived and became a prominent member of the newly-founded community of Melrose.

Meanwhile his son, Charles, lived the life of a typical son of the frontier. His task was to secure food for the family table, a pleasant task for a youth who enjoyed the outdoors more than the confining atmosphere of the log cabin school room. Many hours he spent in the woods, hunting rabbits, pheasants and when luck was on his side, a passing deer. In later life he recalled that at times "there were thousands of duck. . .so many that the sky was blackened." But to school he must go, for the pioneer placed a value on education that has not been surpassed in the area. August, who was instrumental in organizing the first school district in Melrose township in 1861, donated a granary on his farm as the first school building in the area. He was determined that his son should have the best schooling he could supply. Charles was among the first pupils and later in life he recalled how he was embarrassed when his father, in broken English, spoke at the school. As he grew older the elder Lindbergh sent his son to Grove Lake Academy in nearby Sauk Centre conducted by the rather unusual and contentious priest, Reverend Daniel J. Cogan.

The Sauk Centre Academy in which August Lindbergh enrolled his young son Charles was, to say the least, a different and exceptional school. Father Cogan had come to central Minnesota from the diocese of Chicago and took up residence at St. John's Abbey, agreeing to teach for his board and "to keep the rules of the house and to promote its interests." Because of the great number of English-speaking immigrants in the Melrose and Sauk Centre area, Abbot Alexius Edelbrock sent Father Cogan to serve the people in that area in the spring of 1877. His personality was electric and quickly he won the affection and admiration of the people he served. Born in Dublin in 1827, he was educated at Trinity College and possessed all the charm and wit so closely identified with the inhabitants of the Isle of Saints and Scholars. His obituary testified to his charm as the editor of the *Sauk Centre Herald* wrote:

"It is not too much to say that he was everybody's friend. Modest and unassuming in every-day life, yet he was always sparkling and vivacious in conversation, and few suspected, without intimate acquaintance, the profound depths of his learning, which seemed to have grasped the most diversified subjects."

During these years Father Cogan also ministered to the needs of the growing Irish Catholic population of Melrose. In 1877 he opened his private high school on his own authority and under his own responsibility and soon newspapers throughout the area were advertising for candidates to be admitted to St. Paul's School, Grove Lake, Pope County. After meeting success in Grove Lake, he expanded his school and moved it to Sauk Centre, calling it Lake View Academy. The institution had accomodations for seventy-five students and, according to the reports of the time, there was no difficulty in securing that number of students. One authority on the educational system of the area claimed, "He flattered the 'Yankee' by claiming that the design of the school was more like Eastern and Southern institutions which have brought educational refinement into this country." Needless to say, Father Cogan met opposition and his story will be recalled later in these pages. The fact, however, that August Lindbergh would send his son to this institution of learning, rather than to the more stable and traditional type of school that the monks of St. John's were creating in the neighboring Indianbush gives an insight into the daring progressivism of the senior and junior Lindbergh.

No doubt the influences of the then "liberal" Sauk Centre Academy had a profound influence upon the young Charles Lindbergh. From there he went on to law school at the University of Michigan and returned to practice law and enter the political arena in Little Falls. He returned frequently to Melrose in later years, chiefly to visit his aunt, Mrs. Linda Seal. Lindberg made his name known throughout the state and nation chiefly as a progressive Republican congressman from Minnesota and as a candidate for governor of Minnesota on a platform of reform during the turn-of-the-century American protest politics. His son, Charles A. Lindbergh, Jr., would make the name internationally famous by his non-stop air flight from New York to Paris in 1927. The name later would be the subject of sensational headlines in the nation's newspapers in connection with the Hauptman kidnapping case. At the present time the Lindberghs are among the most ardent advocates of environmental survival and control.

The grandfather, August Lindbergh, however, continued to live in Melrose and became one of the village's most prominent citizens. In his lifetime he served as town clerk for eighteen years, village recorder for two years, clerk of a school district for twenty-one years, justice of the peace for sixteen years and postmaster from 1863 to 1865 and again from 1879 to 1887. This service was rendered by a man who emigrated from Sweden at the age of fifty, lost one arm in a farm accident two years after he homesteaded in the area, and gave to our state and nation a distinguished son and grandson. August Lindbergh was, to be sure, an ethnic exception to the local colonization, but his life's story could be duplicated, if not exceeded, by other early immigrants to the Melrose area.

Melrose was less than a decade old and the township less than two years old when the census showed no more than 285 people in the entire township. Many factors contributed to this slow population growth of the area. Both nature and human resources combined to make life for the settler more than normally difficult. Writing of pioneer times in the area of central Minnesota, General Christopher C. Andrews observed that "the worst hard times I ever knew come in the early part of that winter." In 1857 "money all at once seemed to disappear and I found it about impossible to collect much of anything that was due me. These hard times improved but very little until the time of the Civil War." The economic panic of 1857 and the resulting depression was felt most keenly on the frontier. The entire nation was suffering from the economic depression. People were reluctant to take any great economic risks and well they knew that settling on the frontier would be a serious challenge to their ingenuity and industry. With low prices those who had dreamed of the westward venture were content to maintain what they had in the East rather than sell at a loss and move to an unknown and uncertain new land.

Nature, also, afflicted these early settlers. As in these early years of settlement, so two decades later the area would be afflicted with the scourge of grasshoppers. The grasshoppers literally descended upon an area and devoured everything within reach. One early settler recalled that the only things that were not devoured were kept in a barrel and buried in the basement of the farm dwelling. Another pioneer recalled how her father's jacket was devoured by the grasshoppers as he left it laying in the field while he was plowing.

The congressional delay in passing the Homestead Act was another factor. The Free-soil-Democratic convention of 1852 first brought to the public's attention the proposal of giving free lands from the public domain to permanent settlers. The Homestead Act was introduced into the United States Congress in 1859 and met with the solid opposition of legislators from the southern states. They knew that its passage would upset the balance of power between slave and free states. The bill was buried in legislative limbo until 1861 when a Minnesotan, Cyrus Aldrich, again introduced the bill on the floor of the House. It was finally ratified on May 20, 1862. Between 1863 and 1865 the public registers record 9,529 homestead entries for 1,237,722.13 acres of Minnesota farm and timber lands. According to Dr. William Watts Folwell, "between May 20, 1862, and June 30, 1880, there were made in Minnesota 62,379 entries of 7,346,038.96 acres."

Another factor of growth was the freedom from the fear of the surrounding Indian tribes. The Sioux Uprising along the Minnesota River Valley in 1862 and the Battle of New Ulm the same year filled the minds of the people throughout the area with visions of horror and slaughter. People fled their homes and gathered in such centers as St. Cloud, Richmond and Sauk Centre, seeking protection in the safety of numbers. The citizens of Melrose were no exception. Many left home and land to stay with relatives and friends in these fortified centers within the county. The area of Melrose lay in a no-man's land between the Chippewa tribes in the north and the Sioux tribes in southwestern Minnesota. The Indians were not happy with the "treaties" forced upon them by the encroaching white man who had come to despoil their ancient hunting grounds. Nor were the Indians generally happy with the government's financial arrangements, and in some cases the neglect of these arrangements, forced upon them by the overpowering white man.   I. V. D. Heard, an officer on the staff of

General Sibley, wrote about the conditions among the Sioux Indians in 1862:

"The Indians were grievously disappointed with their bargains. They had now nearly disposed of all their land, and had received scarcely anything for it. They were 6,200 in number and their annuities when paid in full, were hardly $15 apiece. Their sufferings from hunger were often severe, especially during the winter previous to the massacre."

The uprising was the immediate result of one young brave's attempt to prove his courage. His three companions, also eager to show how brave they were on that disastrous Sunday night, August 17, 1862, when they went to the nearest house and there shot and killed three white men and two women. The spark of rebellion was already smouldering in the hearts of the Sioux leaders. The preceeding Friday they held council in Redwood Falls with Thomas Galbraith, the government agent, to ask for emergency food and supplies for their starving people because the government annuity had not as yet arrived. Chief Little Crow spoke for his people: "We have no food, but here are these stores, filled with food. We ask that you, the agent, make some arrangement by which we can get food from the stores, or else we may take our own way to keep from starving. When men are hungry they help themselves." Galbraith turned to the traders and asked what they thought could be done. One of them, Andrew Myrick replied, "So far as I am concerned, if they are hungry let them · eat grass or their own dung." After a moment's stunned silence there followed an outburst of angry shouts and then, as a group, the leaders of the Sioux left the council. With a touch of either poetic or Indian justice, Andrew Myrick was killed during the uprising; he was found dead with his mouth stuffed full of grass.

Louisa Lindbergh recounted in later life how one day she confronted a group of Indian braves at the farm. Drunk with firewater the Indians stopped at the house and demanded food. Louisa staunchly refused to serve them. They left grumbling and as they walked away one of the Indians grabbed August's axe from the woodpile. Thereupon Louisa put on her best silk dress to appear as dignified as possible and ran after the small group. After arguing and threatening them, she succeeded in securing the return of the axe, turned away and walked home in triumph. Viewed from the perspective of history one is not surprised that the Sioux revolted; rather, one is amazed that they did not rebel sooner against the flagrant injustices forced upon them by the land-greedy white intruders. Minnesota historian, Theodore C. Blegan, commenting on the revolt, wrote that "the Sioux Uprising was a frontier and national calamity, a blood-spattered commentary on the failure of American Indian policy, a terrible ordeal for the people of Minnesota, a tragic final act in the drama of the Minnesota Sioux."

In spite of those mentioned and other factors that retarded the growth of Adley's settlement, the community did continue to grow. Although the names of the Adley's, the Wheeler's, the Chambers, the Lindbergh's and other pioneers are no longer heard along the streets of the city or roads of the township, there is one reminder of the founders. Although modest it is one of the beauty spots of the Melrose area. It is a small creek flowing from Lake Sylvia in the northeastern corner of the township and emptying into the Sauk River. We call it Adley creek.

CHAPTER TWO

A VILLAGE GROWS
BESIDE THE SAUK

We have room for all creation, and our banner is unfurled,
With a general invitation to the people of the world.

—Early American ballad.

When Moses and Lucinda Adley sold their 160 acres along the banks of the Sauk River for $500.00 to Edwin and William H. Clark on November 17, 1871 neither the seller nor the buyer knew the full dimensions of that financial transaction. Moses, his wife and family, as we have seen, retired to the obscurity of a farm in Getty township and in doing so he made room for the man who deserved to be called the "father of Melrose." Edwin, and his brother William, found a pioneer settlement, scattered, unorganized and aimless in direction. For the next twenty-five years Edwin Clark labored in this frontier settlement and by the time he left it, in 1893, he both witnessed and experienced the transformation of Melrose from a tiny cluster of farmers and merchants into a prosperous, thriving commercial center for an industrious Irish and German immigrant community of rural people.

Edwin Clark was a most unusual character. His life was as varied as any frontiersman on the western reaches of the American republic. He manifested in his own life all the virtues that were held in high esteem by his fellow Yankees — wisdom, thriftiness, creativity and ingenuity.

Born on February 25, 1835 in Grafton county, New Hampshire, he was the son of a Congregational minister, the Reverend John Clark. When Edwin reached the age of eight the family moved to Caledonia county, Vermont and there Edwin was apprenticed to a printer.

1854 the family returned to Grafton county, New Hampshire, and Edwin was with them. He did not remain at home long, however,

21

before the call of the road beckoned him to Boston in 1855, where he spent two years in the printing and lithographing industry. The call of the West was loud and clear and we find the ambitious Edwin Clark moving to the newly created state of Minnesota in 1857 and, with W. A. Croffut as a partner, establishing two publications in the pioneer village of St. Anthony Falls. He became the publisher of the *Minnesota Republican,* a weekly, and *The Falls Evening News,* the first daily paper published in the State of Minnesota. After two years the publishing partnership was dissolved and Mr. Uriah Thomas succeeded Mr. Croffut as Clark's collaborator. The new firm continued publication of the periodicals until 1863 when the establishment was sold to W. S. King, a prominent citizen of Minneapolis.

At this time Clark was appointed a clerk in the United States House of Representatives for the thirty-eighth session, a position, according to his own report, he thoroughly enjoyed. In April, 1865, two days before his assassination, President Lincoln appointed Clark agent for the Chippewa Indians of Minnesota. Clark proceeded to Old Crow Wing, on the present site of Crow Wing State Park, where he administered to the needs of the Chippewa tribe in the area. During this period he supervised the construction of the Leech Lake Agency, now known as the White Earth Indian Reservation. Like so many of his contemporaries and modern day public servants, he was the victim of the spoils system. Shortly after President Andrew Johnson assumed office, Edwin Clark found himself without a government job. Again he was on the road. He certainly had heard about the newly-formed community on the banks of the Sauk River and no doubt had visited this village from time to time in his office as Indian agent. Without a job, Clark went in search of one. Design, not accident, led him to Melrose and to the purchase of Moses Adley's one hundred and sixty acre farm.

Edwin Clark the man, however, was not a hard nosed business-only sort of individual. Reading his correspondence and documents at the Minnesota Historical Society, one discovers that he was a warm, personable and outgoing person. A glimmer of this shows through in his marriage to Miss Ellen F. Rowe, daughter of Morrison and Sally B. Rowe of Belknap county, New Hampshire. It would not, of course, be unusual for a young man to enter into marriage with a young lady from a neighboring village or county. What is significant, however, is the fact that the nuptials took place in St. Anthony Falls on January 1, 1860 — six years after he had left his native New Hampshire! If Melrose subsequently would witness "long distance" romances, this surely must have been the first and one of the longest. Edwin and Ellen Clark gave birth to six children but by 1893 only three remained living, Everett, Mabelle and Walter.

Edwin Clark possessed no small mind. He knew well the happenings in the world at large for, as a newspaperman, he had an abiding interest in the news. From his readings he knew that the "Iron Chancellor" Bismarck was on the point of unifying Germany; that Garibaldi, leading his Red Shirts, had taken Rome in 1869 and unified a tattered and torn Italy. He also read in the weeklies and monthlies that came his way that the European powers were both colonizing and exploiting the natives of the "dark continent" of Africa; that Emperor Franz Joseph was having his troubles keeping the paper of the Austrian-Hungarian empire in one piece. Later he would read how France had suffered a crushing defeat in the Franco-Prussia War of 1870-71. Once again, France would try to become organized under the Third Republic as Frenchmen themselves would ask, "How can you govern a country that makes four hundred cheeses?" Edwin Clark knew that Great Britian was at the zenith of its power and of the proud boast of every good Englishman that "the sun never sets on the British empire." Queen Victoria was the *grand dame* of royalty and her descendants were found among almost every ruling family of European royalty at the time. There were also obnoxious revolutionaries in Latin America, always overthrowing governments and making the southern part of the western hemisphere an impossibly inexplicable area of rebellion, revolution and revisionism. At this time no one really bothered too much nor did anyone really care what was taking place south of the Rio Grande. There was, of course, the fantastic history of France placing a puppet king, Maximillian, on the Mexican throne and the even more unbelievable emergence of a peasant leader by the name of Juarez (who thought himself to be a Lincoln-type) who caused a major revolt — but that was all so far away and so far removed that it did not really concern the majority of the citizens of central Minnesota.

Edwin Clark also read in the same newspapers the regional happenings that concerned him and the Melrose community even more closely. Of course, he read that President Lincoln was shot in Ford's Theatre on the night of April 14, 1865 by John Wilkes Booth. Clark followed the period of Reconstruction after the Civil War in his publications. Like most of his fellow citizens he deplored the scandals of the Johnson administration and welcomed, for better or worse, the inauguration as president the war hero, Ulysses S. Grant, on March 4, 1869. He not only read about the great surge of immigration that passed through the nation's Eastern ports during these years but he was also familiar with these sturdy, stolid German people who found their way to central Minnesota. Honest man that he was, Clark resented the rise of the Know-Nothing Party, for he wanted no part of its blatant bigotry and its militant anti-immigrant and anti-Catholic stance. He knew, as most of his fellow-Americans knew, that "this land of the free and home of the brave" could not, and would not, tolerate such extreme reactionism. Edwin Clark also welcomed the good news of a new gold strike in Colorado, a new silver strike in Nevada. Clark welcomed the westward flow of immigrants to the new territories of the West. He was as much addicted to the "course of Empire" as any other fellow American and he eagerly awaited the day when his country would be united "from sea to shining sea."

No doubt, too, he was tempted as many of his friends and neighbors were, to strike it rich in the Black Hills upon hearing that Maurice Manual, a soldier of fortune, had discovered a rich vein of gold on April 8, 1876. But, fortunately for the future, he remained in Melrose and continued to build a community centering around his flour mill.

Edwin Clark and his brother William were no soldiers of fortune. They came to the settlement on the banks of the Sauk with the determined intention to make use of the water power at the dam and create a business enterprise in that fertile valley. The very year that the Clark brothers came to Melrose they opened a general store. It was only a board shanty, nonetheless, an edifice that would suffice until more permanent structures could be built. The shanty gave way before the snow flew that same year to a more durable structure, which also served as the residence of the Clark's. The following year, the Clark's were busy erecting a mill on the south side of the dam and encouraging the local farmers to bring their grain to be milled at this site. They built their mill on a ledge of very hard, coarse, red granite, which extended about twenty-five feet from the mill and half-way across the waste-way of the dam. The success of the venture is evidence by the fact that the original mill was enlarged on three different occasions in the course of the ensuing years.

The original Clark mill was a modest structure, built in 1867 and which consisted of no more than a forty by forty-foot one-story structure. By 1885 three additions had been added and the mill was the economic and business hub of the continually expanding village and neighborhood. In 1878 Edwin bought out his brother's interest in the mercantile store and mill and became the sole owner. By 1885 the forty by forty-foot mill had doubled in size and the steam plant had been transferred to the west side of the mill, on the north bank of the Sauk River. An early visitor to Melrose made the following observations about the Clark mill:

"The mill is built on a solid granite foundation, this being the only place on the river between Cold Spring and Sauk Centre where the granite crops out, and even here it is too low to quarry. There is no other mill in the above distance of more than forty miles, and this is kept running continually night and day. The river flows through a bed so level, that damming but a few feet will back the water by miles, and being fed principally by numerous lakes above, is not easily effected by drought. The mill can run every day in the year without lack of power. The same newspaper correspondent observed that the Messers. Clark owned one of the two stores: and though they kept a good variety for country trade, would gladly welcome a few enterprising merchants, in various branches of trade."

The Clark papers in the Minnesota Historical Society are replete with references to the business acumen of this early businessman of Melrose. His business dealings were chiefly with the United States Army and throughout the decade of the seventies only the recording angel would know how many hundred pound sacks of flour passed through the Clark mill to the military posts of Fort Totten, Fort Abercrombie, Pembina and Fort Ransom in the Dakota territory. For example, the records of the mill show that on June 13, 1870 the Clark mill supplied 10,000 pounds of flour for Fort Totten, 30,000 pounds for Pembina, 20,000 for Fort Abercrombie and 15,000 for Fort Ransom. A decade later, on June 27, 1880 a government order revealed that the Clark mill had supplied 15,000 pounds of flour to Fort Ransom, 10,000 pounds to Fort Totten, 26,200 pounds to Fort Thomas. For the transaction of 1870 Edwin and William Clark received a check from the Office of the Chief Commissary of Subsistence in the amount of $430.00 for the flour delivered to Fort Abercrombie. In other words, the 20,000 pounds of flour delivered was valued at a little more than two cents a pound. Throughout the coming decade the Clark mill would continue to sell flour to the United States Army, in the early years transporting the flour to the office of Wilder Burbank and Company in St. Cloud by means of wagons along the newly-constructed state road that is now known as old highway fifty-two. Later, after the construction of the St. Paul and Pacific railroad, flour was shipped directly to Breckenridge and Fort Abercrombie.

Edwin Clark was not only a leading merchant and miller in the thriving Melrose village, he also became, knowingly or unknowingly, the founding father of the community. On October 27, 1871 Clark penned a letter to George L. Becker, the president of the St. Paul and Pacific Railroad — forerunner of the Great Northern Railroad. By this letter he literally put Melrose on the map and changed the course of its history for succeeding generations. Clark's letter read as follows:

"Sir:

Being desirous to secure the location of your line of railroad through our proposed town site at Melrose, we make you the following proposition in relation to the same.

1st. We will give the Railroad Company the right of way through our land free of expense.

2nd. We will convey to your Railroad Company by a good and perfect title one half of the lots to be laid out in the proposed town site of Melrose as may be selected by your agent, and also such grounds for depot purposes as he may select.

3rd. Should the owners of land along the proposed line of Railroad in the town of Melrose demand payment for the right of way through said town, then we agree to pay all such amounts as the Railroad Commissioners may adjudge them, unless satisfactory settlement could otherwise be made.

From the Railroad Company we should expect in consideration of the foregoing:

1st. The location of the Railroad through our proposed town of Melrose.

2nd. The location of, and maintenance of, a passenger and freight depot at or near the corner of section thirty-four (34) and thirty-five (35) . . . .

3rd. No other station to be located or established within six miles of said station at Melrose.

All of which is most respectfully submitted for your consideration.

E. and W. H. Clark"

On the same day the letter was received the proposition was accepted on behalf of the St. Paul and Pacific Railroad Company by S. P. Folsom acting as the railroad's agent. A further note on the transaction, dated December 22, 1871 attests to the fact that "a division of lots in the town of Melrose was made and one half deeded the Railroad by the Messers. Clark of that state." Mr. Folsom further added, "The deeds for the right (of way) were delivered December 22, 1873 as required (by) the proposition." On April 10, 1874 both Edwin Clark and S. P. Folsom appeared before a notary public and the transaction was duly certified and recorded. The future growth of Melrose was assured. The railroad would not only facilitate commerce, and especially the commercial output of the Clark mill, but the railroad would be the principal artery connecting Melrose with the outside world, via St. Cloud, St. Paul, Chicago and the East. The same railroad would be the route that the immigrants in the next two decades would follow in search of land, liberty and the good life in the wilderness surrounding Melrose. The iron horse would be the harbinger of cultivation and civilization and be a determining factor in creating a distinct and unique culture out of what was once derisively called the "Melrose bush."

The St. Paul & Pacific Railroad arrived in St. Cloud on September 1, 1866. Six years later, on June 12, 1871 the railroad bridge was completed across the Mississippi at St. Cloud. Rail construction work proceeded rapidly during the summer months and early fall until on November 18th the railroad was completed and trains began running to Melrose. At that time a stage coach made connection for the citizens of Sauk Centre and beyond with Melrose. Much of the grain that previously was loaded at Benson was now loaded on the freight trains at Melrose.

The timetable for the new passenger trains showed that the trains leaving St. Paul at eight o'clock in the morning arrived at Melrose at three o'clock in the afternoon, with stops at St. Cloud at twelve thirty-five. The return trains would leave Melrose at six o'clock in the morning, and arrive at the St. Paul depot at one twenty-five in the afternoon. The local fare from St. Cloud to Melrose was $1.65. In 1889 the St. Paul & Pacific Company was merged with other properties and became known as the Great Northern Railway Company. Four years later the Great Northern was completed all the way to Puget Sound in the far West.

Before the iron horse arrived in Melrose, however, there was already a history associated with railroads on the Minnesota frontier. This book is not the place to recall that story. Suffice it to say that both the state legislature and general public recognized the railroads as an indispensable means for populating and colonizing the state. By the same token, both government and governed were suspicious of the financial practices of these railroads already granted charters by the state legislature. The conflict between the legislature and public and the railroad companies was established early and would continue for several generations.

The first stretch of railroad connecting the area with the outside world was completed on September 1, 1866, with the arrival of a passenger train at the East St. Cloud depot of the St. Paul & Pacific Railroad. St. Cloud remained the terminal point of the railroad until 1872. Almost twenty years before this time the federal government authorized a Pacific railroad survey under the leadership of Isaac I. Stevens. The survey group left from St. Paul, passed through St. Cloud and Melrose following the survey that would eventually become the route of the Great Northern Railroad across the plain states and through the Rocky Mountain passes. Somewhere near Melrose one disgruntled member of the survey party complained about the mosquitoes in the area and recorded in a letter sent back east that the land was "useless and worthless." No doubt he was a man of little vision and less imagination. Although many railroad magnates at this time were no more than land speculators, the same cannot be attributed to the leadership of the St. Paul & Pacific Railroad Company. Control of the company fell into the hands of an exceptional genius, one who would be called the "Empire Builder," James J. Hill. Because the story of his railroad is so intimately linked with the successful growth of Melrose, it is well to record his own recollections of these early days from the report he submitted in a letter to the board of directors of the Great Northern Railroad dated July 1, 1912. He wrote:

"Nearly forty years ago the thought of a possible railway enterprise in the Northwest began to occupy my mind. It was born of experience in Northwestern transportation problems that had occupied most of my early business life, of faith in the productive powers and material resources of this part of the country, and of railroad conditions at that time. The feverish activity in securing railroad concessions in land cash that marked the sixth decade of the last century had been followed by collapse. Doomed as these enterprises were to ultimate failure by their lack of commercial foundation and financial soundness, they were suddenly wrecked by the panic of 1873. Aside from the Northern Pacific property, the lines in the state of Minnesota most important and available if converted into real assets for the development of the Northwest were the fragments of the old St. Paul & Pacific Company. Following the panic of 1873 these were in the hands of a receiver. The holders of their securities in Holland were more anxious to recover what they could from the wreck than to put more money into its completion and improvements that must be made if the properties were to continue to be operated at all. Their value lay to some extent in what was left of a land grant, which would be valuable as soon as the country should be opened, but chiefly in the possibilities of traffic from the millions of productive acres in the Northwest to be opened to settlement by transportation facilities. Yet so great seemed the task and so uncertain the reward, in the general opinion, that any plan of acquiring and reorganizing the property was regarded as visionary in those days by most holders of capital and most men of affairs.

"After long and close study of the situation the slender beginning was made on which we risked our all. Failure would be immediate and final disaster. My associates were George Stephen (later created Lord Mount Stephen), Donald A. Smith (later created Lord Strath and Mount Royal) and Norman W. Kittson. We bought the defaulted bonds of these properties from the Dutch holders. The agreement with the Dutch committee was executed March 13, 1878, and practically all outstanding indebtedness was subsequently secured. The mortgages were afterwards foreclosed and the property was brought in. For those days it seemed a formidable financial undertaking. The stock of these companies aggregated $6,500,000, and their bonded indebtedness with past due interest nearly $33,000,000, aside from floating obligations. These had to be purchased at prices above those for which they had previously been offered in the open market. The total capitalization and indebtedness at that time of the companies taken over was approximately $44,000,000.

"The property secured consisted of completed lines from St. Paul via St. Anthony to Melrose, a distance of 104 miles, and from Minneapolis to Breckenridge, a distance of 207 miles; and of two projected lines, one from Sauk Rapids to Brainerd and one from Melrose to the Red river at St. Vincent on the international boundary line. On these latter some grading had been done and about 75 miles of track had been laid. There were gaps between Melrose and Barnesville, Crookston and St. Vincent, that must be filled quickly. In themselves, had it not been for the promise of the future, these were scattered tracks in a country just being settled, out of which to construct a railway system and on which to base the financing of their purchase and development.

"We advanced the money to build the Red River Valley Railroad, fourteen miles of track from Crookston to Fisher's Landing, on the Red river, making a through route by steamboat from that point to Winnipeg. While negotiations were pending and also after they were concluded but before possession could be secured through the foreclosure of mortgages, an immense amount of work had to be done. The extension from Melrose to Barnesville must be pushed, and was carried thirty-three miles, as far as Alexandria; and ninety miles were built in the Red River valley to reach the Canadian boundary. The former was necessary to save the land grant, whose time limit, already extended, was about to expire. The latter was in addition to connect with a railroad projected by the Canadian government from Winnipeg south. As the properties were still in the hands of a receiver, an order had to be obtained from the court for the completion of the work in Minnesota with funds furnished by us. Money had to be raised to build these lines and to furnish equipment necessary for their operation.

"In May, 1879, the St. Paul, Minneapolis & Manitoba Railway Company was organized to take over all these properties, whose bonds had been largely purchased, whose stocks had been secured and whose assets were to be brought in under foreclosure. It had an authorized capital stock of $15,000,000, limited by its charter to $20,000,000, and made two mortgages of $8,000,000 each. George Stephen was made first president of the company, Richard B. Angus, vice-president, and I was chosen general manager. This placed upon me the practical conduct of the enterprise from its formal inception.

"The lines of the new system turned over to our possession on June 23, 1879, comprised a mileage of 667 miles, of which 565 were completed and 102 under construction. From the beginning its business fulfilled the expectations of its founders. The annual report for 1880 showed an increase in earnings of 54 per cent, and land sales amounting to $1,200,000. And now began the long task of building up the country. No sooner was a mile of road finished than the need of building other miles became apparent. Before Minnesota had filled up, the tide of immigration was passing even the famous Red River valley country and flowing into Dakota. By 1880 it had become necessary to add a line down the Dakota side of the Red river, to plan for many extensions and branches, and two local companies, building lines in western Minnesota, were purchased.

"Only a detailed history of the railroad could follow step by step the progress of track extension and the financial arrangement by which capital was furnished for these constant and always growing demands from this time on. Gradually year by year the lines were extended.

"In 1889 the Great Northern Railway Company was organized, to bind into a compact whole the various properties that had grown too large for the charter limitations of the old Manitoba. It leased all the property of the latter company, and was prepared to finance the undertakings about to be completed or in contemplation. By 1893 the line was opened through to Puget Sound. In the next five or six years many improvements were made by relaying track with heavier rails and by changes in equipment and large additions thereto. Branches and feeders were built to round out the system.

"In 1907 the subsidiary companies controlled by the Great Northern, including fourteen railway companies operated as a part of it, making of these related parts one homogeneous whole. In the same year I resigned the presidency of the system, and became chairman of the board of directors, — the office that I lay down today."

So the railroad came to Melrose and a whole new world was opened for the inhabitants of the community. Melrose would remain the terminus of the railroad from 1872 until 1878 and become an important shipping center throughout those six years, bringing supplies from the East to the farmers on the frontier and sending back produce from the farmers to the commercial centers of the East. At this time Minneapolis, the former St. Anthony Falls, was becoming an international flour milling center. No one has or can itemize the number of bushels of wheat that flowed from the heartlands of Stearns County and the western prairie to the flour mills of the Washburn's and the Pillsbury's that lined the banks of the Mississippi near the falls discovered by Father Hennepin. The railroad from Melrose to Sauk Centre was completed August 1, 1878; from there to Alexandria, December 1, 1878 and from there to Fergus Falls on January 1, 1881. The railroad and its influence upon the community was the beginning of a vital link in the growth, development and the near catastrophe of the frontier community. Meanwhile other activities were taking place assuring the development and growth of the small village on the banks of the Sauk River.

The Clark brothers were still busy developing their commercial enterprises and in 1868 they constructed a saw mill on the north side of the Sauk River, directly opposite their mill. The venture, however, did not prove successful and after a few years they disposed of their interest. Shortly thereafter the saw mill was defunct. In 1869 the far-sighted Clarks realized the advantage of a hotel in the community and thus offered free land to Joseph Moritz if he would come to build and maintain a hostelry one block from the Clark mill. Joseph Moritz obliged and during the same year a hotel appeared on the Melrose scene. Moritz continued to operate his hotel and became one of the leading citizens of the community. The Clark brothers did not have a monopoly on the milling industry. Pillsbury Hulbert of Minneapolis also settled in the area and opened a mill in 1879. Hulbert's mill was operated by steam power with a storage warehouse attached to it. His elevator was twenty-six by thirty-six feet with a storage capacity of thirty thousand bushels. This was during the hey-day of the milling industry in Minneapolis and Minnesota and, Hulbert, no doubt, thought he would be able to find his goldmine in this venture. Unfortunately the Clark's had the corner on the market. The Hulbert mill, however, was not a complete failure. Records tell us the mill produced 60,000 bushels of grain that was transformed into flour.

The thriving community was not without its organizations. Needless to say, religion was primary among the social institutions. Other organizations and institutions bound the local citizenry together. There was, first of all, the establishment of a newspaper. On June 22, 1877 Don B. McDonald began the publication of the *Melrose Beacon,* an ambitious project for a pioneer village. It did survive and on August 7, 1880 he sold the paper to James L. Hendryx, who continued its publication until November 1, when it was consolidated with the *Sauk Centre Herald.* The author of the *History of the Upper Mississippi Valley* also recounts that in 1881 there were two Masonic lodges in Melrose, one organized on May 15, 1876 and the other on February 14, 1881. The first boasted of a membership of sixty and the lodge held its meetings every Saturday night. The second lodge under the Worshipful Master, S. R. Foot and Secretary, Don B. McDonald, held their meetings on the first and third Wednesday of each month in "an elegant hall." The newspaper was started again on January 1, 1881 by Mr. McDonald and his son as the *Melrose Record* and was called by an early historian in politics an "Independent Republican."

The success of Edwin Clark is somewhat reflected in the fact that he purchased the entire manufacturing and commercial interests of his brother, William H. Clark in 1878 and became sole owner of the Clark properties. We do not know what happened to William Clark. He disappeared from the scene and was not heard of again in the area of Minnesota. Most probably he returned to his native New England.

Melrose however, in these days of the seventies was not without leadership. As a matter of fact, it might be safely stated that the community had more ambitious leadership per person than it ever had in its existence. There was not only the enterprising Edwin and William Clark; they were joined in their efforts by other enterprising citizens, such as August Lindbergh, whom we have already mentioned, and William Chambers, who opened his home for the offering of Mass by Father Pierz in 1868 and would become the prototype of the numerous Catholics who would follow. There was B. F. Burrill, from the state of Maine and a veteran of the Civil War, who settled in Melrose in December, 1878 and who took charge of Clark's cooper shops. Another citizen, the first druggist in the community, was N. M. Freeman, born in Massachusetts and an early settler of Paynesville, Minnesota. In 1859 he journeyed to Pike's Peak, Colorado and returned the same year to Richmond, Minnesota. There he operated a mercantile store until the store burned down in 1863. He returned to his native state and enlisted in the Thirty-Seventh Massachusetts Volunteer Infantry. Freeman served three years on the side of the Union in the Civil War. In 1872 he settled in Melrose where he lived on a farm for several years before becoming a bookkeeper in Clark's store. In 1878 he opened his own drug store and proved to be a successful business man of the new community.

Another early settler, also a Civil War veteran, was George L. Grinnel, a native New Yorker, a farmer by birth and vocation. In 1850 he followed the call of the California gold fields but returned a decade later disillusioned and disenchanted. In 1860 he enlisted in the Union Army and was severely wounded in the battle of the Wilderness. After the war he settled in Wisconsin for two and a half years before coming to Melrose, in 1868. Grinnel engaged in farming with the help of his wife, the former Liza Thompson, whom he had married in Pennsylvania in 1863. Another settler, proving the cosmopolitan nature of the early community, was a Mr. D. Grein who was born in Belgium in 1857. Grein emigrated to the United States in 1875 and found his way to St. Cloud. A harness-maker by trade, he was not content to live in either St. Cloud or Sauk Rapids and thus came to Melrose in 1879 and, according to an early historian, had conducted "a thriving business" since that time. Grein was married on March 11, 1880 to a certain Miss B. Folz in St. Cloud. That record leads the present reader to imagine the difficulties that courtship and marriage must have meant on the Minnesota frontier in those early days. Another early pioneer must be mentioned for the name is so well known throughout central Minnesota. A certain M. Gau appeared on the Melrose frontier in 1860. He must surely have been a most unusual, colorful and important personage in the development of the community. The son of a doctor, he was born in the province of Rhineland, Germany. He came to the United States in 1843 and lived in Wisconsin until the Mexican-American War. He served in the American army during that period — perhaps the only citizen of Melrose who ever served in that war — and ultimately settled in Toledo, Ohio. During this period he studied medicine and subsequently moved to Stillwater and Belle Plaine until 1860 when he moved to St. Cloud. After living in St. Cloud seven years he moved to a farm near Spring Hill where he served as both doctor and farmer. He came to Melrose in 1873 where he practiced medicine until the time of his death.

Melrose in the eighteen-seventies, was far from being "Dullsville, U.S.A." Its citizenry was of a cosmopolitan nature and being without radio or television, they exchanged stories of their origins and backgrounds that must have been as thrilling as the latest James Bond movie. Another enterprising pioneer was Volney C. Mead who settled in Melrose in July, 1879. He became the manager of the Pillsbury and Hulbert elevator and proved himself to be a stalwart citizen of the thriving community.

Omer Morehouse, born in Bradford county, Pennsylvania, in 1837, and another Civil War veteran, dated his coming to Melrose in 1879. Another early settler, A. A. Whitney was born in New York State in August, 1846. He also served in the Union army "without a day's sickness or an hour's absence from duty". He came to Melrose in 1871 and taught school for one year before taking over the management of Clark & McClure's lumber business. According to an earlier historian "Mr. Whitney had held a number of important local offices, the duties of which he has discharged with much ability." Another Whitney, W. B., also a native of Oswego county, New York, came to Melrose in 1867 and settled about six miles northwest of the townsite. He also was a veteran of the Civil War and a relative of A. A. Whitney. He lived on the farm until 1873 and then transferred his home to the village of Melrose. A. E. Whittemore, another Yankee, born in Merrimac county, New Hampshire, started with a team of horses for Minnesota, arriving in

Sauk Centre in 1864. The following spring he opened a farm with his wife, the former Miss Sarah Norton, whom he married in 1857. William H. West came to the area in the fall of 1877. A native of Jersey county, Illinois, he grew up in Prescott, Wisconsin. In the fall of 1877 he learned the miller's trade at Hudson, Wisconsin and two years later came to Melrose and was employed by the Clark's flour mills. On December 23, 1879 he was married to Emma Webb, the daughter of O. D. and Esther Webb of Melrose.

These are but a few of the names among those who composed the original settlement on the banks of the Sauk. Most of the names are Yankee, and most of them have already disappeared from our midst. One name, however, was a harbinger of the future immigration that would take place in the area. Even though his name would disappear, his heritage would remain and become the foundation of a community that would continue to grow and prosper along the banks of the Sauk River and, knowlingly or unknowingly, fulfill the prophetic words of Father Pierz as he saw his cross in the sky.

The man who would link the Yankee immigration of the sixties with the German immigration of the eighties was a nondescript Rhinelander by the name of John Wett who was born in Germany in 1840. For two years and nine months he served as a soldier in the Prussian army. He left Germany, obviously in disgust with the course of German political activity, and joined the American army at Fort Ridgley spending several years in military service on the western frontier. In 1870 he purchased a farm near St. Cloud. He was not, however, happy there, and two years later sold his properties and moved to Melrose. Here he was engaged in the selling of produce, which he marketed in Fort Gary (Winnipeg) and other stations throughout the Northwest. He became the first butcher in Melrose, selling his wares not only to distant markets but also to the local citizenry. He married the former Miss T. Nonbaum of St. Cloud and became one of the prominent pioneer families of Melrose. Only imagination can supply how he welcomed his fellow countrymen as they alighted from the immigrant trains at the Melrose station throughout the decade of the eighties.

Without a doubt, the most significant and important development in the history of the Melrose community was the great wave of German immigration of the 1880's and 1890's. One would have to be historically blind not to recognize that these immigrants completely changed, as well as developed, the growth of the community. This phenomenon not only caused the city to be called the home of the "Dutchmen"—a misnomer, by the way, but also advanced a pioneer village to the status of a city. No historian, can ever possibly expect to capture in writing the trials and tribulations, the joys and sorrows, of the pioneers of a bygone era. All he can hope to do is recount these experiences for generations yet unborn and hope that somehow or another they will appreciate what their ancestors did and how they accomplished their work. The following remarks and observations will draw heavily upon the studies of two notable descendants of the pioneers of the area, namely, Dr. John Massmann, who wrote his doctoral thesis on German immigration in Minnesota and Sister Nora Luetmer, O.S.B. who authored a doctoral thesis on the history of the Catholic school system in the Diocese of St. Cloud.

With the railroad came the first wave of immigrants to the Melrose area. Historians of an earlier period would like to lump these immigrants with the original settlers and call them all "Yankees." Nothing, however, could be further from the truth. These first native born immigrants were Irish — and they would deeply resent being equated with the Yankees of the preceeding decades. They came with the railroad and they were the men who laid the ties, kept the books, served as conductors and engineers and kept "Jim Hill's" railroad running from St. Paul to the marvelous unsettled lands of the West. They succeeded the Yankees in taking over the commercial and industrial operations of the area in this latter part of the nineteenth century. Nor should it be forgotten that in 1868 the first Mass offered in Melrose was in the home of William Chambers. And even if little is known about the circumstances, it should not be forgotten that it was an Irish Catholic priest, Father Augustine Burns, O.S.B., who was the first pastor to serve the Catholics of the area. Both facts attest that it was the Irish who not only planted the seeds of Catholicism in the area, but also with names such as McDonald, Stephens, and Donahue developed the professional and business community of Melrose. It was the gallant, daring, noble Irish who created a community. They were the most logical successors of the Yankee, building a bridge between the Yankee entrepreneur of the past and the stable German business man and farmer who were yet to appear on the scene in the coming decade.

Some of these Irish pioneers would be like this writer's own maternal grandfather who would sell his one hundred and sixty acres for a railroad ticket back to St. Paul. Most of them, however, would stay and create a community, a culture and a parish that would co-exist, if not amalgamate until a latter date, with the influx of German immigrants. Gone are the Donohue's, the Stephen's, the Lang's, the Graham's, the Gallagher's. Like this writer's own grandparents, they have gone off to the *city* — wherever that may be. But, recognized or not, they were the builders of the community of Melrose. They did it through the railroad; through their stores; through their law offices; through their church affiliations.

There were some days of conflict, as when the Irishmen told the Dutchmen to get out of "their" church. However, there existed a bond of faith and civic pride which recognized a fellow member of the teeming and exciting new community of Melrose. By the time their German brothers appeared on the scene the initial institutions were already in existence for the latter to develop and expand.

The entrance of the German settlers into the area, begins with the decade of the 1880's. This immigration, which would last until approximately the turn of the century, was one that brought to the community its present stability, growth and individuality. It would be accurate to state that the German immigrants, coming from abroad and from the eastern states, endowed the area of Melrose with a cult and culture that was unique in the western progress of the expanding republic. If we have praised the enterprise of the Yankee on the frontier, if we have paid tribute to the industrious and diligent Irish immigrant of a later period, it would be less than honest to state that the German immigrant was not merely a stranger in the night as the former nor a harbinger of better things to come as the latter. The German immigrant gave the community a particular stamp. He struck his roots firmly and deeply into the rich soil of the area. He perpetuated, and in some cases created more institutions and organizations that would continue until the present day. The Yankees, in those distant days, would scoff at him and label him a "dumb Dutchman," little realizing that he was neither a Dutchman, nor ignorant. The fact that he could not speak or understand the native tongue was neither cause nor reason for labeling him by a term of opprobrium. The fact that the Yankees are no more, that the Irish have moved to the city leaving the so-called "dumb Dutchman" to create a civic and religious culture out of an area that was once a wilderness is evidence that he was neither "dumb," nor was he more "Dutchman" than American. What exists in the Melrose community today is chiefly a tribute to his pioneering ingenuity and creativity.

The immigrant to the United States has been the subject of many scholarly studies. As the Irish, who poured into the country in the eighteen-forties and fifties posed many problems and taxed the resources of the nascent Catholic Church and growing urban areas, so during this period of the eighteen-eighties and nineties the wave of German immigrants would create further challenges for both Church and state. A distinguished historian, Father Colman Barry, O.S.B. has

treated these tensions and conflicts in greater depth than we can here —
in his two historial studies, *Worship* and *Work,* the centennial history
of Saint John's Abbey, and *The Catholic Church and German Americans.*

Another author, Marcus Lee Hansen, wrote about the spirit that
motivated the immigrant in an earlier work entitled *The Immigrant in
American History,* "The odyssey of the immigrant began," Hansen wrote

"when he first dreamed of that far-off land. Week after week that
dream became more real, speculation crystalized into action and, finally,
the day of departure arrived. There was a "last time for everything — a
last Sunday in the Church with the village pastor extending a special
blessing; a last visit to the tavern where the whole company solemnly
drank to the success of the undertaking; a last stroll through the winding
lanes or along the river's bank; a last night beneath the paternal roof.
To hide neighborhood doubts once the decision was made, tradition
decreed that festivity should reign. In Germany, orchestras and bands
of singers serenaded until the doors were opened and all thronged in
for a shake of the hand and a final word of encouragement. . . . Shortly
after sunrise, to the pealing of the village bells, the procession started,
accompanied for a mile or two along the highway by the now weeping
relatives and strangers."

Germans left their native cities and *dorfs* for many reasons. Some of
them because of their opposition to the Kaiser's wars were the predecessors of the current "draft-dodgers" who leave the United States. Others
left because of the religious persecution that followed the *Kulturkamp*
inaugurated by Chancellor Bismarck. Others left for the call to a
better life and the promise of cheap land that was loudly promoted
by missionaries, land companies and state-sponsored land development
offices. "The promise of," wrote John Massman,

"a new Canaan flowing with milk and honey induced thousands of
Germans to desert their looms and shops, farms and cottages for a new
life in the prairie-forest region of Minnesota. They read glowing accounts
by propagandists and believed. They devoured letters penned by missionaries and by friends and relatives in the New World, not failing to
note the repeated references to the good life awaiting them in the trans-
Mississippi West."

So the Germans heeded the call to the West. In 1862 there were
only 27,527 Germans who emmigrated; however, between 1866 and
1870 over a hundred thousand Germans emigrated each year. The
number of German immigrants increased each decade of the second
half of the nineteenth century, from 244,887 in the 1860's to an all time
high of 400,000 in 1890's. A majority of these Catholic Germans did
not remain in the seaboard towns on the Atlantic coast but made the
journey into the heartland of the bustling nation. So vast was their

number that they created what was later called "the German belt" geographically extending in a triangular pattern from Buffalo, New York to St. Louis to central Minnesota. One of the chief reasons why so many of Father Pierz' "dear German Catholics" emigrated was expressed by a Catholic tenant farmer of the Rhineland when he said:

"My landlord gave us free lodging and 23-30 pfenning a day for wages. For this my whole family had to labor on Sundays as well as weekdays. We were obliged to do our own chores during free hours and on Sunday afternoons. If we asked permission to go to Church on Sunday, then the man abused us . . . every time and said: "You won't always need to be running after the priest if you find yourselves in the alms house. And so I am going to America. My acquaintances write from there that they have such good conditions, and on Sundays as many as wish to may go to Church. My children shall not imitate my slavery."

A large number of these German immigrants found their way to the frontier of Minnesota. As their Scandanavian brothers who would follow them twenty and thirty years later, they sought woods and water, an innate love of Germanic people. In 1867 a writer in the *Minneapolis Chronicle* observed that the German immigrants coming into the state "immediately upon their arrival here, they make a bee line for the Big Woods. They cannot stand the prairie, but are at home in the heavy timber, where they grub and clear off the land with all the activity and patience imaginable..." The 1890 census of Minnesota showed that Minnesotans of German parentage ranked first in all the foreign-parentage categories. Over twenty-percent of the citizens had either one or both German-born parents. A further figure showing that twenty-three percent of all the children born in Minnesota between 1871 and 1884 had German-born parents reveals the influence of the German immigrants on the development of our state. In 1890 with a state population of 34,844 over ten thousand were foreign born and the vast majority of these had come from Germany.

It was no easy task, however, to leave family, home and the fatherland and strike out for an unknown and uncertain future. "The several million Germans," wrote John Massman,

"who left their old homes in search of a new chance during the nineteenth century faced a long, and often hazardous journey. Wherever they turned someone seemed to be there to try and take advantage of them. Boarding-house keepers wanted business. Shipping companies looked for passengers. Railroads searched for settlers. Port cities vied for a greater share of the lucrative emigrant trade. Runners, money changers, and thieves tried to relieve them of a part or all of their money and to steal their baggage. To cities, steamship lines, and unscrupulous persons the emigrant offered a means of immediate or potential profit."

In spite of the trials and hardships they still kept dreaming of that day when they could pack family and baggage and set out for the "new world." The journey across the ocean was long and arduous and lasted in some cases as long as two months. The immigrant was sometimes the victim of thieving sailors and other times the prey of unscrupulous steamship agents. Religious leaders frequently complained about the unwholesome and immoral conditions that existed on the ship during the trans-Atlantic voyage. In many cases a wife, a husband, brother or sister died at sea and only the recording angel can tell of the thousands who suffered terribly from that ever-recurring malady, sea-sickness. The cost of so uncomfortable a journey would vary from forty dollars for adults to thirty dollars for children.

Yet by the millions they made the journey overseas, by the thousands they came to central Minnesota and by the hundreds to Melrose. By 1850 over 17,000 had found their way to Minnesota; by 1870 48,457 had arrived; by 1880 over 18,000 and by 1890 there were 116,955 German-born immigrants in the North Star state. At first they arrived in St. Paul by riverboat and later, by railroad. As they went in search of their new land they sang, as all German people love to sing, a popular ballad of the period:

> At last! the cry spreads
> Out you people, there is land
> Balleri, Ballera, Balleri, juchhe.
> Balledri, Balledra
> Now we are in America,
> Balleri . . .
> Then we come to a waterfall
> And thank God for everything
> Balleri . . .

Their joy upon arriving in a new country and the joy of a new way of life, however, did not protect them from further hardships. Some were the victims of inhuman treatment by the railroads carrying them to their new homes. Some travelers were packed into cars behind freight trains and were switched to isolated stops without food or water. The *St. Paul Daily Press* recounted some of these hardships in an article in its May 24, 1861 issue entitled "A Regular Swindle." The author wrote:

"There is a lot of one-horse boarding house keepers in our city, who have commenced practicing a very mean and despicable business towards immigrants who arrive by the boats from below. Only a few days since, a number of German families arrived, and, as is the custom with these economical people, were anxious at once to depart for their destination . . .

one of these harpies — one of their own countrymen — came among them with the lying tale that the Indians were over-running the neighborhood where they were going and murdering all the whites. He persuaded most of them to remain a few days, took them to his house, or the house for which he is a 'runner' and of course made a 'good thing' out of his false story. Without at all finding fault with the present excellent regulations on the levee, we should suggest to the Mayor to detail a day policeman for that service who understands the German language."

The dream which urged the immigrants to take the final step was best expressed in the poem, *"Lose Blatter aus Minnesota's Geschichte"* written by Francis Martin for the *Minnesota Volkszeitung.* Even allowing for poetic license it was then, as now, idyllic, yet it represented the aspirations of millions who came to the western frontier.

> Oh, how many wonderful things
> One hears from America
> There we wish to make our way
> There one has the finest life.
> Here one has his daily strife
> And scarce can find 'nough bread for life
> There one had life's abundance
> In America the beautiful land.
> Now let us on our journey go
> Dear God will stand beside us so
> To shelter us with His own hand
> And bring us to the promised land.
> Also be with us on the sea
> Almighty God with your guardian hosts
> For ev'rywhere you are so near
> Here and also in America.
> The wagon ready stands before the door
> With wife and children we depart
> All you dear and well known friends
> For the last time now your hands extend.
> Dear friends, do not so fondly cry,
> We see you today and then nevermore.

Without railroad service the area might have been much slower in development. The St. Paul and Pacific Railroad included rebates to settlers in order to encourage cultivation. In the 1870's, for instance, the rebate consisted of $2.50 per acre if the settler would cultivate ten of eighty acres; twenty of 160, fifty of 320 and one hundred of 640 within a year of his purchase. "These rebates," Massman concludes, "could total up to three-fourths of the cost of acreage purchased."

Besides purchasing the land, the German immigrant had to purchase the necessary implements to practice his trade. Since most of the Germans who settled in the area were farmers and not businessmen, they would be most concerned with the cost of farming equipment. A yoke of oxen cost $125.00; horses were $300.00; a span harness about $40.00 apiece; wagons were $90.00 each; boards for fencing eighteen cents each; a McCormick reaper cost $200.00; and breaking plows $30.00 each. A hired man could be employed for a dollar a day plus board and laborers during harvest time for $3.50 a day. Henry Petermeier, the son of one of the early pioneers, Stephen Petermeier, recalled that their eight bedroom farm home built in 1895 cost $700.00.

So the German immigrants came to the Melrose area in the last two decades of the nineteenth century. They were seeking prosperity, to be sure, but they were also seeking the freedom to practice their religion without government restrictions. Both natural and spiritual considerations have guided and directed their descendants even to the present day. Father Colman Barry, O.S.B., made the following observation:

"The German Catholics settled together in colonies wherever possible, often by their own choice, more often under the direction of zealous German missionary priests. They desired to have churches of their own in which their traditional religious observances and customs could be carried out, where they could hear sermons in their mother tongue, go to confession as they had learned to confess from early childhood, and take an active part in parish life through their beloved societies. They wanted the order and discipline of parish life as they had known it before coming to the United States."

In Melrose they created a way of life that would be industrious, thrifty, hard-working and religious. They were too busy creating farm land out of the woods and swamps of Melrose township; too industrious in establishing new businesses and industries; too concerned with outwitting and eventually beating the Yankee and Irish at their own business enterprises; and, yes, too concerned with their own family and religious life to give much consideration to the events of the outside world. They read their own German-language newspapers, *Der Wanderer* and *Der Nordstern* and the local *Melrose Sun* that would soon become the *Melrose Beacon*, and in none of them would they find much intellectual stimulation apart from the local happenings of state, county and township and some parochial religious items of more than passing interest.

Little were they aware of the tremendous population growth taking place in their newly adopted country. During the last three decades of the century 11,903,224 immigrants from European countries passed through American ports and of that number almost four million were

Catholics. Nor did it seem important to them that only a few hundred miles to the north a new nation, Canada, was born, created by the British Parliament's North America Act of 1867. Though life was rugged and the major preoccupation in the Melrose area was clearing the land and making of a living, events taking place in the world would profoundly affect the futures of their sons and daughters.

The first year of the 1870's witnessed the proclamation of the dogma of papal infallibility; the birth of Lenin, christened Vladimir Ilyich Ulyanov; and the beginning of the Franco-Prussian War, which ended at Versailles with Germany being proclaimed as Empire. The European intellectuals were discussing a book, *Das Kapital*, written by an unknown author, Karl Marx. Marx's book was published in 1867, the same year that a Swedish chemist, Alfred Nobel, invented dynamite; in future years Marx's book would have more tragic effects on world history than Nobel's invention. Although there would be scant attention given by these sturdy Germans their Irish neighbors were thrilled by the news that Charles Steward Parnell was elected to Parliament in 1875 and revived the movement for Irish independence. These Germans, rather, were discontent with the local Irish and to register their disapproval of the Irish in 1878 fifteen German families left the "Irish" church and founded their own "German" church.

The Germans paid more attention to news events developing in their adopted land. When the first German immigrants began coming to Melrose a financial panic in 1873 caused a depression that lasted five years. By the time most of the German immigrants had arrived and settled in Melrose a financial depression in 1893 resulted in the failure of thousands of banks and commercial establishments. Only in 1897 did the economy recover. The settlers were stunned, as Americans have always been in such crisis, when President James A. Garfield was shot in 1881. The conservative settlers would be shocked and surprised three years later when Grover Cleveland became the first Democrat elected to the presidency since 1860. The formation of the American Federation of Labor in 1886 did not much concern them and the Sherman Anti-Trust Act of 1890 they neither understood, nor even cared about.

They were fascinated, however, by the reports concerning the Indians, as Americans have always been intrigued by the land of the golden West and by the country's original citizens. They read the news of Custer's massacre by Chief Sitting Bull's braves in 1876; the capture of Geronimo in 1886; and the tragedy of the white man's brutality at the Battle of Wounded Knee in 1893, this being the last time the Army of the United States would slaughter the Indians *en masse.* Years later poet Steven Vincent Benét would immortalize the battle with the phrase:

> I shall not be there.
> I shall rise and pass.
> Bury my heart at Wounded Knee.

Commenting upon the American Indian in 1971 historian Dee Brown wrote, "Now, a century later, in an age without heroes, they are perhaps the most heroic of all Americans."

These German immigrants and Irish railroad workers were also concerned about the Pullman strike of 1894 for many a friend or neighbor was employed by the railroad. On April 16, 1894 the trainmen employed by the Great Northern Railroad went out on strike. It was a bitter strike, lasting until May 2, 1894 with court injunctions being issued forbidding the strikers to interfere with the operation of the railroad. The strikers demanded a return to the wage scale that was in effect before the depression of 1893. After lengthy arbitration the strike was settled and the men returned to work. It was more than an inconvenience to all people along the line and business men suffered severe financial losses. Feeling towards the railroad was extremely bitter in St. Cloud, where the division headquarters were then located. Through acts of interference some of the businessmen of St. Cloud provoked the anger of the railroad officials and this appears to be one of the reasons why the Great Northern division headquarters were removed to Melrose that same year. Another reason given is the removal of the first division center from Fergus Falls to Barnesville thus making the division of labor unequal inasmuch as the distance from St. Paul to St. Cloud was almost half as far as the distance from St. Cloud to Barnesville.

The coming of the division headquarters to Melrose was a turning point in the growth of the city and surrounding area. It was marked by the arrival of more settlers; the growth of the city; the expansion of facilities. A spirit of optimism filled the citizens as they stood on the eve of a new century.

An indication of the growth of the community is reflected in the assessed valuations of the city. In 1860 the valuation of Stearns county was $387,198 and Melrose was not even mentioned. Twelve years later Melrose first appeared on the assessed valuations rolls and then was listed at $7,540 with the county listed as having a total valuation of $2,672,419. A decade later the valuations of Melrose rose to $31,995 with the county being listed as $5,123,921. At the turn of the century Melrose was evaluated as $106,649 and the county as $6,526,809. In other words, from the period between 1872 and 1896 the assessed valuation of the county rose 144 percent while during the same period the valuation of the city of Melrose increased 1,314 percent!

Before ending this chapter mention should again be made of some of the pioneers who lived in Melrose and developed the city in the closing years of the nineteenth century. B. F. Burrill is called by the author of the *History of the Upper Mississippi Valley* "a man of considerable prominence." Born in 1836 in Maine he arrived in Minnesota in the fall of 1857 and settled at St. Anthony Falls, remaining there until 1862 when he enlisted in the Sixth Minnesota Volunteer Infantry in which he first served on the western frontier and later was engaged in the Civil War. He arrived in Melrose in December, 1878 and was engaged in the management of Clark's cooper shops.

J. E. Campbell, M.D. was born in Brooklyn, New York in 1852. After pursuing studies in medicine in Aurora, Illinois and Ann Arbor, Michigan he came to Melrose in 1875, succeeding Dr. M. Gau who had arrived in Melrose in 1872. An active man in civic and commercial affairs, Dr. Campbell entered into partnership with his brother, C. R. Campbell and they opened the first livery stable in the growing village. In 1890 he became the publisher and owner of the *Melrose Sun.*

George L. Brinnell, a native New Yorker was born in 1827. At the age of twenty-three he caught "gold fever" and headed for the mines of California. Disillusioned, he returned to Pennsylvania and in 1861 enlisted in the Forty-Fifth Pennsylvania Volunteer Infantry and was severely wounded at the battle of the Wilderness. In 1868 he came to Melrose and engaged in farming.

Charles D. Lamb, a member of the first township board, was born in Bucks county, Pennsylvania on September 5, 1837. He arrived in the Melrose area in 1860 and engaged in farming. The following year he served in the Third Minnesota Volunteer Infantry in the Civil War as well as the Sioux campaign, in the latter suffering injuries at the battle of Wood Lake. For twelve years Lamb was assessor of the township and in 1876 he served as representative in the state legislature for the district. An extremely active man in civic affairs, Lamb also served as postmaster of Longhill for three years.

Donald B. McDonald, a Canadian, was born in Ontario on April 18, 1835. He arrived in the Melrose area in 1866 and settled on a farm about eight miles southeast of Melrose. McDonald moved to the city in 1869 and the following year became postmaster, an office he held for ten years. From June, 1877 until 1881 he served as editor of the *Melrose Record.*

Peter Pallansch, born in Belgium in 1849, came to America in 1868 and settled in Wisconsin where he learned the miller's trade. In 1874 he came to Melrose, after marrying the former Miss S. Heintz of Kandiyohi county the previous year, and became the manager of the Melrose Flouring Mill.

Gerhard Richter, another Rhinelander, was born on May 1, 1843. As a youth he learned the blacksmith trade in various German cities, emigrating to America in 1865. After living for six years in St. Cloud, Clearwater, and Richmond, serving as a blacksmith for the Minnesota Stage Company. Richter came to Melrose with his new bride, the former Miss M. Grunn of St. Cloud, in 1872. Here he became the village blacksmith and engaged in the manufacture of wagons and the sale of farm machinery.

These were but a few of the early settlers of the area with a cross-section of the background and training that prepared them to help create a city out of the growing community on the banks of the Sauk. There were others, to be sure, such as John Wette, who also came from the Rhineland who was both a stockman and butcher; O. D. Webb, who first operated a saw mill in Sauk Rapids and later a flour mill in Paynesville before taking up farming near Melrose in 1878. The names of other early settlers, whose family names are almost legion in the area today, also made their contributions in the establishment of the city and the building of the community. Many of these — such as John V. Free, Henry Loosbroek, Moritz Hoeschen, Dr. August Kuhlmann, Andrew Kolb, Henry G. Meyer, Adam Nickolaus — will be treated in a later chapter.

The economic depression of 1893 affected the entire population of the country, of the county and the Melrose community. Few people in the Melrose area suffered more from the depression of 1893 than the one who would come to be called "the Father of Melrose," Edwin Clark. The year was for him not only a tragic economic one, but also a year marked with personal sadness. His wife died during the same year that he lost control of his business enterprises and was forced to sell his properties and businesses in Melrose. His losses marked the end of an era both for himself and his family as well as for the community at large. Melrose would never again be the same as it had been in the past generation. Edwin Clark and his tragic misfortunes marked the passing of an era.

But Clark was no defeatist. Undaunted by failure, he returned to Minneapolis with his two sons and daughter and there engaged in several business enterprises. He was still well-known among the older citizens of the city by the Falls of St. Anthony and revered by the memory that he was the first publisher of the first daily newspaper in Minnesota in 1857. A man sensitive to history, he purchased the

Godfrey House, now located on University Avenue, the first house built in Minneapolis. He established the house as a museum under the auspices of the Hennepin County Pioneers Association, an organization he was active in until his death on April 27, 1922.

Progress was noted in the hustle and bustle of the frontier community of Melrose. The village needed a larger school to supercede the first school opened by Alred Townsend in 1868. A new and larger school was constructed in 1882. New additions to the plat of the village were added, notably Ayer's and Clark's addition in 1873. On March 3, 1881 the village was incorporated and the first elections were held the following April 5. The first village officers were J. H. Edelbrock, president; Edwin Clark and A. A. Whitney, Gerhard Richter and Joseph Moritz, councilmen; Donald B. McDonald, justice of the peace; Abram Lent, marshall and W. B. Whitney, street commissioner. Henry Borgerding and H. J. Haskamp organized the Bank of Melrose in 1886. There were wooden planks serving as sidewalks with gullies of mud on the streets in spring and seemingly mountains of snow in winter, but the mood of the citizenry was optimistic and, in a phrase that would be developed a hundred years later, all signals were "A-okay."

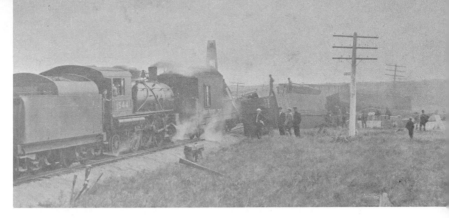

The wreck on the Great Northern east of Melrose in August, 1910.

Adley creek was dredged by workers from Lake Sylvia to the Sauk River in 1914.

Part of the crowd that gathered to view the fire at the railroad depot in 1910.

Homestead of the late Bernard Herzog. The new barn (1) was built by Carl Bruentner about 1907. One of the original buildings, constructed in 1897, still remains on the farm which is now owned by Joseph Weber.

Dillo Hinnenkamp's blacksmith shop has not changed much over the years, except for the wooden sidewalk.

This could be a scene from a Western movie, but it is rather two of the thriving business establishments in Melrose about 1890.

Henry Tieman was the proud owner of the first auto dray wagon in Melrose.

The fire that demolished the Kleber store in 1934 was a major economic disaster for the community.

Long before St. Cloud became known as the "Granite City" Melrose was the center of a thriving granite industry. John Luckemeyer opened this marble cutting shop in 1897.

A group of the granite cutters of Melrose taken in 1909.

Charles "Browney" Hoffman was one of the expert granite craftsmen for many years in the area. He is lettering a headstone in 1928.

For many years Herman Hollermann's woodworks was a landmark in Melrose. This photograph of his employees was taken in 1911.

The first saw mill in the area was opened in 1895 by Henry and Elizabeth Hinnenkamp. Located three miles north of Melrose, it has always been known as the Hinnenkamp saw mill. It is still in operation.

A carpenter crew at the turn of the century worked for a dollar a day and built many of the buildings still standing in the area. They are, seated left to right: August Moorman, Joseph Roering, Michael Hennen, Herman Hollermann; standing left to right, Paul Stadherr, Frank Hinnenkamp, Peter Hinnenkamp and Fred Wessel.

The interior of the Melrose Telephone office as it appeared about 1930 showing operators Marie Stundebeck and Mildred Arvig.

The fiftieth anniversary of the Melrose Fire Department was marked by the purchase of a new Reo chassis with a pumping capacity of five hundred gallons a minute in 1934. Shown above, front row left to right: John Beste, Anthony Primus, Henry Rolfzen, Hubert Beste (chief), U. C. Schlicht (assistant chief), J. T. Angelbeck, Henry Griep, Otto Bringe, H. F. Hinnenkamp, Ignatius Lemmn, H. J. Tieman. back row left to right: Oswald Botz (secretary), Leo Lemm, R. C. Kleber, C. W. Carlson, Herman Hollermann, C. P. Meyer, Joseph Hemmesch, H. C. Tembrock, Joseph Stundebeck, Henry Primus. Seated on the truck is Peter Wilhelm, a retired member at that time.

The original Melrose co-operative creamery located on the north side of the Sauk River.

Before the advent of the beer truck, refreshments were delivered by the barrel.

No one in Melrose was prouder than Matt Winter with his first Model-A car that appeared on the city's streets.

One of Melrose's successful businessmen today is Al Kociemba, manager of the Red Owl Store.

Celebrating an achievement in one of Melrose's far-reaching businesses were these employees of Munson Feed Company; left to right: Ed Munson, Joseph Ellering, Peter Terres, Christ Athman and Vernon Munson.

Officials of the Firestone Tire Company presented Henry Loxterkamp (center) with a Lord Elgin wrist watch after twenty-five years of service to the company.

For thirty-five years Eddie Salzman has been "doctor" to Melrose's machines. The mechincal crew are, from left to right: Louie Rau, Barney Servatius, Connie Salzman, Eddie Salzman.

In 1972 the Melrose Post of the Veterans of Foreign Wars and its Auxiliary observed the silver anniversary of their organizations. Charter members of the post, shown above, are, seated left to right: Ben Tieman, Norbert Renneker, Elmer Eveslage, Ted Welz, Thomas Kennedy; standing left to right: Olaf Becker, Roman Schulzetenberg, Ted Kennedy, Jack Kraker, Eddie Schlzetenberg, Al Thelen, commander, Abe Spaeth and Clyde Tise. Charter members of the auxiliary shown below are, seated left to right: Renee Moening, Ann Otte, Marie Latzka, Johanna Weier, Sophia Loehr; standing left to right: Geri Tiemann, Marie Welz, Delores Kluempke, Rose Moening, Ida Spaeth, Alma Stalberger, Rose Anderson and Francis Monroe.

CHAPTER THREE

A CORD OF WOOD
AND A PAIL OF BEER

If it be true that the past is a prologue to the future, it is most certainly true in the development of Melrose throughout the next twenty years, a period ranging from 1895 to 1915. The pioneers, symbolized by Moses Adley, gave way to the settlers, represented by Edwin Clark. No longer will one or two names dominate the panorama; instead the list will expand to include many of the names still familiar in the area. Many hands and hearts will fashion a community that will become "a thriving and flourishing city in Stearns County." From a population of 611 in 1881, the city will grow by 1915 to a total of 2,500 inhabitants.

One of the older members of the community, Henry Petermeier recalled how in his youth the family would bring a cord of wood to town from the farm and exchange it for a pail of beer. Another elder citizen, Theodore Wessel, recalled the time where a person could row a boat from five miles north to the city, so swampy and full of creeks was that area at the turn of the century.

The most striking sign of growth and optimism was the incorporation of Melrose as a city in 1896, and it still remains one of the three cities in the county, the others being Saint Cloud and Sauk Centre. The first mayor was Dr. P. A. Hilbert. Other officers were Conrad Keppel, president; J. A. McGregor, Joseph Primus, George Rauch and William Schwanke, aldermen; Frank Waldorf, clerk; F. J. Weisser, justice of the peace. A writer in the Melrose *Beacon*, commenting upon the election made an observation as accurate today as it was then:

"The difficulties attending the organization of a city are many and the expenses to be met are numerous and by no means small, while the reward usually given to the first set of city officials consists principally of adverse criticisms. This the new officers received in large chunks, but they met regularly, transacted business as they believed to the best interest of all concerned and retired."

That there must have been some discontent among the citizenry is evidenced by the election returns of 1897 when Dr. J. E. Campbell succeeded as mayor and H. R. Edelbrock as president and William Rahn as alderman. An earlier writer has noted that until this time "Melrose was a sleepy little village of but 847 inhabitants."

The people of this area were becoming more and more interested in the world at large: that interest would be intensified during the succeeding decades. They did not know that Einstein formulated the theory of relativity in 1905 nor did many other people in the world realize the significance of that discovery in the years to come. The social rumbling in the Balkan states in 1908, and again in 1912 spurred the first arms race among the European powers; the murder of Archduke Francis Ferdinand of Austria was the spark that ignited the powder keg into a full blown war in 1914. In 1917, preoccupied with the war in Europe and rumors of the United States getting involved in that war so distracted the citizens from noticing a far more significant and disastrous world event, the Bolshevik Revolution of 1917. The Treaty of Versailles was signed in 1919 and the giddy optimists felt that they emerged with a victory in a "war to end all wars," which was even further confirmed by the formation of the League of Nations the following year.

Once again Melrose was shocked, as was the nation and the world, by the assassination of President William McKinley in 1901, as we who live today were shocked by the death of three great leaders in the sixties, John F. Kennedy, Martin Luther King and Robert Kennedy. With most of their contemporaries they rejoiced upon hearing that the Panama Canal was opened in 1914 for it represented a fulfillment of the expansionist designs of the national government which was led by that exceptional man, Theodore Roosevelt, who created a modern proverb when he said, "Speak softly and carry a big stick." As most of the nation, Melrose was not surprised on April 2, 1917 when President Woodrow Wilson called for a declaration of war against Germany, saying, "We have no selfish ends to serve. We desire no conquest, no dominion. We seek no indemnities . . . no material compensation." And eighteen months later the jubilation in Melrose was just as enthusiastic as in every part of the world because the war had ended.

Life was not all work and business during this period. At the turn of the century the Melrose *Beacon* recorded that "a merry crowd of thirty young people organized a sleighing party, drove down from Sauk Centre. . . . After having supper at Hotel Melrose, they all went to the club dance and spent a few hours in merriment at the ball. They started homeward at about half after eleven." The same chronicler took note of the fact that John Wellenstein's store advertised Dr. Reed's Cushion Shoes, which were "not only divinely suited to strutting about, but helped cure corns, callous spots, bunions, perspiring and burning feet, prevents corns, neuralgia, pneumonia, rheumatism, ciatica (*sic*), etc." A later observer commented, "One helluva pair of shoes for $2.50." The editor also noted that Melrose had only eight saloons left, since Joseph Kleber and J. J. Hilt went out of business. "The $1,000 liquor license went into effect July 1," he stated, "and eight saloons are a great plenty anyhow." The "horseless carriage" made its appearance on the sometimes muddy, sometimes dusty streets and roads. In 1909 the editor noted that the Studebaker "Flanders" was introduced, "featuring four cylinders, 20 horsepower, a 100-inch wheel-base, 32-inch wheels and, of course, a magneto." The same year three million acres of Indian reservation land at Cheyenne River, South Dakota, were thrown open for homesteaders. "To be eligible," the editor wrote, "one would merely register with the Land Office in that state and wait for the raffle-type drawing to determine the winners." And as did every weekly paper, the Melrose *Beacon* carried its "locals." One tells us that the Kraker girls went to Sauk Centre one Sunday and another tells us Mrs. Fred Zisky of Greenwald was afflicted with carbuncles on her back. The editor added, "The dear woman has our sympathies." And during these years the Theodore Hamm Brewing Company was advertising Digesto Malt Extract for workers, housewives, businessmen and all others as a "stimulating tonic that helps relieve the day-to-day pressures encountered by all of us."

There were, too, events of exceptional nature, times when friends and neighbors would gather to celebrate a wedding, pay respects to the deceased and engage in neighborhood parties. Mrs. Frank Hinnenkamp recalled these days when she wrote about life as it was for one of the pioneer families, that of Heinerich "Holzschumaker" Hinnenkamp.

"He was born in Voerden, Hanover, Germany and married Elizabeth Niehaus in 1848. He served in the Franco-Prussian War in 1870-1871 and shortly after came to the United States with their six children. He worked in the brewery owned by his brother-in-law in Cincinnati until he had saved enough money to move to Melrose township where he started farming about 1890, three and a half miles north of the city. His first wife died in 1882 and two years later married Elizabeth Hollermann. From his second marriage he also had six children. Two daughters, Sister Boniface and Sister Gaudentia joined the Franciscan Sisters at Little Falls and one son, Father Frederick was ordained a priest for the Diocese of St. Cloud.

With three brothers, Diederick, Herman and Bernard, they settled near each other north of Melrose and helped each other clear the land, build roads and construct log houses and log barns. Trees had to be cut down with a cross-cut saw and later the stumps had to be cut around the outside, with a grub axe. A 'slip hook' with a long pole pulled by horses pulled out the stumps. The trees were cut down for fire wood and some of this was sold in town and from the money they received they bought groceries for their homes. A few cows were added to the farm every year and they were milked by hand. The milk was brought to the creamery where it was separated and made into butter. At this time butter sold for twenty cents a pound. They raised only very few chickens and eggs sold for about ten cents a dozen.

People husked corn by hand and the straw was saved to feed the cattle. Later a corn shredder was bought and thus corn could be shredded faster and easier. Hired help was cheap. You could hire a man for a dollar or a dollar and a half a day. People worked hard and saved their money and were happy.

But we still had good pastimes playing solo, sixty-six and pinochle. In winter-time about eight neighbors would join together, pack the whole family in a sled drawn by horses and with jingle bells ringing, go off to visit a neighbor. There we would play cards, partake of a good lunch and go home happy.

North of Melrose the people also celebrated the *Schiessenfest*, which was always celebrated on Pentecost Monday. Young and old, everyone was welcome to come. A forty or fifty-foot pole was set up with a bird carved out of wood placed on the top of the pole. The men all brought their guns to take turns shooting the bird down. The one that shot the wings would get one dollar and the man that shot the entire bird was the King of the *Schiessenfest* and he had the privilege to select a Queen for the next year. They had to sponsor the *Schiessenfest* for the next year and entertain the neighbors in the area. They had music and dancing and drinking and a great supper was served one and all. The people always enjoyed the *Schiessenfest* party. Henry "Holzschumaker" Hinnenkamp died on September 13, 1916."

Another event, celebrated by family and friends, was a wedding in the area. In the homes of the early settlers people gathered together to make light work of arduous tasks. Since everyone worked diligently, there was the hum of activity known as a "bee." The women enjoyed these get-togethers because it was a chance to catch up on the news of the neighborhood. Corn-husking, apple-paring and quilt-making were common types of bees.

When a settler was ready to build a new house, the logs were first prepared at the mill for the "house-raising." The men of the area would come together to help neighbor, relative or friend and the women would prepare their choicest dishes for the hungry crew. When news of a wedding spread throughout the community the women of the neighborhood would gather to help the bride-to-be prepare quilts, pillows and other household needs for her hope chest. The feathers were saved from wild and domestic fowl to be made into pillows and feather beds. In the area north of Melrose a custom, dating back to the "old country," was known as the "hanging of the wreath." It took place at the home of the bride on the Sunday before the wedding. A heavy rope of green branches and vines gathered by the young men was interwoven with flowers. The wreath was carried in procession around the house while the young people sang German love songs. The festoon was draped over the door of the home and hung down at the sides. A suitable verse or reading which had been compiled before-hand was read to the young couple about to be married. It told of the good qualities of the couple. Showers, then as now, were held as a means of giving a young couple gifts for their new home. Frequently today the attendants host a shower dance at a public hall; previously these dances were held in the home of the bride. Neighbors and rela-tives would help prepare the wedding dinner in the home of the bride and most of it was prepared in the homes of the area. Besides baking and cooking, decorating the house and bowery, friends and neighbors would assist in the decoration of the church and, never to be forgotten, the "marriage carriage" that was the delightful occupation of the young men of the area.

During these early years of the century weddings were more simple than they are today. The young couple might ride to church in a wagon or a carriage if they were from the country; if from the city, they would walk. Wedding dresses were in a great variety of colors. Old photo-graphs show many of dark hues. In fact, one showed the bride and bridesmaids all in black cashmere gowns with white at the neck and cuffs. Usually a bridal veil was held in place by a wreath of wax blos-soms. A prayer book, rosary or a tiny bouquet of flowers was usually carried by the bride. The groom was dressed in somber black, with a stiff high collar and a large necktie. The photographer arranged a few standard poses, with one of the principals sitting on a fringed, velvet chair and the partner, usually the bride, standing with a hand on his shoulder. Most of the pictures had the couple pose in a serious mien and, in almost all, a steady fixed stare into oblivion.

Long hours of work and the difficulty of travel developed close bonds among the families in a relatively small area. Although Henry Ford had begun his assembly line in 1908 and created the Model T Ford, it would be some time before roads in the area were suitable for the "horseless carriage" and even more years would pass before "motor-ing" would be a familiar sight in the area and a frequently used word in the local gazette. Thus young people would chose their friends from among the neighboring families and ultimately a life partner would literally be in many cases the girl next door. Parents kept their eyes open for a good partner for son or daughter and in not a few cases literally made the arrangements for brothers and sisters in one family to marry brothers and sisters in another. Only after travel became more convenient would the young men of Melrose find wives in the neighboring communities such as Meire Grove, New Munich, Spring Hill, Saint Rosa (which at the turn of the century was called Saint Isabella) and Sauk Centre. This sometimes resulted in a rivalry between factions in the community. "Doesn't he think the people here are good enough to marry?" was a frequent question. At such weddings, before the dance would end and before the bar was closed, there would be a free-for-all to prove which town area was better.

During these early decades of the century the wedding generally took place on Tuesday, with the wedding Mass beginning about nine o'clock, most probably because of the eucharistic fast. Generally only the bride and groom and attendants would receive Holy Communion. After Mass there was the traditional wagon ride throughout the city; a wagon festooned generally by the friends of the groom. The day's festivities were held at the home of the bride where a bowery of trees and a temporary wooden floor for dancing was erected. There was food a-plenty, surpassed in quantity perhaps only by the flow of beer. Music, supplied by the local musicians, was heard throughout the day and in the evening families and friends would gather in singing their favorite German songs. In the evening a charivari (shiveree) was part of the program. People who had not been invited to the wedding "crashed" the party by creating a deafening noise with cowbells, kettles, drums and anything that could be added to the din and clamor. In later years the charivari was held only after the newlyweds had returned to their home.

"Selling" the bride's slipper was also a part of the amusement at the dinner. The highest bidder paid the bride for her slipper. Now as then the young men would "steal" the bride and the young ladies would "steal" the groom and return them to the reception at an undetermined time. A couple who did not go on a honeymoon but went directly to their new home would frequently have an "after wedding" on the following Sunday. Families and friends who helped with the wedding would gather at the home of the newlyweds for an evening of visiting, eating and drinking.

A death in the community was always a major event. When news of a death in the family was announced — and the church bell would toll out the number of years of the deceased — friends and neighbors would hasten to extend sympathy and assistance to the bereaved family. They would clean the house, care for the children, bring food, do the farm chores, deliver messages to distant relatives and help in any way possible to bring consolation and comfort to the family. Before the days of embalming, neighbors would wash and dress the corpse and place it in a casket which was brought to the home in a wagon. The caskets were sold at the furniture store. In the time of an epidemic, such as the flu epidemic of 1918, wooden boxes were made for the burial by local carpenters. In warm weather tubs of ice were placed under the casket to help preserve the remains and a glass lid kept flies off the corpse.

The "wake," a peculiarly Irish custom, was readily adopted by the Germans. In these early days of the century two or three relatives and friends would stay up throughout the night and guard the corpse as it laid in the parlor of the home. The ladies of the neighborhood would serve a lunch to all who came from the food that was donated by them. The rosary was recited at various intervals throughout the day and evening and one of the more pious ladies would be heard exclaiming from time to time, *"Bet mit mir."* The wake took on the nature of a social event when people who had not seen friends and relatives for a long time would have the opportunity to visit and renew acquaintances.

In some homes, at the time of a death in a family, clocks were stopped and mirrors covered or turned to the wall. Sometimes the door was draped in black and a funeral wreath was hung on the outside wall of the house. Older people who anticipated death would prepare for it by placing a complete set of clean clothing in a box to be used for their burial.

In good weather the corpse was carried to the church on a wagon and in winter on a sled, and generally the wagon or sled was draped in a black bunting. Only in later years was the hearse introduced and this was usually framed in glass so that the casket could be seen from the outside. In the city itself the mourners would walk in procession from the home to the church, praying as they walked behind the hearse. The procession to the cemetery was made on foot, as is the case in some parishes even to this day. Flowers were sent as an expression of sympathy for the family. The floral wreath was usually made up of white and purple pieces of flowers. The broken wheel with a spoke or bit of rim missing, a chain with a broken link, a heart pierced by an arrow were some of the more popular symbols used in these floral creations. The "Gates Ajar," modeled after a floral creation in Como Park, St. Paul, was a more elaborate arrangement, expressing the idea that the gates of heaven were now opened for the deceased. The clothing of the mourners were always black with a touch of white. Women wore heavy black veils over their hats, thus hiding their faces and men placed black crepe bands on their hats or arms. These signs of mourning would be worn by the immediate family for several months and in many cases for an entire year. The family of the deceased refrained from attending parties, dances and other social gatherings for a year.

After the burial relatives returned to the home of the deceased for a lunch and some would remain for several days to give consolation and help to the family. Then friends, neighbors and relatives would all depart and the family was left alone to recover from the shock, to recall the kindness of so many friends and relatives and to feel the loneliness in heart and home by the absence of a loved one.

Besides the influx of German settlers to the area surrounding the city, the division headquarters of the Great Northern railroad also brought a great number of city residents, most of whom were of Irish descent. By state law Melrose acquired the title of a city, as did four other municipalities in the state, namely Cloquet, East Grand Forks, Red Lake Falls and Thief River Falls. More than the title, however, was the fact that Melrose was taking on the characteristics of a self-sustaining and self-promoting community. The railroad roundhouse provided around-the-clock work for the men of the city and Clark's mill, now owned by John Hoeschen, continued to expand its business because of the growing number of farms being created by the *bushwackers* of the area. The editor of the Melrose *Beacon* at the turn of the century described the city as "not 'booming,' but just forging ahead at a good, healthy pace."

By 1896 the city had taken the shape that it largely retains to this present time. From Adley's original settlement on the banks of the Sauk, the city had extended to include the Great Northern addition, Ayers and Clark's addition, Freeman's addition, Dederick's addition, Kolb's addition and Borgerding's addition, all lying south of the river and Haskamp's, Kraker's and Hoeschen's additions lying north of the river. The townsite was platted and names were given the streets, names, regrettably, that have recently been supplanted by numbers. Some of the early names given the streets were Fulsom, Morris, McKenzie, McDonald, Deland, Miller, Adley, Freeman, Grove, Borgerding, Rowe, Hoeschen, Hill and Kraker. The map of 1895 shows the site of the Methodist Church where the present Dairy Freeze is located, the Episcopal Church two blocks west on Riverside Avenue, the "Irish Church" on the site of the present Rose View Manor apartments and the "German Church" on the site of the present St. Mary's Church.

In 1896 people had moved to the north banks of the Sauk River, many of them employees of the railroad. Rather than take a long route back and forth to work by way of the bridge by the dam, they joined together in building a "footbridge," thus creating a second span across the Sauk. Although modest in construction, it served its purpose well. In recent years it has been replaced by the present concrete structure even though it is still called "the foot-bridge."

A city needed electrical power if the wheels of industry were to keep turning. Thus in 1895 John Hoeschen, the newly-established owner of Clark's mill, installed a direct current plant and sold electrical power under contract to the city. This arrangement lasted for ten years. In 1905, however, the city undertook the construction of its own electrical light plant, erected a building and installed a Bros Boiler, seventy-five kilowatt two phase generator and a Twin City Corliss 125 horse power engine. In the same year a water works was installed, the source of water being the Sauk River Mill Pond. The following year a two panel switchboard was installed, the distribution system was completed and services were supplied to approximately fifty customers. Further improvements and additions were made over the years until the "great white way" was built in 1925. Due to the inefficiency of the steam generating plant, operations were halted in 1937 and two Fairbanks Morse 2 - kilowatt diesel generating units were purchased to handle the electrical load. Continued demands, reflecting the growth of the city, necessitated the installation of a 467 kilowatt unit in 1938, a 975 kilowatt unit in 1945, and a 1,136 kilowatt unit in 1949 to provide a plant capacity of 2,987 kilowatt power.

On July 12, 1969, the new Municipal Water, Light Plant Building was dedicated. The utility commission members are: Oswald Botz, Norman Bohlig, R. O. Passi, Chairman; Al J. Westendorf, Commission Secretary; John Hinnenkamp, Utility Superintendent. Plant operations personnel include Ves Roering, Ronnie Zirbes, Don Oevermann, Herb Inderrieden, Ervin Vogel, and Rich Klasen. Administrative personnel are Mrs. Martha Meyer and Miss Rose Ann Hellermann, secretarial assistants.

The capacity of kilowatt volume has increased at a rate of 8 percent per year and at the present time the generating capacity of the plant is rated at 8,111 kilowatts per hour at peak load.

The Melrose Water, Light, Power and Building Commission furnishes electric light and power service only to the residents of the city. The Stearns County Electric Cooperative serves the surrounding area. The City Water System is supervised by the Light and Power Commission and supervision and maintenance of public buildings is under the control of the Utilities Commission.

Besides electrical power a city must also have fire protection. The first records of the Melrose Volunteer Fire Department date from 1894. Two units were organized, Hook and Ladder Company Number One in 1894 and Hook and Ladder Company Number Two in 1896. Officers of the first company were Charles Spicer, foreman; B. J. Moritz, first assistant; John Tiedeman, second assistant; Stephen J. Ley, secretary; John A. Schoenborn, treasurer. Officers of the second company were: M. Burton, foreman; M. A. Scherfins, first assistant; T. P. Kitowski, second assistant; W. J. Bohmer, secretary-treasurer. Both companies had members assigned to specific duties such as crankmen, climbers, axemen, horsemen and the like. In 1898 the Fire Department Relief Association was organized in order to give aid to those who were afflicted by serious fire damage. The first officers of the group were George J. Wampach, president; Frank Waldorf, vice-president; H. F. Loosbrook, secretary and John H. Walz, treasurer. The board of directors were P. M. Koenigs, J. W. Helsper, John Tiedeman, Joseph Primus and John Sauer. The finance committee consisted of Charles Kramer, John Krick, Lambert Sonnen, George L. Sauer and Michael Rauch.

The necessity for a Volunteer Fire Department at that time was as obvious as it is today. A catastrophe was reported on February 19, 1896 when a fire broke out in J. J. Hill's livery barn and spread to the feed stable owned by William Unger and Wheeler's livery stable, all of which were destroyed. In August of the same year the Haskamp elevator, managed by M. S. Kolb, was burned, destroying the 4,000 bushels of wheat stored therein. The Catholic church and rectory in nearby Spring Hill was completely destroyed on October 31, 1899 and July 15, 1904 the Great Northern dispatcher's office was almost entirely destroyed, the source of the fire being attributed to the sparks of a passing locomotive. In the same year the Catholic Church in Freeport caught fire on October 19, only five years after it was built at a cost of $25,000 and six years later on January 5, St. Boniface school was completely destroyed by fire. In 1910 also, on June 7, the Great Northern depot was destroyed by fire, again caused by the sparks thrown out of the smokestack of a passing locomotive. The depot, one of the oldest buildings in town, was built in 1871. "It was entirely inadequate for present needs," the local editor stated, "and as stated by the *Beacon* last week Melrose was to have a new depot sometime this summer." A major catastrophe occurred on March 21, 1914 when the high school building was completely destroyed by fire — needless to add, much to the glee of the local scholars. For some of the local and thirsty citizens, however, an even greater tragedy occurred on September 9 of the same year when the Melrose Brewery, valued at $50,000 was totally destroyed by fire. "It was owned by the Melrose Brewing Company," a local historian recorded, "which carried only $10,000 insurance, the loss therefore being heavy."

The Melrose Brewing Company was organized in 1911 to brew a beer called Schatz-Brau. An early historian made a masterpiece of understatement when he said it was "an important institution." Located on the north side of the river, near the present home of Dr. L. B. Kuhlmann, its first officers were Andrew Stalboerger, Peter P. Stalboerger, secretary-treasurer, and John F. Winter, manager. The Melrose keg beer, called "Old Bohemian Style" was in popular demand and the first year of the company's organization it produced over 1,200 barrels of beer. Within three years the annual output rose to over 3,000 barrels annually. The era of prohibition soon sounded the death knell of the brewery as it did to many other small breweries throughout the country. After the days of prohibition, enterprising businessmen tried to resurrect the brewing industry in Melrose. The old Clark mill was refurnished and intended to become a brewery in 1934-1935. However, lack of working capital prevented it from ever producing so much as one bottle of beer. The old mill would be resurrected at a later date as the plant of a now thriving Melrose business, the Kraft Company.

Another business that would bring life to the thriving community, was the Melrose Granite Company. The story of the Melrose Granite Company is one of the unique business enterprizes in the history of the community. Perhaps no other industry has made Melrose so nationally prominent as the development of natural resources conducted by the Luckemeyer brothers at the turn of the century. John and Anton Luckemeyer came to Melrose with their invalid mother from Germany in 1895. John learned the "marble cutting" trade in Germany and Anton received the equivalent of a business college education in his native land. When they came to Melrose they were first employed by John Hoeschen at the flour mill.

In 1897 John Luckemeyer started a small marble-cutting shop and John Hoeschen underwrote the first shipment of marble to help this modest beginning. In later years he told that his working capital was no more than thirty-five cents that he kept in a little cash box. During the day he would travel by bicycle to the neighboring communities soliciting business and at night, by the light of a lantern, cut the marble slab by hand. The following day he would strap the thin marble slab to his bicycle and deliver the monument to the neighborhood cemetery.

The following year Anton Luckemeyer saw the possibilities opened by the business and joined his brother in a business that was called Luckemeyer Bros. Marble Company. The name was later changed to Melrose Marble Works, Inc.

In those early days marble was the only stone used for monumental work because it was soft and could be easily cut by hand with chisel and mallet. After some years the air compressor and pneumatic tools were introduced so that by 1911 the small ten by twelve foot shop gave way to a spacious six acre plant and the incorporation of the organization with John Luckemeyer, president; Anton Luckemeyer, vice president and Henry Kalkman, secretary and treasurer. The business expanded rapidly and the company was soon able, with the use of pneumatic equipment, to manufacture hard granite, abundantly available in the surrounding area, for moumental purposes. Subsequently the company acquired the St. Cloud Red and St. Cloud Gray quarries near St. Cloud and expanded into a growing wholesale granite sales organization by the name of Melrose Granite Company, Inc. The retail business was operated at first under the name of Melrose Marble Works, Inc. and later changed to Empire Memorials, Inc.

In 1908 the company employed about sixty stonecutters and other staff members who long before the rest of the granite industry, were organized into a labor union. To be a member of the granite cutters' union, a two year apprenticeship was required and the qualifications of the applicant were then approved by the union. Achieving the rank of a member of the union was a definite mark of distinction. A visit to any local cemetery reveals the craftsmanship and skill of these early stonecutters, especially when one considers the limited mechanical equipment they had. This skill is a rapidly disappearing art because so much of this work is not designed for mechanical production.

A great loss to the city of Melrose was the removal of the Melrose Granite Company to St. Cloud in 1915. The move was occasioned by the extensive quarry operations in that vicinity as well as the construction of a large plant and office there which was then said to be the largest wholesale monumental plant in the nation with distribution outlets in almost every state of the union. Two years later, however, the Luckemeyer brothers established another wholesale monumental business in Melrose and called it the Wagner Granite Company. After a few years this business, conducted by John Luckemeyer became the Royal Granite Company and subsequently was merged with the parent organization and is now known as the Royal Melrose Granite Company of St. Cloud. William J. Bohmer, a Melrose banker, held a substantial interest in the Melrose Granite Company and after the death of Anton

Luckemeyer he relinquished his banking interest in Melrose and moved to St. Cloud to become the manager of the Melrose Granite Company. John Welle, also a local banker, had financial interests in the company and in 1930 he and his son, Ambrose, established the Melrose Memorial Company which in later years was successfully operated by Ambrose C. Welle as owner and manager. Due to ill health, Ambrose Welle sold his interest in the Melrose Memorial Company in 1966 and several years later the business was terminated.

Upon the death of John Luckemeyer in 1931, Herman J. Lippsmeyer became financially interested in the Melrose Marble Works, Inc. and acquired the majority of the stock held by John Luckemeyer. The business was re-incorporated under the title of Empire Memorials, Inc. with Herman J. Lippsmeyer as president, Charles "Brownie" Hoffman as vice president and manager; H. C. Tembrock as secretary-treasurer and Anthony J. Primus as director. In 1965 Paul J. Dougherty purchased Empire Memorials and assumed management of the business on August 1. The following year he purchased Gopher Memorials Company in Minneapolis which is operated as a subsidiary of Empire Memorials. At the present writing a substantial addition to the plant of Empire Memorials, Inc. is in the planning stage.

By 1913 the Melrose Granite Company was employing about 160 men and the annual sales were valued at $175,000. According to an earlier historian, the plant was the first of its kind to introduce electricity as the motive power for the operation of machinery and the same writer noted "that labor trouble is unknown to this concern."

Another institution was struggling for existence during these early years of the century and only by the end of this chapter in our narrative would it be firmly established as one of the most stable and stabilizing institutions in the area. Melrose's first newspaper, called the *Record,* was begun in 1877 by Donald R. McDonald. After four years it was sold to Charles F. Hendryx who six months later moved it to Sauk Centre and consolidated it with the *Sauk Centre Herald.* This was a blow to the pride of the city fathers and thus another enterprising publisher was welcomed, a man by the name of Campbell E. Dorcy who established the *Melrose Sun.* For several years the paper passed through several owners until 1893 Dr. Campbell acquired full ownership and changed its name to the *Melrose Beacon.* Again the paper went through the hands of several editors until it came into the hands of A. F. Steffin who was one of its vigorous and dynamic editors shortly after the turn of the century. He, in turn, sold the paper to Elmour D. Lum and J. B. Howard in October, 1913. Three months later the struggling publication was in peril and the junior partner, J. B.

Howard appealed to the readers in verse, although not ranking in quality with Shakespeare, did express the sentiments of the new owners:

"Fish down in your pocket and dig up the dust, the editor is hungry and the paper 'bout to bust; we've trusted you for several months, and did it with a smile, so just return the compliment and trust us for a while . . . . Don't give us that old story long gone to seed, 'bout taking more papers than the family want to read; but help feed the printer, and he'll help the town to grow, and thus escape the sulphur in the regions below."

Less than a month passed and Howard was swiftly dispatched and replaced by what the historian of the *Beacon*, Ernest J. Bergeron, called "the handsomely prim, Mary Humphrey." Lum continued as publisher and Humphrey as a live-wire editor. Within a month she penned an editorial whose veracity remains as important today as when she wrote it on May 28, 1914:

"It is impossible to estimate the value to a town of a real live aggressive newspaper that is awake to the needs of its readers. A good newspaper is ever ready to fight the battles in the town in which it is published and to defend the interests of its citizens. No society or individual can or will take the same aggressive stand in public affairs and if they attempted to do so would meet with disappointment."

Miss Humphrey, however, departed from the editorial desk in July, 1916 and was succeeded by an Iowan by the name of Paul H. Appleby who, a year later, bought out Lum and became sole owner of the publication. Less than two years later, after many significant improvements, Cupid shot his dart through the heart of the enterprising editor and he returned to become editor of a larger newspaper in his own and his new bride's native Iowa. In his farewell edition he announced the new owner of the publication, at the time an unknown young man from Gibbon by the name of C. W. Carlson . . . An industrious and diligent man, Carlson would not take too many years before he would make the *Beacon* one of the most influential newspapers in the county. A political and social conservative, he would maintain a middle-of-the-road position, causing offense to few and injury to no one.

C. W. Carlson in the course of the ensuing years would make the *Beacon* not only a successful business enterprise but also a promotional instrument for hometown activities. In the course of time he also became one of the promient citizens of the city and contributed a great deal of time and energy in promoting the civic, religious and educational activities of the community. By some critics he may have been judged too moderate in his political and social views; by no critic, however, could he ever have been accused of religious bias. A staunch Lutheran, he worked within the fabric of a predominantly Catholic community, he continued the original policy of publishing each week's issue "not without several news items of reference to a church gathering, celebration, or observance." In an interview with Mr. Bergeron in July, 1962, C. W. Carlson stated, "To serve the greatest majority in the most valuable way I can, that is my purpose. I prefer to bend over backwards to serve the people rather than to risk any thought of being prejudiced on the subject of religion." Bergeron added, "To the people of the Melrose area, the *Beacon* was a constant expression of C. W. Carlson's most favored phrase, *"Die Kirch ist die hauptasch."*

Worthy of mention at this time is a young man who joined the *Beacon* staff on December 27, 1917 who had previously been employed by the Browerville *Blade* and the Freeport *Informant.* A native of Freeport, his name was Oswald Botz. For over fifty years, first setting type by hand and later by the marvellous linotype machine he, perhaps more than any other citizen, was responsible for the reporting of most stories in the columns of the *Beacon*. Although presently retired, he has still found it difficult to wash "printer's ink" from his hands and continues from time to time to set more than a few columns of type.

At the present time the *Beacon* is owned by Walter Carlson who took over the management at the beginning of 1955. Present employees include Mr. Carlson's wife, Lucy, who has been actively engaged in the business for the past twenty-five years; Doris Weiner, who has been employed for the past twenty years; Daniel Schmidt, who has been employed for the past twelve years. Mrs. C. W. Carlson, who is presently eighty three years old, has worked for thirty-five years on local weeklies in the state.

The present circulation of the publication is 3,045, making it the largest general weekly circulated publication in Stearns county. Approximately one-third of the volume of the Beacon is presently commercial printing.

Tragedies continued to plague the community and the early decades of the century were spared no less than the passing decades of the previous one. Railroad accidents continued to dominate the obituary columns, followed in number by an increasing number of deaths caused by farm machinery. A typical item, dated September 12, 1898, cited the death of "an old gentleman, named Moehrn, father of Casper Moehrn" who while crossing the railroad track near the depot "was struck by a passenger train and almost instantly killed." Another item took note of the death of John Rose in February, 1899 who froze to death in his own field, having been "overcome by the severe cold, the mercury being 25 degrees below zero." The summer of the same year witnessed the death of John B. Harren, "a teacher in the town of Millwood, and Miss Agnes Herzog, his affianced, who were both struck by lightning and instantly killed at the Herzog home." In 1903 an old soldier by the name of Michael Cosgrove fell down the stairs in his home in Melrose and died instantly. Two years later, Edward Atkinson, assessor for Millwood township, was struck by lightning on June 16 at the home of Bernard Boeckermann, "in the performance of his official duties." On August 3 of the same year the nine year old son of Andrew Thull, a farmer living near Melrose, died from injuries received in falling from a wagon. George Weisser, on June 20, 1910 was but one of many victims who drowned while swimming in the mill pond. Lest life seemed a bit routine and monotonous during these years a record dated August 18, 1907 recounts a rather wild incident in the neighboring village of Freeport. "William Ratford, constable at Freeport," the record states

"shot and almost instantly killed John Tonyon in that village on the night of Sunday, August 18. Tonyon was a member of a gang who had been drinking and creating a disturbance, driving through the streets. Repeated warnings from the officer were unheeded. A shot was fired in front of the horses without effect. Another, after midnight, when the men refused to behave, was fired, the bullet taking effect in Tonyon's neck. The constable, who claimed that the shot was fired simply as a warning, was arrested, but was fully exonerated by the coroner's jury. The case was afterwards presented to the grand jury, which refused to return an indictment."

The mention of trials and juries recalls the advent of two distinguished jurists to Melrose in 1896, names of men and their families who would serve with distinction even to the present time in the courts of Stearns county.

William Florence Donohue arrived on the scene at about thirty years of age and shortly after was joined in his law office by a Minnesota College of Law classmate, William J. Stephens. Shortly after these two most eligible bachelors arrived they entered into wedlock; the former marrying Mary A. Graham, daughter of Thomas Graham of St. George township and the latter marrying Ella Barrett, daughter of Michael Barrett of the city. The only indication that the city previously enjoyed the services of an attorney is a comment W. F. Donohue once made to his son, Howard. He told that shortly after his arrival in Melrose a certain Patrick Graham came to his office and told him that the town previously had a lawyer who lasted only a very short time. The gentlemen concluded by saying that he would give Mr. Donohue about six months. Both Donohue and Stephens were active members of the Democratic party and both served with distinction for many years on the local school board.

William Donohue became county attorney and moved to St. Cloud in 1918. William Stephens continued to practice law in Melrose until about 1945 and was widely known as one of the leading citizens of the community. In 1940 he was joined in partnership with a young graduate of the Minnesota College of Law who was born in Duluth by the name of John Lang. The young man was not only a law partner but soon became the senior's son-in-law when he married his daughter Bertha Stephens. Mr. Lang practiced law in Melrose until December, 1960, when he was appointed judge of Probate and Juvenile Court in St. Cloud. Attorney William G. Meyer began practicing law in Melrose in 1954 and ten years later was joined in partnership by his brother, Mark H. Meyer.

The citizens of Melrose generally reflected the political affiliation of their neighbors in Stearns county. We tend to think of the area as predominently Republican and so the voting records of recent years indicate. But it was not always so. During these three last decades of the nineteenth century the nation was predominantly Republican, as was also the state. Stearns county, however, was predominantly Democratic with the Democrats receiving a majority of 285 votes out of a total of 1035 cast in 1859. Democrats again received a majority of 3,469 out of 7091 votes cast in 1914. Between the years 1859 and 1914 there were only three elections won by the Republicans in Stearns county. One election return casts an interesting sidelight on the social customs of the county. In 1873 Samuel Mayall ran for governor of the state on the Prohibition ticket. He received thirty-five out of a total of 2,332 votes cast and of these, twelve were from St. Cloud, sixteen from Maine Prairie and five from Fair Haven. Needless to say, not a one from Melrose.

The city was firmly established and the rural area was already being recognized as one of the best in the state. The younger members of the community were catching on to a new "beat," symbolized by the rising songwriter, Irving Berlin, and his recent song, "Alexander's Rag-time Band." Mothers, however, were singing another popular anti-war song entitled "I Did Not Raise My Son to be a Soldier." American isolationism was the dominant theme of the country and even more dominant in the Melrose area. But secretly all knew that it was only a matter of time before the United States would be drawn into the

European war. The days of "a cord of wood and a pail of beer" were already a memory of the past for the advocates of temperance were active and prohibition was only a matter of time just as the war, suspicions and false accusations were already seen on the horizon. But life did go on and would go on and must go on. The "good old days" would pass into the new days and these in turn would again turn into the "good old days" for an older, wiser and somewhat sadder generation.

CHAPTER FOUR

GOD'S FAMILY IS OUR FAMILY

It is impossible to tell the stories of all the families of the area. An attempt was made, however, to secure the family geneological trees and this chapter will list the family origins as can best be recalled by the present citizens of the city and surrounding area. We have already recalled some of the early families, such as the Adley's, the Lindbergh's and the Clark's. Before listing more recent families we have chosen at random names of some prominent people who lived in the community several generations before the present.

CARL W. CARLSON, publisher of the *Melrose Beacon* for forty-five years, was born in Carver county on 13 May, 1887. As a boy he learned the printing trade in Gibbon and "printer's ink" never got out of his system. He attended Gustavus Adolphus College in St. Peter for two years until he had the opportunity to purchase the *Gibbon Gazette*. On 6 March, 1917 he purchased the *Melrose Beacon* from Paul H. Appleby. Previously on 5 September, 1912 he married the former Charlotte W. Naegli, and with their three children they arrived in Melrose. For twenty years he was cornet player in the city band; for over thirty years he was a member and chairman of the school board; he was also a member of the volunteer fire department as well as a member of the Firemen's Relief Association. He also served as postmaster during the Hoover administration, a member of the draft board during World War II, a member of the city Water and Light Commission and a deacon of St. Paul's Lutheran church for forty-five years.

JAMES FERGUS CROSSEN, for many years a prominent miller in Melrose, was born in Belfast, Ireland on 9 August, 1843. Before coming to Melrose he worked in a mill in Ontario and the Washburn mill in Minneapolis. In 1870 he arrived in Melrose to take charge of the Clark mill. He built the first two-story house in the village and

65

was employed by the mill until 1892 when he retired. For many years he was the justice of the peace and was popularly called "Judge" Crossen. He married the former Hannah Tierney in Toronto, Canada in 1866 and the couple had eleven children. The children had scattered to the four winds except Charlotte who married D. E. Edenbrack and retired in Melrose in later life.

HENRY JOSEPH EMMEL was born in Cumberland, Maryland 17 March, 1844. He came to Stearns county with his parents in 1856, a lad of twelve years old. His father was a prominent painter and church decorater during these early years. He was one of the original six students of what would become in time St. John's University. After being employed in the St. Cloud post office and teaching school in Richmond and St. Augusta, he became a clerk in the general store of J. Schoenborn in Spring Hill. After Mr. Schoenborn's death he married the widow, managed the general store and became one of the prosperous farmers of the area, at one time owning and operating 1,100 acres of land. In 1878 he became a member of the state legislature and after retiring to Melrose in 1907 he was again elected to the lower house of the state legislature. He was the father of seven children whose name is well known throughout the area of western Stearns county.

JOHN V. FREE, a prominent lumber man, was born at Wabasha on 30 October, 1879. He married the former Anna Geyer on 11 November, 1902 and the couple lived in Wabasha several years before coming to Melrose where he was engaged in the lumber business for thirty-five years. He was a candidate for the state legislature in 1934 and served as a member of the city council in 1940-41. The couple had five children.

JOHN JEROME GETTY, the first permanent settler in the township that now bears his name, was born in New York state on 15 September, 1821. In his youth he drove mules on the Erie canal tow path. He came to what is now Getty township on 6 July, 1857 and took land in section nineteen in the area of what used to be called Getty's Grove. He married the former Permelia Jane Layman and the couple had three children. Except for four years during the Civil War the family lived on the farm and Getty was recognized as a leading farmer and citizen of the area. He retired to Sauk Centre in 1891 and died on 12 November, 1895.

HENRY KALKMAN, born in Richmond on 19 December, 1859, was for many years the secretary and treasurer of the Melrose Granite Company. A graduate of St. John's University, he came to Melrose in 1881 as the proprietor of a local mercantile concern. Five years later he sold the store and moved to Duluth, but returned to Melrose in 1904. He married Minnie Pogatchnick, a native of Austria, and the couple had seven children.

FRANK M. MOREHOUSE, SR. was born in Herkimer county, New York on 16 December, 1839 whose father, John, a carpenter by trade, was one of the early pioneers of Melrose. A veteran of the Civil War, he was wounded in the first battle of Bull Run. In 1866 he brought his bride, the former Julia Lowngsbury, to Melrose where he operated a farm a mile out of the village and practiced his trade as a mason. He worked on the first house erected within the present city of Melrose. For thirteen years he served as constable of the village.

ANDREW KOLB was born 9 December, 1868 on a farm in Grove township. As a lad of six he moved with his parents to Melrose and spent almost his entire life in Melrose until his death in 1938. He married Rosalia Hun of St. Cloud on 2 May, 1893. His wife preceeded him in death by only six weeks and his father, George Kolb, Sr., by only one week. He was engaged in the lumber business for many years, the firm being called the A. Kolb Lumber Company. He served as mayor of the city from 1921-1923 and from 1933 until the time of his death. He was known as an ardent sportsman and enjoyed nothing more than an afternoon of fishing in summer and an evening of bowling in winter. For many years he managed the St. Boniface bowling lanes.

JOHN J. KRAKER was born in Albany on 29 June, 1875, the son of Joseph and Maria M. (Bohmer) Kraker. At the age of ten he moved with the family to Melrose which was his home until his untimely death in 1908. With his father as a partner they purchased Dowes Hardware store in 1893 and two years later sold the store to Wardian and Dederick. In 1898 the father sold his interest in the store and Kraker entered into partnership with W. J. Bohmer. In 1900 Kraker and Bohmer opened "The Big Store," the first department store in the city. Besides his commercial interest Kraker was active in many other activities. He was cashier of the Bank of North America in 1903, a stockholder in the Scandinavian State Bank of Brooten, secretary of the Melrose Commercial Club and city treasurer almost to the time of his death. His obituary read, "He was for a number of years one of Melrose's most trusted and enterprising business men. He was a practical matter-of-fact man, but ever ready to extract merriment from life as he went along. He numbered his friends by his aquaintances and was generous to a fault. For years to come, kind memories will endure in the hearts of his friends."

AUGUST KUHLMANN, M.D., one of the early doctors of the community, was born in Hanover, Germany on 27 January, 1876. He attended St. John's University and taught for three years in the rural schools of the county. In 1905 he graduated from the University of Minnesota School of Medicine and after serving his internship at St. Mary's Hospital, Duluth, he began practicing medicine in Melrose. In 1926 he took post-graduate studies in eight different clinics throughout Europe. He was known as "a man of very high character, a good physician, forceful and outspoken in his opinions and had a sincere interest in the welfare of his community. On 9 April, 1907 he married Anna Meyer of Humphrey, Nebraska and the union was blessed with six children."

HARRY E. MEYER, son of Mr. and Mrs. Nicholas Meyer, was born in Melrose on 19 June, 1902. After graduating from Melrose High School in 1920 he attended the University of Minnesota and was licensed as a funeral director and embalmer in 1930. Upon returning to Melrose he established the Meyer Funeral Home with two children before his untimely death at the age of forty-two in 1945.

IGNATIUS LEMM, born on 1 August, 1888 in Luxemburg, Stearns county, was for many years a leading citizen of the community. He graduated from the St. Cloud Teachers College in 1910 and for several years taught school in Watkins, St. Augusta, Lastrup and Melrose. For three years he was engaged in the garage business in Melrose, from 1924 to 1927. From that year until 1931 he served as senator from the forty-sixth legislative district in the state's upper house. In 1936 he was appointed city clerk as well as clerk of the water and light commission, offices that he held until the time of his death in 1954. On 12 November, 1912 he married the former Margaret Weber in Luxemburg and the couple had three children. A son, Homer F. Lemm, succeeded him as state senator.

HENRY F. LOOSBROOK was born in Dyersville, Iowa on 3 April, 1868. As a child he came with his parents who settled near St. Martin. After graduating from St. Cloud State Teachers College he came to Melrose and was employed in the lumber office and store until he started his own general merchandise business in 1898, an occupation he engaged in for the next fifty years. He served as a trustee of St. Boniface church for many years, was a member of the school board for thirty-seven years and president of the Melrose State Bank. He married Margaret Kolb of St. Martin in 1891 who died in Melrose on 26 November, 1895. Three years later he married Anna Caspers of New Munich. Mrs. Alma Pappenfus of Melrose is one of his two daughters.

ANTHONY A. MEYER, M.D., born in Freeport on 5 August, 1885, came to Melrose in 1920 to practice medicine in association with

Dr. P. A. Hilbert. He attended grade school in Freeport and college at Valparaiso University, Indiana before enrolling in the medical school of the University of Illinois from which he graduated in 1914. Before coming to Melrose he fulfilled his internship at University Hospital, Chicago and practiced medicine in Anamoose, North Dakota and Osakis. In 1925 he started a hospital in Melrose and in succeeding years enlarged and improved it until it was sold to the city in 1957. He served the medical needs of the community for over thirty-eight years and acted as mayor of the city for over twenty years, before retiring to live in Minneapolis in 1958.

C. P. MEYER, christened Celestine Peter, was born in St. Joseph on 19 May, 1896 and came to Melrose in 1918. A prominent electrician known throughout the state, he was first employed by Otto Bringe until he purchased the business in 1937. Active in many civic and religious circles, he was a member of the choir of St. Boniface church for over thirty-five years, served as a volunteer fireman for thirty-five years and a member of the board of directors of the Minnesota Electric Association. A veteran of World War I he served overseas in England. He married the former Teresa Schreder on 12 June, 1923 and the couple had seven children.

HENRY MOSER, born 5 October, 1894 in Eden Valley, attended St. Cloud State Normal School in 1911 when its total enrollment was four hundred and ten students. There were only eighty-four men in the entire student body. He taught four years in Lake Henry township rural schools before being inducted in the United States Army in 1918. A year and a half later he was employed as cashier in the Farmers State Bank of Spring Hill, a position he held until the bank liquidated voluntarily with no loss for any depositors. In 1931 he returned to teaching in District number sixty-one, located about three miles west of Greenwald where he remained until he became associated with the Melrose State Bank in May, 1942. He married Eleanor Lieser of Lake Henry in 1922. The couple was blessed with five children, three sons and two daughters.

MRS. AGNES MOENING was born in Neuenkirchen, Germany on 10 June, 1875. As a young girl she emigrated with her parents to the United States and on 20 June, 1899 married John Moening who died on 12 August, 1937. She was a charter member of the St. Elizabeth's CAA Society and the mother of ten children. The family farmed north of Melrose until 1939 when she retired in the city. The "Moening boys" were a legend in baseball circles throughout the county.

ADAM NICKOLAUS, born in Danheim, Germany on 6 February, 1852, was one of the few centenarians of the community, dying one hundred years, seven months and thirteen days after his birth. He was married in Germany to Elizabeth Keller in October, 1875 and eight years later the couple emigrated to the United States. The young couple first settled near St. Joseph and after seven years moved to Elrosa where Nickolaus was engaged in farming and practicing his trade as a mason. His wife died on 11 April, 1929 and in 1943 he moved to Melrose and took up residence with his daughter, Mary.

JOSEPH NIEHAUS, born in Hanover, Germany on 2 January, 1876, was one of the outstanding citizens of Melrose township for many years. With his parents he emigrated to the United States at the age of five, first settled in Cincinnati, Ohio where the family lived eight years before becoming one of the pioneer farming families of Melrose. On 4 May, 1904 he married the former Agnes Wessel and the couple had ten children, three of whom are religious in the community of the Sisters of St. Francis, Little Falls, and one son, Joseph, is the present state representative of the area. Mr. Niehaus played a prominent role in the early growth and development of the community. He served as clerk of Melrose township fifty-four years and was secretary of the Melrose Cooperative Creamery Association for nineteen years. One of his sons, Anthony, succeeded him as township clerk, and still maintains the records of the township that date back to 1873. Another son, Theodore recently recalled that "these records were kept by the township clerks until about 1925. Old death certificates attribute the death of anyone over fifty to 'weakness and old age.' Children died of such diseases as 'cholera morbus,' which was probably food poisoning resulting from lack of refrigeration. The salary for the town clerk," Theodore continued, "being a princely twenty dollars a year. My father was probably inclined to rush a bit and he had a great propensity for abbreviations. In my own birth certificate his name is given as Jos. and mine as Ben. Theo. I am now involved in securing proof that my father's name was Joseph and that I was baptized 'Bernard Theodore'."

DONALD OTTE, one of the outstanding citizens of the community in recent times, was killed while performing his services as an electrician on 2 October, 1961. He was employed by the Meyer Electric Company for twenty years. Born in Melrose on 2 January, 1923 he attended St. Boniface Grade School and Melrose High School. He served during the Second World War in the Pacific theatre with distinction and returned to Melrose as an employee of the Meyer Electric Company. In 1948 he married the former Mary Woeste in Sauk Centre and the couple had five daughters. He was a charter member of the Melrose Veterans of Foreign Wars Post #7050 and served as its commander for two years. In 1954 he was elected commander of the VFW Sixth District and in 1959 was elected the VFW State Department Commander. In this capacity he received the nickname of "Fireball" because of the vigorous administration of his duties. The writer of his obituary made the following observations:

"Don was not satisfied with just doing a job, he was intensely interested in people, his community, his church and his country. This is the reason why he was so loved and respected by those who knew him. He was active in a multitude of enterprises and won the distinction of being one of the most leading citizens. . . . Don was endowed with an infectious personality, a delightful sense of humor, and high standards which he never permitted himself or any other to compromise. We have lost a valuable citizen who will be missed by all who knew him."

HENRY B. OTTE, was born on a farm near Meire Grove on 8 December, 1890. As a young man he was employed as a creamery helper in St. Martin, Long Prairie and Meire Grove and was creamery operator at Albany and Eldred for a short time. He became operator and manager of the Melrose Cooperative Creamery in 1917 when the creamery was located in a frame building on the north side of the river. When he left this position after seventeen years the creamery had its present modern brick building and plant on Main Street. He won the title of state champion buttermaker at the state fair in 1919. For twelve years he was secretary of the Central Minnesota Creamery Operators Association and served as that organization's president for thirteen years. In 1937 he was appointed state dairy and food inspector with headquarters in Duluth. Among the creamery operators that he trained were Julius Otte, Joseph Dufner, John Athmann and Norbert Rolfzen. He married Christine Kramer on 11 November, 1914 who died on 7 August, 1934. The following year he married Margaret Friederichs. He died 20 August, 1952.

STEPHAN PETERMEIER, one of the pioneer settlers of Melrose township, was born in Delbrueck, Germany on 25 April, 1857. He married Theresia Neukirch on 12 June, 1883 in that city and a month later the newly-married couple emigrated to the United States and settled on a farm in the northeast section of Melrose township. The couple farmed there until 1917 when they retired to the city of Melrose. After Mrs. Petermeier's death on 26 December, 1931, Stephan made his home with a daughter, Mrs. Theresia Hinnenkamp. The couple had eight children among whom were the Reverend Monsignor Benedict Petermeier and Sister Aloysius, O.S.F.

CHARLES M. C. PENNISON, retired farmer, veteran of the Civil War and for many years street commissioner of Melrose was born in England on 25 October, 1845, enlisted in the Wisconsin Volunteer Infantry that accompanied General Sherman on his march through Georgia. In 1869 he came to Melrose and spent twenty-one years as a grader of wheat for the Clark mill and also managed an eighty acre farm near the village. He married the former Amelia Witcho of Jefferson county, Wisconsin in 1874 and the couple had four children.

SIMON PFAU, already in 1901 a retired farmer, was born in Germany on 10 July, 1840. With his parents, a brother and sister, he arrived in the United States in 1852 after a voyage of thirty-five days. After several years in Wisconsin the family moved to Oak township in 1865. He served the Union cause during the Civil War and returned to Oak township to engage in farming. He married the former Catherine Metzger, who was also born in Germany, and the couple had two daughters and one son.

JOSEPH PRIMUS, for many years a machinist and implement dealer in Melrose, was born on 18 March, 1857 in Wisconsin. In 1862 his parents settled on a one-hundred and sixty acre farm near Meire Grove in a cabin with no floors, no windows and only the kitchen stove for light. According to an earlier historian, the family "had an ox team for farming, but they had no suitable winter shelter for them, so often on a winter night, the oxen and the members of the family slept in a row on the hard floor, with nothing in the way of a bed but some coarse grass cut from the river bottoms. During that first winter the family had absolutely nothing in the way of purchased provisions except 100 pounds of flour. Their principal fare was deer and rabbit meat cooked in various fashions, and eaten without any vegetables, even potatoes being unknown during the whole winter. After having braved the first winter," this writer continued, "circumstances improved, and the Primus family became one of the first in the community." Joseph Primus married the former Christiana Michaels and the couple had thirteen children. After engaging in farming for several years the couple moved to West Union where he managed a general store. After several years he sold the store in West Union and moved to Melrose where he served for eight years on the city council.

GERHARD RICHTER, the village blacksmith for many years, was born 1 May, 1843 in the province of the Rhineland, Germany. He came to St. Cloud in 1865 and was associated with Peter Shedler, one of the first blacksmiths of the area. The following year he opened his own smithy in Richmond and six years later moved to Melrose. In 1868 he married Margaret Grun, also born in Germany, in St. Cloud and the couple was blessed with nine children. Richter was one of the first councilmen of Melrose, served as a director of the school board for nine years and on two different occasions took the census of the area, once for the state and another time for the federal government.

S. J. ROELIKE, D.D.S. was born near Lake Henry on 12 August, 1892. He graduated from the University of Minnesota School of Dentistry and opened his office in Melrose in 1918. He continued his practice throughout forty-five years, retiring five years before his death in 1962. He married Alma Kummer of Cold Spring on 24 August, 1920 and the couple had two children. A son, Dr. H. H. Roelike is presently practicing dentistry in Melrose.

GEORGE SAMES, a beloved merchant of the community, was born in St. Paul on 8 October, 1888. He came to Melrose in 1950 and opened a general merchandise store, assisted by his two sons. He married the former Cecilia Ebert in St. Bonifacius on 14 November, 1922 and the couple had five children.

AUGUST L. SAUER, a native of Langendorf, Bavaria, Germany, was born on 21 August, 1870. At the age of nineteen he came to the United States and was employed five years as a butcher in St. Paul before coming to Melrose in 1894. He practiced his trade forty years and was known throughout the area as one of the best in the business. His excellence as a butcher made "Melrose sausage" a byword in hundreds of homes and people from throughout the state and as far away as Huron, South Dakota journeyed to Melrose to purchase its famous sausage. He married Lucy Gans of St. Cloud on 29 October, 1907 and the couple was blessed with four children. He was "a man of very strong character, outspoken and fair in his opinions and he had a sincere loyalty for his friends and his community." He served ten years as a member of the city council and water and light board and was a member of the school board seven years at the time of his death.

BEN SCHULZETENBERG, a prominent area farmer and businessman, was born in Meire Grove on 25 February, 1886. He married Rose Welle of Freeport on 17 February, 1914 and after five years of farming in Alberta, Canada, the couple returned to the area and settled on a farm near New Munich. In 1926 he retired from farming and purchased an implement store in New Munich. He purchased the "Our Own Hardware" store in Melrose in 1939 and for several years operated both stores until he finally moved to Melrose and sold the store in New Munich. Upon his death in 1963 the writer of his obituary said, "The deceased lived an active and useful life up until about a year ago when he became ill. He liked work and he liked people, and these two outstanding characteristics contributed greatly to his success in farming and the implement and hardware business."

HENRY SOENNEKER, another prominent pioneer, was born in Neuenkirchen, Hanover, Germany on 7 December, 1860. He came to the United States in 1887 and after working in Cincinnati for two years he purchased a farm four miles northeast of Melrose. He married Mary Wessel on 22 November, 1892 and they were blessed with nine children. One of his sons, Henry, is the present bishop of Owensboro, Kentucky and three of his daughters, Sister Mary Valeria, Sister Mary Elizabeth and Sister Mary Agnes all entered the convent of the Franciscan Sisters of Little Falls.

PETER P. STALBOERGER was born 6 June, 1891 in Spring Hill and attended the district schools and Melrose High School. For many years he was the secretary and treasurer of the Melrose Brewing Company. His father, Andrew, a retired farmer and president of the brewery, was born in Germany and after his father's death, emigrated with his mother and brother, Gerhard, to the United States in 1852. After living in Iowa four years they came to Stearns county where the mother and two boys obtained claims near Spring Hill in 1856. Andrew was one of the men who helped build St. Michael's church in Spring Hill. He married Anna Loehr on 28 June, 1876 and the couple had nine children. Another associate of the brewery was John F. Winter who was born in Spring Hill on 9 November, 1883. A graduate of St. John's University, he married Mary Stalboerger, Andrew's daughter, and became manager of the brewery in 1911.

WILLIAM J. STEPHENS, who died at the venerable age of eighty-seven in Shakopee, was born on 24 July, 1866 on a farm near Hammond, Wisconsin. He attended Valparaiso College, Indiana and received his law degree from the University of Minnesota in 1896 and immediately entered the practice of law with William F. Donohue in Melrose. From 1918 he carried on private practice until 1940 when he was joined by his son-in-law, John Lang, as a partner. For forty-four years he served as president and a member of the Melrose school board, as attorney for the city, as a charter member of the Knights of Columbus council and a member of the Stearns-Benton Bar Association. On July, 1899 he married the former Ella Barrett and the couple had five daughters.

MRS. SOPHIE STILLING, born at Saus, Westphalia, Germany in 1867, came to the United States at the age of nineteen with her father, Joseph, and brother, Ben. After residing in Albany with an uncle, Herman Blenker, for a short time the family purchased a farm about five miles northeast of Melrose. She was married to Frank Hiltner in 1888 and the couple had three children before Mr. Hiltner's death in 1894. In 1901 she was married to Henry Stilling in New

Munich and four daughters were born of this union. In her declining years she resided with her daughter, Alvina, who at the time was housekeeper for Monsignor Mathias Hoffmann.

JOSEPH H. STUNDEBECK, born in Germany on 3 January, 1887, emigrated with his parents to the United States and settled with them in the Melrose area. In 1913 he moved from the farm to the city and started a plumbing and heating business, an occupation he was engaged in until 1956 when he was succeeded by his son, Charles. On 17 May, 1921 he married the former Mary Pfeffer and the couple had two children.

FRANK TIEMAN, born in Hanover, Germany on 23 February, 1872, came to the United States with his parents in 1882. The family settled on a farm near Freeport for two years before moving to a farm north of Melrose. For forty years he served as a director of the Melrose State Bank and for over twenty-five years he was a trustee of St. Boniface church. On 1 May, 1900 he married Johanna Hinnenkamp and the couple had four sons. The Reverend Lawrence Bohnen, S.V.D. also made his home with the family since 1930. Frank Tieman was known far and wide for his generous assistance, especially during the days of the Great Depression, to all of those in need.

JOSEPH F. THEIRS, one of the few members of the community to serve in the Spanish American War, was born near Newton, Illinois on 15 December, 1875. As a young man he clerked in a store in Peoria, Illinois and later managed his father's farm until it was sold. After the war he came to Sauk Centre and entered into a partnership with Peter Robischon in the bottling business. He married Mary Deters of Sauk Centre on 2 October, 1900 and the couple had two daughters. They lived to celebrate their golden wedding about the same time the Thiers Bottling Company marked its fiftieth year in business.

JOHN H. WELLE, the son of a pioneer Freeport family, was born on 7 May, 1879. He began his banking career with the Freeport State Bank and remained there until 1903 when he moved to Melrose with his bride of two years, Ositha Buttweiler. He was employed first with the First National Bank which later changed to the Security State Bank. Leaving that position he was one of the organizers of the German American Bank and when that bank was consolidated with the Borgerding State Bank he continued there as cashier. The latter years of his life he served as vice-president of the Melrose State Bank. Known as "the counselor and the friend of many," he served more than twenty-five years as the treasurer of the school board as well as city treasurer for many years.

MATTHEW J. WINTER, a leading merchant of Melrose, was born 24 February, 1882 in Lake Henry township. After graduating from Sauk Centre Business College he was employed in a hardware store and the Gund Brewery Company in that city. When he came to Melrose he first worked for C. J. Hoeschen in the mercantile store. In 1911 he opened his own furniture store and also became the city's mortician. He married Helen Ostendorf on 14 April, 1906.

ALFRED L. ZUERCHER, M.D., born in Zug, Switzerland on 5 September, 1850, was for many years the "beloved physician" of the community. He studied medicine at the University of Wurzburg and the University of Paris before coming to the United States in 1873 when he settled in New Munich and married the former Mary Broker. Shortly after his marriage he moved to Stillwater where he practiced medicine until 1882 when he and his family moved to Melrose where he continued to practice medicine until his death in 1892. Alfred J. Zuercher, the doctor's son, was born in Stillwater on 11 November, 1877. After attending St. John's University he was employed by a druggist in Melrose and Long Prairie and then entered the College of Pharmacy of the University of Minnesota. For seven years he was the manager of the Helsper Drug Company of Melrose until he purchased the store from W. J. Stock in 1906. He also became the owner and operator of the Lyric Theatre, one of the social hubs of the community in the early years of the century. Alfred Zuercher, whom everyone knew better as "Fred," on one occasion recalled why his father settled in this area. "My father came to this country and settled in Pennsylvania," he said. "There he met a railroad surveyor whom he traveled with until he saw this country. He separated from the surveyor and settled in New Munich." An earlier historian described Alfred Zuercher in these words:

"Mr. Zuercher of Melrose is of 'the old school' and of the 'nice people' category. His smile, shuffling me in his house, serving me refreshments, offering me cigarettes, all were done with 'Dixie' hospitality. Mr. Zuercher has spent fifty of his eighty years as a druggist. His love of people made his work a joy."

*   *   *   *   *

Although some men may be outstanding in a community they are so only because the community expected leadership from them and they were endowed with a natural talent of leadership. Such were the men we already cited. A community, however, is like a beehive — it is only as good as everyone fulfills his special service and talents. Throughout the years every member of the community of Melrose contributed, each in his own way, to the building up of the community. More than that, it is safe to say that the individual was an integral part of the community and both were closely knitted together in religion, culture, social and economic bonds. In order to recognize all the families of the Melrose community as contributors to the history of Melrose we circulated a questionaire through various media at the beginning of this year with the hope that the present families in Melrose would respond. The response we received is recorded on the following pages.

ANDERSON, CLARENCE R. son of Clarence and Alice (Bakkom) Anderson, Sr. *Grnd* of Anton (1882) and Carrie (Pearson-1885) Anderson, Jr. and O. H. (1872) and Mrs. Bakkom. "My greatgrandfather, Anton Anderson, Sr., and a friend jumped a Norwegian freighter in San Francisco in 1849. They did well in the gold fields and went back to Norway in 1850. Seven years later they bought passage to New York and again traveled toward California. Got as far as the Rocky Mountains where they met people coming east, no more gold. They returned to a Norwegian community they had passed through going west and began farming. This community was Greenleaf. Anton and his friend later escaped Indian attacks on their way to Fort Snelling to get troops because of an uprising in the Greenleaf area." *M* Lanita, daughter of Frank and Lucy (Spengler) Zinniel.

ANDRES, LESTER, son of Anton and Christina (Schmidt) Andres. *Grnd* of Peter (1837) and Susanna (Brass) Andres and John (1837) and Ellen (Yager) Schmidt. Paternal *greatgrnd* were Jacob and Margaret Andres. *M* Dorothy, daughter of August (1894) and Nellie (Gummow-1898) Zellner.

ARVIG, "TOM" LEONARD H. son of Thomas L. (1883) and Mildred (Oliver) Arvig. *Grnd* of Thomas S. (1846) and Lena (Roarason-1857) Arvig and Benjamin (1846) and Fidelia (Hasbrouck-1848) Oliver. Maternal grandfather, Benjamin Oliver, fought with a Minnesota Regiment during the Civil War. When mustered out he moved to Sauk Centre and spent a winter living in the abandoned Indian stockade. Paternal grandfather, Thomas S. Arvig, was a Norwegian fisherman. He came to the United States after his boat was wrecked. After arriving in America he homesteaded to Minnesota and later his

---

N.B.: Abbreviations used in this section are; *Great-Greatgrnd* indicates Great-greatgrand parent; *Greatgrnd* indicates Greatgrand parent; *Grnd* indicates Grand parent; (cf) indicates comparison with same name in other paragraphs.

sons built the Electric Light plant at Pine River in 1913. They were pioneers in the development of rural electric power lines and telephone systems. M Marie Elizabeth, daughter of Fred H. (1856) and Elisabeth (Rehkamp) Stundebeck. *Grnd* of John Henry (1816) and Catherine Marie (Mollman-1816) Stundebeck and Henry (1836) and Marie Antonette (Schierberg-1837) Rehkamp. Paternal *greatgrnd* were Bernard Henry (1775) and Marie Elizabeth (Schnaker-1788) Stundebeck and John Henry (1788) and Catherine Marie (Steinkamp-1785) Mollman. Maternal *greatgrnd* were John Bernard (1807) and Elisabeth Marie (Bruns-1811) Rehkamp and Friederich and Gertrude Catherine (Middeke) Schierberg. Parents, grandparents and greatgrandparents were born in Germany. Maternal grandparents, Henry and Antonette Rehkamp, purchased wilderness land northwest of Melrose from Henry and Carolina Borgerding around 1885 when they emigrated to America from Europe, and cleared and farmed it. They were among the early members of St. Boniface parish, and liberal supporters of the church. "My father, Fred Stundebeck, first came to Melrose as a young man in 1886 from Covington, Kentucky and purchased land northwest of Melrose from Henry and Carolina Borgerding. He returned to Covington, Kentucky after six months where he owned the Kentucky Spice Mills and was an importer of coffees, teas and spices. In 1906 he came again to Melrose with his wife, the former Elisabeth Rehkamp, and three children, Fred Jr., Joseph and Marie. He opened a General Merchandise store, and later a Flour and Feed store which he operated until his retirement."

ATHMAN, CHRYS C. son of Joseph and Katherine Athman. *M* Anna, daughter of Joseph and Mrs. (Schultenkemper) Enneking.

ATHMAN, HENRY J. son of Bernard and Veronica Hienze. *M* Regina, daughter of John and Mary (Kolb) Wander.

ATHMAN, NORBERT, son of Henry (cf) and Regina (Wander) Athman (cf). *M* Bernice, daughter of Lambert and Agnes (Ellering) Worms. *Grnd* of Leonard and Anna (Pung) Worms and Bernard (1857) and Anna (Lois) Ellering. Paternal and maternal grandparents each had nine children.

BECKERMAN, JOSEPH, son of Edmund and Rose (Berns) Beckerman. *Grnd* of John H. (1873) and Agnes (Boeckers-1884) Beckerman and Herman (1867) and Wilhelmina (Wehlage-1877) Berns. *M* Joyce, daughter of William and Cecilia (Weber) Kack. *Grnd* of John (1877) and Anna (Kurenbach-1872) Kack and John (1868) and Anna (Rader-1870) Weber.

BERSCHEID, JOSEPH, son of Lawrence and Emma (Hessing) Berscheit. *Grnd* of John and Mrs. Berscheid. *M* Frances, daughter of Bernard (1886) and Rosa (Welle) Schulzetenberg. *Grnd* of Gerhard (1851) and Katherine (Geserchens-1860) Schulzetenberg and William (1863) and Katherine (Wolters-1869) Welle.

BERTRAM, JOSEPH, son of Peter (1850) and Mrs. Bertram. *M* Katherine, daughter of Peter (1852) and Katherine (Mehr) Hemmesch. *Grnd* of Mike and Mrs. (Spoden) Hemmesch and Jacob (1840) and Mrs. (Henges) Mehr.

BEUNING, JOSEPH, son of William (1858) and Bernadine (Peger) Beuning. *Grnd* of Henry and Mrs. Beuning. *M* Mary, daughter of Henry (1848) and Mary (Winter) Reller. *Grnd* of Stephan and Mrs. (Timmer) Reller.

BLENKER, BERNARD, son of Bernard (1872) and Mary (Hellermann) Blenker. *M* Leona, daughter of Frank (1891) (cf) and Elizabeth (Schmiesing) Hinnenkamp (cf).

BLENKER, GERHARD, son of Ben and Mary (Hellermann) Blenker. *M* Thekla, daughter of Ben (1880) and Mary (Angelbeck) Hinnenkamp. *Grnd* of Bernard (1843) and Catherine (Neinaber) Hinnenkamp and Fred (1861) and Caroline (Westerhaus) Angelbeck.

BLENKER, JOSEPH SR. son of Ben and Mary (Hellermann-1877) Blenker. *M* Marie, daughter of Bernard (1858) and Katherine (Gicskc-1858) Bussmann.

BOECKERMANN, WILLIAM, son of Bernard and Catherine (Neinaber) Boeckermann, Sr. *M* Mary, daughter of Bernard (1872) and Anna (Broermann) Kerfeld. *Grnd* of Henry (1846) and Agnes (Kuhlmann-1849) Kerfeld and Joseph and Marie (Unger) Broermann. Parents and grandparents were born in Germany.

BOHLIG, NORMAN M. son of Charles H. (1887) and Magdalen (Athman) Bohlig. *Grnd* of John and Mary (Dufner) Bohlig and Bernard (1854) and Veronica (Heinze-1860) Athman. *M* Renee, daughter of Frederick W. (1887) and Wilhelmina (Fiergolla) Knafla. *Grnd* of Karl (1858) and Wilhelmina (Wittkowski-1860) Knafla and John (1857) and Wilhelmina (Kowalski-1862) Fiergolla. Paternal *grnd* were born in East Prussia and maternal *grnd* in Germany.

BORGERDING, RAYMOND C. son of John (1870) and Caroline (Kolb) Borgerding. *Grnd* of Henry (1836) and Caroline (Kersing) Borgerding and Leonard (1826) and Margaretta (Joa-1830) Kolb. *Greatgrnd* were Christopher (1799) and Elizabeth (Darlinghous-1798) Borgerding and Joseph (1795) and Dorothea (Schmitt-1801) Kolb. Maternal great greatgrandparents were Leonard and Dorothea (Greul) Kolb. *M* Antoinette, daughter of George B. (1864) and Mary (Kerfeld-1875) Rehkamp. *Grnd* of Henry and Marie Antoinette (Schierberg-

1837) Rehkamp and Henry (1846) and Agnes (Wiechman-1849) Kerfeld, Sr.

BOTZ, OSWALD M. son of John F. (1872) and Elizabeth (Wahls) Botz. *Grnd* of Jacob (1845) and Elizabeth (Wolter-1850) Botz and Henry (1846) and Mary (Albers-1856) Wahls. Maternal *greatgrnd* were Henry (1826) and Anna Marie (Panschard-1831) Albers. Paternal greatgrandfather Albers was a volunteer in the Union Army during the Civil War. Died at Freeport in January 1913. *M* Elizabeth, daughter of William and Anna (Peckscamp) Hackmann.

BRAGELMANN, NICHOLAS, son of Leo and Mary (Olk) Braegelmann. *M* Doris, daughter of Henry (cf) and Rita (Schulte) Loxtercamp. (cf)

BREN, MALCOLM, son of John (1880) and Anna (Wraspir) Bren. *Grnd* of Joseph and Emily Bren and Anton (1850) and Winifred (1853) Wraspir. Grandparents came to America from Czechoslovakia. *M* Marie, daughter of Peter (1889) and Mary (Eischen) Thielen. *Grnd* of Matt (1852) and Catherine (Rausch-1855) Thielen and John (1861) and Josephine (Von Bank-1864) Eischen. Great maternal grandparents were Johann (1837) and Anna (Thill) Von Bank. All grandparents were born in Germany and after arriving in America settled around the St. Joseph, St. Nicholas and Eden Valley area.

BRINGE, MRS. ROSE, daughter of George (1857) and Susan (Knapp) Meyer. Maternal grandfather was Adam Knapp. "My father - George Meyer," said Rose, "was choir director, and sang in the church choir for more than fifty years and he also was band director of the St. Joseph Band for over fifty years.

BUDDE, EDWARD, SR. son of Joseph, (1866) and Lizetta (Tape) Budde, Sr. Both parents were born in Germany. *M* Johanne, daughter of Ben (1855) and Katherine (Renneker) Enneking, Sr. *Grnd* of Fredrich and Mrs. Enneking and Fredrich and Gertrude (Gieske) Renneker.

BUDDE, JOSEPH F. son of Joseph (1866) and Lizetta (Tape) Budde, Sr. Both parents were born in Germany. *M* Clara W. daughter of Clemens and Louise (Pape) Schwers. *Grnd* of Herman (1816) and Elizabeth (Kramer-1819) Schwers and Conrad (1838) and Josephine (Winter-1841) Pape. Maternal *greatgrnd* were William (1810) and Margaret (Hoppe Mies-1800) Pape. Maternal greatgrandparents and grandparents were born in Germany and immigrated to New Vienna, Iowa.

BUDDE, RICHARD J. son of Edward (cf) and Johanna (Enneking) Budde (cf). *M* Katherine, daughter of Frank and Alma (Neubeck) Goski. *Grnd* of George and Mrs. (Duda) Goski and John and Anna (Siefert-1882) Neubeck.

BUDDE, SHELDON, son of Lawrence and Helen (Rose) Budde. *Grnd* of Joseph (1866) and Mary (Mueller-1879) Budde, Sr. and Herman (1874) and Theresa (Benolken-1881) Rose. *M* Joan, daughter of Rene and Rita (Theroux) Lizotte. *Grnd* of Paul (1885) and Emma (LaCoursiers-1892) Lizotte and Joe (1891) and Leah (Quensnel-1895) Theroux. Greatgrandparents were Stephen and Ann (Delorme) Quensnel and Louis and Phelemen (Valemout) Theroux.

BUECKERS, ERVIN J. son of Clemens and Lorette (Rakotz) Bueckers. *Grnd* of John (1877) and Frances (Fischer) Bueckers and Anton (1881) and Margaret (Froelich-1889) Rakotz. *M* Bertha, daughter of Henry and Anna (Fuchs) Doll. *Grnd* of Joseph (1887) and Elizabeth (Schaefer-1890) Doll and Joseph (1882) and Bertha (Moser-1890) Fuchs.

BUSSMANN, AGNES, daughter of Bernard and Katherine (Gieske) Bussmann.

BUSSMANN, BEN SR. son of Bernard (1858) and Katherine (Gieske-1858) Bussmann. *Grnd* of Henry and Mrs. Bussmann and Henry and Mrs. Gieske. Ben, parents and grandparents were all born in Germany. *M* Elizabeth, daughter of Ben (1850) and Anna (Vadder-1862) Wenker.

BUSSMANN, EDWARD, son of Ben (cf) and Elizabeth (Wenker) Bussmann (cf). *M* Darlene, daughter of Herbert and Regina (Tschida) Douvier. *Grnd* of Louie (1884) and Anna (Wolbeck-1885) Douvier and Joseph (1893) and Lucy (Fladung-1899) Tschida.

CARLSON, WALTER E. son of Carl W. (cf) and Charlotte (Naegeli) Carlson. (cf) *M* Lucille, daughter of Gustof (1895) and Katherine (Hintzen) Skoglund. *Grnd* of Peter and Kristen Skoglund and Leonard and Elizabeth Hintzen. Paternal grandparents were born in Sconia, Sweden and reared eight children. Maternal grandfather was born in Holland and maternal grandmother was born in Germany. They were blessed with twelve children.

CARSTENS, RICHARD, son of Herman and Katherine (Mohs) Carstens. *Grnd* of Julius (1862) and Marie (Gobel-1872) Carstens and Math (1868) and Lena (Menzurber-1885) Mohs.

CASPERS, JOHN, son of Nick and Susan (Kulzer) Caspers. *Grnd* of John (1855) and Elizabeth (Sonnen-1859) Caspers and Michael (1860) and Mary (Sand-1860) Kulzer. Paternal greatgrandparents of Lawrence (1817) and Anna M. (Zenz) Caspers. Lawrence served in the German Army for two and one-half years before moving to America in 1846. He purchased a farm in Wisconsin and became very friendly with the Indians. Four of his nine children died during the flu epidemic. He later moved to Meire Grove and became a member of the "Schwetzenverein" (A rather exclusive organization similar to a drill team). M Bertilla, daughter of Peter and Elizabeth (Thull) Sand. *Grnd* of Paul (1859) and Christine (Doetkott-1859) Sand and John (1870) and Mary (Schwieters) Thull. Greatgrandparents were Paul (1832) and Catherine (DeDelia) Sand and Herman and Gertrude (Blenker) Schwieters. "My greatgrandfather Paul Sand," wrote Mrs. Caspers, "lived in Brooklyn, New York and married Catherine DeDelia. They traveled to Dubuque, Iowa on their honeymoon and lived there one year. With another couple, named Linnehan, they moved to St. Joseph. The couple was blessed with nine children. The eldest, Paul, completed two years at St. Johns while the second son's schooling was short-lived (six months). He and a friend were caught helping two "Benny" girls out of their dorms after ten o'clock one evening. As a result, greatgrandfather ruled out any further education."

DENNE, RAYMOND J. son of Herman (1885) and Anna (Poepping) Denne. *Grnd* of Herman and Anna (Steffans) Denne and Joseph and Mrs. Poepping. M Anna Mae, daughter of Ben E. (1880) and Katherine (Hemmesch) Otte. *Grnd* of William (1849) and Mary (Mache-1850) Otte and Matt (1850) and Catherine (Schlener-1853) Hemmesch.

DERICHS, ROBERT M. son of John and Mary (Stang) Derichs. *Grnd* of John (1865) and Lydia (Rausch-1876) Derichs and Conrad (1861) and Josephine (Spanier-1866) Stang. M Janice, daughter of Casper and Irene (Walkaurak) Fiedler Sr. *Grnd* of Sylvester and Anna (Fuchs) Fiedler and Joseph and Helen (Bardonski-1897) Walkaurak.

DETERS, FRANK J. son of Henry J. and Catherine (Weiss) Deters. *Grnd* of Henry and Mrs. Deters and Joseph and Mrs. Weiss. M Angeline, daughter of John (1868) and Mary (Smoley) Schumer. *Grnd* of John and Mary (Kosel) Schumer and Gregor and Ursula (Blenkush) Smoley.

DICKHAUS, VERNON, son of Fred and Bertha (Herzog) Dickhaus. M Betty, daughter of Ben E. (1880) and Catherine (Hemmesch) Otte. *Grnd* of William (1849) and Mary (Mache) Otte and Matt (1850) and Catherine (Schlener-1853) Hemmesch.

DOEGE, SYLVESTER, son of Albert Charles (1887) and Rose E. (Pauly) Doege. *Grnd* of Frank Andrew (1854) and Rosina (Prellwitz-1859) Doege and Henry (1861) and Anna (Brang-1871) Pauly.

Paternal *greatgrnd* were John (1815) and Henrietta (Gruen-1821) Doege. *M* Bernice, daughter of Joseph (cf) and Christine (Hinnenkamp) Stadtherr (cf).

DONOHUE, EDWARD J., son of James (1856) and Julia Agnes (Lynam) Donohue. Maternal grandparents were Bartholomew (1814) and Mary (Coughran) Lynam. Maternal great-grandmother was Julia Lynam (1775). Grandparents were born in Ireland. "My father, James Donohue operated a granite shop in Melrose up to 1912." (Edward Donohue is a professional architect living in Havre, Montana.)

DUERR, MARSON G. son of Albin and Marie (Schraut) Duerr. *Grnd* of Anton (1859) and Mary (Schumacher) Duerr and Michael (1876) and Mary (Keller-1881) Schraut. The Duerr family came to Melrose from St. Michael in 1948 when Albin purchased the City Meat Market and operated it until his retirement in 1964. *M* Marlene, daughter of Mathew J. and Agnes Katherine (Schreifels) Fink. *Grnd* of Joseph and Ann (Gill) Fink and Michael (1870) and Ann (Bolfing-1886) Schreifels.

DUEVEL, ANNA, daughter of Henry (1855) and Katherine (Grube-1859) Duevel. *Grnd* of Christopher and Elizabeth (Drelman) Duevel and Bernard and Mrs. Grube. Parents were born in Hanover, Germany. On 30 April, 1884 they were married in Germany and came to America in 1889.

DUEVEL, ERVIN, son of Joseph (1901) and Helen (Schmidt) Duevel. *Grnd* of Henry (1855) and Katherine (Grube-1859) Duevel and Bernard (1875) and Agnes (Rueter-1884) Schmidt. *M* Denice, daughter of Harold and Alice (Zacharias) Rogers. *Grnd* of Wesley (1883) and Dena (Wentland-1888) Rogers and Andrew (1871) and Esther (Ferm-1885) Zacharias.

EGAN, RICHARD B., son of Joseph Michael (1877) and Anna (Anderson) Egan. *Grnd* of James (1826) and Mary (Rooney-1837) Egan and Peter and Anna Marie (1861) Anderson. Greatgrnd were Thomas and Anna (Welch) Egan and Patrick and Ellen (Tracy) Rooney. Maternal *great-greatgrnd* were Michael and Catherine (Canfield) Rooney. Paternal grandfather, greatgrandparents and maternal great-greatgrandparents were all born in County Mayo, Ireland. Paternal grandfather James Egan emigrated from Ireland in 1842 to Quebec, Canada and later to Padua and Bengor township, Pope county. *M* Lucienne Marie, daughter of Philippe (1888) and Cora (Mousseau) Gosselin. *Grnd* of Pierre (1847) and Camille (Lemieux-1855) Gosselin and Atchez and Roseanna (Roy-1822) Mousseau. Lucienne, parents and grandparents except maternal grandmother were all born in Canada.

Paternal grandfather, Pierre Gosselin, was the first baker in Western Canada.

EGERMAN, JACOB, son of George (1866) and Rosina (Rausch-1862) Egerman. *Grnd* of Stephan and Maria (Jondel) Egerman and Peter and Anna (Bell) Rausch. *M* Jean, daughter of Frank and Mary (Reid) Berkeley. *Grnd* of Frank and Mrs. Berkeley and Thomas and Jean (Arnot) Reid. Grandfather Frank Berkeley was a veteran of the Civil War and held the rank of Lieutenant. Grandfather Thomas Reid belonged to a band and was an accomplished cornet player. His band played for Queen Victoria, then the reigning Queen of the British Empire. The cornet enclosed in a wooden case with some sheet music is now the property of our son, Dr. Lyle B. Egerman, Bancroft, Nebraska, with the understanding that after his death it will revert to our other son Mark J. Egerman, of Alameda, California or his heirs, in order to keep it directly in the family.

EHLERT, WALTER, son of John (1881) and Mary (Laing) Ehlert. *M* Adella, daughter of Bernard (1883) and Julianna (Hoeschen) Wenker. *Grnd* of William and Mary (Borgerding) Wenker and Joseph and Agnes (Bergman) Hoeschen.

EICHERS, ERVIN, son of Joseph and Susan (Theisen) Eichers. *Grnd* of Nicholas (1859) and Mary (Nies-1859) Eichers and Mike (1869) and Mary (Biesener-1858) Theisen. *M* Helen Rose, daughter of Herman and Theresia (Benolken) Rose. *Grnd* of John and Mrs. Rose and Frank and Anna (Molitor) Benolken.

ENNEKING, LAVERNE, son of Bernard and Elizabeth (Hinnenkamp) Enneking. *Grnd* of Bernard (1855) and Katharina (Renneker-1861) Enneking, Sr. and Friederich (1851) and Elizabeth (Kruezman-1858) Hinnenkamp. *M* Rita, daughter of Frank and Katherine (Schiller) Scholz. *Grnd* of Frank and Madeline (Reiger) Scholz and John and Mary (Soller) Schiller.

ESSLER, NORBERT, son of Anthony and Agnes (Doege) Essler. *Grnd* of Frank (1865) and Anna (Jung-1870) Essler and Anton (1846) and Augusta (Schurman-1857) Doege. *M* Alice Virginia, daughter of Alfred and Verna (Sanders) Bjoralt. *Grnd* of Hans (1872) and Margaret (1874) Bjoralt and Olavis (1883) and Regina (Munson-1876) Sanders. My father and paternal grandparents were born in Norway.

EVESLAGE, NORA TEMBROCK, daughter of Tobias and Margaret (Olmschenk) Santer. Maternal grandparents were Dominic and Caroline (Grutsch) Olmschenk. Paternal immigrated from Austria.

FERN, RICHARD P., son of Joseph J. (1887) (cf) and Katherine (Zenz) Fern (cf). Paternal greatgrandfather came from London,

England and paternal greatgrandmother, Sara Fern, came from Dublin, Ireland and died in Melrose in 1894 at the age of eighty-three. "On 15 May, 1911 my father Joseph J. Fern," wrote Richard, "began employment at the Melrose City Power Plant when steam boilers were in use. On 1 April, 1919 he succeeded C. Carlson as superintendent. In his span of forty-one years of labor in the power house he saw the plant converted from steam to diesel power and increase in the output of electricity. He retired on 31 July, 1952. Before his employment at the power house he worked for several years at the Clark mill. *M* Violet, daughter of Conrad and Mary (Rakotz) Voss.

FERN, JOSEPH J., son of David (1850) and Magdelena (Philippi-1855) Fern. *M* Katherine, daughter of Nick (1849) and Agnes (Schneider-1850) Zenz.

FICHTINGER, LEO, son of Sebastian and Theresa (Ederar) Fichtinger. *M* Elizabeth, daughter of Frank and Catherine (Eiynck) Mayers. *Grnd* of Michael (1826) and Catherine (Michels-1820) Mayers.

FINKEN, WILFRED, son of Robert and Loretta (Stueve) Finken. *Grnd* of Conrad (1883) and Mary (Stangler-1888) Finken and August (1878) and Agnes (Kleinberg) Stueve. *M* Alice, daughter of Joseph and Marie (Altmann) Dufner. *Grnd* of Nicholas and Louise (Nett) Dufner and John and Mrs. Altmann.

FRIE, JOSEPH HENRY, son of Herman and Anna (Denne) Frie. *Grnd* of Henry and Gertrude Frie and Herman and Mrs. Denne, Sr. Henry and Gertrude Frie adopted four children. Of these four, Joseph was the first. Children to be adopted upon request were brought by train from New York Foundling Home, operated by Catholic nuns, to their destination. *M* Marie, daughter of Peter J. (1880) (cf) and Theresa (Brandtner) Welz (cf).

FUECHTMANN, BEN J. son of Gerhard (1854) and Gertrude (Wenning-1861) Fuechtman. *M* Anna, daughter of Peter (1856) and Barbara (Rahm) Lehner.

FUECHTMANN, BERNARD JR., son of Bernard J. (cf) and Anna (Lehner) Fuechtmann (cf).

FUECHTMAN, HENRY, (same as Ben J. Fuechtman). *M* Bertha, daughter of Frank (1878) and Elizabeth (Grambke-1903) Wielenberg. *Grnd* of Franz (1842) and Maria (Kramer-1841) Wielenberg and Heinrich (1845) and Caroline (Mache-1852) Grambke. Paternal great-grandfather Franz Heinrich Borgerding married Agnes Wielenberg and since she was the heir to the homestead in Germany he changed his name to Wielenberg and his children carried on the name.

FUNK, JOHN HAROLD, son of Norbert and Valerie (Boecker) Funk. *Grnd* of John and Elizabeth (Block) Funk and Bernard (1879) and Frances (Stoerman-1886) Boecker. *M* Dorothy, daughter of Edward and Pauline (Meyer) Imdieke. *Grnd* of Henry G. (1884) and Barbara (VanBeck-1883) Imdieke and Joseph (1876) and Elizabeth (Deters) Meyer.

GALLOWAY, ROBERT, son of A. G. and Ola (Lanford) Galloway. *Grnd* of maternal grandmother Josephine Theo. *M* Patricia, daughter of Frank and Margaret (Prenisol) Mills. *Grnd* of Newton and Mrs. Mills and Joseph and Mrs. Prenisol.

GERDING, WILLIAM J., son of Bernard (1869) and Katherine (Spaeth-1868) Gerding. *M* Bernadine, daughter of Henry (1876) and Frances (Ostendorf-1885) Verkennis. *Grnd* of Leonard (1851) and Bernadine (Bruns-1857) Verkennis and Joseph and Katherine Osendorf. Paternal grandparents reared eleven children.

GIESKE, JAMES, son of Joseph and Katherine (Althaus) Gieske. *Grnd* of Bernard (1850) and Mary (Otte-1878) Gieske and Henry (1881) and Mary (Zitter-1880) Althaus. *M* Ruth Ann, daughter of Anthony A. and Loretta (Weimerskirch) Goerdt. *Grnd* of Theodore (1855) and Margaret (Stoeckl-1865) Goerdt and Nicholas (1876) and Rosa (Singsank-1880) Weimerskirch.

GEBEKE, CHARLES, son of Edward and Rose Gebeke. *M* Mary Ellen, daughter of James and Ruth (Scholl) Graham. *Grnd* of Patrick (1830) and Ellen (Brown-1852) Graham and John (1871) and Mary (Albrecht-1878) Scholl. "Grandfather Patrick Graham was a veteran of the Civil War," wrote Mary Ellen, "and my father's horses pulled the caisson bearing the remains of soldiers returned from overseas for burial in the local cemetery during World War II.

GIESKE, MRS. MARY R., daughter of James (1870) and Bernadine (Roering) Helsper. *Grnd* of William (1820) and Hannah (O'Connel) Helsper and John H. (1826) and Mary (Fleer) Roering.

GOERDT, JOSEPH, son of Anthony and Loretta (Weimerskirch) Goerdt. *Grnd* of Theodore (1855) and Margaret (Stoeckl-1865) Goerdt and Nicholas (1876) and Rosa (Singsank-1880) Weimerskirch. *M* Marion, daughter of Joseph and Katherine (Althaus) Gieske. *Grnd* of Bernard (1850) and Mary (Otte-1878) Gieske and Henry (1881) and Mary (Zitter-1880) Althaus.

GOIHL, JOHN H., son of John P. and Elizabeth (Muellner) Goihl. *M* Carol, daughter of Oswald (cf) and Elizabeth (Hackman) Botz (cf).

GOIHL, LEROY, son of John P. and Elizabeth (Muellner) Goihl. *M* Janet, daughter of Mathew J. and Agnes Katherine (Schreifels) Fink. *Grnd* of Joseph and Ann (Gill) Fink and Michael (1870) and Ann (Bolfing-1886) Schreifels.

GRAHAM, JAMES, son of Patrick (1830) and Ellen (Brown-1852) Graham. *M* Ruth, daughter of John A. and Mary (Albrecht) Schoell. *Grnd* of George H. and Maria (Appeldorn) Schoell and Joseph and Katherine (Becker) Albrecht. Maternal *greatgrnd* were Peter and Katherine (Peiffer) Becker who immigrated from the Saar Region of Germany to St. Paul. Later they purchased a farm near Belle Plain where they started a brickyard. Many of these bricks were used in the building of the St. Paul Cathedral. John A. Schoell started the first telephone company in Belle Plain.

HAIDER, HENRY M. JR., son of Henry and Rose (Fuchs) Haider, Sr. *Grnd* of Lawrence (1857) and Susanna (Haider-1867-no relation) Haider and John (1869) and Mary (Wymann-1875) Fuchs. *Greatgrnd* were John (1832) and Elizabeth (1847) Wymann and Mike and Margaret (Molitor) Fuchs. *M* Marge, daughter of Edward and Pauline (Meyer) Imdieke. *Grnd* of Henry G. (1884) and Barbara (Van Beck-1883) Imdieke and Joseph and Elizabeth (Deters) Meyer.

HAMPER, RICHARD J., son of Peter and Anna (Sperl) Hamper. *Grnd* of Jacob (1867) and Elizabeth (Schmidt-1868) Hamper and Joseph (1869) and Mary (Regenauer-1868) Sperl. Both sets of grandparents came from Germany. Paternal grandparents moved to St. Paul and maternal grandparents to New Ulm. *M* Frances, daughter of Joseph and Veronica (Bijak) Oczak. *Grnd* of Andrew (1842) and Harriet (Wiatros-1847) Oczak and John and Anna (Kolasienski-1856) Bijak. Parents and grandparents were born in Poland.

HARTUNG, FRANK, son of Sebastian and Frances (Young) Hartung. *Grnd* of Charles and Elizabeth (Yunich) Hartung and Jerome and Mary (Riesinger) Young. *M* Evangeline, daughter of Henry and Margaret (Wiebolt) Klaphake. *Grnd* of Clemens (1866) and Frances (Kersting-1871) Klaphake and Bernard (1858) and Caroline (Woerman-1867) Wiebolt.

HELLERMANN, HENRY, son of Gerhard (1845) and Catherine (Brumlage) Hellermann. Henry was born in Hanover, Germany and came to Melrose in 1892 with his parents who farmed and then retired in Melrose. *M* Rosina, daughter of Ben and Agnes (Hinnenkamp) Wessel. *Grnd* of Theodore (1840) and Mrs. Wessel and Theodore H. (1846) and Elizabeth (1846) Hinnenkamp. Parents and grandparents were born in Damme, Germany.

HELLERMANN, PAUL, son of Henry (cf) and Agnes (Hinnenkamp) Hellermann (cf). M Alma, daughter of Ben G. (1888) and Elizabeth (Von Wahlde-1890) Hinnenkamp. *Grnd* of Henry (1846) and Elizabeth (Niehaus) Hinnenkamp, Sr. and Fred (1862) and Elizabeth (Hasmann-1865) Von Wahlde.

HELLERMANN, HERMAN, JR., son of Herman (1883) and Rose (Steineman) Hellermann, Sr. *Grnd* of Gerhard (1845) and Katharina (Brumlage-1842) Hellermann and John F. (1855) and Elizabeth (Dickhaus-1851) Steineman. Father and grandparents were born in Germany. Fiftieth wedding anniversaries were celebrated by parents and both sets of grandparents. M Elsie, daughter of Henry A. (1884) (cf) and Agnes (Pohlmann) Hinnenkamp (cf).

HELLICKSON, ARTHUR N., son of Nils (1833) and Mary (Tollefruel) Hellickson. "My father was born in Numadahl, Norway and my mother in Halingdahl, Norway. After coming to America, my father served in the Union Army for three years and received an honorable discharge in 1865. In 1866 he homesteaded in North Fork township, in Stearns county and became one of the first supervisors. M Marie, daughter of William (1867) and Christina (Discher) Kind. *Grnd* of George (1822) and Anna (Moh-1834) Kind and Fred and Mrs. Discher. My grandfather, George Kind homesteaded a one hundred twenty acre farm two miles southwest of Melrose, which continued to be my parents' home. When St. Paul's Lutheran Church was organized, my parents were among the orginal members and remained as such until their deaths."

HERGES, RITA, daughter of William (cf) and Elizabeth (Angelbeck) Hinnenkamp Sr. (cf).

HILTNER, GEORGE J., son of Frank and Sophia (Blenker) Hiltner. M Agnes, daughter of Bernard (1858) and Catherine (Gieske-1858) Bussmann.

HILTNER, RICHARD, son of George (1894) (cf) and Agnes (Bussmann) Hiltner (cf). M Delores, daughter of Joseph (cf) and Christine (Hinnenkamp) Stadtherr.

HINNENKAMP, ALBERT A., son of Theodore (1875) and Caroline (Kuhlmann-1878) Hinnenkamp. M Marjorie, daughter of Henry and Theresa (Essler) Nugent. *Grnd* of John and Carrie (Thompson) Nugent and Frank and Anna (Jung) Essler.

HINNENKAMP, BEN, son of Bernard (1843) and Katherine (Nenaber) Hinnenkamp, Sr. Ben and parents were born in Forden, Germany. Ten children were born of this union. M Mary, daughter of Fred (1861) and Caroline (Westerhaus) Angelbeck.

HINNENKAMP, BONIFACE B., son of Henry A. (cf) and Agnes (Pohlmann) Hinnenkamp (cf). M Agnes, daughter of Henry B. and Anna (Kettler) Mueller. *Grnd* of William and Katherine (Schmidt) Mueller and Bernard and Anna (Schulte) Kettler. Father and grandparents were born in Germany.

HINNENKAMP, ELMER B., son of Joseph F. and Elizabeth (Dickhaus) Hinnenkamp. M Rose Marie, daughter of Joseph (cf) and Mary (Bussmann) Blenker, Sr. (cf).

HINNENKAMP, ERNEST B., son of Frank (1891) (cf) and Elizabeth (Schmiesing) Hinnenkamp (cf). M Marcella, daughter of Steve (1819) and Josephine (Meyer) Gruber. *Grnd* of Stephen and Theresa Gruber and Joseph and Catherine Meyer.

HINNENKAMP, FRANK G., son of Henry (1846) and Elizabeth (Hollermann) Hinnenkamp, Sr. "My father was a trustee of St. Boniface Church and helped to build the present church. He owned and operated a steam engine which was used as power for threshing machines in the area. He also operated a saw mill which was taken over by Henry A. and Ben G. Hinnenkamp, (sons of Henry Hinnenkamp, Sr.) and today by Leo and Norbert Hinnenkamp, (sons of Henry A. Hinnenkamp). My brother Fred was ordained a priest in 1907 and two sisters became Franciscan nuns and took the names of Sister Boniface and Sister Gaudentia." M Elizabeth, daughter of Henry (1851) and Catherine (Ferneding) Schmiesing. Paternal grandparents were John Henry and Agnes (Wiechmann) Schmiesing.

HINNENKAMP, JOHN, son of Paul and Grace (Ritter) Hinnenkamp. *Grnd* of Bernard (1843) and Katherine (Neunaber-1849) Hinnenkamp and John and Emily (Roth) Ritter. M June, daughter of Alfred and Katherine (Killeen) Pfeninger. *Grnd* of Albert and Elizabeth (Luenmberger) Pfeninger and Barney and Mary Ann (Meagher) Killeen. Paternal grandparents were born in Switzerland and maternal grandparents were born in Canada.

HINNENKAMP, HENRY A. son of Henry (1846) (cf) and Elizabeth (Niehaus) Hinnenkamp, Sr. (cf). (Same as Frank G. Hinnenkamp). Henry A. served on school board, creamery board, worked at bowling lanes in parish hall and was well known for his German singing. M Agnes, daughter of Bernard (1841) and Elizabeth (Overmann) Pohlmann. "Agnes enjoyed doing mission work and was known for her art in making quilts and cooking for wedding dinners."

HINNENKAMP, LEO B. son of Henry and Agnes (Imdieke) Hinnenkamp, Jr. *Grnd* of Bernard (1843) and Katherine (Nenaber-1849) Hinnenkamp, Sr. and Joseph and Elizabeth (Otte) Imdieke. M Monica, daughter of Henry (1872) and Bernadine (Scherping) Herzog. *Grnd* of Frederick and Gertrude (Koetter) Herzog and Gerhard and Gertrude (Bueckers) Scherping. "My father, Henry Herzog, donated the land in St. Rose for the Church and the Rectory.

HINNENKAMP, NORBERT, son of Henry A. (1884) (cf) and Agnes (Pohlmann) Hinnenkamp (cf). *M* Loretta, daughter of Henry (1879) and Agnes (Hinnenkamp) Hellermann. *Grnd* of Gerhard (1845) and Katherina (Brumlage-1842) Hellermann and Theodore H. (1846) and Elizabeth (1846) Hinnenkamp. Henry and parents were born in Ankum, Germany. Agnes and parents were born in Hanover, Germany.

HINNENKAMP, ROBERT, son of Bernard (1880) (cf) and Mary (Angelbeck) Hinnenkamp (cf). *M* Lorrayne, daughter of Anthony and Louise (Osendorf) Van Beck. *Grnd* of Peter and Katherine Van Beck and Joseph and Katherina Osendorf. "My father, Anthony Van Beck, was born on the ship during the trans-Atlantic crossing from Germany.

HINNENKAMP, WILLIAM J. son of Bernard (1843) and Katherine (Nenaber-1849) Hinnenkamp, Sr. *M* Elizabeth, daughter of Fred and Caroline (Westerhaus) Angelbeck.

HOFFMAN, ROGER, son of Henry and Helen (Schulte) Hoffman. *Grnd* of August and Mrs. Hoffman and Theodore (1888) and Theresa (Mayers-1890) Schulte. "Our family", wrote Roger, "was in the tornado twister that hit south of Melrose on 5 May, 1964. It destroyed the home we were living in." *M* Theresa, daughter of Roman and Martha (Harren) Vos. *Grnd* of Anton (1875) and Elizabeth (1878) Vos and Bernard and Elizabeth (1877) Harren.

HOLLENKAMP, ELMER, son of Aloys and Philomina (Finken) Hollenkamp. *Grnd* of Frank and Frances (Stangler) Finken and John and Tillie (Bachel) Stangler. *M* Nora, daughter of Anthony and Agnes Marie (Doege) Essler. *Grnd* of Frank (1802) and Anna (Jung-1807) Essler and Anton and Augusta (Schurmann) Doege.

HOLLERMAN, HENRY, son of Herman (1882) and Elizabeth (Hinnenkamp) Hollermann. *Grnd* of Herman and Mrs. Hollerman and Herman and Mrs. Hinnenkamp. "My father, Herman Hollerman", wrote Henry, "was a carpenter and built the first wood-working shop in Melrose, in a building directly south of his home at three hundred six - East, Second Street South (the house still stands). He built this shop in 1906 and the first church pews manufactured are still in use in the Immaculate Conception church, New Munich and the Sacred Heart church, Freeport. He operated this millworking shop until his death." *M* Eleanore, daughter of Herman and Margaret (Spaeth) Wiener. *Grnd* of John and Mrs. Wiener and John and Mrs. Spaeth.

HOLLERMAN, JOSEPH J. son of Herman (1882) and Mary (Mehr) Hollerman. *Grnd* of Heinerich and Anna (Bosse) Hollermann and Jacob and Margaret (Miller) Mehr, Sr. *M* Mary Ann, daughter of Bernard and Cecilia (Kersting) Feldewerd. *Grnd* of Bernard (1857) and Christina (Struck-1861) Feldewerd and Heinrich and Anna Maria (Kottenhover-1849) Kersting.

HOLLERMAN, VERNON, son of Henry and Eleanor (Wiener) Hollerman. *Grnd* of Herman (1882) and Elizabeth (Hinnenkamp) Hollerman and Herman (1868) and Margaret (Spaeth-1871) Wiener. *M* Barbara, daughter of Lester (cf) and Dorothy (Zellmer) Andres (cf).

HUGHES, FRANCIS S., son of Henry and Gladys (Knutson) Hughes. *Grnd* of Francis (1868) and Anne (Sheridan-1910) Hughes and Solan (Norway-1871) and Anne (Haugen) Knutson. Paternal grandfather was a member of Archbishop Ireland's colony at DeGraff. *M* Bonita, daughter of William and Gladys (Swanson) Boutain. *Grnd* of Edward and Mary Ellen (O'Brien) Boutain and W. G. (1890) and Gerda (Tengwall-1892) Swanson. Paternal grandparents lived on the land that once was the Minnesota French Indian School in Swift county. In both families the paternal side is basically Irish and French and the maternal side Swedish and Norwegian. In the Benson area, from which the family originates, there was formerly a great religious division between Irish and French Catholics and Luthern Scandinavians. Francis' mother was one of the first to cross the line and Bonita's mother followed a few years later.

IMDIEKE, HERMAN PETER, son of Herman G. and Gertrude (Breitbach) Imdieke. *Grnd* of Herman Joseph (1843) and Agnes (Schmiesing) Imdieke and Peter and Katherine (Gau) Breitbach. Paternal greatgrandparents were Gerad and Mary (Leaning) Imdieke and John and Mary (Wiechman) Schmiesing. Maternal greatgrandparents were Nick and Gertrude (Deiderich) Breitbach and Mr. and Mrs. (Schmitz) Gau. "Grandfather Herman Joseph Imdieke started a brickyard in Meire Grove", wrote Herman P., "in 1880 and my father, Herman G. Imdieke, served in the State Legislature for three terms, 1939-1944, when I came to Melrose from Mayowood, Rochester. I began the first milk pasteurising plant in Melrose and operated it until 1951." *M* Wilma Mary, daughter of Paul William and Pauline (Henry) Halbmaier. *Grnd* of William A. and Elizabeth Mary (Lauer-1854) Halbmaier and Louis Augustine (1838) and Mary (Verner-1838) Henry. Paternal grandparents were born in Germany and maternal grandparents were born in France.

IMDIEKE, JOAN, daughter of Herman P. (cf) and Wilma Mary (Halbmaier) Imdieke (cf).

JACOBS, GUSTAV, son of Michael (1881) and Theresia (Utch) Jacobs. *M* Alma, daughter of Tone J. (1886) and Apolonia (Schoenberg-1887) Welle. *Grnd* of Christ and Elizabeth Welle and Martin and Katherine (Gerads) Schoenberg.

JACOBS, NORBERT, son of Michael (1881) and Theresia (Utch-1887) Jacobs. *M* Leona, daughter of Casper (1889) and Anna (Enneking) Wensmann. *Grnd* of August and Mrs. Wensmann and Bernard (1855) and Mrs. Enneking.

JOHNSON, GARLAND L., son of Ole E. (1886) and Mrs. (Kirekadahl) Johnson. *M* Rosemary, daughter of Alexander (1897) and Gertrude (Stumpf) Hartman. *Grnd* of Philip and Elizabeth (Hennen) Hartman and Adolph and Theresa (Hauer) Stumpf. Alexander Hartman came to Melrose in 1935 and opened a clothing store. Today his daughter, Rosemary, and her husband, Garland, operate this store known as "The Garland."

KEMPER, BEN SR., son of Joseph and Minnie (Zurliene) Kemper. *M* Mary, daughter of Joseph (1851) and Elizabeth (Moeller) Stundebeck. Paternal grandparents of John Henry (1816) and Catherine (Mollmann) Stundebeck. Parents and grandparents were born in Germany.

KERKERING, WILLIAM, son of Henry (1866) and Roseanna (Niehoff) Kerkering. *M* Mary, daughter of George and Mary (Primus) Leukam.

KETTLER, FRANK, son of Henry and Agnes (Woebkenberg) Kettler. *M* Agnes, daughter of John Henry (1850) and Katherine (Ferneding) Schmiesing. *Grnd* of John H. and Bernadine (Wiechmann) Schmiesing.

KETTLER, LEANDER HENRY, son of Frank (1885) (cf) and Agnes (Schmiesing) Kettler (cf). *M* Juliana, daughter of George (1891) and Rose (Berling) Leukam. *Grnd* of George (1859) and Mary (Primus-1860) Leukam and Henry (1855) and Elizabeth (Richter-1854) Berling. Paternal grandparents were born in Wisconsin and maternal grandparents in Germany.

KLAPHAKE, ERVIN, son of Henry and Margaret (Wiebolt) Klaphake. *Grnd* of Clemens and Frances (Kersting-1871) Klaphake and Bernard (1858) and Caroline (Warmen) Wiebolt. Paternal and maternal grandparents reared ten and thirteen children. *M* Virginia, daughter of Joseph and Frances (Renneker) Stueve. *Grnd* of August (1878) and Agnes (Kluenburg-1880) Stueve and Bernard (1864) and Lena (Koch-1876) Renneker. Paternal grandparents reared ten children and maternal grandparents nine children.

KLAPHAKE, GILBERT, son of Alphonse and Rose (Thieschafer) Klaphake. *Grnd* of Clemens (1886) and Frances (Kersting) Klaphake and Bernard (1865) and Mary (Imdieke) Thieschafer. *M* Marcella, daughter of Joseph and Elizabeth (Wiebolt) Uphoff. *Grnd* of August (1859) and Mary (Reverman-1865) Uphoff and Bernard (1858) and Caroline (Wensmann-1867) Wiebolt. Grandparents were born in Germany.

KLAPHAKE, JOSEPH, son of Clemens and Frances (Kersting-1871) Klaphake. *M* Amanda, daughter of John and Anna (Bueckers) Klasen. *Grnd* of Herman and Adelhide (Koopmeiners) Klasen and Bernard (1835) and Adelhide (Wilkes-1845) Bueckers.

KLAPHAKE, ANTHONY, (same as Ervin Klaphake). *M* Alice, daughter of Anthony and Hilda (Lieser) Leukam. *Grnd* of George (1859) and Mary (Primus-1860) Leukam and Nicholas (1874) and Elizabeth (Schoenhoff-1878) Lieser.

KLEIN, HERBERT, son of John (1870) and Frances (Hennen-1883) Klein. *Grnd* of Henry and Mrs. (Bishoph) Klein and Nicholas (1844) and Mrs. (Marz-1848) Hennen. "My father John Klein," wrote Herbert, "was born in Baltimore, Maryland and moved with his parents to Florida where they started a fruit farm. As a young man, he married in Florida and after a disasterous freeze to the fruit farm, he and his wife moved to Minnesota where he sought employment on the railroad. He also worked at Kleber's hardware, Empire Memorial and then bought a farm with a milk route that formerly belonged to the Borget's where he lived until his death. *M* Jane, daughter of Aloys and Irene (Schulte) Hemmesch. *Grnd* of John and Mrs. Hemmesch and Henry and Mrs. Schulte.

KLEUMPKE, JOSEPH, son of Gerhard and Dorothea (Koenig) Kluempke. *Grnd* of Herman A. and Elizabeth (Korf) Kluempke and Anton and Katherine (Graf) Koenig. *M* Mary, daughter of Bernard (1850) and Mary (Otte) Gieske. *Grnd* of Bernard (1850) and Gertrude (Vonstraus) Gieske and William (1849) and Mary (Mache-1850) Otte. Parents and grandparents of Joseph and Mary were all born in Germany. Gerhard Kluempke and his mother, Elizabeth, purchased a farm that is now owned by the fourth generation.

KLUEMPKE, ROBERT, son of Herman and Christine (Gieske) Kluempke. *Grnd* of Gerhard (1866) and Dorothea (Koenig-1869) Kluempke and Bernard (1850) and Mary (Otte-1878) Gieske. *M* Bernadine, daughter of Ben and Veronica (Pohlmann) Koopmeiners. *Grnd* of Herman (1865) and Mary (Bueckers-1881) Koopmeiners and Henry (1876) and Bernadine (Boeckers-1882) Pohlmann.

KOCIEMBA, ALOIS, son of Stanis (1896) and Victoria (Wiatrek) Kociemba. *Grnd* of Frank and Johanna (Kiertzman) Kociemba and Andrew and Mary (Stegura) Wiatrek. All four grandparents were born in Poland. *M* Donna Rose, daughter of Albert and Rose Helen (Timmers) Achman. *Grnd* of Joseph and Elizabeth (Solinger) Achman, Sr. and John and Helen (Scherrer) Timmers.

KOLL, AUGUST P., son of Peter and Augusta (Eckermann) Koll. *M* Loretta, daughter of Nicholas and Clara (Segerty) Laubach, Sr. *Grnd* of Joseph and Mrs. Laubach and Joseph and Mrs. (1822) Segerty. Father was born in Germany and mother in Austria.

KOOPMEINERS, EUGENE, son of Henry (cf) and Olivia (Pohlman) Koopmeiners (cf). *M* Joan, daughter of Anton and Bertha (Kenning) Messer. *Grnd* of Michael and Bernadine (Wehlage) Messer and Herman and Mary (Kiffmeyer) Kenning.

KOOPMEINERS, HENRY A., son of Herman (1865) and Mary (Bueckers) Koopmeiners. *Grnd* of Herman Henry (1836) and Gisina Adelieg (Menke-1829) and Bernard (1835) and Adelhide (Wilkes-1845) Bueckers. Herman and parents born in Hanover, Germany and maternal grandparents were born in Prussia. *M* Olivia, daughter of Henry (1876) and Bernadine (Boeckers) Pohlmann. *Grnd* of Herman and Mrs. Pohlmann and Herman and Agnes (Peckskamp-1860) Boeckers. An interesting incident in these two families was five sons of Herman and Mary Koopmeiners married five daughters of Henry and Bernadine Pohlmann, namely: Henry married Olivia, Ben married Veronica, Herman married Florence, Al married Brigetta and Joe married Evelyn.

KOOPMEINERS, HERMAN, son of Herman (1865) (cf) and Mary (Bueckers) Koopmeiners (cf). (Same as Henry A. Koopmeiners). *M* Florence, daughter of Henry (1876) (cf) and Bernadine (Boeckers) Pohlmann (cf). (Same as Mrs. Henry Koopmeiners.)

KOOPMEINERS, JOSEPH J., son of Herman (cf) and Mary (Bueckers) Koopmeiners (cf). (Same as Henry A. Koopmeiners.) *M* Evelyn, daughter of Henry (1876) (cf) and Bernadine (Boeckers) Pohlmann (cf). (Same as Mrs. Henry Koopmeiners.)

KRAKER, JOHN A., son of Alphone H. and Minnie (Schwegmann) Kraker. *Grnd* of Joseph (1843) and Mary (Bohmer-1857) Kraker and Clemens (1867) and Mary (Terwey-1871) Schwegmann. Joseph donated the main altar in St. Boniface church. *M* Lorraine, daughter of Bernard (cf) and Elizabeth (Wenker) Bussmann (cf).

KRAKER, JOSEPH C., son of Alphonse H. (cf) and Minnie (Schwegmann) Kraker (cf). (Same as John A. Kraker.) *M* Florence, daughter of Walter and Clara (Wellenstein) Johnson. *Grnd* of Frank and Mary (Rockstrom) Johnson and John (1856) and Susan (Guidinger-1856) Wellenstein. Paternal grandparents were born in Sweden and maternal grandparents were born in Wisconsin.

KRAMER, GEORGE WILLIAM, son of John R. (cf) and Bernadine (Ahrens) Kramer (cf). M Loretta, daughter of George and Mathilda (Wieling) Schneider. *Grnd* of Henry (1866) and Pauline (Primus-1868) Schneider and Herman (1878) and Wilhelmina (Wolmecke-1881) Wieling.

KRAMER, IRENE, daughter of John R. (cf) and Bernadine (Ahrens) Kramer (cf).

KRAMER, JOHN R., son of Frank (1862) and Mary (Nett) Kramer. M Bernadine, daughter of George (1852) and Elizabeth (Schmeising-1862) Ahrens.

LAMBERT, RUSSEL, son of Harvey and Pearl (Sherman) Lambert. *Grnd* of Charles and Margaret Lambert and Thomas and Clara Sherman. "My father, Harvey Lambert," said Russel, "was a United States marine stationed in Peking during the Boxer Rebellion in the early 1900's. While in Peking he stopped to give a wounded Chinese a drink of water from his flask when the Chinese thrust a bundle into my father's hands as a thank you gesture. Upon opening the bundle he found a set of nuptial sheets and pillow cases made up of solid embroidery and drawn work (today it is a almost completely vanished art). The value placed on these sheets and pillow cases is priceless. M Evelyn M. daughter of Joseph F. and Mary Caroline (Deters) Thiers. *Grnd* of Joseph F. and Margaret (Schultheis) Thiers Sr. and Ferdinand and Helen (Behres) Deters. "My father, Joseph F. Thiers was a veteran of the Spanish American War, Co. M Thirteenth Minnesota All Volunteers, and came to Melrose in 1900 and started his own soft drink bottling works.

LATZKA, WILLIAM B. son of Herman and Wilhelmina Latzka. M Marie, daughter of Domnich and Barbara (Volz) Grein. *Grnd* of Joseph and Wilhelmina (Fogert) Grein and Joseph and Ann (Weber) Volz. William and Marie were married in 1906 and reared twelve children.

LEMM, DELIA, daughter of Joseph (1874) (cf) and Mary Christine (Borget) Tise (cf).

LEUKAM, RALPH, son of Tony (1898) (cf) and Hilda (Lieser) Leukam (cf). M Irene, daughter of Leo and Mary (Scherping) Elfering. *Grnd* of Bernard (1876) and Anna (Altmann-1880) Elfering and Henry (1868) and Frances (Suek-1883) Scherping.

LEUKAM, TONY, son of George and Mary (Primus) Leukam. *Grnd* of George and Susanna Leukam and John and Mrs. Primus. *M* Hilda, daughter of Nicholas and Elizabeth (Schoenhoff) Lieser.

LOECKEN, HENRY, son of John and Mary (Meemkin) Loecken. *M* Mary, daughter of John (1855) and Mary (Korte) Hemmesch. *Grnd* of Mathew and Mary (Spoden) Hemmesch and Henry and Mary (Lembeck) Korte.

LOECKEN, MARGARET, daughter of Henry (1894) (cf) and Mary (Hemmesch) Loecken (cf).

LOEHR, AUGUST, son of Peter and Gertrude (Heiserich) Loehr. *Grnd* of Arnold and Mrs. (Stalboerger) Loehr and Mr. and Elizabeth (Tonagen) Heiserich. *M* Sophia, daughter of Lawrence (1880) and Mary Magdelin (Freese) Schanhaar. *Grnd* of Henry and Mrs. Schanhaar and Clemens (1854) and Sophia (Grass) Freese.

LOXTERCAMP, HENRY, son of George (1877) and Mary (Kampsen) Loxtercamp. *Grnd* of Frederick (1859) and Catherine (1858) Kampsen. *M* Rita, daughter of Henry (1871) and Elizabeth (Nathe) Schulte. *Grnd* of Anton (1834) and Adelaide (1849) Nathe.

MAUS, DONALD, son of Peter (1875) and Mary (Doepker) Maus. *Grnd* of John (1833) and Catherine (Loesch-1854) Maus and Frank and Marie (Phoebe) Doepker. Paternal greatgrandparents were Nicholas and Anna Maria (Kremges) Maus. "Grandfather John Maus was born in Kreis Trier, Germany and came to America in 1856. In October, 1861 he volunteered for the Union Army in the Civil War for a term of three years. He saw action in Battle of Deserted House on 4 January, 1863 and Suffolk on 26 January, 1863. The remainder of term was at various posts on Point Lookout and guarding rebel prisoners. After the war he bought land and farmed near Pearl Lake. He married Catherine and they had nineteen children (three died as infants). In 1954 Father Alban Fruth O.S.B. wrote a history of the Maus family and found one thousand forty-seven descendants including four priests and fifteen nuns." *M* Mary Ann, daughter of Joseph (1899) and Augusta (Ostendorf) Hoeschen. *Grnd* of Benedict and Mary (Roering) Hoeschen and Theodore and Bernadine (Lange) Ostendorf.

MAUS, RAYMOND, son of Peter (1875) (cf) and Mary (Doepker) Maus (cf). (Same as Donald Maus). *M* Agnes, daughter of Joseph (1890) and Elizabeth (Wiebolt) Uphoff. *Grnd* of August (1859) and Mary (Revermann-1865) Uphoff and Bernard (1858) and Caroline (Woermann-1867) Wiebolt. All four grandparents were born in Germany.

MAUS, WENDELIN B., son of Peter (1875) (cf) and Mary (Doepker) Maus (cf). (Same as Donald Maus). M Winifred, daughter of Henry (1895) and Margaret (Wiebolt) Klaphake. *Grnd* of Clemens (1866) and Frances (Kersting-1871) Klaphake and Bernard (1858) and Caroline (Wensman-1867) Wiebolt. Paternal and maternal grandparents were blessed with ten and twelve children.

MAYERS, DONALD, son of Herman and Anna (Moser) Mayers. *Grnd* of Frank (1864) and Katherine (Eynck-1869) Mayers. M Jeanette, daughter of Arthur and Elizabeth (Weisser) Braun. *Grnd* of Peter (1852) and Bernadine (Athman-1861) Braun and Fred (1881) and Mary (Schneider-1886) Weisser.

MESSERICH, DONALD J., son of Raymond and Rose (Orth) Messerich. *Grnd* of Joseph and Anna (Pluth) Messerich and Nicholas (1875) and Katherine (Klein-1875) Orth. M Arlene, daughter of Casper and Irene (Walkaurak) Fiedler Sr. *Grnd* of Sylvester and Anna (Fuchs) Fiedler and Joseph and Helen (Bardonski-1897) Walkaurak.

METZGER, VIRGIL G., son of Hubert A. and Helen (Salchert) Metzger. *Grnd* of George (1879) and Christine (Rieland-1879) Metzger and Joseph (1863) and Mary (Pung-1879) Salchert. M Marty Lou, daughter of Axel and Lucille (Hatcher) Anderson. *Grnd* of Andrew and Anna Anderson and Bertrum and Mrs. Hatcher.

MEYER, CELESTINE P., son of George (1857) and Susan (Knapp-1865) Meyer. M Teresa, daughter of John (1874) and Catherine (Krebsbach) Schreder. *Grnd* of John and Mrs. Schreder and Joseph (1846) and Applonia (Sturm-1849) Krebsbach. Teresa was born in a log cabin and can well remember how life was in the early 1900's.

MEYER, DONALD J., son of John (cf) and Eleanor (Uhlenkott) Meyer (cf). M Geraldine, daughter of Dr. A. H. and Eleanor (Gravelle) Zachman. *Grnd* of John and Mary (Willems) Zachman and Frederick and Pearl (Morgan) Gravelle.

MEYER, JOHN L., son of Nicholas (1863) and Margaret (Friederich) Meyer. Maternal grandparents were Nicholas and Elizabeth (Benolken-1841) Friederich. Nicholas Meyer operated a Men's clothing store in Melrose from 1898 to 1928. Joseph A. Meyer, brother to John L. took over the clothing store in 1928 and continued until 1962. M Eleanor, daughter of George (1850) and Mary (Metzger) Uhlenkott. Maternal grandparents settled on a farm near New Munich. Herman Uhlenkott, paternal grandfather came to Minnesota in the summer of 1859 with grandmother and three children in a covered wagon and homesteaded on land about one mile northeast of New Munich bordering a small body of water now called Uhlenkott lake. In 1901 George Uhlenkott organized the Bank of Freeport. In 1908 the business was incorporated as the Uhlenkott State Bank.

MEYER, LEO A., son of Aloys C. and Elizabeth (Nietfeld) Meyer. *Grnd* of Herman H. (1868) and Pauline (Nathe-1873) Meyer and Henry J. (1852) and Anna (Kerkhoff-1858) Nietfeld. *M* Janice J. daughter of Alphonse and Irmalinda (Rademacher) Schulte. *Grnd* of Clemens (1879) and Josephine (Macke-1879) Schulte and Peter (1870) and Mary (Froehler-1881) Rademacher.

MEYER, LEROY, son of Celestine (cf) and Teresa (Schreder) Meyer (cf). *M* Catherine, daughter of John and Rose (Mache) Nietfeld. *Grnd* of Henry (1852) and Anna (Kerkhoff-1858) Nietfeld and Bernard (1850) and Catherine (Dickhaus-1849) Mache.

MEYER, MARK H., son of John L. (cf) and Eleanor (Uhlenkott) Meyer (cf). *M* Barbara, daughter of Francis and Ruth (Kennedy) Heckler.

MIDDENDORF, FRED, son of Henry (1869) and Mary (Westendorf) Middendorf. *Grnd* of Henry and Elizabeth (Schmidt) Westendorf. *M* Theresia, daughter of George and Appolonia (Meizen) Hiltner. *Grnd* of John Meizen and Anna Eva (Faust) Meizen.

MIDDENDORF, GERALD, son of Joseph W. (cf) and Veronica (Toenyan) Middendorf (cf). *M* Diane, daughter of Bernard and Rose (Austing) Stoerman. *Grnd* of Gerhard and Catherine Stoerman and Melchior and Mary (Bergmann) Austing.

MIDDENDORF, JOHN, son of Fred (cf) and Theresa (Hiltner) Middendorf (cf). *M* Mary Jane, daughter of Joseph and Clara (Ebensteiner) Peters. *Grnd* of George (1867) and Susan (Schutz-1874) Peters and John and Kathryn (Dix) Ebensteiner.

MIDDENDORF, JOSEPH W., son of Henry (1869) and Mary (Westendorf) Middendorf. *Grnd* of Henry and Elizabeth (Schmidt) Westendorf. *M* Veronica, daughter of George (1870) and Bernadine (Albers) Toenyan. *Grnd* of Gerhard and Gertrude (Stilling) Toenyan and Henry (1826) and Mary (Poncho-1831) Albers.

MIDDENDORF, LAWRENCE H., son of Henry and Loretta (Toenyan) Middendorf. *Grnd* of Henry (1869) and Mary (Westendorf) Middendorf and George (1870) and Bernadine (Albers) Toenyan. *M* Rose Mary, daughter of Alfred and Julitta (Meyer) Lieser. *Grnd* of Joseph and Theresa (Hemmesch) Lieser and Ignatius and Martha (Joegel) Meyer.

MIDDENDORF, MARK, son of Herman and Helen (Zwilling) Middendorf. *Grnd* of Henry (1869) and Mary (Westendorf) Middendorf and Nicholas (1870) and Clara (Fruth-1875) Zwilling. M Kathleen, daughter of Joseph (1895) and Christine (Klobe) Ettel. *Grnd* of Frank (1865) and Julianna (Steiner) Ettel and Carl (1865) and Paulena (Teuber-1871) Klobe. Maternal greatgrandparents were Valentine and Catherine Klobe and John and Magdalen Teuber.

MLODZIK, JAMES, son of Walter C. and Mary Ann (Zabrocki) Mlodzik. *Grnd* of Frank (1871) and Josephine (Thomas-1870) Mlodzik and Gracian (1879) and Palagia (Stanislawski-1883) Zabrocki. Paternal greatgrandfathers were Jacob Mlodzik and Thomas Thomas and maternal greatgrandparents were Frank and Frances (Ciszenski) Zabrocki and Stanley and Augustina (Mazik) Stanislawski. M Mary, daughter of Edward and Rose Gebeke.

MOENING, GEORGE B., son of John (1875) and Agnes (Renneker) Moening. *Grnd* of George (1844) and Elizabeth (Heidgerken-1844) Moening Sr. and Frederich and Gertrude (Gieske) Renneker. Grandfather George Moening, was one of the eleven families that originated St. Patrick's Parish. M Helen Overmann.

MOENING, LEO, son of Joseph (1874) and Bernadina (Kerfeld) Moening. *Grnd* of George (1844) and Elizabeth (Heidgerken-1844) Moening Sr. M Mary, daughter of Bernard (1876) and Anna (Altman) Elfering. *Grnd* of Engelberth and Mrs. Elfering and Aloys and Elizabeth (Frevel) Altman. Grandfather Aloys Altman, was a veteran of the Civil War.

MOORE, DONALD C., son of Clarence and Bertha (Spahr) Moore. *Grnd* of John and Lottie Moore and Carl and Mary Spahr. Donald and parents were born in Texas. M Pearl, daughter of John and Lilly (Crowell) Wade. Grandfather John Magrey Crowell, came from Scotland as a stowaway on a ship at the age of fourteen. John Holland, who came over on the Mayflower, is our ancestor on mother's side.

MOSER, HENRY MICHAEL, son of Joseph (1849) and Elizabeth (Wessels) Moser. *Grnd* of Justus and Mary (Bolfing) Moser and Henry and Mrs. Wessels. M Eleanor, daughter of John (1862) and Anna Marie (Winter) Lieser. *Grnd* of Michael and Frances (Kohler) Lieser and Peter and Anna Marie (Miller) Winter.

MUELLNER, RAY STEVE, son of Ray and Agnes (Tieman) Muellner. *Grnd* of Math (1856) and Elizabeth (1865) Muellner and Henry (1866) and Mary Ann (Dickhaus-1881) Tieman. M Regina, daughter of George and Juldah (Buchholz) Schieffer. *Grnd* of John (1881) and Mary (Kohn-1882) Schieffer and Charles and Anna

(Thomas) Buchholz. "One interesting fact in our family history," wrote Regina, "is that twins run in our family. My paternal grandparents had twin boys, my mother had twin girls (of which I am one), and my third oldest sister had twin boys.

NATHE, BERNARD E., son of Fred (cf) and Christine (Gieske) Nathe (cf).

NATHE, FRED V., son of Herman and Catherine (Ortman) Nathe. *Grnd* of Joseph and Mrs. Nathe and Bernard and Mrs. Ortman. *M* Christine, daughter of Bernard and Mary (Otte) Gieske. *Grnd* of Bernard (1850) and Gertrude (Vonstruas) Gieske and William (1849) and Mary (Macke-1850) Otte. Parents and grandparents were born in Germany.

NIEHAUS, ANTHONY, son of Joseph and Agnes (Wessel) Niehaus. *Grnd* of Joseph and Katherine (Nienaber) Niehaus and Theodore and Elizabeth (Wichaus-1841) Wessel. Parents and grandparents were born in Germany. *M* Carol, daughter of Ferdinand and Loretta (Storkamp) Eveslage. *Grnd* of Ferdinand and Catherine (Schwegman) Eveslage and Bernard (1872) and Mary (Kiffmeyer-1875) Storkamp. "Grandfather Bernard Storkamp," wrote Carol, "helped lay the bricks for the former St. Boniface School.

NOHNER, FABIAN, son of Leo and Elizabeth (Mies) Nohner. *Grnd* of Peter and Katherine (Hommus-1864) Nohner and Peter and Susan (Schaefer) Mies. *M* Bernice, daughter of Math and Frances (Dockendorf) Froehling. *Grnd* of John and Margaret (Leisch) Froehling and Math and Susan (Rausch) Dockendorf.

NORDMAN, JOHN, son of Bernard (1850) and Margaret (Hammar) Nordman. *M* Esther, daughter of John (1861) and Margaret (Kuefler) Miller.

NOTCH, LAWRENCE, son of Joseph (1873) and Mary (Wiechmann) Notch. *M* Alma, daughter of Ladislaus and Mary Anna (Eiynck) Butkowski. *Grnd* of Jacob and Mary (Goerka) Butkowski and Henry (1853) and Gertrude (Beier-1859) Eiynck.

NOTCH, MARVIN J., son of Lawrence (cf) and Alma (Butkowski) Notch (cf). *M* Janet, daughter of Ben H. and Theresia (Engelmeyer) Klasen. *Grnd* of John (1873) and Anna (Bueckers-1879) Klasen and Stephan (1872) and Mary (Vornbrock-1882) Engelmeyer.

O'BRIEN, GEORGE A., son of George A. (1890) and Sylvia K. (Danielson) O'Brien, Sr. *Grnd* of Thomas and Bridget (St. John) O'Brien and John F. and Sara E. (Jahanson) Danielson. Paternal grandparents came from Ireland and maternal grandparents came from

Sweden. *M* Barbara, daughter of Charles F. and Mary (Seymour) Schisler. Barbara and parents were born in Baltimore, Maryland.

OEVERMAN, MRS. ALVINA, daughter of Bernard and Mary (Imdieke) Thieschafer. *Grnd* of Joseph and Mrs. (Primus) Imdieke.

OEVERMAN, JOSEPH JR., son of Joseph (1860) and Katherine (VonWahlde) Oevermann, Sr. *M* Kathleen, daughter of Alex and Eleanor (Radermacher) Messer. *Grnd* of Bernard and Anna Messer and Andrew and Helen (Fink) Radermacher.

OLMSCHEID, ALOIS, son of John P. (1871) and Theresa (Kascht) Olmscheid. *Grnd* of John and Anna (Jacobs) Olmscheid and Mathias and Katherine Kascht. *M* Sophia, daughter of Anton (1875) and Anna (Liebing) Brix. *Grnd* of John and Margaret Brix and Frank and Rosina (Rausch) Liebing.

OLMSCHEID, ED., son of John (1871) (cf) and Theresa (Kascht-1872) Olmscheid (cf). (Same as Alois Olmscheid.) *M* Susan, daughter of Math (1863) and Annie (Hoppe) Mayers. *Grnd* of Mike (1826) and Catherine (Michaels) Mayers and Ferdinand (1835) and Wilhelmina (Meyer-1848) Hoppe. Ed and Susan Olmscheid were married in New Munich 30 August, 1921 and celebrated their golden wedding anniversary on 30 August, 1971 in Melrose. Of this union there were eight children.

ORTH, EYMARD, son of Lambert and Mary (Bromenschenkel) Orth. *Grnd* of Nicholas (1876) and Katherine (Klein-1875) Orth and John (1853) and Barbara (Marthaler-1862) Bromenschenkel. *M* Lucille, daughter of Celestine (cf) and Teresa (Schreder) Meyer (cf).

OTTE, JULIUS J. AND MEINULF, sons of Bernard (1856) and Anna (Nathe) Otte. Paternal grandmother Elizabeth DeMarto was born in Paris, France.

PALLANSCH, ROBERT C., son of Charles and Mrs. (Roering) Pallansch. *M* Dorothy, daughter of Donald C. (cf) and Pearl (Wade) Moore Sr. (cf).

PETERMEIER, ANTHONY H., son of Ignatz (1887) and Caroline (Uhlenkamp) Petermeier. *Grnd* of Henry (1852) and Anna (Blome-1858) Petermeier and Frank (1865) and Marie (Inderrieden-1861) Uhlenkamp. *M* Ella, daughter of Henry (1874) and Tillie (Buchholz) Betow and August (1852) and Wilhelmina (Ehlert-1856) Buchholz.

PETERMEIER, BERNARD, son of Stephan (1857) and Theresa (Neukirch) Petermeier. *Grnd* of Conrad (1804) and Angela Maria (Pohler-1814) Petermeier and Henrich (1762) and Anna Maria (Bose-1787) Neukirch. Both sets of grandparents came from Delbruck, Germany. "If my grandfather had not changed his name from Holtapel to Petermeier, my name would be Holtapel today," wrote Bernard. *M* Mary, daughter of Joseph (1867) and Elizabeth (Schultenkamper) Enneking.

PETERMEIER, CONRAD, son of Stephan (1857) (cf) and Theresa (Neukirch) Petermeier (cf). (Same as Bernard Petermeier). *M* Dorothea, daughter of John Henry (1850) and Katherina (Fernading) Schmiesing. *Grnd* of John Henry and Bernadina (Wiechman) Schmiesing and Mr. and Mrs. Fernading. In both families parents and grandparents were born in Germany.

PETERMEIER, HENRY, son of Stephan (1857) (cf) and Theresa (Neukirch) Petermeier (cf). (Same as Bernard Petermeier.) *M* Elizabeth, daughter of Anthony (1867) and Frances (Pelle) Zirbes. *Grnd* of Peter and Christina (Benolkin-1844) Zirbes and Mr. and Katherine (Wilde) Pelle. Paternal grandparents reared eight children and maternal grandparents eighteen children.

PETERMEIER, JAMES, son of Conrad (cf) and Dorothea (Schmiesing) Petermeier (cf). *M* Betty, daughter of Frank and Margaret (Uphus) Deters. *Grnd* of Frank and Anna (Hens) Deters and Ben and Anna (Kulzer) Uphus. Paternal and maternal grandparents had sixteen and twelve children.

PETERMEIER, JOSEPH C., son of Henry (1887) (cf) and Elizabeth (Zirbes) Petermeier (cf). *M* Patricia, daughter of Leo V. (1890) and Anna (Mertes) Skeffington. *Grnd* of Patrick and Johanna (Leehan) Skeffington and John and Theresa (Jahrmer) Mertes.

POHLMANN, JOSEPH, son of Bernard and Mrs. (Oevermann) Pohlmann. *M* Mary, daughter of Henry and Mary (Wessel-1841) Soenneker.

POHLMANN, JOSEPH F., son of Joseph (cf) and Mary (Soenneker) Pohlmann (cf). *M* Caroline, daughter of William (cf) and Rose (Austing) Wiechmann (cf).

PRIMUS, ALBERT M., son of William J. (1895) (cf) and Rose (Meyer) Primus (cf). *M* Marie, daughter of Henry A. (1884) (cf) and Agnes (Pohlmann) Hinnenkamp (cf).

PRIMUS, ANTHONY J., son of Joseph J. (1857) and Christine (Michaels) Primus. *Grnd* of John and Catherine (Nathe) Primus. Anthony was fire chief for the City of Melrose Fire Department from 1935-1952 when his son Donald became chief. *M* Clotilda, daughter of John and Mary (Kolb) Wander. Paternal grandfather Casper Wander, and his wife had six children. Five of these children died about the same time of diphtheria.

PRIMUS, DONALD J., son of Anthony (cf) and Clotilda (Wander) Primus (cf). *M* Lois, daughter of S. W. and Ella (Emmons) Gilley. Paternal grandparents were John and Martha Gilley. Lois, parents and grandparents lived in Texas.

PRIMUS, HENRY A., son of John (1862) and Theresia (Schneider) Primus. *Grnd* of John (1824) and Catherine (Nathe-1829) Primus and John and Mary Anna (Schulte) Schneider. *M* Mary Magdalen, daughter of Joseph and Katherine (Goeser) Athman.

PRIMUS, URBAN H., son of William J. (1894) (cf) and Rose (Meyer) Primus (cf). *M* Mary Ann, daughter of Henry (cf) and Rosina (Wessel) Hellermann (cf).

PRIMUS, WILLIAM, son of John (1862) (cf) and Theresia (Schneider) Primus (cf). (Same as Henry A. Primus.) *M* Rose, daughter of Henry G. (1865) and Elizabeth (Imdieke) Meyer. *Grnd* of Henry (1835) and Elizabeth (Schulte-1835) Meyer and Henry (1835) and Elizabeth (Macke-1842) Imdieke. Both sets of grandparents were born in Germany.

RADEMACHER, NORBERT, son of Carl (1875) and Frances Rademacher. *M* Priscilla, daughter of Ben E. (1880) and Catherine (Hemmesch) Otte. *Grnd* of William (1849) and Maria (Mache-1850) Otte and Matt (1850) and Catherine (Schlener-1853) Hemmesch.

RAEKER, ANTON, son of Herman (1850) and Anna (Richter) Raeker. *M* Clara, daughter of Nicholas (1853) and Bertha (Herberger) Hockert. *Grnd* of Joseph (1814) and Elizabeth (Heintz) Hockert and Fred and Ottilia (Breigly) Herberger. "My father and grandparents were born in Germany," wrote Clara, "and grandfather Fred Herberger, and his brothers Carl and George started the first brewery in St. Cloud."

RAEKER, JOHN C., son of Anton and Clara (Hockert) Raeker (cf). *M* Lucille, daughter of Herman and Pauline (Nathe) Humbert. *Grnd* of Ben (1862) and Elizabeth (Schweiters-1868) Humbert Sr. and Frank (1864) and Catherine (Pfeffer-1870) Nathe.

RAUCH, MARY MARGARET, daughter of George A. and Anna (Fuhrmann) Rauch. *Grnd* of George and Margaret (Winter) Rauch and Frederich and Mrs. Fuhrmann.

REHKAMP, LOUIS, son of Fred (1866) and Clara (Westbrock) Rehkamp. *M* Mary, daughter of Joseph (1860) and Katherine (Von-Wahlde) Oevermann. Louis and Mary were both born in Melrose.

REHKAMP, ROBERT AND WALTER, sons of Louis (1896) (cf) and Mary (Oevermann) Rehkamp (cf).

REIMAN, LEO, son of Henry and Anna (Krienert) Reiman. *Grnd* of Herman and Mary (Herlist) Reiman and Joseph and Mrs. Krienert.

M Margaret, daughter of William and Anna (Kroenke) Vakiner. *Grnd* of Hartmann and Anna (Schrumf) Vakiner and Joseph and Anna (Werblow) Kroenke.

RENNEKER, ALCUIN, son of Ben (cf) and Rose (Beste) Renneker (cf). *M* Loretta, daughter of Louis and Frances (Kruse) Dullinger.

RENNEKER, BEN, son of Ben and Magdelene (Koch) Renneker, Sr. *Grnd* of Frederich and Gertrude (Gieske) Renneker and Gotlieb and Regina (Sweep) Koch. "Ben Renneker, Sr. left Germany to avoid the draft and later he provided the money so that his parents, brothers and sisters could come to the United States." *M* Rose, daughter of Anton and Mary (Hoppe) Beste. *Grnd* of Henry and Josephine (Dinnobecker) Beste and Joseph and Elizabeth (Rieland) Hoppe. "Joseph Hoppe was a stowaway on the ship bringing the immigrants over. He hid between barrels until the ship was out at sea. Upon arriving in the United States he rode a pair of oxen from Louisana to California to mine gold. Because of some rule the gold mined had to be returned to the property of the mine but Joseph kept enough to make a wedding ring for his wife. The ring was handed down to a grandchild."

REVERMANN, JOSEPH, son of Bernard (1869) and Agnes (Kettler) Revermann. *Grnd* of Mr. and Elisabeth (Roverkamp) Revermann and Bernard and Anna (Schulte) Kettler. Parents and grandparents were born in Germany. *M* Lorraine, daughter of Anthony (1895) (cf) and Clothilda (Wander) Primus (cf).

RIPKA, KENNETH, son of John (cf) and Veronica (Spaeth) Ripka (cf). *M* Alice, daughter of Conrad and Mary (Rakatz) Voss. *Grnd* of John (1867) and Anna (Kubecheck-1863) Voss and Frank (1873) and Catherine (Gerada-1876) Rakatz.

RIPKA, JOHN, son of John and Mary (Miller-1866) Ripka. *M* Veronica, daughter of Matt and Catherine (Schumacher) Spaeth.

RITTER, ALCUIN, son of Joseph (1887) and Catherine (Vornbrock) Ritter. *Grnd* of John (1857) and Amelia (Roth-1863) Ritter and Mr. and Katherine (Buattner) Vornbrock. *M Vera,* daughter of Nicholas (1871) and Anna (Olberding) Sand. *Grnd* of Michael and Mrs. Sand and Henry and Bernadine (Kramer) Olberding.

RITTER, ROMAN P., son of Joseph (1887) (cf) and Catherine (Vornbrock) Ritter (cf). (Same as Alcuin Ritter.) *M* Edith, daughter of Peter (1875) (cf) and Mary (Doepher) Maus (cf). (Same as Donald Maus.)

ROELIKE, ALMA, daughter of Michael and Sophia (Von Loosbroeck) Kummer. *Grnd* of Matthias (1814) and Mrs. (Moes-1809) Kummer and Henry and Margaret (Heissler) Von Loosbroeck. Alma is the wife of Dr. Stephen J. Roelike, a practicing dentist in Melrose from about 1920 until his death.

ROELIKE, JOSEPH, son of Othmar (cf) and Frances (Stein) Roelike (cf). *M* Marguerite, daughter of Walter and Florina (Brixius) Dobmeier. *Grnd* of Lawrence (1880) and Mary (Sieben) Dobmeier and Jacob (1864) and Maria (Joa-1877) Brixius.

ROELIKE, OTHMAR, son of Joseph and Elizabeth (Meyer) Roelike. *M* Frances, daughter of John and Mary (Hinnenkamp) Stein. *Grnd* of John and Mrs. Stein and John H. and Anna (Feldhaus) Hinnenkamp.

ROERING, BERNARD, son of Albert and Mrs. (Beckermann) Roering. *Grnd* of Herman and Elizabeth (Housman) Roering and John and Mrs. (Luckmann) Beckermann. *M* Kathleen Dorothy, daughter of Joseph and Elizabeth (Kolb) Wensmann. *Grnd* of Philip and Theresia (Walentiny) Kolb and August and Josephine (Beyer) Wensmann.

ROERING, SYLVESTER H., son of John B. and Theresa (Hiltner) Roering. *Grnd* of John and Mary Roering. *M* Margaret, daughter of Anton and Margaret (Klein) Nathe. *Grnd* of Joseph and Elizabeth (TeMarto) Nathe and Henry and Ursala (Bischoff) Klein. Margaret wrote about this incident in their family history - "When my greatgrandfather Christopher TeMarto came across from Germany, a son died on board ship and was buried at sea and again when my Grandmother Mary Ursala Bischoff, came from Germany her mother who accompanied her, died on ship and was buried at sea.

ROLFZEN, JOSEPH F., son of Herman Henry and Agnes (Sundenberg) Rolfzen. Parents were born in Germany. *M* Hildegarde, daughter of Frederich (1875) and Katherine (Wuebkers) Wessel. *Grnd* of Theodore (1840) and Elizabeth (Wiehaus-1841) Wessel and Herman and Maria (Otte-1851) Wuebkers. "My grandparents, Herman and Maria Wuebkers built the first frame house north of Melrose in 1886," wrote Hildegarde.

SALZMANN, EDWARD, son of Reinhold (1876) and Katherine (Jaspers) Salzmann. *M* Mildred, daughter of Fred (1875) and Katherine (Wuebkers) Wessel. *Grnd* of Theodore (1840) and Elizabeth (Wiehaus-1841) Wessel and Herman and Maria (Otte-1851) Wuebkers. "My father, Fred Wessel, came to Melrose from Germany in 1890 accompanied by his friend, August Kuhlmann who later became a practicing physician in Melrose for many years," wrote Mildred.

SANDBRINK, ANN, daughter of Joseph B. and Margaret (Hilger) Sandbrink. *Grnd* of John A. and Anna K. (Wehlage) Sandbrink and William F. and Anna Clara (Ulmann-1828) Hilger. "Joseph B. Sandbrink became a citizen of the United States in 1881 and moved to Melrose in 1886 where he bought all of Block Fifty-nine, 5th Ave. N.E. in 1906 and lived there until his death."

SCHANHAAR, LEO W., son of Lawrence (1880) and Mary (Freese) Schanhaar. *Grnd* of Henry and Mrs. Schanhaar and Clemens (1854) and Sophia (Grass) Freese. *M* Lois, daughter of Paul (1898) and Beata (Hofmann) Buttweiler. *Grnd* of Peter (1855) and Agnes (Barthle-1865) Buttweiler and Julius (1868) and Mary (Auer-1870) Hofmann. "My paternal greatgrandparents homesteaded in the area between Freeport and St. Rose and settled there in 1868," wrote Lois.

SCHIFFLER, LORDELL, son of Wilfred and Ann (Silbernick) Schiffler. *Grnd* of John and Mary (Frye) Schiffler and Joseph and Katherine (Deters) Silbernick. *M* Susan, daughter of John B. and Barbara (Duclos) Thelen. *Grnd* of Hubert and Susan (Nett) Thelen and John and Katherine (Hoffman) Duclos.

SCHLICHT, URBAN C., son of Michael and Anna (Wohls) Schlicht. *Grnd* of Peter and Mary (Micklish) Schlicht. *M* Rose, daughter of Carl J. and Dela (Neveaux) Eiler. *Grnd* of Henry (1832) and Karen Elizabeth (Hansen-1834) Eiler and Thomas (1835) and Rosalia (Trudeau-1849) Neveaux.

SCHMIDT, ETHEL, daughter of Joseph and Anna (Uphoff) Schmidt Sr. *Grnd* of John J. and Maria G. (Mescher) Schmidt and Herman and Mrs. (Maurer) Uphoff.

SCHNEIDER, EARL M., son of Frank (1888) and Ida Rose (Ramacher) Schneider. *Grnd* of Anthony (1860) and Mary (Halfman-1860's) Schneider and Christ (1860) and Mary (Moehler-1860's) Ramacher. Maternal grandparents came from Holland. *M* Genevieve, daughter of Henry C. (cf) and Eleanor (Santer) Tembrock (cf).

SCHOLZ, FRANK J., son of Frank and Magdalena (Rieger) Scholz. *M* Katherine, daughter of John G. and Mary (Soller) Schiller.

SCHWIETERS, HENRY, son of Joseph and Catherine (Hallermann) Schwieters. *Grnd* of Herman and Elizabeth (Blenker) Schweiters and Henry (1854) and Mrs. Hallermann. *M* Rose, daughter of Bernard and Gertrude (Jenniges) Otte. *Grnd* of Bernard (1836) and Anna (Nathe) Otte and Matthias and Gertrude (Eichten) Jenniges.

SCHWIETERS, NICHOLAS, son of Herman (1866) and Katherine (Roering) Schwieters. *Grnd* of Ben and Mrs. Schwieters. *M* Helen, daughter of Ben and Catherine (Spaeth) Gerding. *Grnd* of Henry and Mrs. Gerding and John and Mary (Weber) Spaeth.

SERVATIUS, GEORGE C., son of Math and Anna (Henry) Servatius. *Grnd* of Peter and Jennie (LaBudde) Henry. Maternal grandmother came from France. *M* Nellie, daughter of Frank and Mary (Trobec) Siminich. *Grnd* of Mr. and Mrs. Siminich and Frank and Annie (Schumer) Trobec. Nellie wrote, "Bishop Trobec was my great-great uncle and Monsignor Joseph Trobec was my great uncle."

SIEBEN, DAVID H., son of Omer (cf) and Clara (Lembeck) Sieben (cf). *M* Bernadine, daughter of Mike J. and Adela (Meyer) Welle. *Grnd* of Hubert and Elizabeth (Sand) Welle and Joseph and Elizabeth (Deters) Meyer.

SIEBEN, OMER, son of Aloys (1894) and Anna (Wheeling) Sieben. *Grnd* of Jacob and Veronica (Pfiefer) Sieben and Carl and Mary (Wieber) Wheeling. *M* Clara, daughter of Henry W. (1871) and Emma (Utecht) Lembeck. *Grnd* of William and Mrs. Lembeck and Alexander and Mrs. Utecht.

SOENNEKER, JOSEPH A., son of Henry and Maria (Wessel) Soenneker. *Grnd* of John Frederich (1831) and Elizabeth (Reising-1831) Soenneker and Theodore (1840) and Elizabeth (Wiechman-1841) Wessel. *M* Magdaline, daughter of Frank and Elizabeth (Grampke) Wielenberg. *Grnd* of Franz (1842) and Marie Agnes (Kramer-1841) Wielenberg and Heinerich (1845) and Caroline (Macke-1852) Grampke. The Soenneker family has a paternal family tree dating back to 1661 and the Wielenberg family have a paternal family tree dating back to 1672.

SPAETH, ALLEN, son of Henry and Rose Spaeth, Sr. *M* Betty Lou, daughter of Ed (cf) and Susan (Mayers) Olmschied (cf).

SPAETH, THEODORE, son of Matthias (1866) and Katherine (Thull) Spaeth. *M* Alvina, daughter of Bernard (1871) and Mary (Klein) Kramer.

STADTHERR, JOSEPH M., son of John P. (1872) and Maria (Zins-1873) Stadtherr. *Grnd* of Wencil (1832) and Ursula (1833) Stadtherr. Grandparents were born in Germany and celebrated their diamond jubilee in Melrose in 1912. *M* Christine, daughter of Henry (1871) and Agnes (Imdieke-1900) Hinnenkamp, Jr. *Grnd* of Bernard and Mrs. Hinnenkamp and Joseph and Mrs. (Primus) Imdieke.

STALBOERGER, DONALD L., son of Henry C. and Bernadine (Schoenberg) Stalboerger. *Grnd* of Andrew and Anna (1851) Stalboerger and Peter (1860) and Agnes (Moorman-1862) Schoenberg. M Lorraine, daughter of Michael (cf) and Bernadine (Verkennis) Haider (cf).

STILLING, ALVINA, daughter of Henry and Sophia (Blenker) Stilling. *Grnd* of Joseph and Elizabeth (Heskemann-1836) Blenker. Parents and grandparents were born in Germany.

STROEING, ALCUIN, son of Henry and Anna (Nathe) Stroeing. *Grnd* of Herman and Katherine (Ortman) Nathe. M Merena, daughter of Tony and Apolonia (Schoenberg) Welle. *Grnd* of Christ and Elizabeth Welle and Martin and Katherine (Gerads) Schoenberg.

STUEVE, OSWALD, son of Henry (1865) and Theresa (Bormes) Stueve. Parents were born in Germany. M Catherine, daughter of Joseph and Cecilia (Loosbrock) Gillitzer.

SUNDERMAN, VICTOR, son of Tony and Anna (Volbert) Sunderman. *Grnd* of Ben (1853) and Bernadine (Tieman-1854) Sunderman and Herman (1850) and Elizabeth (Hewing-1870) Volbert. M Dorine, daughter of Joseph and Katherine (Althaus) Gieske. *Grnd* of Bernard (1850) and Mary (Otte-1870) Gieske and Henry (1881) and Mary (Zitter-1880) Althaus.

TERRES, PETER, son of Frank and Harriet (Shay) Terres. M Dorine, daughter of Paul (1893) and Margaret (Kampsen) Rieland. *Grnd* of Joseph (1864) and Mary (Welle-1870) Rieland and Bernard (1856) and Josephine (Zaph-1853) Kampsen.

THELEN, ALPHONSE A., son of John and Mary (Goihl) Thelen. *Grnd* of Martin and Mary Anne (Laubendahl) Thelen and John and Anna (Schneider-1859) Goihl. M Jeanette, daughter of Peter and Rose (Weymann) Klapperich. *Grnd* of Jacob and Appolona (Homburg) Klapperich and John (1868) and Mary (Ahles-1877) Weymann.

THEILER, PHILIP F., son of Joseph (1882) and Mary (Ecker) Theiler. M Agnes, daughter of Ed (1892) and Mary (Buechele) Weisbrich. *Grnd* of Joseph and Mrs. Weisbrich and Max and Mrs. Buechele.

THIESCHAFER, JOSEPH HENRY, son of Bernhard (1865) and Mary (Imdieke) Thieschafer. M Marie, daughter of Joseph (1882) and Frances (Hunhoff) Wiechmann. *Grnd* of Frank H. (1844) and Elizabeth (Kuhlman-1857) Wiechmann and Bernard and Barbara (Moeller) Hunhoff.

TIEMAN, CHRIST, son of Frank (1872) and Johanna (Hinnenkamp) Tieman. *Grnd* of Henry (1839) and Elizabeth Tieman, Sr. and Herman (1849) and Marie Hinnenkamp. Parents and grandparents here born in Germany. M Irene, daughter of Ben E. (1880) and

Katherine (Hemmesch) Otte. *Grnd* of William (1849) and Marie (Mache-1850) Otte and Matt (1850) and Catherine (Schlener-1853) Hemmesch.

TIEMAN, EDMUND, son of Bernard H. and Elizabeth (Kluempke) Tieman. *Grnd* of Conrad (1841) and Katherina (Kreutzmann-1848) Tieman and Gerhard (1866) and Dorothea (Koenig-1869) Kluempke. Greatgrandparents were Henry and Gertrude Tieman. Paternal and maternal grandparents were among the first pioneer settlers in Melrose. *M* Geraldine, daughter of William and Amy (Holmberg) Cumming. *Grnd* of George and Isabelle (Gray) Cumming and Nels and Caroline (Hendricks) Holmberg. Paternal grandparents were born in Canada and maternal grandparents were born in Sweden and Norway.

TIEMAN, FRANCES, daughter of George and Mary Katherine (Hinnenkamp) Tieman. *Grnd* of Conrad (1841) and Katherine (Kreitzmann-1848) Tieman and Herman (1849) and Maria (Friederich-1849) Hinnenkamp Sr.

TIEMAN, WALTER J., son of Bernard H. (cf) and Elizabeth (Kluempke) Tieman (cf). (Same as Edmund Tieman). *M* Anne Marie, daughter of Francis Wm. and Lydia Z. (Lucier) Helsper. *Grnd* of James Wm. and Bernadine (Roering) Helsper and John and Mary Elizabeth (Pratt) Lucier. Greatgrandparents were William H. and Johanna (Connolly) Helsper. "My greatgrandparents were the first couple on record to be married in St. Paul, when it officially became a city," wrote Anne Marie. "Greatgrandfather William Helsper, also was the first to organize a unit of Guardsmen that are referred to as the Minute Men. He and the company were the first to volunteer to fight during the Civil War from Minnesota and was decorated for bravery receiving a citation personally from President Abraham Lincoln. He was among the first of the early pioneers of this area."

TIMMINS, JOSEPH F., son of Francis and Mildred (LeMoine) Timmins. *Grnd* of Frank and Belle (Bradley) Timmins and John Antoine (1885) and Florence (Doebler-1885) LeMoine. *M* Carol, daughter of Edward Carl and Mary Blanche (Roney) Goellen. *Grnd* of Mathew and Augusta (Kaske) Goellen and Charles and Honora (Tobin) Roney.

TISE, JOSEPH, son of John and Maria (Wurtzel) Tise. *M* Mary Christine, daughter of August W. (1852) and Margaret (Bettendorf-1859) Borget.

TOBROXEN, RICHARD, son of Bernard and Katherine (Schieman) Tobroxen. *Grnd* of Henry (1859) and Bernadine (Duevel-1846) Tobroxen and John (1859) and Catherine (Schmasel-1860) Schieman.

M Edna, daughter of Paul and Angeline (Rossmann) Rausch. *Grnd* of John and Susan (Eickers) Rausch and Frank and Amelia (Jopp-1868) Rossmann.

TOMSCHE, EDWARD J., son of Emil and Christine (Broker) Tomsche. *Grnd* of Joseph (1856) and Theresia (Kampa-1859) Tomsche and Henry (1885) and Anna (Lucken-1890) Broker. *M* Theresa, daughter of Fred and Mrs. (Boyle) West.

TRAEGER, GEORGE, son of Anton and Marcella (Theisen) Traeger. *Grnd* of George and Agnes (Widman) Traeger and Henry and Katherine (Koppy) Theisen. *M* Ruth, daughter of Joseph (1894) and Hilda (Borgerding) Overman. *Grnd* of Bernard and Bernardina (Treinest) Overman and Joseph (1856) and Anna (Bergman-1867) Borgerding.

VAN BECK, RICHARD, son of Anton (1884) and Louise Mary (Ostendorf) Van Beck. *Grnd* of Peter and Catherine Van Beck and Joseph and Katherina Ostendorf. *M* Rose, daughter of Joseph F. (1895) (cf) and Hildagarde E. (Wessel) Rolfzen (cf).

VAN HAVERMAET, LAWRENCE, son of Bernard and Susan (May) Van Havermaet. *Grnd* of Joseph (1863) and Annie (Claude) Van Havermaet and Joseph (1863) and Mary (Wahl-1868) May. Paternal grandfather immigrated from Antwerp, Belguim. *M* Lorraine, daughter of Theodore (cf) and Alvina (Kramer) Spaeth (cf).

VAN HEEL, RICHARD, son of John and Mary (Beckers) Van Heel. *M* Adeline, daughter of John A. (1885) and Caroline (Dickmann) Stalboerger. *Grnd* of Andrew (1844) and Anna (Loehr-1851) Stalboerger and Bernard (1857) and Elizabeth (Hilger-1857) Dickmann.

VERBEKE, REMI, son of Louis and Julia (Goemaere) Verbeke. Remi and parents were born in Flanders, Belgium. He was also awarded the Distinguished Service Cross on 14 December, 1918. *M* Irene, daughter of Joseph and Katherine (Zenz) Fern. Joseph Fern was Superintendent of the Water and Light Department for forty-one years.

VOGEL, ERVIN H., son of Joseph C. and Catherine (Poepping) Vogel. *Grnd* of Carl and Mrs. Vogel and Joseph and Elizabeth Poepping. *M* Susan, daughter of Herman and Clara (VanHeel) Arnzen. *Grnd* of Gerhard and Katherine Arnzen and Andrew and Katherine (Woeste) VanHeel.

VOIT, GREGORY, son of Wolfgang (1841) and Anna (Gretch) Voit. *M* Elizabeth, daughter of John (1871) and Anna (Deters) Woeste. *Grnd* of Frank and Anna (Hens) Deters and Anton (1834) and Mathilda (Westbrock) Woeste.

VON WAHLDE, HENRY, son of Fred (1862) and Elizabeth (Huesman) VonWahlde. *Grnd* of Carl and Mrs. Huesman. *M* Collette, daughter of Ben (1880) and Mary (Angelbeck) Hinnenkamp. *Grnd* of Ben (1843) and Katherine (Nienaber) Hinnenkamp and Fred and Caroline Angelbeck.

WANDER, MARTIN L., son of John (1857) and Mary (Kolb) Wander. *Grnd* of Casper and Mrs. Wander and Leonard and Mrs. Kolb. *M* Margaret, daughter of John (1872) and Anna (Rothstein) Frank. *Grnd* of Anton (1843) and Margaret (Meyer-1852) Frank and John and Mrs. (Thelen) Rothstein.

WEBER, ANTHONY T., son of Anton and Ida (Scholz) Weber. *M* Elizabeth, daughter of Joseph (1889) and Anna (Herzog) Thieschafer. *Grnd* of Herman (1855) and Mary (Jansing-1858) Thieschafer and Bernard (1853) and Gertrude (Schweiters-1856) Herzog.

WEBER, Anthony, son of Barthel (cf) and Catherine (Mehr) Weber (cf). *M* Martha, daughter of Joseph F. (1895) (cf) and Hildagarde E. (Wessel) Rolfzen (cf).

WEBER, BARTHEL, son of Jacob (1863) and Josephine (Pirz) Weber. Father Pierz was a close relative of Josephine. *M* Catherine, daughter of Anton (1851) and Margaret (Schaefer) Mehr.

WEBER, JOSEPH J., son of Barthel (cf) and Catherine (Mehr) Weber (cf). *M* Dorothy, daughter of Otto and Frances (Miller) Koeckler. *Grnd* of Otto and Mrs. Koeckler and Nicholas and Mary (Hemmesch) Miller.

WEHLAGE, JOSEPH H., son of Bernard and Philomina (Imdieke) Wehlage. *Grnd* of Henry and Elizabeth (Korf) Wehlage and Henry and Elizabeth (Macke) Imdieke. *M* Rose Ann, daughter of Frank and Helen (Deters) Faber. *Grnd* of Frank and Anna (Hens) Deters.

WEISS, NORBERT E., son of Joseph and Mary (Schendzelos) Weiss. *M* Margaret, daughter of Mr. and Mrs. Orbeck.

WELLE, HERBERT L., son of Peter and Isabelle (Heinen) Welle. *Grnd* of Hubert and Anne (Sand) Welle and Peter and Anna (Michaels) Heinen. *M* Rosalie A. daughter of Edward H. and Pauline (Meyer) Imdieke. *Grnd* of Herman G. and Barbara (VanBeck) Imdieke and Joseph F. and Elizabeth (Deters) Meyer.

WELLE, HUBERT J., son of Hubert S. (1873) and Anna (Sand) Welle. *Grnd* of Christopher (1841) and Elizabeth (Primus) Welle and Paul and Mrs. Sand. *M* Dorothy, daughter of Sebastian (1873) and Mary (Roos) Janson. *Grnd* of Joseph and Mrs. (Fuchs) Janson and Mr. and Mrs. (Huever) Roos.

WELLE, THOMAS ERWIN, son of Wilfred and Ledvina (Berns) Welle. *Grnd* of Joseph and Anna (Schoenberg) Welle and Herman and Wilhelmina (Wehlage) Berns. *M* Margaret Ann, daughter of Hubert and Lidwina (Heltemes) Buettner. *Grnd* of Michael and Anna (Knese) Buettner and Joseph and Margaret (Wegscheid) Heltemes.

WELZ, EDWARD P., son of Peter J. (cf) and Theresa (Brandtner) Welz (cf). *M* Marie, daughter of John (1875) and Agnes (Renneker) Moening. *Grnd* of George (1844) and Elizabeth (Heidgerken-1844) Moening, Sr. and Frederich and Gertrude (Gieske) Renneker.

WELZ, PETER, son of Robert and Mary (Prem) Welz. Peter was a member of the Melrose city council for many years and was mayor in 1948. *M* Theresa, daughter of Carl (1844) and Mary (Iletsko) Brandtner. "Carl Brandtner and his wife were born in Austria and came to America in 1882. They settled around Sauk Centre where Theresa was born and later moved to Melrose. In 1890 Theresa attended school in the old sisters house where four classes were held. These classes were taught by the following sisters: Sister DeSales, Sister Folgentia, Sister Athanasia and Sister Ehrentrude."

WENKER, CLARENCE, son of Bernard (1894) and Rose (Kortenbusch) Wenker. *Grnd* of Bernard (1850) and Anna (Vader-1862) Wenker and Anton (1843) and Katherine (Korf-1855) Kortenbusch. "Paternal and maternal grandparents were born in Westfalen, Germany." *M* Mary Ann, daughter of John B. (1897) and Caroline (Anton) Meyer. *Grnd* of Clemence (1874) and Mary (Imdieke-1875) Meyer and Frank (1870) and Mary (Blumhofer-1876) Anton.

WENSMAN, RALPH, son of Casper (1889) and Anna (Enneking) Wensman. *Grnd* of August (1861) and Mrs. Wensman and Bernard and Bernadine (Renneker) Enneking. *M* Armella, daughter of Frank (1888) and Mrs. (Heine) Zwack. *Grnd* of Wolfgang (1851) and Anna (1862) Zwack and Henry (1854) and Philomina (Ruppert-1875) Heine.

WESSEL, THEODORE A., son of Ben (1865) and Agnes (Hinnenkamp) Wessel. *Grnd* of Theodore (1840) and Mrs. Wessel and Theodore H. (1846) and Elizabeth (1846) Hinnenkamp. Parents and grandparents came from Germany. "In April, 1917," wrote Theodore, "our house burned down, killing my thirteen year old sister and four year old brother. My mother and brother Paul were severely burned but survived." *M* Veronica, daughter of Joseph (1863) and Elizabeth (Schutenkemper-1871) Enneking.

WESTENDORF, ARTHUR N., son of Bernard (cf) and Ludwina (Lahr) Westendorf (cf). *M* Cherylene, daughter of George T. and

Rita (Athman) Ritter. *Grnd* of John (1895) and Augustine (Bloch-1897) Ritter and Joseph (1888) and Anna (Waldorf-1893) Athman. Maternal greatgrandparents were John (1863) and Katherine (Weller-1874) Waldorf and Bernard and Veronica (Heinze-1860) Athman. Paternal greatgrandparents were Theodore and Katherine (Feldgers-1863) Ritter and Joseph (1861) and Mrs. Bloch.

WESTENDORF, BERNARD, son of Joseph (1873) and Mary (Duevel-1885) Westendorf. *Grnd* of Henry (1838) and Elizabeth (Schmidt-1838) Westendorf and Henry (1855) and Katherine (Grube-1859) Duevel. Paternal greatgrandparents were Mr. and Mrs. Westendorf and Theodore and Marie (Hausfeld) Schmidt and maternal greatgrandparents were Christopher and Elizabeth (Drelman) Duevel and Bernard and Anna Grube. Parents and grandparents were born in Germany. *M* Ludwina, daughter of Nicholas (1878) and Elizabeth (Erz) Lahr. *Grnd* of Peter and Margaret (Morbach) Lahr and Matthias and Gertrude Erz.

WESTENDORF, HERMAN, son of Joseph (1873) (cf) and Mary (Duevel-1885) Westendorf (cf). (Same as Bernard Westendorf). *M* Norma, daughter of Edward (1898) and Johanna (Enneking) Budde. *Grnd* of Joseph (1866) and Elizabeth (Tape-1868) Budde and Bernard (1855) and Katherine (Renneker-1861) Enneking. "My grandmother, Katherine Enneking was killed instantly by a Great Northern train near the Melrose Produce on her way to church on 4 April, 1941."

WESTERHAUS, HENRY T., son of Bernard Taubke (1855) and Bernadine (Grote-1857) Westerhaus. Henry was born in Oldenburg, Germany in 1895. *M* Mary, daughter of Anton (1861) and Catherine (Bruns-1868) Fisher.

WESTERHAUS, JOHN HENRY, son of Henry T. (cf) and Mary (Fischer) Westerhaus (cf). Henry has in his possession the paternal family tree that dates back to the year 1651. *M* Jeanette, daughter of Henry and Florence (Eischens) Braun. *Grnd* of Math (1870) and Mary (Ballman-1867) Braun and John M. (1887) and Magdalen (Bairel-1888) Eischens. "Grandmother Braun was the first postmaster of St. Leo and she was also the first switchboard operator for Bell Telephone System. Both of these operations took place in her home."

WIECHMAN, ERVIN, son of William (cf) and Rose (Austing) Wiechmann (cf). *M* Viola, daughter of Herman (1895) and Katherine (Meyer) Korf. *Grnd* of Gerhard (1851) and Pauline (Klausing-1864) Korf and Joseph (1876) and Elizabeth (Deters-1878) Meyer. Maternal greatgrandparents were Frank and Ann (Hens) Deters and Henry and Elizabeth (Schulte) Meyer.

WIECHMAN, FRANK, son of Frank H. (1848) and Elizabeth (Kuhlmann) Wiechmann. M Walburga, daughter of George (1870) and Bernadine (Albers) Toenyan. *Grnd* of George and Mrs. Toenyan and Henry and Mary (Panchor-1831) Albers. Grandmother Mary Albers, lived to be one hundred and two years of age.

WIECHMAN, WILLIAM, son of Frank H. (1848) and Elizabeth (Kuhlmann) Wiechmann. M Rose E. daughter of Bernard (1889) and Bernadine (Henkenbernz) Austing.

WOESTE, ANDREW P., son of Victor (1868) and Anna (Nathe) Woeste. M Ann, daughter of Frank (1892) and Mary (Altendahl) Brickweg. *Grnd* of Herman and Bernadine (Homer-1858) Brickweg and Bernard Joseph (1837) and Elizabeth (Lienesch-1847) Altendahl.

WORMS, LAMBERT, son of Leonard and Anna (Pung) Worms. M Agnes, daughter of Bernard (1857) and Anna (Lois) Ellering.

ZACHMAN, JOHN F., M.D., son of Albert and Eleanor (Gravelle) Zachman M.D. *Grnd* of John K. and Lena (Willems) Zachman and Frederick N. and Pearl (Morgan) Gravelle. M Kathleen, daughter of Theodore J. and Rose C. (Welle) Moening. *Grnd* of John (1875) and Agnes (Renneker-1875) Moening and Hubert S. (1873) and Anna (Sand) Welle.

ZENZEN, EDWIN H., son of John (1881) and Amelia (Scholz) Zenzen. *Grnd* of Joseph (1839) and Mary (Beck-1854) Zenzen and Frank (1858) and Magdalena (Rieger-1862) Scholz, Sr. M Selestia, daughter of Bernard and Elizabeth (Hinnenkamp) Enneking, Jr. *Grnd* of Bernard (1855) and Katherine (Renneker-1861) Enneking, Sr. and Fredrick (1851) and Elizabeth (Kreuzman-1858) Hinnenkamp. Both sets of grandparents were born in Germany.

ZENZEN, RAYMOND, son of John (1881) (cf) and Amelia (Scholz) Zenzen (cf). (Same as Edwin H. Zenzen.) M Laura, daughter of Frank (1898) and Mrs. (Feldeward) Brake. *Grnd* of Joseph (1869) and Josephine (Lampmann-1876) Brake and Bernard (1857) and Christina (Strucke-1861) Feldeward.

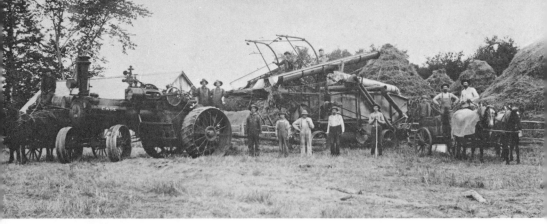

Threshing team on the Joseph Nathe farm, the site of the new Senior High School. Driving the team of horses is Robert Nathe who later was ordained a priest.

After 54 years Father Niehaus swears in his son as Melrose township clerk.

Henry Petermeier with his favorite horse, Dan.

Funeral procession in 1918 for Leo Kolb, the first casualty of World War One.

Left: Vincent Schanhaar, casualty of World War Two.

Below: Edward Schanhaar, second from left in front row, casualty of World War Two, after whom the Melrose Veterans of Foreign War Post is named.

Below: The wedding of H. W. Broker in 1910 as the groom was escorted by friends past the Kraemer saloon and Gau's hotel.

The wedding "carriage" of Mr. and Mrs. Henry Roggenkamp in 1910. Seated above, front seat, are Joseph Roggenkamp and Mary Schmiesing; second row: Henry Roggenkamp and Bernadine Schmiesing; back row: William Otte and Frances Macke.

Everybody's friend for two generations was Auty Ostendorf, shown above with a friend.

One of the oldest and best loved citizens of the community, Mrs. Sophie Stilling, by her Christmas tree the year before she died.

Two young ladies "all dressed up and no where to go" in the first decade of the century were Agnes Hinnenkamp (now Sister M. Gaudentia, O.S.F.) and Agnes Pohlmann (now Mrs. Henry A. Hinnenkamp).

Four men "on the town" at the turn of the century were August Ostendorf, Peter Detrick, Ben Saleman and William Schwanke.

That great day in a lifetime: Miss Alvina Stilling on First Communion Day.

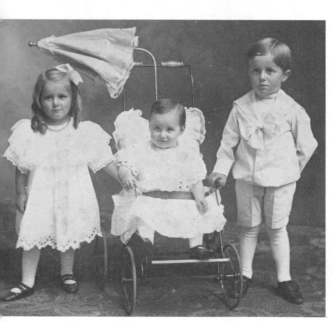

Three children: Monica Welle O'Connor, Florence Welle Edelbrock and Ambrose Christian Welle.

Five first communicants: John, Mary, Ben, Joseph and Henry Hinnenkamp.

Mr. and Mrs. Herman F. Hinnenkamp (nee Agnes Mueller) with Fritz Hinnenkamp and Mary Mueller.

Mr. and Mrs. Frank Wielenberg with, back row, Anna Kamphake, Gen Rolfzen, Joseph Tieman and Mary Kampsen.

Mr. and Mrs. Herman Hollerman (nee Elizabeth Hinnenkamp) with Henry Hinnenkamp, Clara Brickweg, Ben Hinnenkamp and Mary Hinnenkamp.

Mr. and Mrs. Frank Wielenberg, married, 1903.

Below: Mr. and Mrs. Frank and Elizabeth Hinnenkamp, married, 1915.

Mr. and Mrs. Herman Hellermann, Sr. (nee Rose Stienemann), married, 1912.

The guests at the wedding of Henry Tieman.

The Henry Hollermann family.

The relatives and friends at the Christ Bruggenties home.

The family of Mr. and Mrs. Henry Rolfzen.

Below: The family of Mr. and Mrs. Herman Hinnenkamp.

The family of Mr. and Mrs. Henry John Hinnenkamp.

CHAPTER FIVE

HOME AGAIN WITH THE FOLKS

The family may be regarded as the cradle of civil society,
and it is in great measure within the circle of family
life that the destiny of states is fostered.

— *Pope Leo XIII*

Before school and churches, organizations and businesses, special
events and daily routines, the family comes first. As a matter of fact,
all other institutions are designed and exist for the good of the family
and the individuals in each family unit. The families that came to
the Melrose area throughout the decades came to strengthen family
bonds either through economic progress, religious freedom, climatic
conditions and personal development through the strong ties of the
family. No one had to tell the Yankee, Irish and German pioneers
these facts for they instinctively knew the truth of Tolstoy's saying,
"All happy families resemble each other, each unhappy family is unhappy in its own way."

As a community Melrose has been blessed throughout the years
with a strong sense of family unity and pride. Family ties were
strengthened on such occasions as baptisms, weddings, anniversaries,
graduations and deaths. Sunday dinner "with the folks" is a tradition
that antedates the automobile and in many cases as sacred a ritual as
Sunday Mass or religious services. In the "locals" of the weekly newspaper no word, perhaps, was used more frequently than "motored,"
for on any Sunday children and parents, relatives far and near would
gather around the family table.

As in every community there was in Melrose also some exceptional
events concerning family life. A national record was set when five
brothers married five sisters between 1925 and 1945. The five sisters
were Olivia, Florence, Evelyn, Brigitta and Veronica Pohlmann; the

115

five brothers were Henry, Herman, Joseph, Al and Ben Koopmeiners. At the present time Al and Joseph are deceased.

Twins were not too unusual over the course of the years but when Mr. and Mrs. George Nathe became the proud parents of triplets the event was duly noted. Previously the Nathe's had six other children. Four generations of living members in a family was not too unusual and the *Melrose Beacon* regularly published photographs of such an event. Worthy of front page notice, however, was when a family could boast of five generations, such as was recorded with the family of Mrs. Elizabeth Pung whose daughter was Mrs. Chick Molitor, her grandson Donald Molitor, her great-granddaughter Mrs. Daniel Meyer and her great-great-grandson, Jason Alexander Meyer. If twins were not too exceptional and if triplets was remarkable, three sets of twins in the same family was sensational. That is exactly what occurred in 1962 when Mr. and Mrs. John Kraker became the parents of Pamela Jean and Patrick John. Their previous sets of twins were Jean and Joan and Michael John and Mary Jane.

Double weddings, when two sisters married two brothers, were not uncommon events. The number of these cannot be tallied but they were frequent occurrences, especially during the early years of the community. An indication of the healthiness and hardiness of the early families of the community was the exceptionally large number of married couples that celebrated their golden wedding anniversaries. It would seem that what today is a rather unusual event in the life of a family in previous decades was more common. One couple, Mr. and Mrs. Joseph Bertram, lived to celebrate the fifty-fifth anniversary of their wedding in 1957. The couple had ten children, fifty-four grandchildren and twenty-six great-grandchildren. Mrs. Bertram, the former Catherine Hemmesch, still resides in the home the couple purchased after retiring from farming near Lake Henry. Another couple, Mr. and Mrs. Joseph Schmidt, Sr., lived to observe the sixtieth anniversary of their wedding. They were married in Melrose on 30, October, 1884 and were the parents of nine children. Except for three years spent in Pennsylvania they lived their entire lives in Melrose where Joseph was engaged in general merchandise, implement and stock-buying businesses.

Every community has its "professional letter writer" and Julius Otte holds this distinction for Melrose. His letters have appeared in numerous publications throughout the state and nation and his name is familiar to numerous editors. He developed his interest in national and international affairs in 1924 while listening to the radio programs of Father Coughlin. "Since then," he said, "I have read everything I can get my hands on." Evidence of his wide range of reading appeared in his letters. In one he quotes Henry David Thoreau who wrote, "If a man does not keep step or pace with his companions, perhaps it is because he hears a different drummer." In another, defending old age, he recounted that Henry Ford "who at 40 didn't know where his next meal was coming from, built his huge empire after that." Again in a letter he recounted that he served as custodian of St. Mary's parish under six different pastors, namely "Willenbring, Schirmers, Haupt, Hoffman, Julig and Lutgen. The former five have gone to their reward and now Father Lutgen has left for greener pastures." Interviewed by the St. Cloud *Photo News,* Otte said, "Apathy in people is the most disturbing thing. There are too many people like that around. You know, they don't give a dam about anything as long as they get their social security. This attitude is going to catch up with us some day." He also commented on readers' reactions to his letters. "A fella a couple of weeks ago called me long distance," he recalled. "He called me every name in the book for almost forty minutes, and I never even found out his name — but he paid the bill. I had one letter that brought eighty-three letters — most of them against me." Julius would use every device imaginable to see that his letters were published. On one occasion he wrote to the editor of the *St. Cloud Visitor* in German. That letter deserves printing in full for the sake of posterity. He wrote:

"Dear Editor,
        Nicht zuschauen-aber-mitmachen!
        Micht kritisieren-aber-besser machen!
    Die meisten Organisationen und Vereine haben heute ein gemeinsamen Problem, naemlich das Fehlen an Interesse zur aktiven Mitarbeit. Die Neigung zum Zuzammenschluss mit Gleichgessinten isst gerade noch vorhanden, doch kommt es zur Frage der Mitabeit, so isst man erstaunt, wie viele Ent-schuldigungen und Vorwaende aus einem Munde sprudeln koennen.
    Wir leben in einer Zeit des Tempos in der wir moeglichst viel erreichen und viel "money" machen wollen. Warum sollen wir daher "brethern." Wir koennen ja alles erhalten "readymade." . . . Mahlzciten his zu fertigen Veranstaltungen. Von "easy-payments" zur Politik. Wenn uns etwas nicht gefaellt, sind wir jedoch schnell mit einer Kritik zur Hand und vergessen dabei, dass wir durch Passivitaet oder stillsschweigender Duldung selbst daran schuld sind. In einem demokratischen System wird sowohl die Mitarbeit als auch-die Kritic gebraucht. Mitarbeit zum Fortschritt und Aufbau, Kritik zum Verbesserung und zur Wachsamkeit.
    Es isst ein Irrtum zu glauben, "sie werden es schon machen" . . . Wir muessen persoenlichen Anteil und Einflus nehmen in unsere Organisationen. Wir duerfen uns nichts vorsetzen lassen und muessen selber mitmachen.

Der beste Platz dafuer sind die Versammlunger — Dort werden Vorschlaege gemacht, Beschluesse gefasst, dort reifen Ideen . . . . Dort isst auch der Plats zu kritisieren und wird immer wilkommen sein, wenn die Kritik etwas Konstrktives an seine Stelle zu setzen hat, sonst wird es einfach mechern genannt.
Herzliche Gruesse an Alle Leser.
Julius J. Otte"

Many columns in neighboring weekly and daily newspapers were brightened by the comments Julius Otte expressed in the "Letters to the Editor" section. In his writings he gave voice to the sentiments of his many friends and neighbors in the Melrose area.

One of the pioneer families of Melrose was Mr. and Mrs. John Tiedeman. On 1 February, 1959 Mrs. Tiedeman recorded in the pages of the *Melrose Beacon* her recollections of family life in Melrose during the last decade of the preceeding century. It offers an insight into the lives of some of the early families of the community. She wrote:

"We moved to Melrose in the spring of 1892. Della (her daughter) was six. Mr. Tiedeman had bought the Harness Shop owned by Dominic Grein. Harness shops in those days were interesting. Harnesses, collars, bridles, and lap robes filled the shop. Leather things were all cut and sewed by hand. Our shop was on the west end of the middle block of main street. The last time I was in Melrose that building was still there. Our neighbors on the east were the Unger family — on the west was Kleber's Grocery Store.

"Wellenstein's had the shoe store and shop a few houses over. Jimmy Ahern's Jewelry Shop was across the street with Krick's Shoe Shop and Thul's Barber Shop right there also. Nick Meyers lived over his store. All of us and our families and businesses were in one block. Other people living there were the Herman Fuessneers, Wampachs, Wetleys, Borgerdings, John Kolbs, Hoeschens, Loosbrooks, Schmidts, Siems, Schultenovers, Clarks, Ulmers, Sandbrinks, Townsends, Krakers, Peter Wilhelms and Borgerts. Sidewalks were wooden and the streets were sandy.

"Life was quiet. The Great Northern had come through a few years before. People had little time to play. Women all did their own sewing, cooking, baking and cleaning. Sometimes on birthdays, we had coffee together, but it was not until many years later that we played cards. We also had a few surprise parties too, when everybody brought food and then we played cards.

"In 1896 we moved to Riverside where we built a house. Andrew Kolb and the Kricks were our neighbors there. Nick Meyers came to the Kolb house shortly after and our children had good times together. About six years later we moved our shop to our new building where Angelbeck's and Lamberton's store is. Wellensteins and Thuls again were our neighbors. Schmidt's Store and August Sauer's Butcher Shop were soon there. We used to get together with Thuls, Wellensteins and Ungers for cards.

For fun before the movies came, we took walks, going across the river on one bridge and coming back on the other, picking berries. Once in a while we hired a rig and went to Birch Lake on a picnic. This took all day — it took two hours to get to the lake and two hours to get back.

"In the winter our children went sliding with some homemade sleds on Pennison's Hill, skated on the river and went bob sled catching. Dog and pony shows and medicine tent shows came to town in the summer. We always went to the fires and run away horses caused some excitment. Our main life was our families and our work."

In spite of religious conflicts that arose between the early Protestants and the more recently arrived Catholics, a strong community bond was strengthened through the closely-knit family relationships. Pride in one's family has always been a distinct characteristic of the people of the Melrose area. An example of this is found in an early issue of the weekly newspaper. Although the verse might never be preserved in future anthologies of great English poetry it expressed at the time of the subject's death the esteem of family and friends.

TO LEO LEMM
(By His Friends)
Though he now has left us,
His memory lingers still;
He raised many a downtrodden man
By his kindness and good will.
He brought much happiness to us all
By his kindly, friendly wit,
And just to tell him of our troubles,
Seemed to ease the load a bit.
All who knew him, loved him,
And all were cheered by his smile
For his grin and homely wisecracks
Made life seem more worthwhile.
And though he now is gone,
To a place that is far more fair,
We know that Heaven is a brighter place
Since Leo Lemm is there!

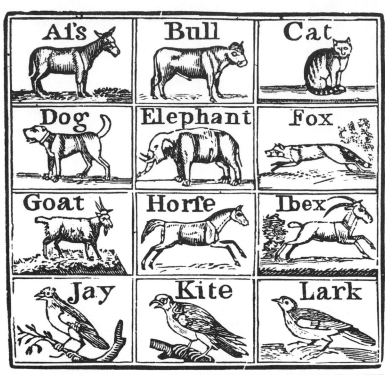

As	Bull	Cat
Dog	Elephant	Fox
Goat	Horse	Ibex
Jay	Kite	Lark

Monkey	Nag	Otter
Parrot	Quail	Raven
Sow	Tiger	Vulture
Wolfe	Yellowhammer	Zebra

CHAPTER SIX

BY THE ROD AND BY THE BOOK

School days, school days,
Dear old golden rule days.
Reading and writing and 'rithmetic
Taught to the tune of a hickory stick
You were my queen in calico,
I was your bashful barefoot beau.
When you wrote on my slate
"I love you, Joe" when we were a couple of kids.

— An American folk song

No one man living today better personifies all the good that has been achieved in Melrose and the surrounding area than Mr. Norbert Weiss. For thirty-eight years he was associated with the Melrose school system, serving as principal, industrial arts teacher and vocational occupations teacher. He founded the Area Teachers Education Association and served as its president for many years. The community recognized his services on May 19, 1969 when the mayor proclaimed the day to be "Norb Weiss Day." Shortly after that date WCCO radio station saluted him with its Good Neighbor Award. He was also recognized by state and local fraternal, civic and professional organizations. This chapter is the work of Norbert Weiss; he researched it and he wrote it. It is a tribute to a great educator, a good neighbor and friend to thousands of young people who were influenced by his learning and his example.

Strange as it may seem, the history of education in the Melrose area begins with the Northwest Ordinance of 1787. Although Melrose was not a part of the Northwest Territory which was bounded on the west by the Mississippi River, the following land ordinance influenced future territorial development in Minnesota. It stated: "This public land was divided into townships six miles square. Section sixteen of each township was set aside for the support of education and four additional sections were set aside for the government." When the present area of Minnesota was acquired from France by the United States, Melrose was a part of this purchase. The pattern of the Northwest Ordinance was applied to this new territory and land was set aside for public education in Melrose township.

It is difficult to say much about the early history of education in Stearns county because the records of the superintendent of schools were kept in the old court house, built in 1864, and were lost in the process of moving to the present court house in 1922. It was, then, necessary to interview people in the area who were able to recall the early days of education in Melrose. This chapter will first discuss the rural schools of the area and secondly, Melrose district 740 and, finally, some observations concerning athletics in the area.

RURAL SCHOOLS

The achievements of the rural schools in the development of the children of the area was, to say the least, phenomenal. Even with limited facilities, finances and instructional aids these schools performed an outstanding service in preserving and perpetuating the rural culture and heritage of the community. From these schools came some of the finest spiritual, civic and professional leaders of the area, state and nation. The "hickory stick" of the old song was used to give a pat on the back, but low enough to motivate the student to better apply himself. Many of those who have passed through these schools nostalgically recall the sweet young girls with their braided pigtails with a starched bow at the end. The rural schools were familial institutions. Looking back upon them now the families fondly recall the Christmas programs, the school plays and the spring picnics. Although these rural schools are no more and, although it is still debatable whether or not they should have been suppressed by state law, no one can deny the invaluable service they performed in the formation of thousands of young people of the area. There was, as we have seen earlier, the strong desire, even ambition, of the pioneers to have their children educated. They sensed that education was a primary means in promoting the financial, civic and religious welfare of their children. They felt, too, as parents always feel, that they wanted their children to have more opportunities in the future than they themselves enjoyed. So beginning with the Lindbergh school in late 1800's, the settlers established their schools at the same time they were building their homes. One resident of the area, John Bergman, recalls how he walked through the woods, about five miles back and forth each day, to attend "the little red school house." The same man in later life would see to it, at a price of many sacrifices, that his twelve children would all become graduates of Melrose High School. Another example of the pioneer interest in education is the number of rural schools that were built. In 1860 there were ten schools; in 1869-1870 fifteen new schools were erected; in 1870-1871 four more were built. And so the building of schools continued throughout the succeeding decades.

A word, too, must be added concerning the teachers of the rural schools. In the area of Melrose the schools were "quasi-Catholic" in nature. In the early days more frequently than not the teacher was a layman who had received his education at the Catholic Normal School in Milwaukee or at St. John's University. As the *scholemeister* or *kirchenlehŕer* he was a prominent member of the community and exerted a great influence over the young people. The authority on this subject, Sister Nora Leutmer, O.S.B., states that over fifty of these dedicated men taught in the rural schools of Stearns county. As shall be seen, several of these men taught in the rural schools of this area. Later, however, the lady teacher staffed the rural schools. One of these early teachers was Anna Kennedy who taught in Melrose from 1896 until 1904. Some of her letters to her mother are preserved in the Minnesota Historical Society archives. On April 5, 1896 she wrote, "The school house stands in the woods and it is like an oven." Frequently she complained about the loneliness of the rural teacher and was delighted to have the opportunity, the summer of the same year, to attend the University of Minnesota. While attending the University she stayed with the Benedictine Sisters in Minneapolis and wrote excitedly to her mother about field trips to Minnehaha falls, Fort Snelling and a boat excursion from St. Paul to Hastings. Upon returning to Melrose she reassured her mother by writing on August 8th, "I went to Holy Communion, three Masses and Vespers today, so you see I have not been so very bad." The life and experiences of Anna Kennedy would be duplicated by hundreds of teachers in the rural schools of those early days.

The first eight superintendents of schools in the county were: N. F. Barnes, Henry Krebes, Dr. Moody, C. Tolman, M. Perz, Peter E. Kaiser, P. B. Gorman, Henry Krebes (reelected) and Lorenzo J. Rocholl. During the latter's term the use of free text books was introduced, library aid was paid and teachers certification was required from the state superintendent of schools. Charles Weber was the ninth, and Paul Ahles, in 1902, the tenth county superintendent of schools. In Ahles' term new certificating laws were introduced, schoolroom heating and ventilating systems were required, and examinations for eight grade diplomas were demanded. The eleventh county school suprintendent was William Boerger who served the longest term in that office, from 1910 until 1934. On his office letterhead was printed the slogan, "The home and the school, let us bring them nearer together." He inaugurated school exhibits at the county fair and inaugurated a project to encourage the raising of potatoes in the county, which proved to be a great economic boost for the farmers. Each child in the rural schools was encouraged to raise potatoes both for the family's use, and for exhibiting at county contests. Boerger also encouraged county-wide spelling bees and county-wide 4-H clubs. Foreign languages, such as German, Swedish and Polish were also taught in some of the rural schools. The fourteenth and last superintendent, preceeded by Garland Taylor and Al Schmidts, was Carl Ohman. The elimination of the office of county superintendent of schools marked the passing of an era and an institution, the rural school, an institution which had served the citizens of Stearns county exceptionally well.

During the period of their existence, however, the state legislature passed laws for the improvement of the quality of education in the rural schools. In 1909 the first compulsory education law was passed, requiring children between the ages of eight and fourteen to attend school regularly, unless excused by the board of education. Grounds for excuse were physical inability, mental deficiency and unreasonable distance from school. Children between fourteen and sixteen years of age could be excused between April 1 to June 1 and September 1 to November 1 to assist in necessary farm work. In 1914 the requirements for state aid and the continued existence of a rural school were: the teacher must hold a complete grade certificate; no less than eight months of school must be held; there must be one hundred square feet of blackboard, one unabridged and five academic dictionaries, two sets of supplementary readers, a case with nine maps, a twelve inch globe, ten dollars worth of primary construction material, a library which must have at least ten dollars worth of books added each year, a heating and ventilating plant, sanitary drinking vessels, foot scrapers, erasers and two well-kept screened outhouses at least thirty feet apart. If the teacher had a first grade certificate the district would receive $150. in state aid; a second grade certificate would merit only $100. in aid. If the district voted a seven month school term it received $75. The apportionment for 1914 was six dollars per pupil who attended forty days of schooling.

Before briefly examining the various district schools in the area a word should be added concerning the "father of education" in Stearns county, Father Cornelius Wittmann, O.S.B. "This zealous young man," wrote William Boerger

"Observing the utter absence of institutions of learning, added to his already long list of strenuous labors the hard task of teaching school. It was in the dwelling of Joseph Edelbrock, who, with the openhanded generosity of pioneers, cheerfully donated the use of one of the rooms, that Father Cornelius, in the early fall of 1856, taught the first school within the present boundaries of Stearns county. It was thus a free school in the fullest sense of the word, for no tuition was asked, and the teacher received no pay!"

Father Cornelius was thus not only the first teacher in the first school of the county but also the prototype of the Benedictine monks who would establish St. John's University which has had and continues to have a decisive influence on education in the county and throughout the state.

DISTRICT 41 (1946)

This district, located a few miles west of Melrose, was on the old stage coach road running from Melrose west to the Sauk River where the road crossed the Stewart bridge. The stage road was later known as highway number four to Sauk Centre. The bridge received its name from the Stewart family who had settled on the banks of the river at that point. In 1897 Charles Lamb sold three-fourths of an acre to the school district for the building of a school. The first school stood on a rise of land near the river north of the John Kemper farm. The early settlers discovered that the water level of the river was uncertain and thus moved the school to higher elevation of land on the John Kemper farm. The site of this school if it still existed would be in the shadow of an outdoor billboard sign north of the Kemper farm. Interstate Highway number ninety-four would pass through the front yard of the old school house. The school building was moved and is now on the Albert Meyer farm near Meire Grove.

This school was in existence before the village of Melrose. In its early days children attended school only four months a year and then during the winter months. The students remained in school until they satisfied their educational needs. Some pupils attended until they were eighteen years old. The subjects taught from furnished text books were reading, writing, arithmetic and religion. Writing materials were primarily slates and slate pencils. It is said that August Lindbergh taught in this school for some time although the first record shows that Minnie Newman taught during the year 1903-1904. No classes were held from 1925-1926, 1949-1958 and 1961-1965, the year the district was dissolved. James Winter, a nearby farmer recalls that his teacher in 1906 was Mr. Eckenrood. The last teacher on record was Mrs. Geraldine Frieler. Both the lack of students and the rising costs of education forced the closing of the school in 1960 when the district joined Melrose district 740.

DISTRICT 73 (1976)

Located near the Henry Hellermann farm on highway 13, District 73 was known as "the little red schoolhouse." In 1873 Alfred Townsend, Melrose's first teacher, and his wife, Sylvia, after whom nearby Lake Sylvia is named, purchased part of the Herman Hellermann farm and sold one acre to the district for the building of a school. This information is found in the deed of the land now in the possession of Ted Wessel.

A typical school day began with prayer, the pledge of allegiance to the flag, the singing of songs of the seasons for fifteen minutes and then classes. Recess lasted from ten o'clock until ten-fifteen and back to classes until the noon lunch hour which lasted until one o'clock. Classes resumed again until two-thirty o'clock followed by a fifteen minute recess. Every Monday morning the "Busy Bee Club" met and elected pupils to do the household and yard chores of the school.

There were also the special holidays and occasions. Halloween was spent bobbing for apples, playing witches and indoor games. Christmas programs were presented at which St. Nick made his appearence with goodies for all and gifts were exchanged among pupils. In February valentines were exchanged and the young scholars made booklets about Abraham Lincoln and George Washington. Easter was marked by the traditional egg hunt. One day in Spring was set aside and everyone pitched in to clean the school grounds. This cleaning bee was followed by a traditional marshmallow roast. The annual spring school picnic took place in May, with many of the parents joining the children for the day. Mothers chatted among themselves and exchanged items of local news while children played games, ran races, held tug-of-war and pie-eating contests.

The school district was organized March 10, 1869 and paid Townsend three dollars for the acre of land now located on the Herman G. Hellermann farm.

In 1881 the school site was moved across the road to section three, northeast corner and the moving of "the little red schoolhouse" was an event noted throughout the country. The three acres needed for the new location were purchased from John and Emma Hanna. In 1900 the boundaries of the district were again changed because of the disagreements between the German and Irish settlers. Parts of sections 12, 13, 14 and 15 left the district. As years passed hostile feelings were forgotten and the farmers in sections 4, 5, 6, 7, 8 and 9 rejoined the district. The boundary line was moved north, taking in parts of sections 33, 34, 35 and 36. The other sections joined districts north and west of Ward Springs.

German Catholic farmers settled in the district during the decade of the 1890's. They wanted religion taught in the school and so waged a campaign to elect all German Catholics to the school board. By 1904 they had secured control of the school board and ordered that religion be taught. This angered the Yankees in the area and they began to sell out. Each child was asked to pay five cents a month for his religion lesson. Some of the parents did not approve of this arrangement and did not allow their children to study religion. The teachers' contracts stipulated that the German language must be taught one hour a day and two hours of religion after school each week.

One of the prime social events in this district was a "basket social" that took place on a given evening at the schoolhouse. Each young lady prepared a basket of food that would be auctioned at about nine o'clock. The attending young men would bid on the baskets and the highest bidder not only obtained the basket of food but also the privilege of eating the lunch with the girl who prepared the basket. The baskets were decorated with various ribbons and fashioned in such a way that the boy friend would recognize his girl's basket. If another young man was a bit jealous or just down right mean he would force the bidding higher and higher in order to outbid the young lady's boy friend. The receipts from these socials were put into a fund for school purposes.

Records show that in 1914, the school term lasted eight months for which the teacher's salary was $300, the fuel bill was $25, and the cleaning bill was three dollars. For the same year the receipts were $137.54 from apportionment, $267.14 from a special tax and $40.59 from the local one mill tax. The votes from the election held in 1917 approved the construction of a new school that cost approximately $3,000. Of the forty ballots cast there were twenty-eight for and twelve against the new building. The bond was granted with an interest of four percent and Fred Wessel was contracted to build the new school. The teacher's salary in 1917 was $500. The following year the old school house was sold to John Matties for $212. After moving the building to his land north of the school site Matties used it as a home for his family. Later his farm was sold to Henry Hellermann who again moved the school house into a wooded area east and closer to Ward

Spring and there used it as a granary. Still later Richard Hellermann moved the "little red schoolhouse" to a farm on the Melrose - Ward Springs road. It now stands on the Francis Hertzog turkey farm.

In 1918 the water pail and dipper was replaced by a modern drinking water fountain and a flag pole was erected. In 1921 the teacher's contract stipulated that German was still to be taught one hour a day and religion to be taught at least twice a week after school. In 1927 a new well was drilled on the school grounds for the use of the fifty-one pupils enrolled that year. In 1930 the teacher's salary was still recorded as $500. In 1929 Alice Graham started her first of thirty-one years as a teacher in the district. The first nine month school term was ordered in 1931. Eight years later the school library numbered 220 volumes. Electricity replaced oil lamps and a coal stoker was added to keep the building heated day and night. In 1945 a new, shingled roof was added and in 1947 Leo Hoppe began a bus route which transported three pupils to the school. *Current Events* magazine was introduced into the school the same year.

The new school came to be known as the Hellermann school about 1917 because of the number of Hellermann children who attended it. One of the early teachers was Minnie Pitzlin who taught during 1902-1903 and the last teacher was Mrs. Robert Peschel who taught from 1961 to 1968. During the twenty-nine years of Alice Graham's teaching tenure the largest enrollment was fifty-eight and the smallest number of pupils was thirty-six. The salaries for teachers ranged from $50 in the early years to $327.65 a month, the highest ever, paid during the last year of the school's existence. Members of the school board from 1904 to 1968 were Anthony Zirbes, Gerhard Sunderman, Gerhard Hellermann, Fred VonWahlde, Frank Wilenberg, Frank Hinnenkamp, Joseph Tieman, Joseph Zirbes, Henry Hellermann, Herman Hellermann, Lawrence Tieman, Rosina Hellermann, Edmund Pohlmann, Roman Hellermann, Lawrence Pohlmann and LaVerne Hollenkamp.

Some of the events in more recent years included the installation of plumbing in 1951 and joining of the Stearns county film service in 1953. The following year the county library book service was added. In 1955 free milk service was offered the children. In 1957 the district number was changed from 73 to 1976. In 1960 Alice Graham died and the remaining two months of the school term were taught by the deceased's sister, Nell. In 1963 public prayers were stopped by law in the school and a few families withdrew their children from the district school. In 1968 a special election was held to determine if the district should be dissolved and become part of the Melrose district, with the results being eleven affirmatives and four negatives. The school was put up for bids with highest bidder being Ted Wessel with the sum of $1,200. Mr. and Mrs. Wessel have remodeled the school and added a garage to the property. It is now the Wessel home.

Some of the pupils of this school who distinguished themselves in various ways were Mary Wicks (now Mrs. Cedric Marshus), winner of the Stearns county spelling contest in 1933; Reverend Ervin Zirbes, pastor of St. Mary's Church, Park River, North Dakota; Mildred Zirbes (Sister M. Kenneth, O.S.F.); Rita Pohlmann (Sister M. Paula, O.S.F.); Anna Mae Herzog (Sister M. Lawrence, O.S.F.); Bertha Wielenberg, a teacher.

DISTRICT 164 (2046)

Better known as the Petermeier school, this district lies in the northeast corner of Melrose township and was organized by Stephen Petermeier, an early pioneer, in 1892. The building that still stands is the original one built in 1892 at a cost of $400 by John Beste of Melrose. John Siefert was the first teacher and his salary was $28 per month. Dr. August Kuhlmann taught school in this district before he began the practice of medicine. Mrs. Phyllis St. Martin was the last teacher when the district was dissolved in 1967. Henry Petermeier was one of the first pupils in the school. He recalled that the children sat on benches and wrote on slates. The pupils noticed with some trepidation the big stick that stood in the corner of the school room for more than once it was used to motivate a youngster to do better work. Mrs. Wimmer, one of the early teachers, was the proud owner of a bicycle. Whenever a visit from the county superintendent was expected Mrs. Wimmer would hide the bicycle so that he would not know how wealthy the Wimmer family was.

Some of the graduates of this rural school who have distinguished themselves in later life are the Most Reverend Henry J. Soenneker, Bishop of Owensboro, Kentucky, Monsignor Benedict Petermeier, Elizabeth Petermeier, (Sister Aloysius, O.S.F.), Sister Valeria, O.S.F., Sister Agnes, O.S.F., Sister Elizabeth, O.S.F., three Soenneker girls who are sisters of the bishop, and Sister Julitta, O.S.B., a Westendorf daughter. Eunice Petermeier was a lieutenant in the United States Navy. Stephen Petermeier was the first president of th Adley Creek 4-H club and he named the club after the Adley creek that flows near the family farm. Martha Lippsmeyer also attended this school. She served as secretary to the American delegation of the United Nations at the London conference in 1945. She is presently a tax consultant to the Internal Revenue Service in San Diego, California.

DISTRICT 165 (2047)

This district school, known as the Flahaven school, was located northwest of Melrose. There are no extent records from the early years of this district school. However, according to the age of the people interviewed by the writer it would seem to have been in existence prior to 1885. The original schoolhouse, in the course of time, was moved to the Brian Flahaven farm and a second frame school was built. This in turn gave way to the existing building of brick construction that is presently used as a home. For several years the second school was used as a meeting house and a dance hall. According to some of the older people of the area this building burned in 1918.

One of the first teachers in this school was Henry Adrian. One year he had sixty-one pupils in all eight grades! Another early teacher was Barbara Krik during 1902-1903. The desire for furthering one's education is evidenced by one of the early pupils in this school. Herman Sunderman's parents lived in White Earth where there were no schools at the time. They sent Herman, as a small boy, to live with his uncle, Henry Tieman, in order to attend this district school. The thriftiness of the early settlers was reflected by the custom of the children removing their leather shoes as soon as they returned home from school and putting on wooden shoes for doing their chores about the farm. According to some who wore the wooden shoes they were not only more durable but also more comfortable.

The last teacher in this school was Mrs. Alma Gibson who taught from 1960 to 1966 when the district was dissolved and joined with the Melrose district.

DISTRICT 187 (2062)

This district's school was known as the Hinnenkamp school because of the large number of Hinnenkamp children in attendence at the school. It may also have received its popular name because it was located on land owned by Herman Hinnenkamp across the road from the Anthony Niehaus farm. The school was built in 1900 by Fritz Wessel. The first members of the school board were Herman Hinnenkamp, Sr., Joseph Oevermann, Sr. and Joseph Niehaus, all grandparents of the present generation.

Miss Hattie Himsel was the first teacher and she roomed with various families living near the school. The last teacher was Mrs. Ruth Huber who taught from 1965 to 1967 when the district was dissolved and joined with the Melrose district. Other teachers lived in Melrose and either rode in buggies or in sleds coming and going from school. Ann Sandbrink and Clara Sandbrink, who taught in this school, lived in Melrose and rode to school on their bicycles from their homes in Melrose. The early records list the salary for the teacher as $70 a month of which ten dollars was allotted for room and broad and laundry and a certain percent withheld for pew rent. Another teacher, Mary Kobetich lived in Melrose and walked each day to school. This was no mean task when the thermometer would drop to 25° below zero! With the advent of the automobile teachers would often drive to school. One teacher, Helen Luckroth, had a fatal accident one day while on her way to work.

The annual report of this school district for 1911 gives an indication of the thriftiness of these stolid and sturdy rural families. The teacher's yearly salary was $432. The fuel and school supplies together totaled $5.67! Library books cost $5.00 and text books and maps $17.40. Other expenses totaled $41.15 and the perennial tell-tale sign of the school boy at his recreation — twenty-five cents for a broken window pane.

A portable drinking fountain was provided in 1917 and each child had his own drinking cup. A kerosene stove was a welcomed addition that year. The teacher and older girls could now make hot chocolate for the noon lunch. It was the older boys who had the duty of keeping the wood box filled with wood for the furnace. An able-bodied boy who lived near the school had the responsibility of arriving early to start the fire. The desks in this school were hand-me-downs from the old Melrose public school and with so many deep carvings cut into their tops, it was difficult to write on them. As in the other district schools most of the writing in the pioneer days was done on slates. In 1962 an addition was added to the building and lavatories were installed. Five years later the district was dissolved.

Some of those who attended this school were Sisters Inez, Helen and Venard Niehaus, O.S.F., Sister Gaudentia Hinnenkamp, O.S.F., Joseph T. Niehaus, state representative and the deceased Julitta Niehaus, Ensign, U.S. Navy.

It is not the intention of the writer to incorporate in this chapter the histories of St. Patrick's, St. Boniface and St. Mary's schools. These will be treated in the chapters concerning the histories of these parishes. It would, however, be a serious oversight if mention were not made of the contributions these schools made to the growth and development of the Melrose area. By not mentioning these schools in this chapter the author in no way means to overlook their invaluable contributions. It was felt, rather, that their histories should be recorded in connection with the chapters dealing with the religious development of the community.

MELROSE DISTRICT 740

The early history of this district is nebulous and hazy. Two of the earliest references to the school appear in the 1891 issue of the *Melrose Sun*. On June 5th the editor noted that school closed for summer vacation after nine months of studying. On September 4th he further noted, "Our school will commence next Monday. Books and slates must be looked up and all necessary preparations made at once for the time is short between this and the opening of school." Mr. Earl Seal discovered a photograph with the caption, "Senior Class, Melrose 1893, W. M. Vanderwater, Principal" but other facts about the school, where it stood and what happened to it, could not be uncovered. The first common school in the area, District 48, was taught by Alfred Townsend in 1868 but there are no records as to where the building was located. Possibly in the parlor of some family's home. Mention is also made of the Gerhard Richter family attending school in a store building that stood on the corner of what is now the former Ford garage. And mention has been previously made that August Lindbergh's granary was used as a school with fifteen students being taught by Miss Jennie Simonton of Sauk Centre. Two "alumni" of that granary-school were Charles A. Lindbergh, Sr. and Myron Taylor who later became a district judge in St. Cloud.

A second school is said to have been located two miles west of Melrose on the then Doe farm and now part of John Kemper's farm. Little is known about this school. As the village was growing the site of the school on the Doe farm proved insufficient and thus land was purchased on Riverside Avenue and a frame building of two rooms was constructed there. This building was later torn down and replaced by a brick structure of four or five rooms. This school building stood at 203 West Riverside Avenue, the site of the former John Welle residence. As the village continued to grow with the advent of the railroad and increased immigration, this school also proved inadequate and was replaced by an imposing new structure in 1903. The bricks and windows were salvaged and used in the construction of the George Rehkamp residence on the north side of the river. The Rehkamp house was built in the shape of the original school building and still stands at 411 East Third Street North. The abandoned school property on Riverside Avenue was purchased by William Bohmer and is presently owned by Ervin Dettler. Some of the early teachers in this school were Anna Hannon, Miss Sweet, Nellie Barrett who later married William Stephens, Nellie Staunton and Miss Lehman.

The new grade and high school built in 1903 was located in the block of the present Junior High School. It was destroyed by fire during the winter of 1913. During the process of constructing a new building, the pupils attended school wherever space was available, such as in the city hall, the city jail, St. Boniface church basement and private homes. The graduation of 1914 took place in the auditorium of the city hall.

In 1896 the district was changed from a common to an independent school district. Superintendents were: Mr. Smith, H. W. Shoyer, J. H. Seal, E. J. Sweeny, E. M. Kane and J. J. O'Donnel. Other superintendents of the school district will be mentioned later. Despite the changes of buildings and locations, courses of study, teaching personnel, school boards and administrations, the process of education continued throughout the years. The value of education was not only appreciated by the members of the community at large but highly treasured. Few questioned the need of a good education and almost all recognized its importance as a social, economic, political and religious influence.

One of the first school boards in these early years consisted of William F. Donohue, president; John Hoeschen, treasurer; Frank Mohs, secretary; William Rahn, James Taylor and John Cannon, directors. The first high school graduate — in a class of one — was William Maguren. The commencement excercises were conducted in the city hall with Dr. Schumaker, president of the St. Cloud Normal School, as the principal speaker. Mr. Stephens presented the diploma, a task he continued to fulfill for all high school graduates until 1947. Mr. Maguren, who graduated in 1904, was later employed as the station agent of the Great Northern Railroad at Alexandria.

Ben Eveslage was the first graduate of Melrose High School to attend the University of Minnesota. Howard Quinn and Steven Roelike were the next two graduates of the University of Minnesota. The Melrose High School class of 1913 consisted of five graduates: Caroline Moots, Oswald Kolb, John Meyer, Steven Roelike and Bertha Thull of Freeport.

One day, the president of the city council, Henry Tieman, brought an old school notebook to the office of the *Melrose Beacon*. While making alterations in the city hall the workers found the book. It contained notes from English class numbered 111 and was written by Genevieve Louise Seal, daughter of August Lindbergh, and now Mrs. Percy Huntemer of Chicago. The date written in the book was April 1, 1914 and the note book reveals that classes were then being conducted in the city hall. The back cover of the book listed the members of the junior class. They were Lidvina Helsper, Jack Helsper, Celia Donohue, Mary Barrett, August Eveslage and Genevieve Seal. The teacher was Miss Whaley. The book also revealed that it had been purchased at the Zuercher Drug Store for ten cents.

The class of 1914 deserves further examination because it offers an insight into high school education in Melrose at the beginning of World War I and serves as a comparison with the developments to take place in the succeeding decades. One member of the class, August Eveslage, was the prototype of hundreds of young men who would follow. He played basketball each year that he attended the high school, beginning in the eighth grade. He missed one year of school and still finished the curriculum in three years. In 1914 the Melrose basketball team, with "Gus" as the sparkplug, played twelve games, winning ten of them. This gave the team a high percentage and entitled it to a berth in the state tournament. Due to some technical misunderstanding the team was canceled out of the tournament. Another graduate of the class, Howard Quinn, became a teacher in El Paso, Texas.

Mrs. Nora Eveslage recalled that the school building which burned in 1913 had no indoor plumbing. The assemblies for special events were held in the auditorium of the city hall. She further recalls that there were thirteen graduates in the class of 1914 and when it marked its golden jubilee in 1964 eight of the class returned. In those days the basketball team played its games in the basement of St. Boniface School. There were four iron posts in the hall to support the upper story. Frequently a player would make contact with one of these posts and literally put himself out of the game. This meant a delay in the game because there were no substitutes. There were no cheerleaders then so the student spectators would spontaneously make up their own yells.

After one of these games the freshmen girls were going to sponsor an ice cream social. It did not take place, however, because a few of them stole the ice cream and then, to make matters worse, had their picture taken with the caption "On the Freshies".

Mrs. Eveslage recalled the domestic science classes (today called home economics). The girls would use wood to fire the stoves for heating the ovens and only for smaller projects could they use small electric plates. Whenever all the plates were turned on at the same time a fuse would blow and the girls would be frustrated because they were then unable to complete their projects. In these years each student paid for his books and materials.

The curriculum for the senior class of 1914 consisted of English IV, geometry, bookkeeping, typing, shorthand. A school day lasted from nine o'clock in the morning until four o'clock in the afternoon with one hour for lunch. There was no such thing as hot lunches served at school, and everybody went home for lunch except on cold winter days students were permitted to carry "baggie lunches."

Mrs. Alma Pappenfus, another graduate of 1914, recalled an embarrassing moment in the life of one of the girls in the class. The annual faculty dinner was a time for the girls in the domestic science class to display the excellent quality of their dishes. One girl tripled the amount of red peppers in the hot dish she prepared to the consternation and indigestion of the faculty. Mrs. Pappenfus also related the great fuss that was made over the senior class. In the spring of the year there were three days of special activities for the seniors, one called Senior Class Day, another Junior-Senior Day and finally Commencement Day. Junior-Senior Day consisted of symbolically passing "the torch" and the program for such a day in 1914 was as follows:

Special Meeting of the Senior Class at the City Hall
Thursday evening, May 28th at 8:00

Come wearing the Red and Black class colors;
wear your class flower, the American Beauty,
and bring your class motto, "Reap Only the Best."

Program

A Glance Back	Florence Wellenstein
Roll Call	by the Class President
Report of Committee	
On Senior Dignity	Nettie Behkamp
On Cast of Togs to Juniors	Alma Loosbroek
On Photos	Salvius Helsper
Point of Order	Cecelia Donohue
On the future	Henry Rehkamp
	Eva Fake
On Rewards of Merit	Christine Kraker
A Point of Order	Jennie Little
Passing of Talisman	Florence Albers
Acceptance	by Junior Clarence Anderson '15
Report of Committee of Whole	
"Oh Promise Us"	August Eveslage
Motion to Adjourn	

* * * * * *

Superintendent of the school during the first decade of the twentieth century was J. H. Seal, a highly respected citizen of the community and able school administrator. He retired as superintendent in 1908 and subsequently served the community for thirteen years as the city postmaster. E. J. Sweeny succeeded to the office in 1909 and was a well-beloved man by both faculty and students. The bond of friendship that he established with his students is evidenced by the fact that in 1920, Ben Eveslage, a former student, resigned his office as a high school principal on the Iron Range to return to Melrose and teach under Mr. Sweeny. The pair hunted in the woods around Melrose on Saturdays and during the winter months engaged in boxing sessions in the gymnasium.

The first football team of Melrose High School was organized in 1900. The team practiced, then as now, after school hours and, unlike the present time, the season schedule consisted of one game with Sauk Centre. Sad to state, Melrose lost by a humiliating score of 70 to 6. Ben Eveslage also recalled that the 1911 graduating class consisted of five members: Rose Sandbrink, Nora Donahue, Norbert Borgerding, Win Tyrell and himself.

Another member of the class of 1914, Mrs. Raymond Borgerding, nee Nettie Rehkamp, recalled that the girls in the domestic science class could not turn the ice cream freezer without a special and peculiar hold on the freezer as the cream became stiffer. One girl sat on the freezer while two other girls held her down and a third girl would turn the churn. On another occasion the girls had the project of sewing flannel night gowns. There was only one pattern and it had to be shared by all the girls in the class. One of the girls sewed a sleeve into the neckline instead of the opening where the sleeve belonged, causing frustration to the instructor and exasperation to the one who was expected to wear it. Such were but a few of the numerous incidents that occurred in the early days of Melrose Senior High School. The Melrose Schools, as did the schools in the neighboring communities, contributed not only to the educational development of the area but also to the cultural and religious formation of the children and grandchildren of the German immigrants. This caused one foreign visitor, Xavier Geyer, to observe in 1926 that "all in all Stearns County is the finest and best developed area of German Catholic background that I saw in the whole country."

In continuing the history of Independent School District 740 it is deemed best to present a chronological record of the more significant developments from 1918 until the present time. In such an overview many events and developments may be inadvertently forgotten; nonetheless, a general view will provide the reader with the names of persons and events that have contributed in making the Melrose school system one of the strongest in the state.

1917 - John Kolb was president of the school board, W. J. Stephens was the clerk of the board and H. F. Loosbroek the treasurer. Teachers salaries ranged from a beginning salary of $55 a month to the highest salary of $82.50 a month. Some of the bills paid in May, 1917 were as follows: grade school textbooks, $64.93; high school textbooks, $19.78; periodicals for the library, $1.50; heating, $800.; athletic supplies, $8.15. Students were encouraged to perform their "patriotic duty" and thus the boys went out in search parties seeking scrap iron, while the girls were knitting mittens and scarfs. Sometimes a girl, with a romantic gleam in her eyes, would stuff a note into a mitten and ask the soldier who might receive it to write to her.

1918 — During this term the superintendent's salary was $2,200 and the school staff consisted of eleven people. Two new names appeared as members of the school board, John Welle and C. W. Carlson.

1919 — It was duly noted in the minutes of the board that the school had hired a probation officer. There was also a lively discussion about installing a manual training department, now known as industrial arts. In the annual school board election only seven votes were cast. At this time the school purchased its steam from the city power plant which was steam operated. The exhaust steam was piped underground from the location of the present powerhouse to the present junior high school. Some residences along the street were also benefited by being connected to this steam service heating system.

1920 — The annual report shows that during this year the high school enrollment was eighty-six pupils and the grade school numbered one-hundred and five pupils. Eleven high school students paid non-resident tuition.

1921 — A movement was inauguarated to build tennis courts for the use of the students. St. Patrick's four year high school was discontinued.

1922 — E. M. Kane was elected the new superintendent. The high school curriculum read as follows: English I, II, III, IV; community civics, economics, modern history, American history, American government, social problems, general science, biology, botany, physiography, physics, elementary algebra, plane geometry, Latin, Caesar, animal husbandry, field crops, mechanical drawing, foods and cooking, clothing and textiles, related arts, shorthand and typing, commercial arithmetic, music. Many of these subjects were taught for only one semester and entitled the student to only one-half credit toward graduation.

1923 — A new name, Joseph Thiers, appeared among the officers of the school board for the first time. St. Boniface High School was discontinued.

1924 — Nothing of significance happened during this time. Apparently the citizens were satisfied with the operation of the school. The census of the district revealed a total of six-hundred and forty-one children between the ages of six and sixteen enrolled in the district.

1925 — This was one of the most peaceful years in the history of the schools—perhaps an omen of the trials to come with the great Depression and drought. Miss Loretta McBride was appointed principal.

1926 — August Sauer was appointed a member of the school board to fill the vacancy created by the resignation of John Kolb who had moved to St. Cloud.

1927 — Henry O'Donnell was elected as superintendent. The school census showed a total enrollment of 566 students. During this time the school board rented the old St. Boniface hall that stood at the north end of the present St. Mary's School. The public school used this hall for such activities as basketball games, class plays and socials. Another attempt to start a Parents-Teachers Association also failed. A combined city and school library was established, located in the high school building, with both departments sharing the operations.

1929 — An example of a school calendar at this time is reprinted here.

September:
        Registration
        Seniors organize
        Class rings selected by seniors
        Football season tickets on sale
        First football game of the season with Albany

October:
        Six weeks examinations
        Student Council organized
        Football game at Glenwood. Melrose lost. "M" club dance.
        Homecoming bon-fire and snake dance
        Homecoming dance
        Freshmen initiation

November:
        Senior-Junior Annual Party
        Minnesota Education Association meeting
        "M" club dance
        Annual High School Carnival

December:
        Absence because of the flu epidemic
        Magazine drive
        Football banquet
        Christmas program

January:

  School reopens after Christmas holidays

  Semester examinations

  Preliminary declamatory contest

February:

  Girls entertain the boys at a party as result of magazine drive

  All school program

  Sub-district declamation contest

  4-H club organized

March:

  District basketball tournament

  District declamation contest

  Inter-class basketball tournament. Seniors are champs.

  "M" club initiation

  Regional declamatory contest

  Easter vacation

April:

  School reopens after Easter

May:

  Junior and Senior Banquet

  Class play

  Senior and Junior Picnic

June:

  Baccalaureate

  Commencement

The elementary school returned to a two-grade teacher plan because of the drastic drop in enrollment during the past few years. Two new grade school teachers were hired, one teaching grades from one to four and the other teaching grades five to eight. There were sixteen members of the senior class.

1930 — This year the number of non-resident high school pupils began to increase. Non-resident pupils were those who did not live in the district but whose tuition and transportation were paid for by the state. There was a total of nine teachers in the high school, with the superintendent teaching Latin. Emphasis was placed on the "Good Citizenship" program and Herman J. Hoehl was awarded the best school citizen citation. His picture was prominently printed in the front part of the *Mel-Hi* before all other personnel and activities. At this time there were three grade school teachers and eight high school teachers, with the superintendent again conducting a course in Latin. The basketball team scored a total of 479 points against the 367 points made by its opponents. This team captured the Ninth District Basketball tournament as the baseball team captured the same district tourney. Henry Schwegman won the district oratorical contest and Dorothy Stephens was the winner in the district dramatic contest. A Parents-Teachers Association was finally organized. Melrose and five other rural schools also formed a district 4-H club. During this year the state legislature enacted a law providing transportation aid for all students with the plan to secure the education of all children in the state.

1931 — The bus transportation act was an historic high-water mark in the education of the young people of this area. Previously non-resident students provided their own transportation or boarded in the city during the school term. Bus transportation provided the opportunity of hundreds of students in the outlying areas to take advantage of a high school education. It would take several years before this legislative action would be carried out but only those who have benefited from it can tell of its merits.

In 1937 Otto Harren of Freeport bought a bus from St. John's University for bussing the children of that village to Melrose. In November, the same year, Joseph Nett bought the bus from Otto Harren. Since that time Joseph Nett has been the bus owner and operator. His first bus was known as the "Blue Goose" because it was painted blue. At the present time Joseph Nett is operating five school buses for the Melrose school district. In August, 1948 Elmer Thelen of New Munich entered into the school bus business with one bus. At the present time he is operating six buses and a twelve-passenger station wagon to transport students. The previous bus operators were William Schiller, Joseph Wimmer, Herman Osendorf, Jack Kraemer, and Hubert Heinen.

Leo Hoppe served the northern area of the Melrose area. The previous operators of this line were Herbert Schulte, Jack Kraemer, and Charles Froelie. At the present time Jack Kraemer operates eight buses, the smallest having room for forty-eight passengers and the largest accommodating ninety passengers. Ervin Mayers entered into the business with one bus and now operates four buses and one station wagon. In 1955 Joseph Revermann bought two school buses from Andrew Woeste and presently operates five buses. Riding the school bus today is a far and distant cry from the days when pupils would walk three or five or seven miles to school or live in the home of a relative or friend in order to have the opportunity of a grade or high school education.

1932 — These were the "hard years" not only for Melrose but for the nation. One entry: Philip Thielman started the first Melrose High School Band.

1933 — At this time the members of the school board were Henry Loosbroek, president, and C. W. Carlson, John H. Welle, J. F. Thiers, August Sauer and W. J. Stephens. W. J. Weinberger was elected superintendent in 1934. During this period the state established a payment plan for school districts to be taken from the income tax. The state paid a proportionate amount from the income tax fund for each pupil between the ages of six and sixteen living in a school district. The school census showed how many pupils were entitled to this aid. The state aid at this time was fixed at $10 per pupil. Lambert Baumgartner was chosen as principal during this year.

1935 — Dr. S. J. Roelike and Dr. A. H. Zachman were elected as members of the school board. Federal funds were supplied to furnish meals to needy students. The schools, as the rest of the community, suffered intensely from the economic depression and drought that lasted from 1929 to 1936. A track and field meet was held in Melrose during May. Nineteen rural schools participated and prizes for the event were donated by local businessmen. The school was also the center of a relief sewing project. Women sewed and repaired clothing for needy families in the county.

1936 — The release-time religion courses were introduced, allowing the students to attend religious instructions in their respective churches during school time. Instead of the students returning to their respective communities for religious instructions priests of the neighboring parishes would instruct the pupils at centers established either in St. Patrick's or St. Boniface's parish to give an hour of religious instruction. At this time it was also established that the schools of the district would close on holydays and begin classes one hour later on the first Fridays.

The Melrose Lumber Company sponsored a bird house contest for the boys and girls in the grade schools to see who might be able to construct the finest bird house. The joyful signal that many of these young scholars waited to hear was a blast from the steam whistle at the power plant at seven-thirty in the morning. This meant that because of inclement or extremely cold weather there would be no school that day. The rains finally came breaking the drought and conditions improved. The school board talked about establishing a kindergarten, discontinuing the W.P.A. projects and eliminating the shoe-repair shop in the basement of the school. Everyone was singing, "Happy Days are Here Again".

1937 — The nation and its schools were absorbed with the rumors and rumblings of war in Europe. Interest in European geography ran high in the Melrose schools.

1938 — Two prominent men graduated this year. One was the Reverend Arthur Hoppe, presently pastor of St. Mary's Church, Alexandria, and the other, Dr. Harold Roelieke who followed in his father's footsteps as the local dentist in Melrose.

1939 — Three seemingly contradictory innovations took place this year. The football field was lighted for night games; financial aid to needy pupils was inaugurated; a work-program was established for students who worked about the school at a pay rate of thirty cents an hour. A forty-five minute activity period at the end of the day was introduced, allowing time for music practice, club meetings, athletics and private tutor sessions for teachers who had pupils with particular difficulties in their academic work. The addition to the school was completed, allowing the school to take a greater role in conducting the sub-district and district basketball tournaments. The new auditorium also opened the school for such activities as rural district school's graduations, annual 4-H club meetings and other gatherings of a charitable or civic nature. A nominal fee was charged for non-educational activities. The new addition also encouraged an increase in enrollment with a registration of an all-time high of 333 high school students. There were at this time seventeen teachers and, as in the past, the superintendent was still teaching Latin. There were also three grade school teachers.

Members of the school board were John Welle, C. W. Carlson, William Stephens, Dr. S. J. Roelike, Henry Loosbroek and Dr. A. H. Zachman. M. J. Weinberger continued as superintendent. This year the *Talisman,* the school yearbook, made its first appearance. It took its title from the novel by Sir Walter Scott of the same name. Since a talisman is an amulet or charm, the staff expressed its hopes that the book would bring good luck and many happy memories to its readers.

This year also witnessed the completion of an addition and the renovation of the old building in order to accommodate more students. A new gymnasium, auditorium, five classrooms, administrative offices, industrial arts and home economics departments were added. A bronze tablet on the north wall of the existing building marks the completion of the Works Project Administration in 1939. Besides the physical improvements in the plant there was also a great improvement in the educational formation of the student body at this time. A forty-five piece band was organized and an acappella choir was formed as well as a freshman chorus. Those interested in journalism inaugurated the Quill and Scroll society and the "M" club was organized to promote a healthy school spirit. The previous year the baseball team won the Granite Six championship title and thus the school was afflicted with "baseball fever." A unique institution was the formation of the two basketball teams within the high school, one called the 'Country Dogs" and the other the "City Dogs". History does not record which of the two was the winner in the spirited intramural games. This year also witnessed the winning of the light heavyweight Golden Glove State championship by John Kleber. One of the graduates of this year's class was Edmund Tieman, a member of the community who served for twelve years in the Minnesota legislature and is presently a lieutenant colonel in the state National Guards. The previous year a certain young man by the name of Norbert Weiss ran for the office of county superintendent of schools. He lost. Edward Kellen was appointed principal of the high school.

1940 — The school year proceeded without any significant developments. A new name was added to the members of the school board. Henry Stalboerger was appointed to fill the vacancy created by the death of John Welle.

1941 — A war was raging in Europe and the United States became involved. This was not a time for innovations in education.

1942 — "War is hell!"

1943 — The high school was approved by the state department of education to offer high school courses to returning veterans. Norbert Weiss was appointed principal.

1944 — The high school offered evening classes to prepare people to work in defense plants. Norbert Weiss acted as supervisor and Christ Athmann as instructor. The present city attorney of Melrose, William Meyer, graduated.

1945 — W. J. Murphy was elected superintendent. The school board approved the employment of a community nurse for the school district. Dorothy Lippert introduced art as a course in the school curriculum and was a great promoter in starting the hot lunch program. Gerald Korte, who subsequently received his doctor of philosophy degree, graduated this year.

1946 — The hot lunch program was in full swing in a cafeteria installed in the former St. Patrick's building. The students walked from the public school to the hot lunch room. The school also established a cannery above the present creamery building, where people could bring their vegetables to can at a modest cost. The cost of operating the cannery was covered by charging for the cans used by the patrons. The agricultural department of the school raised vegetables for the hot lunch program, including a great quantity of cabbage.

1947 — The Community Church Services rented the school auditorium for divine worship on Sundays, but the program did not continue very long. The Central Six Conference was started, consisting of boys from the neighboring communities and from Melrose who came to the gymnasium on Saturdays to practice basketball. Members of the high school basketball team would act as coaches and drill the boys. On Sunday afternoons the six teams would play a round robin tournament to see which school would become the Central Six champions. The program is still in operation and includes teams from Freeport, New Munich, Meire Grove, Greenwald, St. Mary's School and St. Patrick's School. The football team shut out all its opponents except Alexandria, which game ended in a tie. The basketball team was going strong throughout the season until it met Osakis, and defeat in the first game of the district tournament. The work experience class was started as a vocational occupations course under the direction of the principal and coordinator. Its specific objective was to develop employable citizens. Instructions were given in the morning at the school; in the afternoons students worked in various business enterprises. Credits were given toward graduation for the work aspect of the program.

At the end of World War II the school and community participated in the "Ground Observer Corps" for several years. This was a branch of the overall Civil Defense Program. Because the country was in a dangerous position from air attack across Canada the government saw need for a chain of human observers to watch for enemy planes day and night in addition to the existing radar stations. By the establishment of the "Ground Observer Corps" the government felt it would be possible to plug any holes in the existing radar system. To fill this need the faculty, students and members of the community volunteered their services. The first observation post was in the belfry of the city hall. There was room in this tower for two people to sit and watch for enemy planes. The Melrose Telephone Company wired the location with a telephone for the observers to use. This telephone was in direct connection with the air control filter center in Minneapolis. If the caller reported an unfriendly plane orders were immediately issued to fliers stationed at World-Chamberlain Air Field to intercept the unknown or enemy plane. Almost every town of any size had an observer post during this time. Because of the unbearable heat and the presence of innumerable mosquitoes the belfry of the city hall became unusable, the post supervisor received permission from the Kraft Cheese Company to move the observer's post into a high tower at the plant. Each ground observer was furnished with a book showing the appearance and insignia of the United States planes and enemy planes in order to recognize them more easily. Each post usually had two observers who worked together as a team. The code-name for the post above the city hall was Love Abel, 1-4 black, Alpha.

Many citizens, both men and women, volunteered to assist with the ground observers corps which demanded a twenty-four hour watch. After the federal government built enough electronic radar tracking station across the northern part of the United States and Canada there was less need for the corps. At this time the system was moved to the high school where faculty members and senior students were trained to carry out the program.

This year, 1947, witnessed the introduction of the school song, "Buckle Down," a rouser that would instill school spirit into the succeeding generation of Melrose High School students. Members of the school board were Henry Stalboerger, president; Al Westendorf, C. W. Carlson, John Lang, Dr. L. B. Kuhlmann and Dr. A. H. Zachman. The agricultural education department was expanded and offered agriculture courses to the returning veterans as well as evening classes to the local adults. The grade teachers directed a combined grades' presentation of "Hansel and Gretel." A student finance committee was introduced. A student committee also took charge of the activity fund money and a student council was organized. A strange new piece of athletic equipment was purchased, called a trampoline. The program of "practice teaching" was inaugurated in conjunction with St. John's University, the College of St. Benedict and the St. Cloud State College. One of the outstanding graduates of this year's class was Anthony Schulzetenberg who would later receive his doctor of philosophy degree in library science.

1948 — This was a year of expansion rather than innovation. The hot lunch program, the vocational, veteran's agriculture, home economics, shop and science departments were all improved by additional equipment. The football team was undefeated and Ray Caspers was chosen as guard on the all-state team. The basketball team captured the district championship for the first time in twenty years. The fund-raiser popcorn machine became a familiar sight at various athletic events. Awards Day was inaugurated to single out the achievements of individual students. One of the graduates this year was John Meyer who would later become an attorney.

1949 — This year witnessed the enrollment of the largest freshman class in the school's history with 107 new students. It also observed the largest number of graduating seniors with eighty-two graduates.

1950 — The school board approved the inauguration of a kindergarten class. The grade school continued to have four teachers with two grades assigned to each teacher. The extra curricular activities that we experience today were already quite firmly established by this time. They included such events as homecoming, junior class play, senior class play and such organizations as the dramatics club, the *Script* and *Talisman* staffs, the library club, cheerleaders, Girls Athletic Association, band, majorettes, mixed chorus, Girls' Glee Club, Boys'

Glee Club, Hot Lunch Club, Industrial Arts Club, Home Economics Club, Future Farmers of America and the "M" Club. The basketball team won the district championship and were runners-up in the regional tournament held at Fargo. In baseball the "Dutchmen" won three trophies, capturing the Lake Region Conference title, the district and the regional championships. The track team won the district title at the meet held in Glenwood.

1951 — The *Talisman,* the school annual, was dedicated to Joseph Trisko who served as janitor of the school for twenty-four years. Mr. Gust Rubash was appointed the new superintendent. An architect was employed to draw up plans and specifications for a new addition to be added on the south side of the school. Thomas Zachman, who would later receive a doctor of philosophy degree, graduated at the end of this term.

1952 — Construction on the new addition to the high school began, providing two new classrooms for the high school, a cafeteria, teacher's lounge, agricultural room, farm and metal shops, four grade school rooms and a kindergarten room. The school district also purchased the Gallagher property on the northwest corner of the school block and thus the school property covered the entire city block. The basketball squad won the district championship and the baseball team gained the runner-up position in the state tournament held at Owatonna. The track team won the District 22 track meet.

1953 — The new extension to the high school was completed and dedicated the following Spring. Mrs. Ben Volbert, supervisor of the hot lunch program, moved into the new cafeteria and prepared the first hot lunch in the new addition. Religious release time courses continued to be conducted by the churches of the area and were functioning well. A new service of the school, called "driver's training" appeared on the scene about this time. The athletes again made impressive showings in football, basketball, baseball and track.

Throughout these years the Melrose school system actively participated in such events as American Education Week, Veterans Day, Citizenship Day and other national and religious holidays. The Melrose Education Association was formed among the teachers of the area and it met at various times throughout the school year to study and implement better teaching techniques and aids. Problems affecting the schools were aired and discussed at these meetings.

1954 — Members of the school board at this time were Dr. A. H. Zachman, John Lang, H. C. Stalboerger, W. E. Carlson, Dr. L. B. Kuhlmann and Al Westendorf. Student counseling became a vital part of the services provided by the administration and proved to be of great assistance to the students. The high school's first exchange student, Jose' Gomez of Mexico City, was warmly accepted by the student body and resided with the family of Dr. and Mrs. A. H. Zachman. One of the graduates of this year's class was Mark Meyer, presently an attorney residing in Melrose.

1955 — This year the school's annual, the *Talisman*, was fittingly dedicated to Norbert Weiss who served the community and school for twenty-five years. William Sundell was appointed superintendent of the school. A department of speech correction was established. The baseball team won the sixth consecutive championship of the district tournament.

1956 — As the nation experienced a time of quiet and peace under the Eisenhower administration, so also did the Melrose school district.

1957 — Members of the school board were now Al Westendorf, William Meyer, H. C. Stalboerger, Dr. A. H. Zachman, Dr. L. B. Kuhlmann and Joseph Brus. The short-lived Edsel car made its appearance on the city's streets and the homecoming king and queen made use of it during the parade. A new bridge was constructed across the Sauk River near the Kraft Food plant, reminding the students that they would be called upon to cross many bridges in their life. The age of Sputnik was duly noted and the students were conscious of the fact that the human race had entered upon a new era. Two of the graduates of this year's term were James Zachman and James Meyer who subsequently became medical doctors.

1958 — This year witnessed the enrollment of 128 freshmen students. The year also marked the inauguration of special education classes for handicapped children. At this time the Melrose fire department began supervising athletic events in order to assure the safety of the crowds that gathered. During this year the high school administration undertook a survey of its facilities and personnel to see whether or not it would qualify as a member of the North Central Association of Schools. Unfortunately, the survey was never completed. The baseball team again won the district championship.

1959 — The election of members to the school board resulted in the installation of these members: Dr. H. Roelike, William Meyer, Rene Lizotte, Dr. A. H. Zachman, Dr. L. B. Kuhlmann and R. O. Passi. The new superintendent was John T. Provinzino. The senior class of the high school started with a class of 170 freshmen. The "Melrose Highlanders," a colorful school band, made its first appearance at this time. Joseph Trisko retired as chief custodian. The baseball team was runner-up in the state baseball tournament.

1960 — A full-time student counselor was hired, a first in the history of the high school. Students and faculty participated in Plowville, U.S.A. that took place in the community this year. At this time "Parents' Night" was initiated as a time for parents to visit with teachers and discuss the progress of their children. Two graduates of the class of 1961 were Russel Sieben and Richard Provinzino, both doctors of dental medicine at the present time.

1961 — A glance of the calender of activities for this academic year reveals the type of education that was being offered by the Melrose High School during these years. The calender, of course, does not reflect the day-by-day series of classes nor does it record the many extra-curricular activities. It does, however, present an overview of the school year at this time.

Teachers' Workshops	August 31
School opens	Tuesday, September 5
Homecoming	September 29
Fire Prevention Week	October 8-11
Christopher Columbus Day	Thursday, October 12
M.E.A. Convention	October 19-20
M.F.T. Convention	October 19-20
All Saints Day	November 1
American Education Week	November 5-11
Senior Class Play	November 18-19
Thanksgiving recess	November 23-24
Feast of Immaculate Conception	December 8 - No school
Christmas Vacation	December 22 - January 8
Minnesota School Board Convention	January 15-17
Lincoln's Birthday	February 12
Washington's Birthday	February 22
Easter Vacation	April 17-23
Ascension Thursday	May 10 - No school
Baccalaureate	May 27
Memorial Day	May 30 - No school
Graduation	May 31
Closing Date	June 1

1962 — Members of the school board were Eugene Herges, Dr. L. B. Kuhlmann, William G. Meyer, R. O. Passi, Drs. Harold Roelike and A. H. Zachman. Santa Claus continued to make his rounds of the grade and high school students, visiting believers and unbelievers alike. For a number of years the health department had been conducting immunization and polio vaccine clinics.

1963 — Mr. Francis Hertzog was chosen principal of the senior high school. The jest of the year was offered by the student council in these words: "The long bus rides, band trips, the incessant testing, and Latin banquets, the stage decorating, the crowded lunch rooms, the dances and the tedious studying have all gone into our molding. Does anyone say the final sculpture is bad?"

Melrose High School received statewide recognition as the only high school that claimed six sets of twins in the freshman class. The twins were Sharon and Shirley Borgerding, daughters of Mr. and Mrs. Robert Borgerding, Freeport; Sharon and Shirley Nohner, daughters of Mr. and Mrs. Fabian Nohner, Melrose; Darlene and Marlene Scherping, daughters of Mr. and Mrs. Jerome Scherping, Freeport; Bruce and David Kuhlmann, sons of Dr. and Mrs. L. B. Kuhlmann, Melrose; Victor and Victoria Burg, son and daughter of Mr. and Mrs. Leo Burg, St. Martin; and Bernard and Urban Beuning, sons of Mr. and Mrs. Alphonse Beuning.

1964 — The complexion of the school board changed once again. Its members were: Lyle Olmschied, Dr. L. B. Kuhlmann, Dr. Harold Roelike, Warren Anderson, Eugene Herges and William Meyer. John Provinzino continued as superintendent and Francis Hertzog remained as principal. Both men would hold the same offices up to the present time. The Girls' Athletic Association expanded its activities to girls' basketball. A Youth Corps program was established with ninety-percent of federal, and ten percent of local funds to provide jobs for young people. Summer school classes in typing and English were offered during the end of this school term.

At the end of this term the district rented the former St. Boniface School to house seventh and eighth grade classes. An intensive vocational night was established with representatives from area vocational schools, colleges and business colleges invited to promote the opportunities their respective institutions would be able to provide. At this time the records also show that it cost approximately $400 to educate a grade school pupil and $600 to educate a high school pupil per year in the Melrose school district. During this year the records also show that the school district enrollment was 754 and a total of 55,073 hot lunches were served the students during the academic session. Another foreign exchange student, Bertha Sanchez from Bolivia, was enrolled in the high school and lived with Ralph Worms family of New Munich. The school board was also discussing the "closed school bill" recently introduced into the state legislature. This bill provided that schools within a high school area which had no district high school would have to join a district that offered high school services. This was the beginning of the end of the rural or common school.

1965 — This year the basketball team won the regional tournament and went on to the state tournament. Although defeated in Williams Arena it was still hailed as a hero-group by the local citizens. Six of the rural school districts joined the Melrose district this year for the convenience of bus transportation. The rising cost of local education forced these districts to close as has already been noted in the earlier pages of this chapter. Dr. Edward Tomsche became the sole new member of the school board in this year's elections. The growth of the district was evidenced by the fact that the members of the graduating class numbered 146 and there were seventy eighth graders and seventy-six seventh graders. Junior high school basketball and football were introduced during this year.

1966 — Liliana Mange, a native of Costa Rica, was the exchange student this academic year and she lived with the Robert Sames family. A new name was added to the school's administrative team. He was James Ricklick who became principal of the junior high school. The baseball team won the consolation trophy at the state baseball tournament and a member of that team, Glen Klimmek, was named to the all state tournament team.

1967 — The community was growing and also the school system was expanding. For several years there had been talk and rumors about the need of a new facility. At the beginning of this school term statistics revealed that there were 125 kindergarten children, twenty-five in special education programs, seventy-four enrolled in grades one through six, and 991 in grades seven through twelve, giving a total student population of 1,215. The present facilities were obviously inadequate. Plans were made for a completely new senior high school plant, separated from the junior high school plant and to be built on the north side of the city's limits. Federal aids were sought to cover some of the proposed construction. Following the directives of the National Defense Education Act it was felt that financial support could be sought under Title One for summer school courses offered in English, mathematics, science, reading, speech correction and kindergarten; under Title Two aid could be found for building up the library and under Title Three for development in the areas of science and physical sciences. At a meeting of the school board in May, 1968 approval was given to begin construction of the new high school at a cost of $2,100,000. A new era in the development of education in the Melrose area was inaugurated at that historic meeting. The die was cast. The past was prologue to a future once again. Through the vote of this school board the citizens of Melrose had again opted for an unknown and uncertain future rather than the tried and trodden paths of the past. The vote represented not only the traditional appreciation and estimation of the need for education of youth; it was, more than that, an expression of confidence in the future.

1968 — A new era in education began on May 2, 1968 when the school board approved a $2,100,000. building bond bid. Piper, Jaffery and Hopwood of Minneapolis was awarded the bond issues. The previous October 5th the voters of the school district had approved the bond issue. The school board had accepted the low bid of the following firms on April 30, 1968: $975,388 for general construction by the Wahl Construction Company, St. Cloud; $579,212 for ventilating, heating, plumbing and temperature control by Weidner Plumbing and Heating Company, St. Cloud; $178,233 for electrical installations by Midstate Electric Company of Willmar; $165,708 built-in equipment to be shared by several contractors; $119,000 for other building costs, fees and expenses.

The new senior high school, designed by the architect, Al Weigleitner, was built to accommodate 750 students. Situated on a tract of land north of the center of the city it included thirteen general class rooms, two science laboratories, one lecture room, an audio-visual center, a general industrial arts shop, a vocational agriculture shop and agricultural classroom, an electronic shop, an art room, two home economic rooms, a library, a larger lecture room, a lunch room and kitchen, four business education rooms, administrative offices, vocal and instrumental music rooms, a physical education room and locker room and a swimming pool. The building is fireproof and adequate to take care of senior high school enrollment for many years to come.

In the spring of 1968 active work began on the new High School building across the river on the site of the former Frank Tieman farm. The enrollment in 1967 showed 125 kindergarten, 25 in Special Education, Grades 1-6, 74; grades 7-12, 991 or a total of 1215 pupils. In 1968 the school board was expanded to seven members. Federal Aid was brought into the picture under three titles; Title I - summer school was offered in English, Mathematics, Science, Reading, Speech Correction, and Kindergarten. This was to give instructions to pupils that have serious learning problems. Title II - was for library aid, and Title III was for reimbursement for National Defense Education Act. These were the years of space flights and moon flights. Mr. Berling became a new board member. The long hair style began to make its

appearance. The Dutchmen cross country track team won the conference meet with a perfect score and continued on to win the district meet.

1969 — A break down of the costs for the month of January in
1969 might give the reader a new perspective of the magnitude of
school work:

Instruction	$ 6,499.78
Administration	504.36
Health Service	13.50
Transportation	11,601.70
Operation of plant	2,134.77
Maintenance of plant	1,433.24
Fixed charges	245.00
Capital outlay	377.30
New Building Fund	43,088.51
Debt Redemption Fund	88,512.23

The era of Confraternity of Christian Doctrine instructions began.
Pupils went to their respective churches or homes in the evening for
religious instruction. The last senior class graduating from the old high
school building was one hundred eighty students. Now the long hair
and beards came on the scene. WCCO radio officials named the
Melrose Pep Band the "Band of the Week." Two new bands appeared.
They are the Concert Band and Varsity Band. Girls gymnastics were
presented in this period of school. MDVC - Minnesota Diversified
Vocation Club changed its name to DECA or Distributive Education
Club of America. Melrose is a member. The Spanish Club had developed into a prominent position. This was the year the football team
was the 1968 Conference Champions. Matt Herkenhoff was named an
All-State by WCCO radio station. The track team was District 22
Champions. May 19, 1969 was Norb Weiss day. His friends and associates and former students observed the day with a banquet at the
VFW club rooms. He received many complimentary awards and citations for this thirty-nine years of unselfish services to his school, community and church. He taught grade school seven years and was a
shop teacher for seven years. He was the principal, teacher and coordinator for a combined twenty-five years.

1970 — Hartmunt Wiedemann, an exchange student from Germany
and Alicia Mange, an exchange student from Costa Rica attended
school here and lived with the Robert Sames family. The school board
changed again with the following members: Henry Berling, Dr. Edward
Tomsche, Wilfred Humbert, Warren Anderson, Dr. L. B. Kuhlmann,
William Meyer and Lyle Olmschied. Administration included Super-

intendent, John Provinzino; Senior High Principal, Francis Hertzog; Junior High Principal, James Ricklick and Grade School Principal, Frank Hughes. The first graduating class from the new Senior High School numbered one hundred eighty-five. A new band was introduced and became widely known as the Marimba Band. The style of girls' wear changed considerably since the early high school days. Melrose basketball team won the District tournament, Regional tournament and the State Consolation. The Senior High School now has a marvelous swimming pool that is used throughout the year for physical education. Certain evenings in the week the pool is open to the public and in the summer it is part of the summer recreation program. Rosa Leona Cervantes, an exchange student attended school in the summer and lived with the David Wander family.

1971 — The school board consisted of the following members: Henry Berling, Dr. L. B. Kuhlmann, Dr. Edward Tomsche, William Meyer, Wilfred Humbert, Warren Anderson and Mrs. Elaine Niehoff. The administration remained the same. Lilia Glarza, an exchange student from Peru attended school here and lived with the James Ricklick family. Josc' Corrca from Chile also attended school here and lived with the Herman Westendorf family.

1972 — The number of administrative and teaching personnel in the Melrose School District in 1972 consists of the following: Administration, four; teachers, ninety-nine; supplemental teachers, thirteen; teacher aids, seventeen. This comprises quite a substantial payroll in the district. The enrollment for 1972 showed Special Education, 8; Trainable, 11; Kindergarten, 191; Grades 1-6, 573; Grades 7-12, 1262 or a total of 2052 pupils. Whether the enrollment will go up or down remains to be seen in the future. Rebecca Elguezahal from Mexico attended summer school. The Melrose Dutchmen won the State Class A basketball championship.

Class mottoes come and go, but one chosen years ago typifies the spirit that instilled students, faculty, parents and citizens throughout the years. It was, "The Stone of the Future is in our hands; we must carve it into a statue of success." That spirit has dominated not only the Melrose school system but also the thousands who were a part of it over the past one hundred years. Although class mottoes have changed year after year and class flowers and colors have changed their hues, the spirit has always remained the same, expressed so well in the slogan on the letterhead of William Boerger, "To bring the home, the church and the school closer together for a better society." Long before the present generation was born and, hopefully, long after the present generation was born and, hopefully, long after the present generation has gone to its reward, there will be students of Melrose High School who will continue to sing the school song:

> Hail to the Dutchmen, they're our team
> Let us cheer them as they go on
> To win this game and bring Melrose fame.
>
> Rah - Rah - Rah
>
> So raise your voices high and shout
> With a mighty cry,
> "Hail to the victors bold
> The purple and the gold."

District school number 41, west of Melrose on the Albert Meyer farm.

District school number 187 was known as the Hinnenkamp school and was located a few miles north of Melrose. All the children on the picture were members of the various Hinnenkamp families except one, Joseph Overmann, the last pupil in the first row.

Miss Hattie Himsel, a popular teacher in the Hinnenkamp school.

The pupils of District school number 187 as they appeared in 1918.

Pupils of District school number 165 at their annual picnic in th early years of this century.

Herman F. Bentfield, teacher in District school number 165 in 1897.

SOUVENIR

School District No. 16

Melrose

Stearns Co., Minn.

Oct. 4, '97—June 4, '98.

District school number 164 was known as the Petermeier school.

The pupils of District school number 164 posed for this picture at the turn of the century.

Above: The pupils of District school number 73, known as the Hellermann school.

Right: Miss Alice Graham, beloved teacher for many years in the Hellermann school.

The first public school in Melrose was located on Riverside Avenue.

The second public school, built in 1903, was destroyed by fire in 1913.

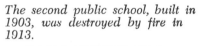

Members of Melrose High School posed for this picture in 1903 in front of the entrance to the new school building.

Above: Members of the eighth grade public school graduating class of 1911 were, left to right, Georgia Zieske, Emily Matson, Genevieve Seal, Goldie Johnson and Cordelia Lambert.

Left: The "cooking class" of 1912 consisted of, front row, left to right: Nora Santer, Florence Wellenstein, Alma Loosebrock; second row left to right: Cecilia Donahue, Nettie Rehkamp; back row, left to right: LeVerna Helsper, Rose Schmidt, Georgia Zieske, Goldie Johnson and Genevieve Seal.

Having a good time at the expense of the "freshies" were William Tirell, Norbert Borgerding and Paul Saulmers.

The Melrose High School crest, suggested by superintendent Maurice J. Weinberger in 1935, depicted the reconstructed view of Melrose Abbey, Scotland.

The architect's view of the new Melrose Senior High School, completed in 1969, with a view of the proposed athletic fields in the background.

The State Class "A" Basketball
champions of Melrose High School
in 1971. They are, first row, left
to right: Coach Frank Shelton,
Tom Walz, Tom Herges, Dave
Schneider, Paul Meyer, Martin
Meyer, Ken Rausch, Coach Del
Schiffler; second row, left to right:
John Thelen, Ron Maus, Richard
Beuning, Randy Douvier, Mike
Hertzog, Herbert Ehlert, Dean
Westendorf, Coach David Linehan;
third row, left to right: Don
Radamacher, manager, John
Herkenhoff, Herman Moening,
Neil Thelen, Bruce Schulzetenberg,
manager.

The Melrose basketball
team in 1923.

The basketball team in
1909 lacking one uniform.

The Melrose football
team in 1900.

THE BEST GAME OF THE SEASON
MELROSE VS. ST. CLOUD.

The baseball field in Melrose at the height of its popularity.

Two frequent visitors and swimmers at Birch Lake, Ray and Nettie Borgerding, model the latest in swimming attire for 1932.

Four women prove they can match the men when it comes to fishing. Left to right: Mrs. Henry Steinemann, Sr., Rosina Hellermann, Hilda Rolfzen and Mary Pohlman.

A hunting we will go! Shown on a hunting expedition about 1900 are Fred Studebeck, George, Fred and Henry Rehkamp, on the Rehkamp farm about four miles northwest of Melrose.

The city park as it appeared a generation ago.

Snowmobile blessing in near-by St. Rosa in 1972.

CHAPTER SEVEN

"A MALICIOUS HOLD-UP
IN BROAD DAYLIGHT"

> Take me out to the ball game,
> Take me out to the crowd.
> Buy me some peanuts and crackerjacks,
> I don't care if I never get back.
> Let me root-toot-toot for the home team,
> If they don't win it's a shame
> For it's one, two, three strikes you're out
> At the old ball game.
>
> —An American Folksong

Elsewhere in this book early settlers have recorded that pioneer life was rough and rugged and that no one would deny. They recounted that life in the early years of the community was one of hard work with only an occasional gathering of the family circle and immediate neighbors. That, too, is understandable. Travel was both difficult and limited; and, more often than not, by the time one arrived at his destination it was almost time to begin the homeward trek. The coming of the railroad and the improvement of the rig or buggy helped to overcome these obstacles and, since man by definition is also a social animal, it was only to be expected that he would seek out the companionship of friends and neighbors in an ever-broadening circle.

One activity that captured the imagination and energies of the Melrose community was athletics. In an area populated with enterprising, energetic young men who inherited a highly competitive spirit from grandfathers and fathers, it was only natural that they would strive to exhibit their prowess in sports. Another factor for this great interest in athletics arose from the very nature of the society that was being created on the western frontier of Stearns county. The nature of their work demanded that young men would be forced to work many and long hours by themselves and, even though there was a respect and reverence for the family circle, there was also the abiding desire to associate with one's peers and exchange — generally over a friendly glass of beer or two and more — the experiences and the discoveries of the previous week or two. Finally, athletic contests were not only a time when families and neighbors might exchange local tidbits of information before, during and after the game, but, not to be overlooked in a culture that enjoyed neither radio nor television, a social event when young ladies might view — under the watchful eyes of fathers — the eligible young men of the community. An interest in athletics was born in the community. Throughout succeeding decades sports were cultivated until at the present time sports have almost reached an obsession with a goodly number of the citizens. Four activities stand out, baseball, football, basketball and resorting; these shall be treated in this chapter. In more recent years such activities as track, swimming, wrestling, bowling, and golfing also became popular athletic activities; lack of historical records, however, prevents recording much of these sports.

Bowling was for many years a popular winter past-time for the people of the community. It began on some distant day in the basement of St. Boniface Church, with wooden bowling balls and hand-made pins. Progress was made when Father Willenbring constructed the St. Boniface parish hall with alleys and regular teams were organized. Several present and former members of the community acted as managers of the bowling "alleys" — a word that came into use in the early 1930's because bowling lanes resembled the alleys of a city. Even before the bowling alleys in the parish hall were demolished, a new bowling alley was opened on Main Street, on the site of the present VFW clubrooms. At the present time, a sparkling new bowling alley is located in the southeast corner of the city and currently has sixty active teams in various leagues. An event of note occured on February 20, 1963, when Marge Hinnenkamp bowled a six hundred and five series at the Modern Lanes — the first time any woman in the area had ever bowled a six hundred series in Melrose. Her record was only broken in 1972 by Mary Brickweg who bowled a six hundred and twenty-six series. A native of London, England, Mary started bowling in 1967 in Shape, Belgium.

Golf-fever came to Melrose with the organization of the Meadowlark Country Club in 1962. Land was purchased from the Herman P. Imdieke farm the following year, greens were planted and in 1965 the loud cry of "Fore" was heard throughout the area. Officers of the organization for the first three years were John Provinzino, president; Ted Welz, vice-president; William G. Meyer, secretary; Donald Stalboerger, treasurer.

The organization began with one hundred and forty-seven stockholders and at the present time numbers well over two hundred stockholders.

"Play ball!" was the sound that inaugurated the oldest and most venerable sport in Melrose. In 1893 there is a record of a baseball team in the village which appeared to be no more than what we would call today a "sandlot" team. In 1910, however, Melrose boasted a Junior baseball team with Bill Thull as its manager. Members of the team were Joe Harren, Harry Morehouse, Norb Borgerding, Nick Krick, Clarence Gummerum, Frank Primus, Harry Waldorf, William Atkinson, Otto Wellenstein and George Primus. Only ten players and only one substitute! Baseball was Melrose's first love and only in recent years has it been replaced by an emphasis on softball, slow pitch or fast pitch. In a hurry-up society the reason for this might well be that a softball game can be played in one third of the time it takes to play a baseball game and, at the same time, allow more participants in the various leagues.

Early issues of the *Melrose Beacon* record as many as nine teams based in Melrose during the 1910's and 1920's. Most of these were teams that would come together on a Sunday afternoon for recreational and social purposes, but there was also some baseball of extremely high caliber played during this decade. The Melrose All-Star team was an aggregate of the good local amateurs combined with some recruits from Minneapolis and other places. Often the recruits were negro players who would come on the train to Melrose from Minneapolis for just one afternoon's game. The schedule of the Melrose All-Stars was somewhat irregular, mostly of a "barn-storming" variety. The team would play whatever teams it could engage and some of these teams came from as far away as Fargo, Minneapolis and St. Cloud. No accurate records were maintained but according to local reports the Melrose All-Stars . was a team of exceptional repute. Incidentally, the *Melrose Beacon's* writer pulled no punches in reporting the news as he saw fit. In the issue of July 12, 1912, he reported, "The failure of the umpire to call a runner out who left the base before a fly ball was caught robbed Melrose of the game at St. Cloud last Sunday. It was a malicious hold-up in broad daylight."

The Melrose baseball teams always played to near-capacity crowds at what is now called the Legion Park. Many people in the city can still recall going from church on Sunday directly to the ball park to insure a good vantage point for watching the day's game. (A comment on the length of the sermons delivered in those days!) It was a common place sight to see cars parked two rows deep around the entire field. Often fans of the teams from the opposing town would come to Melrose on the railroad train to support their teams. Reports of the games were always given prime space with ample (and editorialized) headlines on the front page of the *Melrose Beacon*. The sports were always colorful and gave due credit to both home and visiting teams, but very seldom complimented the umpires.

Organized baseball in Melrose began when the city entered a team in the regular league schedule of the southern half of the sixteen-team Ottertail-Todd-Wadena (O-T-W) League in 1931. The eight teams in the southern division were Bertha, Henning, Parkers Prairie, Swanville, Sauk Centre, Long Prairie and Melrose. Then, as now, the greatest rivalry was between Sauk Centre and Melrose. The roster of the original Melrose team included Roman Sandbrink as manager and players John Gerdes, George Gerdes, Frank "Bud" Matchinsky, Jim Matchinsky, Ben, Tony, Fred and Herman Moening, Al Rehkamp, Arnold Kuhlmann, Aloys Kramer, Carl Welz, Leo Lemm, Homer Lemm, Harold Thompson and Ted Wurst. The following year Melrose joined the newly-formed Central Minnesota League which included teams from seven communities, namely, Sauk Centre, West Union, Belgrade, Regal, Brooten, Grey Eagle and Melrose. The local team captured the league championship with a nine to three record.

In 1934 Melrose entered the Great Soo League, the teams included Holdingford, St. Joseph, Freeport, Albany, New Munich, Eden Valley, Watkins, Avon, Cold Spring and Melrose. Eugene McCarthy, the former senior senator from Minnesota and recent presidential contender, recounted some of his experiences in this league in the appendix to this chapter. Melrose fielded teams in this league in 1935 and 1936 and went independent in 1937 for a year until it joined the renewed Central Minnesota League consisting of St. Martin, Brooten, Belgrade, Lake Henry, Elrosa and Melrose. Again Melrose won the league championship. In 1939 the Melrose team again preferred to be independent until the leagues were disbanded during the war period of 1941 to 1945.

Upon the return of the veterans in 1946, Melrose joined the Stearns County League with Lake Henry, Freeport, Roscoe, Elrosa and Paynesville. Again Melrose won the league title but was eliminated in the regional play-offs by St. Joseph. The following year New Munich and St. Martin were added to the Stearns County League and again Melrose seized the league championship. During this same year Melrose High School baseball team went to the state tournament and received the consolation trophy. The high school team lost the opening round to Duluth Denfeld but went on to beat Crookston and Westbrook, finishing with a nineteen to one record.

The Stearns County League was re-organized in 1948 to include Lake Henry, New Munich, Elrosa, St. Martin, Paynesville, Brooten, Roscoe, Belgrade and Melrose. Once again Melrose took the league championship but went on to defeat by the hands of Albany in the regional finals. Again in 1951 Melrose captured the league championship. In 1953, however, Melrose entered the Big Dipper League (named because a line connecting the towns on the map formed a dipper), including Little Falls, Cold Spring, Albany, Paynesville, Sauk Centre and Melrose. The formation of the new league was but one indication of decline of interest in Sunday afternoon baseball in the smaller communities of the area. The automobile was beginning to take its toll as far as local interest in baseball was concerned. Other factors were the formation of the St. Cloud Rox Club and later the inauguration of major league baseball with the coming of the Minnesota Twins. In 1955 Melrose again entered the Great Soo League, including Cold Spring, St. Joseph, Paynesville, Albany, Sauk Centre, Pierz, Grey Eagle and Melrose. The Great Soo League is still the oldest organized baseball league in the state.

In 1958 the death knell sounded for organized baseball in Melrose, chiefly for reasons already cited as well as for a growing community interest in golf, water-skiing, fishing, resorting and the availability of attending games of a higher professional quality. Other contributing factors to its demise was the expense of providing equipment for the team, the lack of night-lighting facilities and the availability of major league baseball on television. An era had passed and with it, to a degree, a culture that three generations developed. The "good old days" had come a long ways since that dismal day when Melrose lost a baseball game to Sauk Centre by the score of sixty-five to fifteen in 1891! Perceptive observers noted the change of the times when the grandstand in the Legion Park was torn down shortly after the Second World War. When youngsters no longer knew that Frank "Bud" Matchinsky, who played from 1930 until 1948, was one of the finest pitchers in the area, or that Homer Lemm had served twelve years as an outstanding manager — then even the not so keen observers knew that the days of organized city baseball were finished. It was, however, a grand and glorious era and served the needs of the community exceptionally well. Now all that is left is the memory of the "Fighting Dutchmen."

But not quite "all." Another generation came and its members brought new honors to the city. They were not "Dutchmen" anymore than their fathers were; the title was but an Anglo-Saxon corruption of *Deutschman,* the name given a citizen of Germany or his descendants. It was, and is, an honorable appellation for it recalls all that is good and true and manly about a noble people. If interest in organized baseball declined, the new interest of the community would be inaugurated in a football game of utter disgrace. In 1900 Melrose High School lost their only scheduled game to Sauk Centre "Mainstreeters" by a score of seventy to six. It was a bitter, but a good, lesson. The humiliation provided the stimulus to "try harder" and so the Dutchmen did. So mighty would be the efforts put forth in the coming years that Melrose would become known throughout the state as a "football town." Little is known of the intervening years except the fact that Melrose High School was bound and determined to make its mark. A bright young coach arrived on the scene in the late 1920's by the name of Frank O'Rourke. In spite of coaching football, basketball and baseball, his first love was the former and from a struggling ensemble of defeatists he whipped together a first-rate team. One member of the team of 1927, Theodore Niehaus, recalled that O'Rourke "was a good coach but was tough." No one, perhaps, has done more to bring football to the attention and prominence that it enjoyed for two decades in Melrose than Frank O'Rourke. Among some of his early players were Henry Griep, Leonard Sauer, Ray Unger, Leo Althaus, Ted Niehaus, Ervin Hoffman, Mocco Rehkamp, Mort Lent, Arnie Kuhlmann, Jim Campbell, Dan O'Rourke, Hugo Kuhlmann, Jerry Lamberton, Guy Thompson, Art Strommen, Jim Ahmann, Bob Maas, Gilbert Thompson, Jim Matchinsky, Paul Zirbes, Ed Theisen, Ed Maas, Ed Trisko, Fred Kuhlmann and Bob Snyder.

Lambert Baumgartner, Marvin Wrucke and Robert Drescich succeeded O'Rourke as football coach. In 1946 a new coach inaugurated the "golden era" of football in Melrose. His name was Omer Sieben. He coached fifteen seasons, had a record of seven undefeated years and finished with an overall record of 86-25-7. This record included an eighteen-game winning streak, at which point Melrose was ranked tenth in the state. During his tenure the team participated in the Granite Six, the Lake Region and the Central Gopher Conferences at one time or another. During this time also junior league football was inaugurated in order to supply a "feeding" line to the high school team. One of the stellar performers of the Melrose Dutchmen was Bill Daley who went on to play for Michigan and was named an All-American player. He was honored at the Minneapolis Quarterback Club meeting in 1949. On another occasion four players coached by Omer Sieben were honored by the Melrose Chamber of Commerce. They were Val Riley, John Worms, Lyle Olmscheid and Bill Braun. Sieben throughout his fifteen years as football coach brought many honors to the team, the high school and the community. During part of this time, from 1949 to 1965, he also acted as athletic director of the high school. In recent years he has been succeeded as coach by James Miller, Ross Fortier, Robert Swatosch and Sieben's son, the present coach, David Sieben.

Times change, interests change. Enthusiasm for football began to wane in 1961 when for the first time in its history Melrose High School secured a berth in the State Basketball Tournament. Basketball was no innovation in the Melrose area. Already in 1914 Melrose boasted a Catholic Young Men's Basketball Association team consisting of "Peco" Stalberger, Kelly Stalberger, Nick Krick, Leo Michels and Frank Schmidt. In these early years basketball was played in the basement of St. Boniface grade school and this continued until 1939. At that time the present band and chorus room of the Melrose Junior High School was completed and became the basketball floor. In 1954 a new addition was built which continues to house the basketball games for Melrose High School.

One of the reasons for success in basketball endeavors in the area has been the Central Six program, a Sunday afternoon basketball program involving boys from the fifth through the eighth grades in the schools of the area. There are twelve teams drawn from the school district, giving boys the opportunity of playing before an audience and using the facilities of the gym. The teams are presently coached by players on the high school teams. The program, inaugurated in 1946, has proven to be exceptionally successful. Another factor in the present success of basketball may be the fact that in 1929 Melrose High School basketball team captured the old district nine title and a spirit of competition was passed on from father to son.

Coach Otto Schaefer's Dutchmen that year were a relatively small, hustling and unknown club that won the District 22 title in 1960 defeating Detroit Lakes and Crosby-Ironton in the Region Six Tournament. It was the first time in history that Melrose was represented in a state tournament and the city literally went wild. Dinners were scheduled in honor of the coach and the team; Confirmation was cancelled in the local parish; welcoming parades were planned to meet the team in Freeport. The city and school was struck by "basketball fever" and all other interests and activities appeared to be of no consequence. The team went to the state tournament and lost its first game to Granite Falls and then went on to defeat Thief River Falls and Chisholm to capture the consolation trophy. Members of the team were Russell Sieben, Richard Koll, Thomas Ahlers, Thomas Arvig, Jerry Arvig, Reuben Nathe, Merle Laumeyer, Henry Middendorf, Ronald Roering, John Rose, "Bud" Ostendorf, Richard Provinzino, Melvin Beste and John Lieser. "Once you get the fever," said one prominent citizen, "you never say die."

Ten years later the scene was repeated when the Dutchmen went to the state tournament at Williams Arena in Minneapolis. Again the team returned with the consolation trophy and the usual parades, dinners and pep fests followed. A spirit was abroad, however, and that spirit spelled "We Shall Return." And return the team did the following year after capturing the regional title in Breckenridge. Four juniors who spark-plugged the team the previous year returned. They were Herman "Butch" Moening, John Thelen, Martin Meyer and Michael Hertzog. They were participants in a new format for state tournaments that divided teams into Class "A" championship and Class "AA" championship. Melrose captured the Class "A" championship and then went on to lose a heartbreaker in the playoff to Duluth Central, winner of the Class "AA" championship. They still returned as heroes. In 1960 Russell Sieben was selected as a member of the All-State team and in 1970 John Thelen, Herman Moening and Ronald Maus were members of the All-State team, with Thelen and Moening returning the following year for selection as members of the All-State team.

In recent years a new development occurred on the high school sports scene. It was no longer just the city boy who would be actively engaged in athletic events. More and more rural youths would become the football and basketball heroes. In the early 1950's two would be outstanding for their exceptional ability, Anthony Massman of New Munich and Anthony Petermeier of rural Melrose. On more than one occasion a parish priest would drive one or the other home after an evening practice. This trend developed in succeeding years as school bus rides were made available to those who participated in after-hours activities. One outstanding athlete who took advantage of this opportunity was Matt Herkenhoff who, in 1968, achieved the singular distinction of being named a member of the All-State teams in both basketball and football the same year.

Baseball, football and basketball made up only a small part of the community's athletic and recreational activities. The proximity of so many lakes in the area produced an abundant number of the apostle followers of Peter and Andrew, James and John, who were also fishermen. A pleasant Sunday afternoon was spent in a rowboat by many farmer or merchant on one of the numerous lakes in the area while matching his skill against an unwitting walleye, crappie, sunfish, northern or bass. Only God knows how many stories were told about "the one that got away" and "I swear it was *this* big." In the early days all a person had to do was drop a hook in the nearby stream or lake and come home with the evening meal. Later, as state conservation laws became more stringent, there was always the ever-present fear of the game warden who might check the limit or the equipment.

The game warden, the first of a new generation of conservationists, was the harbinger of a new society. Never a beloved man, the warden was, and is a most important man who performs an essential duty in conserving and preserving natural resources for generations yet unborn. Unfortunately, he will never be a "popular" man in the community. This was evidenced already on January 3, 1918, by a poem composed by the late Frank Stanczyk who lived near Lake Sylvia. The poem was sent to the editor of the *Melrose Beacon* by an anonymous Charlie Flintenputzer, Blackoak Township, with the postmark of Brooten. It would seem that Mr. Stanczyk had some difficulty with a game warden from St. Joseph by the name of Michael Loso for his poem reads as follows:

A FISHERMAN'S PRAYER

A fisherman's luck — wet feet and hungry gut
I caught some bass and I caught some pike,
And who caught me? Of course, 'twas Mike.
He took my net and went to town
And told my wife I should be around.
When we went before the court,
Mike told me I was a sport.
He then asked me, "Is this your net?"
I stood with smiles and said, "You bet."
Mike took the net and sent it away,
Then all was o'er but the fine to pay.
When to this I answered, "Nay,"
Mike said, "We'll see what the judge has to say.
The judge he spoke and took his book,
"Thirty dollars." Said I, "Doggone the luck."
The judge was good, and always was, and said:
"Ahem, my man, $27 or 30 days, herein mit Ihm."
When Monday came and I took the train
The policeman said, "It is too bad."
When the deputy came, I was ashamed;
He took the key and said, "My lad,
Behold your home, 30 days to be."
Then I started to pray:
"Vater unser ver du bist,
Ich bin ja nur ein armer Christ,
Da sprach der Herr —
Versage nicht, du frommer Christ;
Und ven du auch in Gefangniss bist.

Der deputy der ist ein gutter Man;
Der zeight dir eine Zelle an.
Die Zelle ist huebsch und fein
Und ein Bettlein steht da drein.
Ein Eimmer und ein Wasserkrug
Da habt ich den ganzen Tag genung, AMEN."

Frank Stanczyk was but among the first of many who would come into conflict with game wardens. Although considered by some sportsmen as "necessary evils" the game warden was still appreciated by most sportsmen as necessary for maintaining an ecological balance in the area surrounding Melrose.

The Melrose area was blessed with a natural resource that was not fully appreciated in its pioneer days, namely, the close proximity to so many lakes and rivers. The pioneers were so busy clearing the land and striving for survival that they had little time for enjoying the lakes and woods that surrounded them. In those early decades hunting was not a sport; it was a necessity to keep the wolf and coyote away from the door. Four decades would pass from the days when Charles A. Lindbergh, Sr., was sent into the woods to fetch some game for the family dinner before the *Melrose Beacon* would report that three hunters from Melrose bagged one hundred and six ducks while hunting one day near Osakis in 1912. Hunting would continue to be a popular sport among the citizens of the community down to the present day. This writer can recall many a fine afternoon when the pastor of St. Patrick's would call and say, "It's such a beautiful afternoon; let's go out and see how the squirrels are doing in the Ward Springs' woods." Only a recording angel can tell how many wives felt they were left as widows when the "call of the north" would summon their husbands during deer hunting season.

But the most natural environmental and recreational area in close proximity was that chain of lakes we know today as the Big Birch, Little Birch and Sylvia lakes. It was here that Michael Loso, the game warden, apprehended Frank Stanczyk. Here, too, the Chippewa Indians located a village on the northern shores of Big Birch Lake. Here, before the coming of the white man, was the traditional boundary line between the Sioux and Chippewas. Writing in 1832 the explorer Henry Schoolcraft noted that no dwelling place, "not even a temporary wigwam" could be observed in the area. The Indians called these lakes "Gawigwassensikag Sagaiigun" — the place of the little birches lake. The first white men in the area knew Little Birch Lake as Birch Bark Fort and Big Birch Lake as Middle Birch Bark Lake. The smaller lake from which flowed Adley Creek was called Lake Sylvia in honor of the wife of Alfred Townsend who homesteaded in the area. Decades later "Chick" Molitor would build and operate one of the most elite summer spots in the area on the shores of Lake Sylvia, known far and wide as Chick's Chicken Camp.

On the western shores of Little Birch Lake a townsite appeared about 1865 with the arrival of Patrick Grimes and Henry Burke, both Canadians, who homesteaded in this area. Early records show that a Michael Burke was baptised in New Munich in 1867, a Julia Costello in 1869 and a Sarah Grimes in 1870. Mention was also made of this settlement by the pioneer missionary, Ignatius Thomazin. The early deeds of the land surrounding this lake area show that the early settlers were mostly Irish Catholics . The township of Birchdale was organized in 1869 and an unsurfaced and often muddy road wended its way from Sauk Centre and Melrose about 1880. Interest increased with the coming of the branch line of the Northern Pacific Railroad between Morris and Little Falls, passing through the newly platted village of Birch Lake City, as it was called in 1881. Four years later a hotel was built in the village and during this period a school district was organized, a saloon was opened. Joseph Kraker's elevator was operated and a small stockyard was opened beside the railroad track. Birch Lake City attracted many tourists from Sauk Centre and Melrose because of its proximity to the lake region. Its permanence seemed to be assured when Bishop Otto Zardetti of St. Cloud established a Catholic church in the community in 1892. The town-site platted by J. W. and Martha J. Ward, however, did not become the thriving metropolis of Birch Lake City that was anticipated in those early days. We know it today as Ward Springs.

Nonetheless, Ward Springs and the area surrounding the lakes became a mecca for city-weary people in succeeding generations for many people from Melrose, Sauk Centre, St. Cloud and Minneapolis. One of the early visitors to the area, Raymond Borgerding, recalled the experiences of his youth in these words:

"When I was a lad of about six years (1903) my parents would go camping out at Middle Birch Lake. They would camp on property owned by Eric Erickson (now owned by Mr. Bitts). There was an old deserted log cabin there that served as living and eating quarters. Dad had a tent with side walls three feet high that served as our sleeping quarters. When Dad had a sectional wood floor built for the tent, we thought that was the 'ultra' of camping.

"Uncle William Broker of Royalton, would camp every summer at 'Ves' Breese's place on Middle Birch by the creek coming from Big Birch, and we would then pole our way up the creek to Big Birch.

There was no dam in the creek then. We would row to the Breese's place. Ves Rose's Resort and Nestle Inn are located on some of the Breese's property. It was a long row but there were no Johnson's or Evinrude's in those days. After a few years Uncle Bill coaxed Dad to camp also at the Breese's place.

"We would drive with horse and buggy to a place close to where 'Chick' Molitor now has his lake home. A wood-cutter by the name of Burns had a log cabin there. Our boat was hid in the creek that now flows by the Schmidt cottage. We would row across the lake from there to the Breese's place.

"Sylvester Breese was a 'character'. He was a bachelor. He always had a number of dogs. At one time the lake water had made an island of some of his property. He raised skunks on this island. As it was surrounded by water they could not get away. He would wait until winter, when the skunks were sort of hibernating and not very active. He would start a smoky fire at the mouth of the den, the smoke would make the skunks unconscious and he would then dig them out and kill them for the fur. The skunks were unable to 'perfume' in this unconscious state. 'Ves' also had a couple of black bears who were a great attraction for us kids.

" 'Ves' made money raising vegetables, selling ice, and catering to the needs of the campers. He often told of the big steamship that went steaming into Hunter's Bay and was never heard of again.

"After we camped at Breese's place a few years, other Melrose people started camping there. Among them were John Kraker, John Selfinger, Dr. Claude Campbell and Herman Fussner. The row across the lake from Burns' cabin was always uncertain on account of wind. After Uncle Bill died Dad tried to buy land from Frank Reller who owned the land where the Burns' cabin was located. Mr. Reller would not sell, but told Dad to camp there to his heart's content. We camped there for three years.

"Dad had his eye on a place a little to the north of the Burns' cabin, but again Mr. Reller would not sell but told Dad to build there as he would never bother him. We built a road to this point, by following a cow trail and chopping our way through the woods. Dad built a cottage on this point. We and other people called it Pike's Point, as there was good pike fishing close by. Many was the time we caught our limit of pike less than a block from the shore. In those days the limit was twelve walleyes.

"It was a busy day in those times. On a weekday, there were no more than three boats out fishing. Transportation was by horse and boats were scarce. There were only three cottages on the lake front, not counting the Grey Eagle frontage on the lake. These were located on what is now known as Sandy Beach, and were owned by Messers. Gordon, Tanner and Turner. These people were from Little Falls and the place was known then as the Little Falls Camp. There were some cottages on the Grey Eagle end of the lake. Some of these people were the Wilkie's, Sliter's and others. Some of the permanent settlers around the lake were the Link's, Rhode's, Cole's and Whitney's.

"A year or two after Dad built his cottage, John Kraker, John Selfinger and Dr. Campbell built a combination cottage and boat house over the creek where Mr. Wilhelm now lives. Pike's Point got to be a popular spot and a number of people camped there — some only for a week or two. I can recall that among these people were the Tise's and the Fussner's.

"After camping on the Point for a few years Dad contracted tuberculosis and the doctors told him to get away from the Point as it was too drafty and would make him subject to colds and impair his health. Dad sold his place to Anthony Kraker and it has since been known as Kraker's Point.

"At one time Dr. A. A. Meyer and my brother Norbert, owned most of the Sandy Beach. They sold lots and urged people to build cottages. This was the start of the cottage 'boom' at Birch Lake.

"My brother Norbert also had a cottage on the lake which I believe is now owned by Ted Kluempke; at least it is close to it.

"I built a cottage on the lake in 1929; put my initials and date on the sidewalk leading from the cottage to the lake. It is now owned by Leo Peyton, a retired game warden."

Throughout the years the people of Melrose took an ever-increasing interest in the Birch Lakes area. At one time "Chick" Molitor owned thirteen miles along the lakes' shores which he sold to friends and neighbors for the building of cottages. When the Birch Lake Association was formed for the preservation and conservation of the lake area the people of Melrose, St. Rosa and Freeport areas were among the most active in the organization. At the present time, of the 145 members of the organization, forty-one — almost one-third — are from Melrose. No longer is it an all-day outing to picnic or fish at Birch Lake. Many an eager fisherman steals away from the office, shop, farm or rectory to spend a few hours matching his wits against a witless fish for an hour or two in the early morning or late afternoon. The weary wives of fishermen would be the only ones who could tell the exact number of hours — and they won't tell.

Snowmobiling, one of the nation's and state's most rapidly-growing sports, hit Melrose in 1967 with the sale of twenty-two machines and two years later the number of sales had increased to eighty-two machines. Since then the number of sales has been constantly climbing. Among the first to purchase machines were Wendell Rausch (father of six boys), Lawrence Scherping, John Kettler and Victor Elfering. Richard Van Beck, the Johnson dealer in Melrose, recalls the first year that he and his family took up the sport of snowmobiling. He had one machine with six eager riders. Most snowmobilers prefer their individual machine and at most one rider. For the true snowmobiler a Sunday afternoon of winter recreation consists of following trails through wooded hillsides and across frozen lakes, especially in the St. Rosa area, and ending with a picnic lunch of weiner roasts together with the whole family in the fresh, frozen air.

Besides serving as an instrument of recreation the snowmobile has also served the needs of neighbors. Many a snowmobiler has brought supplies to people snowbound, helped electricians repair rural outages, rescued stray dogs and taken fishermen to and from their fish house. In 1964 there were only three hundred and twenty-five people employed in the snowmobile industry in Minnesota and only three thousand machines were manufactured. At this writing there are approximately eight thousand people employed directly in manufacturing one hundred and fifty thousand snowmobiles which are distributed by over two hundred distributors who employ an average of twenty-five employees each and approximately ten thousand dealers with an average of three employees each. According to recent figures the snowmobile industry contributed more than twelve million dollars to the state of Minnesota and according to evidence gathered by snowmobile associations the snowmobile has caused no permanent damage to the environment. At the present time there are over one million snowmobiles in the United States and twenty per cent of these are in Minnesota, giving the state a record of one snowmobile for every twenty-one residents. The first snowmobile blessing in the world was held at St. Rosa in December, 1969, and since then the custom has spread throughout the local area to such centers as Sauk Centre, Greenwald and New Munich as well as to other areas in the United States and Canada.

APPENDIX

MY LIFE IN THE GREAT SOO LEAGUE*

by Eugene McCarthy as told to Fred Katz

From time to time youngsters have asked me what I did for entertainment while growing up in rural Minnesota during the 1920's and 1930's. It is a perfectly reasonable question. Commercial television was non-existent, of course, and few towns had motion picture theatres. Perhaps a dozen golf courses blanket the area today, but there were not many back then. And while most of the lakes in the Land of 10,000 Lakes already had been formed, motorboating remained something for the future. So the range of activities was limited, and the lack of spending money during the Depression narrowed the range even more.

Fortunately, there were two inexpensive and popular pastimes available on Sunday afternoons in our area. One was listening to Father Coughlin on the radio; the other was watching or playing baseball in the Great Soo League. The only problem came if one happened to like both. Then he had to make a choice, because Father Coughlin came on while the games were being played. For me, however, the choice wasn't very difficult. Father Coughlin, a priest in Detroit, was a radical social and political reformer. He was a kind of socialist when it came to the economy, believing in the distribution of the wealth. His foreign policy was of another order, based to a large extent upon his acceptance of the Protocols of Zion as true.

The Great Soo League, in which I played for five years, belonged to a baseball era that is fast fading. It was a time when there were few distractions from the outside world, and all attention focused on the local team. If you were fortunate enough to make the lineup, you possessed an automatic mark of distinction. Or if you were a fan, you went out on Sunday afternoons and rooted for the farmers and blacksmiths and school teachers and students and merchants who represented the community on the ballfield. We took the games seriously, which was part of the fun. And it was a pretty good brand of baseball most of the time.

Although the Great Soo League was typical of the country baseball leagues that existed in Minnesota and other states, I suspect it was a bit more organized and successful than some of its counterparts. It began operation as an eight-team league in the late '20's and lasted nearly 40 years. The teams came mostly from the farming areas northwest of Minneapolis-St. Paul. Some towns dropped out along the way, but there were always replacements.

The name of the league was an amalgam of the two east-west railroad lines — the Saulte Sainte Marie (known as the Soo Line) and the Great Northern,

* The author makes grateful acknowledgement to the editors of **Sport** for their kind permission to reprint this article that first appeared in the November (vol. 52, no. 5) 1971 issue of **Sport**, pp. 6-14, 118.

169

which ran parallel to the Soo and about 15 miles to the north. Originally, half the towns in the league resided along one line and half along the other. A cousin of mine, who was there when the league was founded, has told me there was a great discussion in deciding the league's name. But rational men prevailed, and their final choice was a fine tribute to the art of compromise. Henry Clay would have been proud.

The founders of the league also drew up a strict set of bylaws designed to make the Great Soo truly an amateur league. One of the rules provided that a team could not have a player who lived more than five miles from that town. If a player was fortunate enough to live within five miles of more than one town, he could pick his own team. But if he was from outside the five-mile limit, there was rather serious debate as to whether he was eligible. One year, in fact, the championship was taken away from Eden Valley by invoking a technicality of the rule. It seemed Eden Valley had a catcher named Riley who was working on a farm for the summer. One corner of the farm was within the five-mile limit, but the residence and principal part of the farm was out-side it, and so the championship was awarded instead to Albany. But it wasn't the distance so much as that it was known that Riley was a ringer. If he had been a native son of the farm, he probably would have been allowed in.

The effect of all this was to force teams to develop players from local talent. If your team was short a catcher, you had to search the countryside or try out people in town. If you lost a pitcher for some reason, you had to develop another one; you just couldn't hire one from Minneapolis. There were other leagues, however — leagues not as pure as the Great Soo — who weren't above raiding from afar, and who lured a coveted player with a little money. To counteract this, a slight bending of the Great Soo's amateur rules was per-mitted. If an outstanding pitcher from say, my hometown of Watkins had been offered $10 or $25 a game to pitch for non-league towns like Watertown or Delano, Great Soo officials might say, "Well, under those circumstances. . . ." And then Watkins would be permitted to match the offer. But by and large, things were kept honest and amateur.

One nice thing about the league was that age was no barrier. My brother Austin, a pitcher, made it when he was fourteen. I started when I was sixteen and a freshman in college. I played until I graduated, then came back home for a summer when I was twenty-nine and played another year. I had a pretty good season, but I had lost some of the batting eye that I had had at nineteen, when I hit around .380 in my best year.

We had perhaps eight or ten players who turned pro, with a couple getting as high as Double A ball. Our only major-leaguer was George Fisher, who came down to the Great Soo, rather than rising from it. He's listed in the Encyclopedia of Baseball as "Showboat" Fisher, and it says that he played the outfield in 88 major-league games between 1923 and 1932. I still recall his first time at bat in the Great Soo. My brother threw two fastballs by him and then struck him out with a curve-ball. (Fisher denies this.) That was a good sign that he wasn't going to burn up the Great Soo. But he was still a mean, lefthander hitter. I was a first baseman, and I always gave him a couple of yards when he was batting.

Fisher played for Avon, a town of about 400. Richmond was around the same size. My hometown, Watkins, was one of the smaller ones too, at about 600. Eden Valley was around the same. Then there was Paynesville down the road, with 1200. Besides similarity of size, Watkins and Eden Valley had something else in common. Both were Irish towns and Catholic, at least Irish enough to have a nice mixture. Paynesville, though, was mainly a Protestant town, and it was considered a major breakthrough when it came up with a pitcher named Father Kunkel, a Catholic priest.

Eden Valley had still another distinguishing characteristic: An unending supply of erratic pitchers. Lefty Arnold was one of them. He'd have great days, and then he'd go wild with his control and just be terrible. Everybody was pretty shy of Lefty Arnold. His favorite pitch was referred to as the "side-hill gouger."

Watkins had a good catcher and a pretty good batter named Pep Weber, whose big reputation was that he wasn't afraid of pitchers. To prove his fearlessness, he'd bat with his head right over the plate. He got a lot of walks that way. He also got hit a lot. But he was proud of his reputation. People would say, "He has such a good eye, he can really lean over that plate and watch the pitcher all the way."

Some of the other towns in the league at one time or another were Cold Spring, Albany, Holdingford, New Munich, Melrose and Rockville. There also were St. Anthony, St. Martin, St. Joseph and St. Cloud, which made the Soo sound suspiciously like a church league. But there was no danger of the misconception lingering long if you attended any of the games in the predominantly German towns along the Great Northern. It was there, right in the middle of Prohibition, that one could quench his thrist — if he knew the right place in or behind the stands. The Germans in those towns had never morally accepted Prohibition. So when it came, they made their own beer and developed a reputation for pretty good moonshine. Their most famous product was a corn liquor called Minnesota 13, which was processed from, and named after, a hybrid corn developed at the University. The drinking at the games never presented a problem, however, and in fact it may have attracted some of the better umpires from Minneapolis, who otherwise might have been reluctant to make the trip.

Speaking of umpires, I think one of the things that made the Great Soo unique among amateur leagues was its early use of an organized group of umpires to call the games. The first group was the Northwest Umpires Association and was made up of old ballplayers, some of them former major-leaguers. They traveled seventy miles or so from the Twin Cities and were paid $15 or $20 a game. Once the Depression was over, the league was able to afford two umpires a game. This was a definite improvement over the one-umpire days and less dangerous for umpires. It was generally held that an umpire's hearing was more important under these circumstances than was his eyesight. In a game at Avon, with a runner on first, umpire Nelson, working the game by himself, went out to stand behind the pitcher. The next batter came up and hit a groundball to third. Naturally Nelson turned to watch the play at first. He never saw it. The third baseman's throw hit him in the back of the head and knocked him out. While he lay unconscious, the runner from first made it around the bases.

There was always great concern about how to score a play like that, or any other controversial play. Should the batter be given a hit? Should he also get a run-batted-in? How would it affect the pitcher's earned-run average? Naturally we all cared about the final score, but we also cared about our individual statistics, so the selection of scorekeepers was very important. It was said that the scorer had to have at least two qualifications. It was not enough that he be a cashier at the local bank. But if he were the cashier and was also trusted to clerk a country auction, he qualified; that indicated a sharp eye, nimble mind and great readiness.

We came up with a fine solution in Watkins. Our scorekeeper was deaf and also unable to speak. His four brothers played on the team, but he himself couldn't play very well, so we made him scorekeeper. After a game, both teams would go down to the local restaurant and check the final box score. If a visiting player started to complain to our scorekeeper, he soon discovered that the young scorer couldn't hear him. If the player still persisted, our scorer would use hand signals to demonstrate how the ball went up, like this, or how it bounced out of a glove, like that. He was like Zacharias in the Bible: "I have written." It was written, and there it is: An error or a hit—forever. He would just wipe them out. Dan Manuel was his name, the best scorekeeper anyone ever had.

Despite the fact that many of the country roads in our our area were gravel back in the '30's, traveling in the Great Soo League wasn't especially difficult. We would go in private cars, or sometimes rent a school bus, and the farthest distance anyone had to go was 40 miles. If you played a town no more than eight or ten miles away, you would dress at home. But if you had to take the "long" trip, a team with style would rent a couple of rooms at the local hotel and dress there.

It was figured that a team's expenses — bus rental, the hotel, the ballpark, bats and balls, umpires, a policeman to keep law and order, and maybe a pitcher

— ran about $100 a week. At least that was the minimum amount a team tried to make from gate receipts and program ads. At 35 cents a head — 25 cents for children — and with an average turnout of three to four hundred people, most of the teams achieved their financial goal. Fortunately, we didn't have to worry about buying uniforms. The idea was to get local merchants to pay for them, and then try to talk them out of putting their names on the back. The merchants in Watkins, though, wanted the glory — not to mention the free advertising — and so I was the first baseman with "Steman's Cafe" on my back for three or four years. It could have been worse; some players represented the local undertaker.

It would make a quaint touch to say that the fields in the Great Soo were really pastures, but this wasn't quite true. As a boy, I can remember playing ball where the cattle had been put out, but in the Great Soo every town had a ballpark. Of course, the conditions from town to town varied considerably. Richmond was notorious for the sandiest infield. Most of the diamonds had sand infields, because grass was too hard to keep up. But nobody had sand like Richmond, which was located in an old river bed. First base was like a pit, and you felt you needed a shovel rather than a mit to dig out the ball on a low throw.

In the outfields around the league you sometimes found yourself sinking into a little valley as you chased a flyball, or perhaps catching your spikes in a gopher hole. More serious was the problem of the tall grass that had been cut but not raked. Since a team only played at home once every two weeks, farmers who cut the grass for hay liked to let it keep growing until the Friday before the game. But if it happened to rain on Saturday, or if the farmer was just too lazy to rake it, you would end up playing in deep windrows. I saw a fellow hit a ball to the opposite field one time, and the fielder didn't get a line on it. By the time he got to the general vicinity of the ball, it was temporarily lost in the hay. By the time the fielder actually found it and threw it in, the hitter was on third. Not long afterwards the league decreed that these hits would be ground-rule doubles.

Home runs were hard to come by in the Soo League because few parks had fences. If there was a fence, it was usually in just part of the outfield, and then only because it really belonged to the adjoining pasture or cornfield. The ruling was that you had to run out everything that wasn't hit over a fence, and it seemed to me that those accidental fences were always in rightfield. It seemed that way, of course, because I was a right-handed pull hitter.

The one time I figured I had an advantage was when we played a park where there was a cemetery out in leftfield. New Munich had one, and I think St. Martin. The idea was to try to hit the ball among the headstones, figuring that the leftfielder wouldn't chance stepping on his grandfather's grave just to chase a ball. I always aimed for the cemetery when I had the opportunity. In the Great Soo, that was considered place-hitting.

I think it's apparent by now that these games were very serious affairs. Little touches of sportsmanship — such as picking up the catcher's mask after he chased a foul ball — were considered a sign of weakness in the Great Soo. What you did was kick the mask out of the batter's box and let the catcher pick it up himself. On a rainy day, you might catch it on the end of your bat and hold it out to him as he returned from a futile rush to the fences.

The deadly earnestness made the manager's job a difficult one. If a team kept losing, it would change managers just like in the majors. Only the winners stayed on. Joe Meirhofer of Watkins and Mike Ebnet of Albany always seemed to do well, so they rolled along, something like Stengel and Alston. It was a risky office. Ebnet owned a meat market and stood to lose a good portion of his business if he didn't make the right decisions. A manager had to be especially careful, because in the German towns families were large. If a manager benched a member of the family, the whole family just might start shopping elsewhere for their meat. Our manager, Joe Meirhofer, didn't have it as bad. He was in the produce business, and there weren't any ballplaying families in Watkins quite as large as among the Germans. Certain qualities seemed to run in the families. The Glatzmeiers of Albany all seemed to turn out to be infielders. The Ebnets at Holdingford were lefthanded pitchers, and so on.

The entire season led up to the playoffs, and at that point the tension mounted to the level of warfare. Even the mere discussion of where the games were to be played had to take place in neutral territory. After that was settled, it wasn't unusual for the two managers to bet each other in the out-come. Wagering took place throughout the season, but those were generally $2 or $5 bets. The two-out-of-three playoff series was a time for serious betting, and the wagers were up to $50.

The playoffs also required a little more police protection. In the '20's, when they had home umpires, there were a lot of fights involving both fans and the players. The restraining fences weren't very good, and you could get 40 or 50 people on the field pretty fast. There was always a policeman around, threatening to arrest someone, but I don't think it ever happened.

I remember the playoffs with fondness, because Watkins was in a good period when I was playing, and we won the championship four times. We were sort of the Yankees of our time. Our strength was good balance between the pitching and hitting. And it's funny how other teams also took on patterns that seemed to resemble major-league teams. Holdingford was like the Dodgers. It generally had good pitching, but the lineup was full of little guys and they had to get their runs one at a time. And there was St. Joe, who were like Detroit; they would go in streaks — some years good, some years bad. You never knew why. Albany had good hitting.

So that was the Great Soo League: a league with its clowns, its bad guys and good guys, and some who got drunk on Saturday night but who could play ball pretty well on Sunday if you got them sobered up enough. And a league with a great family heritage. When I was campaigning for the Senate in 1964, I'd occasionally be in the Great Soo area and, of course, I'd stop off and see how they were doing. I found some of the sons of men I'd played with who were now on the teams, playing the same position their fathers did.

The league is gone now. Some teams disbanded entirely, while others joined other leagues. The loss of amateur baseball is a serious one. It destroys the basis for realistically comparing your skills with someone else. In the Great Soo, you could say, "Well, gee, I think I can play first base as well as my cousin. I can play in this league." Compare that with the feeling that a Little Leaguer has, whose only grown-up models are the Carl Yastrzemskis and Henry Aarons that he sees on television or at the major-league ballpark. He may be discouraged before he's begun.

Another value of the Great Soo League in particular, and of baseball in general, was the nakedness of each situation. A man was out there in the open, with several hundred eyes upon him. When the time came for him to perform, everyone knew who was responsible. It always seemed to me to be different in football, where a man could fall down in the line and get up with mud all over him and no one except a couple of other players really knew if he had done the job. And it seemed different in basketball, too, where just the positive things — the points scored — were recorded in the paper, but never the errors. The baseball books, like bank statements, are always balanced. In the Great Soo League though, as in the major-leagues, it was always an individual and personal thing at the critical moment, and you hate to think that that is gone now.

CHAPTER EIGHT

JOIN NOW -- PAY LATER

> Hail, hail the gang's all here!
> What the hell do we care -
> What the hell do we care.
> Hail, hail the gang's all here!
> What the hell do we care now.

The beginning of the story of man reveals that his social nature demanded that he join with neighbors and friends in organizations. No ethnic group enjoyed the activities of organizations more than the Germans. They appreciated not only the strength that comes from unity but also the pleasure of one another's company. The lack of distractions and the often loneliness of life among the early settlers of the area caused them to welcome any and every opportunity when they could gather and meet with friends and acquaintances. Civic pride was also a factor in the establishment of many organizations and the building up of a strong parish spirit also determined the beginning of many organizations. The story of a community would be a sad one if it did not recount the history of some of the organizations that fostered the promotion of both church and state.

One of the oldest societies in the area is the St. Bernard's Catholic Aid Association Society, founded on June 5, 1905. At that time the parent organization was known as *"Die Deutsch Romish Katholishen Unterstitzungs Geselschaft Von Minnesota."* The date of June 5th was chosen because it also marked the one thousand and one hundred and fiftieth anniversary of the death of St. Boniface, patron saint of the German people. The original organizer of the society was George Stelzle and at the first meeting there were thirty-five members with eighteen of these signing the charter. At the present time three of the charter members are still living and they are Ted Walentiny, Bernard

Hinnenkamp and John Kramer. At this meeting Joseph Sandbrink, Joseph Seal and Herman Thielen were appointed *"Vier Ortnung zu Halten."* The delegates elected to attend the convention in New Ulm that year were Reverend Francis Zitur and Herman Thielen. The first officers elected on June 18, 1905 were Edward Dingmann, president; Nicholas Meyer, vice president; "Schmeister" Joseph Nathe, treasurer; Peter Moritz, marshall; Joseph Sandbrink, "fannentrager;" John Hilt, financial secretary and members of the audit committee, Henry Niehoff, Herman Och and George Tiemann. Local dues were $1.20 a year and the first financial report showed a total of $78.05 assets. In 1907 the society voted to purchase a banner "at a cost not to exceed $85.00: and in 1909 they voted that a Requiem High Mass would be offered for every deceased member. In 1911 the society purchased its first record cabinet "at an extremely high cost of $10.50."

The St. Bernard's Society donated $25.00 toward the decoration of the new St. Boniface church and presented Father Bussman with $50.00 on the occasion of his first Mass. Henry Wessel was elected president in 1922 and held the office until 1934. In 1926 the society invited the Catholic Aid Association to hold its convention in Melrose and, when held, it proved to be the largest event ever in the history of Melrose. The following year the members decided *"Es verde beshlossen das vier alle applicationan und druchsache in Deutsch haben vollen"* (we wish to have all application forms and news items printed in the German type). Joseph Sandbrink, served as financial secretary from 1908 until 1933, when he passed to his eternal reward.

The president of the society from 1934 to 1935 was Henry A. Hinnenkamp. In 1934 the members voted to have at every meeting a song and prayer and the meeting ended with the singing of *"Maria Zu Lieben."* Times change and customs change and not too surprisingly the ended society voted by forty-one to eight to have all minutes and correspondence in the English language. The following year, Leo Beste was elected president and since then all meetings are conducted in English. The social, which the society sponsored that year, realized a profit of $13.00 and this was divided between the parish and the society. A quotation from the minutes of 1937 states that, "upon motion made and passed via the black and white ball system, Bernard John Bosel was accepted into our society." During the same year, the society deposited $50.00 in its first savings account and a note in the records stated: "In the sixty years of existence the Association never was in serious trouble and that a sixtieth anniversary drive should be conducted in each subordinate council." In 1940, Herman F. Hinnenkamp was elected a delegate to the national convention and the following year the annual convention was again held in Melrose with a notice that the society had purchased new processional torches at a cost of $26.00. In June the society voted that it would exchange meeting rooms with the women provided the men be given free lunch for one year.

In 1945 Louis Kunkel was elected president, an office he held for five years until he was succeeded by Joseph Mischke. In 1942 the society erected church signs along the highways and it was duly recorded that "this proved to be money very well spent." In 1955 the society celebrated its golden jubliee and two years later the society sponsored a celebration marking the sixty years that Sister Celsa had taught in St. Boniface school. In 1968 the society donated one room for the new hospital and joined in the golden jubilee of the St. Elizabeth's society. In 1960 the society honored the pastor, Father Francis Julig on the silver anniversary of his ordination and the following year assisted in the celebration honoring Henry Soenneker's appointment as bishop of Owensboro. In 1963 the society presented fifty year plaques to thirteen members and in 1971 did the same for six members who had belonged to the society for sixty years. At the present time the society numbers one hundred and eight adults and one hundred and eighty-five juvenile members and has a valuation of $1,119.28.

St. Bernard's sister society is St. Elizabeth's Catholic Aid Association Society which was organized April 6, 1909 by the following twenty charter members: Katherine Bohnen, Katherine Gresser, Anna Kuhlmann, Bernadine Moening, Anna F. Kuhlmann, Mary Niehoff, Elizabeth Stein, Margaret Sandbrink, Caroline Somer, Mary Thelen, Josephine Weisser, Frances Wehlage, Rosalia Ebnet, Anna Wiehoff, Margaret Loscheider, Theresa Walentiny, Susan Bohnen, Agnes Moening, Katherine Wiehoff and Kunigunda Plettle. The first president was Mrs. Anna Kuhlmann and the meetings were held in the church basement after Sunday Mass. After the first year Katherine Bummerim was elected president and served in that capacity for six years. The membership increased considerably during these years and in 1911 the Mass Fund was organized. The next president, who held office for three years, was Mary Weyman. On November 12, 1918 the first member of the society, Bernadine Moening, died. During each of the years from ten to fifteen new members joined the society. In 1921 Mary Thelen was installed as president and held that office for the next decade. Membership continued to grow and meetings were now held in the basement of St. Boniface school, usually ending with a card game and lunch.

Katherine Wessel was elected president in 1931 and was succeeded by Anna Osendorf the following year, when the former moved away from the area. Katherine Wessel was re-instated when she returned in

1934 and remained as president for six years. In 1936 the minutes were written in English for the first time. In 1939 Katherine Schmidt took office as president and in 1942 Anna Haider was elected financial secretary, an office she held for twelve years. The society participated actively in the Catholic Aid convention that was held in Melrose in 1940. Elected in 1943, Mrs. Lucy Zinnel served as president for the following nine years. During the years of World War II the society performed many acts of charity and offered numerous prayers for peace and victory. In 1946 the society numbered one hundred and ninety insurance members and two hundred and six social members and for the first time in its history admitted juvenile members. Mrs. Hilda Rolfzen was elected president in 1952. The society sponsored its first juvenile party under the leadership of Mrs. Rolfzen, Mrs. Paul Olmscheid, vice president; Theresa Meyer, recording secretary; Anna Haider, financial secretary; and Frances Tieman, treasurer. During these years Monsignor Mathias Hoffman was the spiritual director.

The word "charity" has been synonymous with the St. Elizabeth Society ever since its inception. As early as 1912 substantial amounts were given towards decorating the church, the Red Cross and other organizations. Every year a substantial donation was made towards the care of the sanctuary, flowers for the altars and shipping charges resulting from the clothing drives.

In 1959 Mrs. Hilda Rolfzen was again installed as president and remained in that office for ten years. During this year the society celebrated its golden jubilee with five charter members still living, namely, Katherine Wiehoff, Susan Bohnen, Agnes Moening, Katherine Gresser and Kunigunda Plettle. At this time the adult membership was two hundred and ninety-one, juvenile membership was one hundred and twenty-three, social membership was one hundred and ninety-three and Mass Fund membership was two hundred and seventy-three. The following year a standing lunch committee was organized and for the first time door prizes were awarded. In 1962 Mrs. Amanda Welle was elected president and the membership kept growing. In 1965 Mrs. Elsie Hellermann took office as president. During this year the society inaugurated the custom of having a Mass offered once a month for the sick members rather than the sending of get-well cards. Mrs. Ruth Graham was elected president in 1967 and the meetings were again held in the church basement. The hour of recollection was begun during this year preceeding the monthly meeting that fell during the Lenten season. The society has for many years been sponsoring birthday parties for residents of Pine Villa and once a month the ladies help at Pine Villa entertaining the residents.

In 1969 Mrs. Elsie Hellermann again took office as president and the society marked the sixtieth anniversary of its founding with two charter members still living, namely, Mrs. Agnes Moening and Mrs. Kunigunda Plettle. The society continues to grow and attract new members. It continues to carry on a ceaseless round of religious, civic and social activities that foster the welfare of home, church, school and community.

Another one of the older organizations in the community is the Melrose Council 1633, Knights of Columbus. Founded in 1912 the council numbered among its charter members four priests and seventy-one Catholic laymen. The council was formed only thirty years after the first council was established in New Haven, Connecticut. It was one of three located in central Minnesota at that time, the other two being in St. Cloud and Long Prairie. The first grand knight was W. J. Stephens and other initial officers were W. J. Sweeney, deputy grand knight; George Borgmann, chancellor; J. Weiser, lecturer, M. L. Gallagher, recording secretary; W. J. Unger, financial secretary and Monsignor Bernard Richter, chaplain. During these early years the club rooms were located over the Security State Bank for which the council paid $20.00 a month rent.

The council grew rapidly in the following decade so that by the early years of the 1920's it possessed an all-time high of membership of seven hundred men enrolled on its roster. The depression of 1929, combined with the removal of so many men who were employed by the railroad, was a serious blow to the effectiveness of the council and at the same time a serious decline in membership. At this time there was even some talk of dropping the charter temporarily. Several members, however, would not tolerate such an action and they revamped the council, set up council chambers in the theatre building and carried on the council's activities against seemingly insurmountable odds. Father Willenbrink was a great supporter of the Knights of Columbus and his constant appeals for people to rely upon God more than natural resources was a sustaining and supporting element in the survival of the council. By 1935 the council was again on the move and the Zuercher hall was rented as a council chamber. By May, 1943, however, the membership dropped to an all time low of one hundred and sixty-nine, due largely to the fact that so many young men were away serving their country during World War II. Another factor in the decline of membership was the organization of several new councils in the area. During April, 1953 the Albany council was organized and this meant a loss of ninety-five members from the Melrose council. Six years later the Sauk Centre council was formed and this new council also took one hundred and forty-two members from the Melrose unit. Later the formation of the Paynesville and Osakis councils drained membership from the parent unit. Another feature of council growth was the formation of subcouncils, or K.C. Clubs, in several of the surrounding communities, some of which still exist. From its beginning there has always been many members of the fourth degree from the council. The present council membership now stands at five hundred and thirteen with one hundred and twenty-seven of them being insurance members.

Chaplains of the council always exerted a definite influence on the activities of the council. The Melrose council was fortunate throughout its history in having the clergy of the area support and promote its activities. Among the better known chaplains were Monsignor Peter A. Lorsung, Father Edwin Kraemer and Father Francis Julig.

Among those items close to the heart of any good Knight of Columbus is the initiation which certainly deserve to be mentioned. These were held in the basement of St. Boniface school during the early years and many of the older members can still vividly describe the ceremonies held there. In May, 1954 the council moved its club rooms into St. Patrick's hall and began also to hold initiations there. The council held its meetings there until 1970 when the building was razed to make room for the Rose-View Manor housing project. At the present time the council chambers are in the basement of St. Mary's church. Dues were $4.00 for insurance members and $6.00 for others until September, 1952 when they were raised to $7.00 for every member and finally, in 1961, were raised to $10.00. Since 1919 meetings have been held on the second and fourth Tuesdays; before that time there were meetings on Saturday evenings. In 1944 it was decided to make the second meeting of the month a club social. In 1953 W. J. Stephens, the first grand knight died, thus signalling the end of the council's infancy.

The success of any organization is revealed by its activities and their lasting value. Masses were provided for at the death of a member and his immediate family just as the Rosary was recited at the wake of a deceased member and his immediate family. Gregorian Masses were offered for deceased priest-members at the request of the council. Quarterly Communion Sundays followed by breakfast had long been an event held in the various parishes of the area both for members and their families. Requests for donations to seminaries, schools, hospitals, homes for the aged, convents, many civic needs and drives were constantly being made throughout the years. Members of the council actively participated in blood banks and for some time actually operated its own blood bank. The charity done for brother knights cannot be overlooked, both through insurance benefits as well as person-to-person assistance. The only limitation on all these charitable works has been the limited resources available. The council also assisted in sponsoring radio and television programs, especially over KASM radio and KCMT television, in order to assist in the Church's work of teaching all men. Through the per capita assessment the council also participated in the many works of charity, education and public relations carried on by the state and national units.

Working with and for young people has been a constant concern of the council. The Columbian Squires were organized in June, 1937 and were very active for many years. Sometime after their organization they were the state champions in athletic contests with other Squire Circles and at one time took thirteenth place in the nation. Two men who worked actively with the Squires were Father Frank Ebner and Val Marchildon. For many years the club rooms were used for teaching release-time religion classes and the council was asked in 1946 to assist in the grade school catechetical contest staged by the fourth degree knights. The council also supported and assisted with retreats for the high school seniors for many years.

The council also concerned itself with combating indecent literature on numerous occasions. In 1953 it wrote the state's U.S. senators requesting them to support a bill curtailing the sale of pornographic literature. The council distributed to dealers of the area a list of recommended publications from the National Office for Decent Literature and urged the merchants to follow it. In 1949 they sought to obtain a city ordinance to prevent the sale of pornography. A newsletter had been published occasionally in former years but the first regular publication of the *Courier* began in September, 1951. Each member at the present time receives it ten months during the year and it keeps him informed of activities of the council.

As other organizations, so also the council suffered during the war years. Records show that the council set aside $50.00 during World War I to pay the dues of delinquent members in the armed services. In 1917 a $1,000.00 Liberty Bond was purchased to help the war effort and during World War II the minutes show that the council bought a dozen packs of playing cards for the men in the service.

Throughout the years the council carried on an adult education program in religious instruction through films, group discussions, talks by prominent speakers. The Lenten quiz was another training means employed and in 1962 the council took first place in the district competition. As early as 1937 the members of the council engaged in a thorough study and discussion of communism and conditions in Russia. Local pastors and chaplains of the council frequently addressed the members on matters of religious importance.

Recreation and entertainment was also a part of the council's activities. In 1913 a billiard table was purchased for $300.00 to be used by the members in the clubrooms and in the early 1920's joint picnics were held with the Long Prairie council at Lake Osakis. Tom and Mike Gibbons were chairmen of these picnics and in 1924 Mike Gibbons was engaged to give a boxing exhibition at the annual Buttermakers' convention in Melrose. At this time the minutes read, "A boxing bout was put on by the lecturer which was appreciated by all present." The lecturer was Dr. A. P. Limperich. The records of these early days also reveal that a considerable amount was spent on cigars! Skat tournaments were begun in the winter of 1940 and annual dances were sponsored for members and their partners for many years. Every year the council sponsors a picnic for its members and their families. One item of interest under entertainment is the controversy that arose over playing poker. In January, 1919 the council voted that playing poker in the clubrooms be prohibited. Two months later it was again allowed until ten o'clock with a twenty-five cent limit, the poker games being either straight, draw or "spit in the lake." Finally, in September, 1921 at a special meeting of the officers it was decided that no gambling in any form be allowed in the clubrooms and violaters would be subject to expulsion from the order.

The Melrose Council, Knights of Columbus, has aided the work of the Church, the welfare of the community and the material and spiritual good of its members for sixty years. In the course of these years the council has had thirty-five grand knights, three of them serving two terms, namely, W. J. Stephens, Joseph F. Michels and Norbert E. Weiss. The present officers are: Reverend Raymond Lang, chaplain; Ignatius Pung, grand knight; Kenneth Kulzer, deputy grand knight; Paul Wuertz, chancellor; Virgil Silbernick, treasurer; Donald F. Schwegman, advocate; Frank Maleska, warden; Ray Maus, inside guard; Walter Walz, outside guard; James Mlodzik, financial secretary; Joseph W. Beckermann, John E. Speldrich and Raymond Barten, trustees. Members of the council are drawn from the parishes in Melrose, Freeport, Elrosa, Spring Hill, Meire Grove, New Munich, St. Rosa, Sauk Centre, Ward Springs and Greenwald.

CONFRATERNITY OF CHRISTIAN MOTHERS

The Confraternity of Christian Mothers was founded in Lille, France in 1850 and made its entrance into the parishes of the United

States in 1881. At one time there were two Confraternities of Christian Mothers in Melrose; the one of St. Boniface parish was organized in 1892 and the other of St. Patrick's parish in 1913. At the time of the organization there were nineteen women enrolled but no record of their names has come to light. The records of St. Boniface's Christian Mothers were misplaced and cannot be found. The records of the St. Patrick's Christian Mothers are only preserved from 1934. Both groups joined in 1958 to form the Confraternity of Christian Mothers of St. Mary's parish. At the present time the organization has a membership of five hundred and ninety-nine. According to Mrs. Peter Welz, who came to Melrose in 1890, Mrs. Frank Weisser was the first president and Mrs. George Moening, Sr. was the first secretary of the St. Boniface group.

The organization's principle source of income is the dues paid by the members although other income is derived from such projects as card parties, mission groups, bingo, raffles and stands at the annual bazaars. This revenue is used chiefly for the Mass Fund for all deceased members of the society. Other projects the Christian Mothers carried out over the years were supplying flowers for the altars at Christmas and Easter, supplying gifts for the priests, sisters and school children, vestments for the church and cassocks for the servers, household needs for the sisters, cleaning the church, managing the Thanksgiving clothing drive, donations to the missions, hospital, Pine Villa and other religious and civic projects.

The Christian Mothers faced a financial crisis in 1918 when the influenza epidemic severely decimated the organization's ranks. For several years they did not meet at all until the danger of the epidemic passed. The Christian Mothers then re-groupd and all the members were asked to pay one dollar for all past dues. At the present time a special fund is set aside to avoid any further financial crisis.

MELROSE STUDY CLUB

Another organization that marked its golden jubilee last year is the Melrose Study Club, founded on February 16, 1921 at the home of Miss Mary Pfeffer (now Mrs. Joseph Stundebeck). The first officers of the club were Miss Mary Pfeffer, president; Mrs. W. Kay, vice president; Mrs. A. J. Kohls, secretary; and Mrs. Rudolph Spieker, treasurer. A month after its founding the club joined the Federation of Women's Clubs. The club's motto was, "Not how much but how well;" its colors were blue and gold; its aim was service and study. Charter members were: Mmes. William Key, E. Stone, Ray Borgerding, A. J. Kohls,

A. A. Meyer, Jacob Meyer, M. Powell, Rudolph Spieker, Frank Schmidt and Mlles. Anna Meyer, Mary Pfeffer, Helen Beste. The following year Mrs. C. W. Carlson joined the club and was elected reporter, an office she held throughout the existence of the organization.

During the early years the meetings were held each month in the homes of members, then transferred for several years to the music room of the public high school and again in the homes of members. Twelve members formed the club and at one time it reached a membership of twenty-five members but generally varied from twelve to sixteen members. Upon marking its golden anniversary on April 29, 1971 the club came to the end of its existence.

Throughout the years, however, the club performed many services to the community. In 1930 it donated $300.00 for shrubbery for the grounds of the present Junior High School, donated prizes for the garden club, books to the library, trophies for the winners of the high school declamatory contests (the first winner was Bertha Stephens, now Mrs. John Lang), presented a medal each year to the highest ranking student of the junior class. The members of the club also took turns as librarians in both the high school and city library which at that time was located in the high school building.

Although few in numbers the number of activities that the club engaged in were amazing. They worked with the city council in promoting stricter supervision of movies, dances and milk delivery, sponsored pre-natal classes for young married couples and were instrumental in securing the services of a county nurse in the area. They also made capes for the members of the high school band, conducted drives for the Red Cross and sold Christmas seals for many years. In order to carry on these projects the club sponsored card parties and dinners. In the fall of 1924 the club served lunch to the public on the occasion of the opening of the pavement on Main Street and served dinner for the convention of educators held in the city in 1933. At each meeting for two years every member was assessed ten cents to help defray the expenses of the golden anniversary of the Stearns county federation of Women's Clubs. As part of its social activities the club sponsored dinners, picnics, tours, plays and the annual Christmas, St. Patrick's and "dress-up" parties.

At their meetings the members studied a great variety of subjects and frequently invited guest speakers to address them, presented slide shows, movies, tapes and record programs. Members of the club who at one time or another held offices in the county organization were Mmes. A. A. Meyer, H. J. Lippsmeyer, Joseph Stundebeck and Miss Nell Graham.

DAUGHTERS OF ISABELLA - JOAN OF ARC CIRCLE

Another woman's organization founded on June 11, 1933 was the Joan of Arc Circle of the Daughters of Isabella. Charter members were Margaret Orbeck, Frances Blommel, Isabelle Miller, Ella Stephens, Mary Schanhaar, Pauline Koeckler, Agatha Anne O'Donnell, Mary Stundebeck, Eleanor Zachman, Alice Meyer, Evelyn Kohls, Margaret Cruse, Jean Egerman, Nell Graham, Alice Graham, Eva Carpentier, Cecelia Majerus, Etta McCarthy, Katherine Flynn, Frances Kukowski, Cecelia Allen, Luella Bringe, Elisabeth Broker, Alice Burke, Cora Clarey, Helen Hentges, Sarah Hentges, Minnie Kraker, Antoinette Meyer, Eileen Rehkamp, Bertha Stephens, Emma Then, Anna Wampach and Anna Zuercher. The first regent was Evelyn Kohls and the first vice regent was Alice Graham. From the original thirty-four members the organization has grown to include one hundred and forty-three members at the present time.

In the course of the years the circle sponsored such activities as a troop of Ukrainian dancers, a boy's chorus, a glee club composed from its own members, study courses, the Sacred Heart radio programs, silver teas and volunteer service at the hospital and participation in Red Cross drives. One of the largest undertaking by the circle was acting as host to the state convention of the Daughters of Isabella on 27-29 April, 1962. The convention chairlady was Mrs. Victor Messerich and the principal speaker at the banquet was Bishop Peter W. Bartholome of St. Cloud. The theme of the convention was, "So Let Your Light Shine" and commenting upon it Bishop Bartholome said, "Every woman must develop her character and personality to conform to the principles of Christ, and then she will be able to let her light shine upon all around her." Over three hundred delegates from the twenty-three Daughters of Isabella Circles throughout the state were present for the convention.

The newly-organized members of the Joan of Arc Circle Choir first performed at the state convention. Members of the choir were: Carol Dierkhissing, Irene Free, Marge Kennedy, Marie Timp, Geraldine Meyer, Edith Messerich, Teresa Tomsche, Vi Berns, Briget Worms, Rosemary Osendorf and Jenny Toenies.

Throughout the years the circle has contributed financially to numerous religious and civic projects. Within the last fifteen years the circle has contributed over $2,181.00 to such worthwhile projects as Father Flanagan's Boys Town, the Red Cross, Christmas seals, St. Benedict's building fund, the D of I Journalism Scholarship, the Poor Clare sisters, the Sacred Heart program, the new Melrose hospital and the convents of sisters in the area, to name but a few of many donations. Members of the local circle who also served in state offices were Alice Meyer, Mae Lippsmeyer, Florence Kraker, Clara Schulzetenberg, Teresa Tomsche, Marguerite Winter, Irene Free and Mary Ellen Gebeke.

The motto of the Daughters of Isabella is, "Charity - Unity - Friendship." The purpose of the organization is "to unite all Catholic women into a fraternal beneficial social society in order to promote friendships and establish a bond of unity and truth that will be of mutual interest in time of trouble and distress."

AMERICAN LEGION POST 101

In response to the urgent appeal of President Woodrow Wilson, the first contingent of World War I troops departed from Melrose on September 20, 1917. The predominantly German community, determined to demonstrate its loyalty, had staged a two-day patriotic observance to mark the departure. On that occasion the American Legion unofficially began in Melrose. The country called and the response was attended by a comradeship, a common danger, a united effort and the defeat of the enemy. The returning veterans, possessed of similar memories and incidents, maintained the comradeship that only they could understand. Buddies had fallen and the returning veterans grieved for the widows and orphans. They also knew about broken bodies and shattered minds and somehow they instinctively knew, even though the war was over, their service to community, state and nation had only begun.

Twenty-one veterans of the Melrose area met in the old Knights of Columbus clubrooms on August 20, 1919 resolved to apply for a local post charter from the national department of the American Legion. Dues for the group were a mere twenty-five cents a person and qualifications for membership were an honorable discharge preceeded by a minimum of ninety days of service in any of the armed forces of the United States. The charter was granted and the first official meeting was held on September 17, 1919. The first commander was Leo Mahoney, with H. L. Rehkamp, adjutant, and H. C. Stalboerger, treasurer. The first activity was to have the post act as the area agency in processing applications for the state soldiers' bonus.

The present fine facilities in the Melrose recreation and tourist park is the direct result of a 1919 proposal the post made to the city council to purchase the area, previously known as Braun's pasture, for a recreational park. The proposal met with enthusiastic support from the citizens and a bond issue of $5,550.00 was upheld in a public referendum. For many years the members of the post sponsored dances, plays, films and athletic events to finance the purchase of equipment. They also devoted countless hours of manual labor in leveling, seeding and beautifying the area. In 1920 the city council formally dedicated the park to the memory of the World War I veterans and to this day the park is known as the Legion Park.

By 1920 dues were raised to one dollar for the one hundred and twenty-five members who re-elected Leo Mahoney as commander and welcomed the formation of the local American Legion Auxiliary — and then promptly raised the dues to three dollars! With community activities proceeding at full speed the energy of the young veterans was evidenced by their interest in extending and coordinating the work of the Legion throughout central Minnesota. Thus in September, 1921 the post invited representatives from all the posts in Stearns county to assemble in Melrose for the purpose of forming the Stearns County Council of the American Legion. The purpose of the Council, which exists to this day, was, and is to coordinate the activities of the separate posts. A second purpose of the Council was to create a Sixth District level of the American Legion which would in turn call conventions of county and post officers.

The first decade of the local post witnessed a continued growth in membership, self-appointed responsibilities and community dependence upon the energies and civic pride of the Legionnaires. In 1921 these young men formed the first independent basketball team and defeated practically every other team from St. Cloud to Long Prairie. Commander Charles "Brownie" Hoffman's basketball team formed the basis and the post co-sponsored the 1922 community baseball team which was coached by legionnaire Isidore Schultenover (King Dodo). In 1922 four juvenile legion inter-city baseball teams were organized and "Dillo" Hinnenkamp pitched his way to local fame. In 1923 the local post and its auxiliary sponsored dances and parties to raise funds to begin the construction of a community skating rink. By 1925 the post sponsored local dog derbies with Dr. Paul in charge of local eliminations. Five years of local inter-city juvenile baseball blossomed into a county-wide sport and the Legion County Council assumed sponsorship. In 1927 the local "Dutch Hall" viewed its first Legion bowling team. The 1920's inaugurated the traditions of Christmas gifts to disabled veterans and great patriotic parades under the direction of John Meyer. Legion picnics helped to fill the need of community socials and there was always music by the American Legion Flapper Band under the direction of Dr. S. J. Roelike. Home talent shows looked to the Legion for both participation and sponsorship. In 1929 the post staged an event called "Aunt Lucia" with over one hundred actors, singers and dancers. The old Olympic theater was jammed for each performance to watch Tony Raeker in the role of "Peaches Browning." The post rounded out its first ten years of existence by moving out of the old Knights of Columbus clubrooms and into its new home in Zuercher's hall above the drug store. The foundations had been solidly laid.

The depression-ridden dawn of the 1930's momentarily temporized the high-flying and fun-loving posts and its meetings voiced an urgent demand for passage of bonus legislation. A "job for veterans" committee was organized. The depression blues drove the legionnaires from their plush home in the hotel building to the drab but rent-free city hall. In those dry and dusty "thirties" the legion could laugh and help keep the city alive with home talent plays such as "Life Begins at 66 and 3 Months," and musical concerts by Dr. Roelike's Legion Orchestra. By 1935 Fourth of July celebrations were the specialty of the legion committees and although the depression had reduced its membership to fifty-seven, the surviving personnel made up for its dwindling membership with intensified dedication. Hand labor was resumed at the Legion Park and the post created a welfare department to collect and distribute used clothing to needy families. Turkey parties provided food for the poor. Ray Kleber was commander during most of these lean years. With the faint glimmer of prosperity on the horizon, H. C. Stalboerger became post commander and some of the increasing revenue began to trickle to Mayo Hospital in Rochester for the benefit of some needy war veterans as well as aid to the flood victims in Ohio. Even in these hard years the local post had enough surplus funds to build a bath house in the Legion Park for the children of the area. In 1937 the junior baseball team sponsored by the local post received a gift of six bats, six balls and a bat bag from General Mills. Perhaps because of this windfall in equipment the team went on to become district champions that year. Twenty years old in 1939, the post was already a strong, healthy and influential community institution with a proud and meaningful heritage of its own.

The early 1940's was a time for acute national awareness, intense patriotic enterprise and collective bereavement when the dreaded telegrams announced the death or "missing in action" of a loved one. The years were also a time of vivid recollection of a long-ago conflict and an empty sense of helplessness in a world gone mad amid the ugliness of war. Old soldiers recalled their sense of obligation to a new generation of war widows, orphans and the maimed. By 1944 meeting notes were filled with projected plans to welcome the returning soldiers and to present them with an active and vibrant organization ready and willing to promote their welfare and rehabilitation.

In 1946 post commander C. P. Meyer determined that the returning veteran would find room in local business enterprises and thus engineered the purchase of the Louis Kind Bakery building and turned it into a temporary clubroom. Almost immediately plans were initiated to construct new clubrooms on the same site. Membership grew and contributions were eagerly accepted. It soon became apparent, however, that the necessary funds were beyond the post's means and construction was delayed. The following year commander Robert Meyer continued to seek subscriptions and with the help of Father Henry Retzek as post chaplain, yards of bunting were purchased to decorate the church for Memorial Day observances. Raymond Borgerding agreed to tear down the old Legion structure and replace it with a two story building and allow the Legion to use the upper-story rent free for a number of years. The membership agreed to the proposal and the clubrooms were established in their present location in 1950 under the command of Roman Athman. The following year the post first commenced one of its lasting educational programs in Americanism known as Boy's State. The program was promoted by Philip Goerger, Frank Matchinsky and Robert Meyer and has continued uninterrupted to the present day.

In 1952, the local post was host to the Sixth District Convention, the largest single Legion event ever held in Melrose. Chairman of the convention was Walter E. Carlson and post commander was Omer Sieben. It was an exhausting but excitingly successful venture. A year later commander Warren Anderson proved instrumental in starting a local Legion drill team which has performed with distinction at many parades, conventions and local military burials for many years. Commander Frank Matchinsky inaugurated Legion sponsorship of a new Americanism program known as "Boy's County" which has become an annual event. Under the directorship of Commander Matchinsky the post enrolled many Korean War veterans in 1955. The post proudly presented the city with an ice rink warming house for the use of the young of Melrose. In 1956 Commander Roy Meyer presented the city with a Legion-purchased drinking fountain and the following year Commander Gordon Radke recalled the memory of the veterans of the First World War with a gigantic dinner party. The bingo parties inaugurated in 1954 under the command of Robert Sames provided a revenue fund which resulted in the contribution of a thousand dollars to the Melrose hospital in 1959 under the command of Homer Lemm. At this point the post was forty years old and age, responsibility, experience and wise leadership had made it a post of which Melrose can be justly proud.

Commander Ernie Bergeron ushered in a new era in 1960. Recognizing their inestimable and loyal services, Commander Bergeron hosted a memorable past-commanders dinner party in their honor, witnessed by Legion dignitaries from throughout the state and district levels. In 1961 Commander Leo "Bart" Schanhaar promoted the Legion's role in the community through the construction of mobile floats that appeared in almost every parade held in the communities throughout the area. The following year Commander Robert Nelson promoted several trips to the Twins baseball games for the members of the local school patrol, a custom that continued for many years. Commander Eddie Herzog, remembered by many as "Mr. Legionnaire," was literally tireless in his personal membership drives. His loyalty, dedication and contagious enthusiasm won for him the deep admiration of his post and community and also the rare honor of re-election in 1964. One of the prime concerns of Commander Elmer Thielen in 1965 was revitalizing an active interest in the County Council affairs. Commander Mel Bren successfully negotiated a new lease for the post on the present location on Main Street the following year.

In 1967 Commander Clary Raeker and his comrades established a bicycle safety program for Melrose and the neighboring communities. The following year Commander Donald Stalboerger and the post found genuine satisfaction in the rediscovery and restoration of a long-forgotten cemetery in the woods near Saint Rosa and a year later the new commander, Melvin Roehrl and the members of the post recognized a joyous milestone by commemorating the golden jubilee of the American Legion and the local post. Under the direction of a committee consisting of Warren Anderson, John Raeker, Anton Raeker and Ernie Bergeron the occasion was marked with an evening of music, dining, memorials and nostalgia. Ten of the original twenty-five charter members were awarded golden anniversary pins and a roll call of all past commanders was read.

The files of the American Legion Post 101 are filled with cards of gratitude, commendation and appreciation. The walls of the clubrooms are covered with awards for child welfare and Americanism. These are but hints of the fifty-some years of dedication and service to community, state and nation. The preamble to the American Legion begins with these words: "For God and country, we associate ourselves together. . . ." So it was in the beginning and so it will continue to be as long as there is a Melrose, a Minnesota and a United States of America.

AMERICAN LEGION AUXILIARY

The first group of the American Legion Auxiliary met in the home of the elected president, Philomena Kennedy, in 1919. For several years the group met and sewed bandages for the Veterans Association Hospital in Minneapolis. After several years the Auxiliary was disbanded.

The organization was re-grouped on January 2, 1935 with twenty-three charter members. Ann Otte was the first president and held that office for about eight years. The auxiliary group had charge of Memorial Day services and the decorating of the graves on that day. From the inception of the auxiliary to the present day the group has been carrying out this function. At the present time there are eighty-nine members of the auxiliary.

SCHANHAAR VETERANS OF FOREIGN WARS POST 7050

The post, named after the Schanhaar brothers, Edward and Vincent who were both killed in action during World War II, was instituted on April 28, 1946. The first commander was Ted Welz and other officers during the first term were George Winter, senior vice commander; Donald Primus, Jr., vice commander; Joseph Kraker, quartermaster; Urban Schulzetenberg, adjutant; Donald Otte, judge advocate; Warren Winter, chaplain; Dr. L. B. Kuhlmann, surgeon; Leander Korte, Alphonse Thelen and Alcuin Enneking, trustees.

Twenty-nine veterans were the charter members of the post. Throughout the twenty-five years of its life, membership of the post has increased to three hundred and seventy-four members representing Melrose, Freeport, St. Rosa, Albany, Meire Grove, New Munich, Greenwald, Spring Hill, Grey Eagle and some former residents who have moved from the area.

Over the years the community service chairman and the members have sponsored youth groups, children's picnics and a hospital program making available free hospital beds, wheel-chairs and crutches for the needy. In 1950 the post erected a memorial in the city park to commemorate those who had given their lives in the First and Second World Wars. American and papal flags were presented to most of the churches in the area and American flags were purchased and are displayed on Main Street on all civic holidays. In previous years the post sponsored a "Speak Up for Democracy" program over radio station KASM and continues to sponsor the "Voice of Democracy" program in the high school. The post also sponsors a midget baseball team whose members later go on to play in the American Legion baseball league.

In 1971 the post erected the lights in the Legion Park for night-time softball games.

Schanhaar V.F.W. post started very small and was financially as poor as the proverbial church mouse. A club room was opened and a license to sell refreshments to members was obtained. Proceeds were used to improve facilities and sponsor the various programs of the post. A chicken fry is held annually for the benefit of the insurance and special funds and each member is able to carry accident and health insurance at the rate of $1.80 a year.

One member of the post, Donald Otte served as state commander and four members have served as sixth district commanders, namely, Ted Welz, Donald Otte, James Enneking and Herbert Thelen. Welz, Otte and Enneking have also held national positions.

The V.F.W. drill team, commanded by Marson Duerr took first place in state competition in 1953, 1954, 1956, 1958 and 1959. They also performed in numerous parades and local military funerals.

The objectives of the V.F.W. post are fraternal, patriotic, historical and educational. The organization strives to preserve and strengthen comradeship among its members, to assist needy comrades, to perpetuate the memory of the fallen and to assist their widows and orphans. Through an active program the post fosters patriotism and loyalty to the United States. The local post is affiliated with the National Veterans of Foreign Wars Organization, the oldest veterans organization in the country. It was organized in the Philippines after the Spanish American War in 1898. At the present time the post numbers among its membership veterans of the Spanish American War, World War I and II, the Korean conflict and the Vietnam war. The present commander of the post is Herbert Thelen.

AUXILIARY OF SCHANHAAR VETERANS OF FOREIGN WARS POST 7050

Less than a year after the V.F.W. post was organized the Auxiliary of the V.F.W. Schanhaar Post 7050 was organized on March 3, 1947. Beginning with sixty-seven members the auxiliary presently numbers two hundred and thirty-nine members. The first president of the auxiliary was Mrs. August Loehr and the other officers elected for the first time were Mrs. Louis Anderson, senior vice president; Mrs. Jane Braun, junior vice president; Mrs. Mary Kennedy, secretary; Mrs. Erwin Hinnenkamp, treasurer; Mrs. Lawrence Schanhaar, chaplain; Mrs. Albert Hinnenkamp, conductress; Mrs. Julius Otte, guard; Mrs. Ralph Baltes, historian; Mrs. Leo Lemm, patriotic committee; Mrs.

Charles Monroe, musician; Dorothy Wensing, Mrs. John Hinnenkamp, Mrs. Al Rehkamp and Evelyn Schulzetenberg, color bearers; and Mrs. Jake Egermann, Mrs. Theodore Kluempke and Mrs. Anthony Moening, trustees.

Among the activities that the auxiliary has participated in are the presentation of flags to schools, churches and organizations in the area; sponsorship of the essay contest on patriotism in the schools of the area; donation of food baskets to needy families and the presentation of favors to patients in the hospital at Thanksgiving and Christmas. The auxiliary also conducts the annual Poppy Day sales for the veterans' relief fund, the cancer drive and many other drives for worthy causes. In more recent years the members of the auxiliary have sponsored birthday parties for the guests of Pine Villa Nursing Home as well as parties for teen-agers and children of the area.

Members of the auxiliary also engaged in such fund-raising events as bake sales, sewing parties, basket socials, carnivals and dinners for various community events and organizations. From this income they were able to make donations to every project sponsored by veterans through-out the state. They sponsor annual dances at the St. Cloud Veterans Hospital as well as assist the veterans at the hospital in bowling and carnivals. Throughout the years several members of the auxiliary have held state and district offices. In the twenty-five year history of the auxiliary there have been fifteen different presidents with Mrs. Julius Otte serving the most number of years, first from 1951 to 1955 and again from 1965 to 1967. The present president is Mrs. Gordon Peschel.

MELROSE COMMUNITY LIBRARY

In 1942 Stearns county organized a county library service for the areas outside of St. Cloud. This began as a modest endeavor which, in the course of time, expanded into one of the best mobile library services in the state. On March 16, 1948 Mrs. Maurice Hoeschen requested the services of a library station in Melrose. One day less than a month passed when the self-service library station was opened in a space provided by Leo Schanhaar at the Swany White Bakery. Members of the Minerva Study Club made the necessary arrangements for tending to the library and three hundred and fifty books were provided for the first collection. In the first six weeks of its existence there were two hundred and fifty-two books circulated from shelves donated by the Melrose High School.

At the beginning of 1951 the library was moved to the Wellenstein building and again the members of the Minerva Study Club were active in the actual moving as well as initiating a subscription drive for new linoleum and furniture. The city of Melrose paid $10.00 monthly rent and Urban Schulzetenberg donated an oil burner. Two years later the library was moved to its present location in the old village hall and again the Minerva Study Club continued to be library attendants on a volunteer basis. Some of the names of the women who staffed the library during these years were Mmes. H. J. Lippsmeyer, Ignatius Lemm, Ruth Graham, Henry Luetmer, J. H. Studebeck, C. W. Carlson, Rose A. Kramer, K. Tuttle, Maurice Hoeschen, George Freeman, Omer Sieben, Walter Hubbell, Harold Sorkness, Mark McCarthy, L. B. Kuhlmann, F. S. Matchinsky, John L. Meyer, Dewey Stowe, Joseph Angelbeck, H. C. Lamberton, Peter Sorkness, George McGarry, Fred Stockman, U. C. Schlicht, Jean Egerman, Mary Schanhaar, John Lang, A. A. Meyer, Edward Gruenke, Julius J. Otte, A. A. Zachman, Richard Rokus, John Provinzino, Joan Schneeweis and Mlles. Alice Graham, Gertrude Klassen, Helen Beste, Bernadine Tillman, and Rosalyn Moening.

The city fathers took cognizance of the library in 1954 and agreed to pay the library attendant thus allowing the library to open for twelve hours a week. In 1959 and again in 1961 additional book shelving was added and new doors were installed, thanks to funds provided by the State Library Aid Fund. A significant event occured in October, 1969 with the formation of the Great River Regional Library which was designed to serve the city of St. Cloud and the surrounding counties of Benton, Morrison, Wright and Stearns. The following year the Great River Regional Library began to pay all branch library attendants and the number of hours that the library was opened increased to twenty-four hours a week. In 1971 the Melrose library was painted and the floors carpeted, thus providing an attractive library room. During this year the Melrose library contained five thousand nine hundred ten books with numerous encyclopedia and magazine subscriptions.

At the present time Mrs. Dorothy Weber is the library attendant, assisted by Mrs. Nettie Meyer. The volume of books that have been checked out increased from two thousand four hundred and eighty-five in 1948 to eight thousand five hundred seventy-eight in 1971. An all-time high in the number of books in circulation was reached in 1970 with a total of twelve thousand four hundred thirty-nine.

MELROSE HOSPITAL AUXILIARY

On September 13, 1956 an invitation to all the ladies of the Melrose area was issued to attend an organizational meeting of a hospital auxiliary. The meeting was held at the city hall and Mrs. Mary Braegelman acting as temporary chairman presided. There were fifty-seven charter members of the auxiliary which presently numbers three hundred and twenty-nine members. The first officers were Mrs. Urban Schlicht, president; Mrs William Sundell, first vice president; Mrs. Leo Peyton, second vice president; Mrs. Edwin Kuhlmann, secretary; Mrs. Donald Meyer, treasurer; Mrs. Frank Matchinsky, Jr., historian; Mrs. Walter Carlson, publicity; Mrs. B. Fierabend, Mrs. Edward Salzman and Mrs. Ben Loxtercamp, trustees.

One of the most successful projects of the auxiliary was the establishment of nursing school scholarships. Over the years this has helped provide a constant supply of nurses for the hospital and during the past six years the auxiliary has raised $2,750.00 for this cause. The auxiliary has also sponsored the ambulance fund drive, purchased equipment for the hospital, acted as hostesses for open houses and bazaars, assisted in the classes for expectant parents, compiled a cook book, made draperies, furnished one hospital room and bought many pieces of equipment. Excluding the ambulance fund drive the auxiliary has contributed $11,032.12 between the years of 1956 and 1971.

The auxiliary also sponsored the Candy Stripers program that has involved hundreds of high school girls over the years. In the past fifteen years the auxiliary has spent almost $600.00 for uniforms, pins, caps and awards for the Candy Stripers. Girls that have received scholarships to attend schools of nursing include Janet Schmidt, Geraldine Sand, Leah Butkowski, Marlene Fuchs, Maria Billefeld, Katherine Latzka and Caroline Hellman.

The purpose of the auxiliary was clearly defined in its constitution. "The object of this auxiliary," the constitution states, "shall be to cooperate with and to give assistance to the hospital board for the comfort, well-being and care of the patients of the Melrose hospital." Its secondary purpose is to raise funds through various activities for the needs of the hospital as requested and approved by the executive board of the auxiliary.

MELROSE SENIOR CITIZENS

A group that seems to have more fun than most others is, surprisingly, the Melrose Area Senior Citizens. They laugh, dance and sing their way to good physical and emotional health and the organization proves to be truly a celebration of the "golden years" for most of its members.

In October, 1962 four high school teachers and Mrs. Joseph Rolfzen were called to a meeting at the home of Mrs. Joan Schneeweis by Father Henry Lutgen. Nine days later the inaugural meeting was held and by the end of that year there were already one hundred and fifty members of the Melrose Area Senior Citizens club. To be eligible for membership a person had to be at least sixty years "young" and there was to be no dues for the members. When a need arises the hat is passed and needs are immediately fulfilled. The club is completely self-supporting. On November 30, 1962 officers were elected and these were Mrs. Hilda Rolfsen, Mrs. Mary Braegelmann and Benedict Enneking. Father Lutgen served as the group's advisor. The group flourished and included members from Freeport, New Munich, St. Rosa, Meire Grove and Spring Hill. For many years the club honored a king and a queen, the oldest man and woman in the group. In recent years this practice has been discontinued and instead the club honors couples who celebrate their golden wedding anniversaries.

The Melrose Senior Citizens' "Singing Group" has already achieved the status of a local institution and performs at many religious and civic functions. The group entertains the guests of Pine Villa at the monthly birthday parties there and also travel to Albany, Cold Spring, Brooten, Belgrade and St. Cloud to perform similar service at nursing homes. The "Singing Group" is generally accompanied by an impromptu band consisting of a guitar, two violins, harmonicas, an accordian and a mandolin. The musicians have also appeared on KCMT television, at hobby shows throughout the area and as far away as Breckenridge.

The organization also participates in various events in neighboring communities such as the Melrose Harvest Festival, G'Suffa Days in Albany and the centennial celebration in Holdingford. It has also planted flowers and assumed perpetual care of the grotto at St. Mary's church. Each year the group holds an annual picnic and from time to time, such as in 1968 when forty-three members visited the grotto at West Bend, Iowa, it sponsors trips throughout the United States.

This group of "youngsters" generates more enthusiasm among its members than most other organizations in the community. There are always over a hundred members at their monthly meetings and the trite phrase — "a good time was had by all" — proves to be a truism at every one of their gatherings. Frequently they entertain guests from similar clubs in Albany, Paynesville, Richmond, Cold Spring and St. Cloud and are also entertained in return by these groups. The historian of the group recorded an activity of 1971 worthy of more than casual notice in these words:

"One of the highlights of the past years was a picnic held at the lake home of Ben and John Enneking at Birch Lake. Over 300 attended. Two chartered buses were not enough to bring friends from the St. Cloud club.

Some had to come by car. Speed boat riding was the chief enjoyment of the afternoon."

Past presidents of the organization are Mrs. Mary Braegelman, Mrs. Joseph Rolfsen and Ed Olmscheid. Throughout the years two of the lively spark plugs of the group have been Henry Petermeier and Theodore Wessel.

MELROSE LIONS CLUB

This club was organized June 19, 1958 with twenty-five charter members. The first president was Edmund Tieman with Donald Stalboerger as secretary-treasurer. In the last fifteen years the club has grown in number to fifty members. The present president is Lyle Olmscheid. The primary purpose of the Lions Club International is sight conservation. The local club supports the Lions Eye Bank and the Lions Eye Clinic. The biggest project that the club participated in was the construction of the Lions shelter building in the Legion Park which, after its completion, was donated to the city. The present secretary of the organization is Warren E. Anderson.

MELROSE VOLUNTEER FIRE DEPARTMENT

The Melrose Volunteer Fire Department was unofficially organized in 1885, although the first minutes state that the organization held a meeting on May 22, 1894 to form the Hook and Ladder Company. The first officers were Charles Spicer, foreman; B. J. Moritz, first foreman; John Tiedeman, second foreman; Stephen Lay, secretary; John Schoenborn, treasurer. The first organization consisted of sixteen members. Although membership has varied throughout the years, in recent years the average number of members has been thirty.

The fire department is a volunteer organization. A portion of their funds is derived from an annual dance which has been sponsored for many years and is a social highlight of the fall season.

The Melrose Fire Department Relief Association was organized and incorporated in 1898. The first officers were: George J. Wampach, president; Frank Waldorf, vice president; H. F. Loosbroek, secretary; John H. Walz, treasurer. The board of directors were P. M. Koenigs, J. W. Helsper, John Tiedeman, Joseph Primus and John Sauer. The finance committee was Charles Kramer, John Krick, Lambert Sonnen, George L. Sauer and Michael Rauch. Over the years only five men have served as fire chiefs. They were Charles Spicer (1894), J. W. Helsper (1907), Henry Primus (1908), Anthony Primus (1935) and Donald Primus (1952-1972).

Another striking characteristic of the department is the longevity of service rendered by many of its officers. Henry Primus was chief for twenty-seven years; Anthony Primus for seventeen years and Donald Primus for twenty years. Oswald Botz served as secretary for thirty-two years. Present officers are Donald Primus, chief; Walter Williams and Richard Klasen, assistant chiefs; Marson Duerr, president; Thomas Reller, vice president; John H. Goihl, secretary; Melvin Roehrl, treasurer; James Mlodzik, chaplain.

Many of the present member recall that the largest fire in the community occured in 1960 with the holocaust at the Melrose Produce plant. In March, 1970 the department purchased a new fire truck from the Laverne Fire Apparatus Company. This new truck, with two other trucks, provides the community with modern fire-fighting equipment. The fire department also instructs the school children in proper procedures for fire drills. Members also attend many work-shops throughout the year pertaining to safety, first aid and emergency treatment. A fireman is eligible to retire after completing twenty years of service.

Throughout the years organizations which have come and gone give evidence to man's innate desire to join his fellowmen in promoting the common good of the community. No one can actually assess the tremendous good that has been performed for the welfare of church and state in the area of Melrose by the numerous religious, civic and service clubs that have come and gone, and still remain an essential part of the life of the community. Financial reports cannot begin to evaluate the beneficial results of man serving his brother-neighbor. Names of officers who come and go can only reflect the interest and concern of a loyal, dedicated membership. Without the organizations that have been listed here, as well as others that have not even been mentioned here (but will be mentioned elsewhere) Melrose would not have achieved the accomplishments that it now enjoys. It is much more than a matter of "Hail, hail the gang's all here." In most cases, this writer suspects, it was a response recorded in scripture centuries ago, "Speak, Lord, thy servant heareth."

A friendly day in Pete Herges' Bar before the days of prohibition.

In the happy days long before prohibition these local citizens ~~p~~osed in front of Tony Tehrahe's Bar.

~~Be~~low: The Melrose Brewery that ~~wen~~t "broke" because of ~~pr~~ohibition. Bill Hinnenkamp is ~~u~~sed on the beer wagon.

A stock certificate issued by the Schatz-Brau Brewing Company to Herman Hellermann on August 9, 1934 for the produce of a brewery that never opened.

A sample of a ballot distributed throughout Stearns County to show the voters how to vote against the Volsted Act.

Form of County Option Ballot
How to Vote Against County Prohibition

Shall the Sale of Liquor be Prohibited?

Yes	
No	**X**

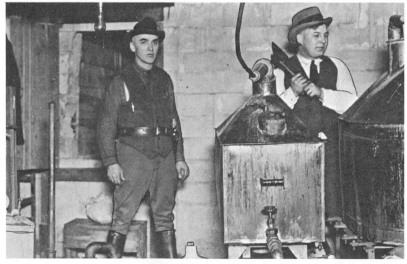

A typical raid, showing federal agents destroying a still in St. Paul in 1925.

Federal agents destroying "moonshine" stored in the Minneapolis court house during the "roaring twenties."

Below: "Stills" confiscated by federal agents are shown here stored in the Minneapolis court house in 1923.

Members of the committee planning "Plowville - U.S.A." are studying the plans for the national event that came to the Melrose area in 1960.

Two prominent speakers at "Plowville - U.S.A." were former governors Elmer Anderson (left) and Harold E. Stassen.

Below: The queen candidates for "Plowville - U.S.A." are shown with Mrs. Joseph Rolfzen (center) and Mr. Norbert Weiss, who acted as chaperones.

Bernard Nietfeld of Greenwald, (right) is congratulated by Herman Imdieke, general chairman of "Plowville - U.S.A." upon winning the state contour plowing championship.

A youngster is amazed by "Mr. Tracto," one of the many exhibits at "Plowville - U.S.A."

A stump-puller, much in use in the early days of the Melrose "bush" was owned by Henry Mueller. Among the group shown above are Henry Mueller, Anna Mueller, Joseph Determan, Agnes Mueller and Henry Kettler, Sr. and Jr.

A steam engine fired with coal or wood used in the area north of Melrose about 1915 was on display during "Plowville - U.S.A."

A typical winter scene in the Melrose area was captured in 1956 on the Joseph Rolfzen farm about five miles north of Melrose.

Sister Celsa, O.S.B., beloved teacher of three generations of children and great woman of God, knew how to win the hearts of children.

Monsignor Matthias Hoffmann, pastor of St. Boniface parish, congratulates Sister Celsa, O.S.B. on her sixtieth year of teaching in Melrose.

Below: The State Catholic Aid Convention, held in Melrose on September 26, 1926, was called, at the time, the largest gathering of people who ever congregated in Melrose.

In 1918 "Loyalty Day" was held in Melrose with the bishop of the diocese and the governor of the state emphasizing in their speeches the "patriotic duty" of every American.

One of the many parades that passed down Main Street, Melrose, was the Fourth of July parade in 1925.

The first Civil Defense Unit of Melrose consisted of the following members: front row left to right: Richard Van Beck, LaVerne Enneking, Eddie Arent, Ervin Althaus; second row, left to right: Ray Althaus, Ted Kramer, Robert Derichs, Kenneth Meyer, and Joseph Meyer.

Melrose Harvest Festival

Friday, Saturday and Sunday
SEPTEMBER 11, 12 and 13

Friday's Program---

AGRICULTURAL ENTRY DAY
$400 IN CASH AWARDS

8 P.M.—

FOOTBALL Game
ALBANY vs. MELROSE
Played on New Athletic Field

Sunday's Program---

Giant Parade 2 p.m.

Many Floats, Bands, Drum & Bugle
Corps. Also 4-H and Farmer Floats!

After Parade—Softball Game
Farmers vs. Melrose Businessmen

Mod. Airplane Demonstration
AT THE LEGION PARK

Nelson Carnival Show
ALL THREE DAYS

Fireworks Display at Legion Park Sun. 8:30 p.m.

Saturday's Program---
KIDDIE PARADE 1 p.m.

Candy Scramble 2 pm
3 Airplanes will drop Bubble Gum,
Suckers, etc., at the Riverside Airport

2:30 pm—Free Softball Game
Two Farm Teams—Winners will play
Melrose Businessmen team on Sunday

8 to 9 p.m.—
AMATEUR PROGRAM

9:30 p.m.—

$200 Cash Drawings
$50 Button prize - 1-$40 - 1-$25
1-$15 - 1-$10 - 12-$5
All the Money will be Given Away
You must be Registered in the Melrose
"Good Will Day" Program

ADDED ATTRACTION
Drum & Bugle Corps, Legion Post 208
of Minneapolis, 45 members with 3
Majorettes, to perform Saturday evening and in the Parade Sunday.

*A typical program for the Melrose Harvest
Festival that has been conducted by the
Chamber of Commerce.*

*Below: The Melrose City Band, conducted
by Dr. Roelkie a generation ago.*

CHAPTER NINE

NEXT DOOR TO MAINSTREET

"There's a fine class of people. I don't like some of these retired farmers who come here to spend their last days— especially the Germans. They hate to pay school-taxes. They hate to spend a cent. But the rest are a fine class of people."

— Sinclair Lewis, *Main Street*

The recorder of life in Gopher Praire which today we know as Sauk Centre was exhibiting a typical prejudice when he had one of his characters exhibit his prejudice of the thrifty and far-sighted German immigrant. Sinclair Lewis was a product of a Yankee culture that has ceased to exist in the western part of Stearns county. The German immigrant, on the other hand, has created a lasting social fabric that is unique in the annals of American life. In 1900 Woodrow Wilson would proclaim that "the history of a nation is only the history of its villages written large." Fifteen years later Edgar Lee Masters would write of the "revolt from the village" in his *Spoon River Anthology*. And in 1922 the critic Robert Littell wrote, "If *Main Street* lives, it will probably be not as a novel but as an incident in American life."

Presidents, authors and critics notwithstanding, the American village and small village has shown throughout the decades of our century a remarkable resiliency. The current trend of moving from metropolis to "hinterurbia" is but one example of many in the ever-recurring American desire to experience the freedom, the leisure and the amenabilities of small town and rural living. Population figures for the city of Melrose also show this national and regional desire. In 1920 the population of Melrose was 2,529 and the population count then nosedived during the following decade — chiefly because of the closing of Great Northern division headquarters — to 1,801 in 1930. Each succeeding decade, however, has witnessed an increase in population from 2,015 in 1940 to 2,106 in 1950 to 2,135 in 1960 to 2,273 in 1970. The snobbery manifested by Carol Kennicott in *Main Street* as well as the "revolt from the village" proclaimed by Edgar Lee Masters were, perhaps, more figments of authors' imagination than a realistic appraisal of the American spirit.

The "fine class of people" that Lewis' character George Edwin Mott described lived not only in Sauk Centre but also next door to Main Street, in Melrose. These were not only the sturdy pioneers who had retired after decades of hard labor on the surrounding farm lands; they were also the railroad workers, the shop-keepers, the stone masons and the traditional "butchers and bakers and candlestick makers." They were a hardy, industrious and thrifty lot. They survived two world wars, the most serious economic depression in the nation's history, the most serious drought the area had ever witnessed and were still able to sing with a smile on their faces, "Yes, We Have No Bananas." They built an economic community, supported religious and civic projects, paid taxes and contributed to worthy causes. No one remembers that they also served as leaders and members in the building of a religious and civic community whose organizations we recounted in the previous chapter.

By the turn of the century their Yankee predecessors had almost completely disappeared from the local scene. They had either not reproduced themselves, or their children whom they generally sent "back East" for an education never returned. Enterprising and ambitious sons of the German immigrants, many of them educated at St. John's University, took over the commercial and business enterprises of the growing city. This practice, begun some seventy years ago, has continued to the present day. It is a story that can best be recalled by the histories of the business establishments of the city.

An additional word – one must not underestimate the two factors which contributed to the building up of the economic community of Melrose. The first was the German Catholic heritage that the immigrants brought with them from the "old country." This was nourished and perpetuated through their religious organizations and chiefly through the influence of the Benedictine monks from nearby St John's Abbey who not only served in many of the parishes of the area but also taught the sons of the immigrants. Significantly the commercial arts department of the college was for many years a most popular and essential part of the education program of many of the pioneer businessmen of Melrose and the area. Secondly, in the thriving, bustling new state of Minnesota there existed an innate desire to "make good" and promote the local enterprise. Songs such as the following were not only sung at the local "bierfest" but were also considered a credo for every aspiring young business-man:

> The Gopher girls are cunning,
> The Gopher girls are shy,
> I'll marry me a Gopher girl
> Or a bachelor I'll die.
> I'll wear a stand-up collar,
> Support a handsome wife,
> And live in Minnesota
> The balance of my life.

In defense of the German immigrant against the flagrant prejudice as manifested in Lewis' *Main Street* one should recall at this point the words penned by Theodore C. Blegen in his book, *Minnesota — A History of a State.* Dr. Blegen writes:

"The Germans were hard-working, systematic farmers who sought out the rich river valleys, notably the Mississippi and the Minnesota. They built flourishing farms. But they spread into many parts of Minnesota, far from these favored valleys. They also went to towns and cities where their skill in trades made itself felt. From early days they were repelled by the Puritanism of New Englanders, and this sentiment, here as in other states, tended to draw many of them away from the Republican party, which in its earlier years was influenced by temperance sympathies. . . The Germans, as farmers, craftsmen, bankers, and business managers, made efficient progress, their traits exhibiting themselves in organizations such as the Turners, in music, a "language press" of their own, schools of their devising, and a way of life that grew out of their heritage but was modified by middle western mores."

MELROSE STATE BANK

The history of the Melrose State Bank *is,* when all is said and done, the economic and commercial history of a community. It is by far the much more important story of people who serve people than one of debits and credits. The history of the Melrose State Bank is essentially a story about people, composed by one of the best-loved citizens of Melrose in recent years, Henry M. Moser. This history of the Melrose State Bank is the result of many hours of painstaking research on the part of Henry Moser who became the cashier of the bank in 1942 and rose to the office of president of the bank in 1969. Henry Moser, as cashier, vice president and president carried throughout thirty years a sense of service to the community that has made the Melrose State Bank one of the most stable and progressive institutions in the economic life of the community.

The Bank of Melrose was organized by Henry Borgerding and H. J. Haskamp in 1885. These gentlemen wielded a great influence over matters of finance throughout Stearns county. They were progressive, energetic and aggressive bankers. In the course of many years of association they amassed a considerable fortune. They continued their banking association until 1907 when they incorporated under the name of the Borgerding State Bank with a capital of $50,000.00.

H. J. Haskamp's mother was a sister of Henry Borgerding. The two bankers assisted the Luckemeyer brothers who came to Melrose from Germany in the late 1890's to open a granite and marble works. Borgerding, Haskamp and the Luckemeyer brothers all came from Damme, Oldenburg, Germany and called themselves *"lands'mann."* The German custom was that *"lands 'mann"* or *"lands 'leute"* would help each other, especially the poorer members. Haskamp was widely known for the personal assistance that he extended to the poor. In the early years of the 1890's Haskamp built a general merchandise store where the Melrose Creamery is now located. Later he converted this into a hotel and apartment house. A few years later he erected the Melrose Hotel and since his wife's maiden name was Edelbrock, he named it the Edelbrock Hotel in her honor. Some years later Haskamp moved to North Dakota where he managed two banks, becoming extremely wealthy. Somehow he was involved in a controversy with the United States government because of taxes and as a result he took citizenship in a South American country. In his later years he developed a nervous condition resulting in his death in a nursing home in California.

Christopher "Stoffel" Borgerding was born December 24, 1798 and his bride, Elizabeth Dalinghaus was born February 13, 1799 in Damme, Oldenberg, Germany. They were married in their native village on February 5, 1828. They had two children, Henry, and a daughter. They were very poor having only one cow and a small piece of rented land outside the village. In those days poor people in Germany were known and registered as *"kleine"* while the wealthy were known as *"grosse."* Christopher Kleine Borgerding. After struggling for survival for twenty-two years in their native village, Christopher and Elizabeth Borgerding harkened to the call of the frontier in America and settled in New Munich. They made their home with their son, Henry, who had already staked his claim in New Munich and was operating an ox cart freighter service between Minneapolis, Fort Abercrombie and Fort Totten in the Dakota territory. In 1866 and 1867 a typhoid fever epidemic swept the New Munich area and Elizabeth Borgerding and a grand-daughter, fourteen year-old Marie, fell victims of the epidemic.

When the Great Northern Railway was extended to Melrose in 1872, Henry Borgerding and his family and his father, Christopher, moved to Melrose. At this point Christopher was awarded the government contract for the freighter service from Melrose to Winnipeg, Canada. Christopher bought cows and heifers in the surrounding area and herded them along with oxen to Winnipeg. This proved to be a profitable business. Christopher, according to local legend, never really cared much about money and therefore was apt to spend it in the company of his closest and nearest friends. He never wore a cap or hat, but only a scarf around his neck in both summer and winter. When it was cold he would wrap the scarf around his head. Summer and winter, Christopher wore wooden shoes. He had a habit of carrying a large piece of cooked bacon in his pocket on which he would nibble when hungry. When there was nothing else to do he would be seen sitting quietly knitting stockings or mittens. He was known as a jolly, kind, good-natured and entertaining man and, in later years when he had become feeble and blind, Christopher was known to have retained his keen mind. He died on May 24, 1898, just seven months short of his hundredth birthday! Christopher Borgerding was buried in St. Mary's cemetery.

Henry Borgerding was born on July 31, 1836 in Damme, Germany. The Borgerding's stopped for some time in Cincinnati before relocating in New Munich. He took a claim in Stearns county at a point where the Soo Line Railroad crosses the Sauk River, southwest of New Munich. According to an early historian the romance of Henry Borgerding is told in these words:

"Henry got busy and built a cabin. A year or so later he went back to Cincinnati, Ohio to visit an old acquaintance. His sister had established her home there. The sister pleaded with Henry not to return to his claim alone. Henry told his sister that he had not seen a young woman whom he cared to have as his life partner. The sister told Henry that his old time sweetheart, Caroline Kersing, had just arrived from Damme, Oldenburg, Germany. He went to see her. They soon got married in St. Joseph's church in Cincinnati, Ohio. Henry was very poor and did not have a suit to wear for the wedding day. A friend let him use his suit for the occasion. Henry had just two dollars in his pocket. So he hired a rig to take his bride for a ride, their wedding trip."

After a short time the newlyweds arrived in St. Paul on a steamboat and then by stage coach to New Munich. Henry was drafted twice during the Civil War but according to the custom of the times bought his way out from military service. In 1874 Henry, his wife and eight children moved to Melrose. His children were John, Christian and Elizabeth (Broker), Anna (Sister Dominica, O.S.B.), Agatha (Hilbert), Mary (Schoener), Mathilda (Rose), and Catherine (Spieker). Henry became an enterprising merchant in Melrose, first by organizing the second general merchandise store in the city and later by taking an interest in th local grain elevator. He formed a partnership with H. F. Loosbrock and the two opened a grocery and dry goods store. Henry Borgerding died June 3, 1909 in Los Angeles. Henry, like his father, is buried in St. Mary's cemetery in Melrose.

John Borgerding, the first son of Henry Borgerding, was a good, kindly family man who married the former Lena Kolb of St. Martin in St. Boniface church, Melrose, on June 9, 1891. The couple was blessed with five sons and two daughters, namely, Norbert, Lenora, Raymond, Leonard, Martha, Wilbert and Aloys. John's father, Henry, had already purchased the Kraker lumberyard. John's keen foresight was that a hardware store was needed in connection with the lumberyard. He built the two-storied building which has been in later years occupied by John Thelen as a liquor store. The building was purchased by the Melrose State Bank and demolished and the lot is now to be used as a drive-in facility for the bank. In 1903 John Borgerding built the Anna Zuercher home presently owned by R. H. Paschke.

After the incorporation of the Borgerding State Bank in 1907 Henry Borgerding was elected president, John was elected vice president and C. C. Schoener, cashier. The position of vice president gave John Borgerding ample time to engage in other businesses. In 1908 and 1909 he started lumberyards and elevators in Elrosa, Greenwald, New Munich, Holdingford, Brooten and Pierz. Since he did not have sufficient funds to engage in these enterprises he borrowed the money from the Borgerding State Bank. Even after the death of his father in 1909 and his election as the president of the bank he continued to expand his interest in lumberyards in Sauk Centre, Browerville, Clarissa and Sebeka. He also purchased an interest in the lumberyard in Albany, and the Kolb lumberyard in Melrose.

All of this demanded capital and some of the directors of the bank were reluctant to approve the amounts of loans that John requested. Accordingly John resigned his presidency and purchased the controlling interest of William J. Bohmer of the First National Bank of Melrose. John changed the name of the bank to the Security State Bank. The following year he contracted tuberculosis and began divesting himself of his commercial interests. He was disposing of many of his commercial interest at the time of his death on April 21, 1919 in Sierra Madra, California. John Borgerding was buried in St. Mary's cemetery, Melrose. His wife, Lena, who would survive him until February 9, 1956, was buried at John's side.

Christian Borgerding, the second son of Henry, would take his father's mantle and become one of the successful bankers of the present generation. He began his business career as assistant cashier in the

Borgerding State Bank and was soon advanced to the position of a director. With his father's advice and blessing he went to Belgrade and there organized the Bank of Belgrade. In 1907 he incorporated the North American State Bank with a capital of $20,000.00. He held the office of president of this bank until his death. Christian was succeeded as president of this bank by his son, Henry Borgerding, the grandson of Henry Borgerding of Melrose.

At the first meeting of the stockholders of the Melrose State Bank, Henry Borgerding was elected president, John Borgerding, vice president and C. C. Schoener, cashier.

Following the death of the elder Henry Borgerding in 1909 the directors and officers were elected annually. Henry was succeeded by his son, John Borgerding, president; Christian Borgerding, vice president; C. C. Schoener, cashier and John L. Meyer, assistant cashier. At this time the board voted and passed that the Borgerding State Bank have no less than five and no more than seven directors and that the annual meeting of the stockholders be held on the first Tuesday after the first Monday in January. These officers held their offices until January 1, 1912 when C. C. Schoener was elected president; Christian Borgerding was elected vice president and H. D. Tembrock, cashier.

The first Call Report of December 3, 1907 listed the resources of the Borgerding State Bank as $441,240.83 of which $36,355.78 was cash on hand and $386,995.79 was on loans and discounts. The transfer of the Great Northern Railroad division to St. Cloud severely affected the banks in Melrose. The Security State Bank was requested to close its doors by the state banking department in 1923 and the same state office ordered the Borgerding State Bank to close its doors on February 21, 1927. Five months later, on July 22 the state banking department allowed the Borgerding State Bank to open its doors for business again. On August 3 the Security State Bank was consolidated with the Borgerding State Bank. At this time the name of the bank was changed to the Melrose State Bank and possessed a capital stock of $25,000. The officers of the consolidated Melrose State Bank were Henry F. Loosbrock, president; John H. Welle, vice president, H. C. Stalboerger, cashier.

Previous to the merger of the two banks, and combined with the transfer of the railroad division, Melrose suffered an economic depression which caused many farmers to lose their land. This was partly due to the land speculation that followed the boom years of the World War I. Many farmers, who owned one farm would mortgage that farm to buy another farm. With the decline in prices for his produce, he would not be able to make payments and subsequently would lose both farms. Before World War I wheat was sold at from eighty cents to a dollar a bushel; during the war wheat was sold for as high as $3.40 a bushel. Before the war oats was sold for twenty-five to thirty-five cents a bushel. During the war oats sold for $1.25 a bushel. By 1923 the price for a bushel of wheat dropped to sixty cents a bushel, oats to thirty cents a bushel and corn to as low as twenty cents a bushel!

Economic conditions did not improve with time. The New York Stock Market crash of October, 1929 brought about the most serious depression the nation and world ever experienced. Milking cows were sold for as little as fifteen dollars. The drought years of the early 1930's intensified the poor economic condition of the area. In 1934, for example, there was very little snow and no rain until the middle of June. Many farmers hauled or drove their cattle as far as two hundred miles to the northern part of the state for pasturing. Other farmers who were not so fortunate were forced to sell their cattle. In these years a good milk cow sold for about fifteen dollars and a good heifer sold for about twelve dollars. Hogs were sold for one or one and a half cents a pound. Eggs sold for five or seven cents a dozen. By 1935, with more soil moisture, the rural economy took an upswing.

During the years of the depression there was little demand for cash money and, accordingly, the banks paid only one percent annually on time certificates. This remained the condition until 1949. From 1949 to 1955 the banks paid two percent annually. By January 1, 1962 the banks paid a four percent interest rate annually. An index of the growing economy was reflected in March, 1966 when the banks paid four and one half percent annually. This increase of interest has steadily climbed since that time due to inflation and a strong demand for capital monies.

Another index of the economic growth of the community is provided by the annual statements published by the Melrose State Bank. The statement issued at the end of 1930 shows a total of resources of $472,084.51. Three years later the resources declined to $346,916.23, an all-time low during the years of the depression, a low that has not again been reached in the history of the Melrose State Bank. Two years later the bank statement registered resources at $433,699.99 indicating not only that the drought years were past but also that the area, the state and the nation was on the road to economic recovery.

During these lean years the banks did not have sufficient cash money to make real estate loans. Consequently insurance companies and federal land banks started to make such loans to farmers. Since prices on the farm products continued to be meager for several years, instead of foreclosing the delinquent loans the insurance companies and land banks allowed farmers an extra year without payments (which these companies were entitled to do under the Foreclosure Act). For this privilege the former would surrender his deed to the land and the insurance company would re-sell the farm again for the amount of the mortgage and past-due interest. Most of these farms were sold for twenty-five to thirty dollars an acre. Towards the end of the 1930's farm prices increased and farmers had enough cash money income to pay for their farms in full. In the Melrose area there were not many mortgage foreclosures. It is safe to say that there were probably no more than five farmers who lost their farms during these years.

Another economic asset to the community was the Clark mill bought by John Hoeschen in 1893. He remodeled the mill so as to be able to furnish electricity to the city, a venture which yielded Hoeschen an income of $800.00 and $900.00 monthly. When Hoeschen moved to Canada to enter the brewery business he sold the mill and electric power business to a St. Cloud firm headed by Enright and Mund. He continued, however, to receive a monthly payment of $800.00 until the city built its own electrical power plant, thus forcing the closure of the mill and its power plant.

During these years C. C. Schoener served as cashier in the bank. He was the son of Casper and Mary (Insebsperger) Schoener, natives of Bavaria, Germany. The couple emigrated to the United States in 1859 and after working on the canals in Ohio for nine years settled in Oak township, near Freeport, in 1868. One of their sons, C. C. Schoener was first employed in the Freeport State Bank. During this time he married Mary Borgerding, daughter of Henry Borgerding and shortly thereafter resigned his position in the Freeport State Bank to become cashier in the Borgerding State Bank in 1907. Two years later, after the death of Henry Borgerding, he was elected president of the corporation with John Borgerding as vice president and John H. Welle as cashier. He remained as president until 1916 when, due to the illness of his wife, the family moved to Los Angeles. At the end of World War I, Mrs. Schoener regained her health and the family returned to St. Cloud where, with George Meinz and three other men, he helped to establish the American National Bank of St. Cloud with a capital investment of $100,000.00.

Another prominent citizen in banking circles was Henry F. Loosbrock who arrived in Melrose in 1891 and was employed by the Borgerding Lumber Company. 1898 Loosbrock erected a grocery store and general merchandise store in partnership with Henry Borgerding on the site that is now occupied by the Athman Furniture Company and the G & R Hardware store. After the death of his first wife Loosbrock married Anna Caspers of Albany in 1898. He proved to be successful in the merchandising business and expanded his interests into the retailing of small grain. In this venture he also succeeded. Active in civic affairs he was one of the first members of the Melrose Fire Department and also served as a member of the Melrose school board for thirty-seven years. He was president of the Security State Bank at the time it merged with the Borgerding State Bank. At the first meeting of the stockholders of the newly-created Melrose State Bank Loosbrock was elected president, a position he held until the time of his death in June, 1948. He performed a great service to the area during the time of the depression. When the state banking department requested that real estate mortgages be charged off he come to the rescue of the bank by buying these mortgages himself. Many times these mortgagors came to him to hand back their real estate mortgages. Henry was lenient and extended the time of payment, giving encouragement and advice to all those in trouble. The mortgagors took courage and eventually paid off the entire mortage. In the words of one who knew him well, Henry Loosbrock "was a truly civic-minded, dedicated church member, successful and popular businessman."

The history of the Melrose State Bank concerns people, both those who served and those who were served by it over the years. Another member of the community closely associated with the bank over the years was Frank Tieman, born in 1872 in Hanover, Germany. With his parents, Henry and Elizabeth Tieman, and five other families he emigrated to the United States at the age of nine and settled near Freeport. Henry Tieman engaged in farming three miles west of Melrose and after some time bought another farm two miles north of the city for his son, Frank. By this time Frank had married Johanna Hinnenkamp, daughter of the pioneer Herman Hinnenkamp, in St. Boniface church. The couple were blessed with four children; Joseph, Andrew, Lawrence and Christ.

An orphan boy, Lawrence Bohnen, lost his mother, Mary Bohnen, when he was only two years old. His father, Thomas Bohnen, a popular and hardworking blacksmith, subsequently remarried. When Lawrence was seven years old he had the added misfortune of his father's death. Since his stepmother did not wish to raise the boy she turned the boy over to the care of Father Willenbring, the pastor of the parish. The pastor, in turn, committed the boy to the care of Mr. and Mrs. Frank Tieman who provided a home and secured an education for the youth. After completing St. Boniface grade school, Lawrence enrolled in the seminary of the Society of the Divine Word and was ordained on August 15, 1944. He is presently a professor in the congregation's seminary at East Troy, Wisconsin.

Frank Tieman was a director of the Security State Bank from June, 1925 until the time of its consolidation with the Borgerding State Bank. At that time he was elected a director of the Melrose State Bank and held this office until his death in 1961. Tieman was a man of exceptional Christian charity. During the hard days of the depression he frequently came to the aid of the bank and also helped make loans under easier terms for those who were financially distressed. He re-vamped loans on many occasions by giving a lower rate of interest and lower monthly payments to many debtors. At times Frank would personally visit some debtor and accept payment on a loan in such produce as grain, poultry or cattle and offering them a higher price for such commodities than the market would allow. He would then credit their loans with a price higher than the market would earn. He would also support the farmer by giving manual aid and supplying moral encouragement. He was, as former associates recall him, "a shrewd, kind collector and hard-working, intelligent man."

Another prominent director of the bank and leading citizen of the community was Dr. A. A. Meyer. In January, 1928 he was the fifth director added to the board of directors. A native of Freeport, he chose to practice medicine in Melrose after completing his education. He was mayor of Melrose for many years, while operating his own hospital in the city. At the annual stockholders' meeting in 1933 he declined re-election due to ill health and, in turn, moved that Joseph A. Meyer, a successful merchant in Melrose, be nominated to succeed him.

In 1936 H. C. Stalboerger was elected as a director to fill the vacancy caused by the resignation of A. L. Sauer. The son of immigrants from Prussia who settled near Spring Hill in 1889, Henry Stalboerger moved to Melrose when his parents retired. He was a member of the first basketball team of Melrose High School. Being of small stature and exceptionally fast, he received the nickname of *Pecco*. Soon after his marriage to Bernadine Schoenberg, the daughter of the successful farmer, Peter Schoenberg, he began his banking career in 1912 as assistant cashier of the Security State Bank. He was soon promoted to cashier and remained with the bank until its consolidation in June, 1928 with the Borgerding State Bank. At the first stockholders' meeting of the Melrose State Bank he was elected cashier. In 1941 upon the death of John H. Welle he was elected vice president and seven years later, upon the death of Henry Loosbrock he was elected president. He held this position until January, 1969 when he retired due to ill health.

Henry M. Moser was employed as cashier in May, 1942. He had been teaching in rural schools near Greenwald and Spring Hill and was previously employed by the Farmers State Bank of Spring Hill for eleven years until it voluntarily liquidated in 1931. In 1962 he was elected vice president and in 1969 president of the Melrose State Bank. In 1950 the bank undertook a thorough repair and remodeling project and built an addition to the west side of the building.

In 1954 Donald L. Stalboerger, the only son of H. C. Stalboerger, was employed as assistant cashier and the following year elected a director of the bank. A graduate of St. Cloud State College he married the former Lorraine Haider and is the father of five daughters. He was elected executive vice president shortly after his father's retirement, an office he held until the present year when he succeeded as president upon the retirement of Henry Moser.

Other employees of the Melrose State Bank at the present time are Donald J. Meyer, cashier; James G. Matchinsky, insurance department and member of the board; Rosalie A. Welle, assistant cashier; Dorothy Funk, Mary Spanier, Irene Meyer and Katherine Bertram, bookkeepers. Donald J. Meyer, also a member of the board of directors, was formerly president of the Meyer Lumber Company before coming to the Melrose State Bank. He is married to the former Geraldine Zachman and the couple has six children. He is also known to be one of the best saxophone players in the area. James "Gary" Matchinsky came to the Melrose State Bank on May 3, 1971. He is married to the former Roselyn Moening and the couple has four children. Before joining the bank he was a salesman employed in the insurance business as a special agent for five years. Rosalie A. Welle has been associated with the bank for many years. She is married to Herbert Welle and is the mother of two daughters and three sons. According to one who knows her well "she is a lovely young lady and has an uncanny ability to work with figures along with an amiable personality to maintain the degree of professional rapport with fellow employees and business acquaintances."

In recent years the Melrose State Bank carried out an extensive remodeling program that was completed in March, 1969. The Meyer Clothing Store building was combined with the bank building and the John Thelen Liquor Store was purchased and demolished to make room for the drive-in window facility. A completely new front was placed on the east side of the bank. On April 11, 1971 the bank suffered a fire but due to the early alarm received at the Melrose Power House and the efficiency of the fire department the fire was checked immediately and kept from spreading and causing serious damage.

As the community grew and prospered so also did the Melrose State Bank. Always conscious of the needs of people, the story of a bank, as the story of every business establishment, is one of people. The local bank, as the local citizens survived the hard days of the depression and drought and lived to see better days. At the present time the resources of the Melrose State Bank total $7,717,496.84. This includes $504,231.65 cash on hand and due from other banks; $1,584,961.02 invested in United States Government bonds and securities; $1,089,288.28 in bonds and securities; $4,369,311.90 in loans and the remainder in furniture, fixtures and other assets. The economic security of the Melrose State Bank is but a reflection of the steadiness and sturdiness of the other business establishments and farmers of the community. It is a tribute to the industry and enterprise of not only men such as Borgerding, Hoeschen, Welle, Stalboerger and Moser but also to the people who made Melrose a distinctive and distinguished community in the state and nation. This chapter would not be complete without a mention of the other business establishments that served the community and area so well in the past and the present.

AL'S RED OWL STORE was founded in 1950 by Al Kociemba who bought the business from the National Tea Company. Previously the store was a part of the Gamble's chain which was bought out by the National Tea Company. This transaction, however, lasted for only a brief period of time. Three years later the store moved to Sames Red and White Store across from the Meyer Lumber Company and in February, 1960 the present Red Owl Super Market was built. By way of coincidence the first year that Al Kociemba operated the store the assistant pastor of St. Boniface church — the present writer — won the drawing for a turkey given away by Kociemba's store. Ten years later, upon the opening of the new Red Owl Store a two hundred pound hog was given as a door prize and won by the sisters of St. Mary's school.

AMERICAN FAMILY INSURANCE COMPANY was begun in 1959 with Daniel Baltes as the local agent. Previously the insurance agency was owned and operated by Joseph Benolken and later by John Nathe before the present agent was appointed. Although the business is operated out of the village of New Munich there are many subscribers in the Melrose area.

ANDERSON FLORIST is located in Sauk Centre and has been serving the Melrose area since 1948, the year that Mr. and Mrs. Alexander "Gus" Anderson opened their shop. Gus and his brother Lyle, who now operates a flower shop in Tucson, Arizona, were educated in the floral business by their father who operated a florist shop in Alexandria for many years. In 1953 Gus became sole owner of the Sauk Centre shop and his brother moved to Tuscon. After renting space in a downtown store for twenty years the Anderson's built a shop of their own in 1968 and have carried on their services there from that time. The business is a family affair with the Anderson's being associated with their sons James, Charles and William. Since Melrose has no florist many of the people of the area rely upon the Anderson Florist for their needs.

ATHMAN FURNITURE COMPANY was purchased by Norbert Athman on September 1, 1956. The store was previously known as Unger Furniture Company and was established by William F. Unger in 1915.

BOHLIG CLEANERS began in 1948 when the Bohlig family purchased the plant and equipment from Howard Greenagle. The business is now owned and operated by Norman M. Bohlig. In 1949 Sylvester Bohlig left the Melrose business and founded Bohlig Cleaners in St. Cloud and some time later Charles Bohlig founded a business in Little Falls. Besides the cleaning firm in Melrose Norman Bohlig also owns and operates a laundry and dry cleaning business in Sauk Centre. Bohlig Cleaners services business establishments and homes in a twenty mile radius of Melrose. The company presently employs seven people.

BUECKERS SANITARY SERVICE, begun in 1956, was an answer to the growing national and regional concern for the ecology. Ervin J. Bueckers started with only two consumers and a car and trailer. From such a modest beginning Bueckers built up a business that presently employs eight people, hauls rubbish for approximately 1800 - 2400 customers in fourteen communities of the area and, as he says, "hopes to succeed in making people happy." The same year he started the Sanitary Service he also began Bueckers Auto-Wrecking Company. He again began modestly; year after year as the number of wrecked cars increased, his business also increased.

CEIL'S CAFE, a popular spot for businessmen as they discuss the issues of the day during the morning coffee break and an even more popular gathering place for high schoolers after the hours of classes, has been operated by Cecelia Frank since 1967. It succeeded Betty's Eat Shop, owned and operated by Mr. and Mrs. Paul Kast. At the present time there are six employees.

CITY MEAT MARKET opened its doors in 1888 by August Sauer, the first butcher in the community. He was succeeded in the business by Henry Wagner, George Maus, Albin Duerr and the present owner, Clarence B. Schwegman who purchased the establishment on October 1, 1964. The shop has developed its own pork sausage which is widely known as Melrose sausage. The firm makes its own baloney and has recently developed a turkey sausage.

CURLY'S BAR has been a landmark in Melrose since 1953. The present owner, Ralph J. Wiehoff, succeeded Edwin Wiehoff, his brother, who then called the establishment Wiehoff's Bar. The first owner was Charles B. Wiehoff and the original bar was located at 111 South Fourth Avenue.

DEL'S CAFE was opened in 1967 by Mrs. Delphine Marty on its present site of 401 East Main Street. The interior was remodeled and new furnishings installed shortly after the opening. It is presently the bus stop for the Greyhound Bus Company.

DUERR INSURANCE AGENCY began operating in 1965 by Marson Duerr with an office located in the former theatre building. Presently he services a large number of subscribers in the Melrose and surrounding areas.

EDDIE'S AUTO AND MACHINE SHOP was purchased in 1927 by Edward Salzmann who continues to be owner and operator of the business. He became a mechanic in 1925, using as a hoist a big tree in his father's yard located on Third Avenue South. That same year the Osendorf brothers built a one hundred by sixty foot garage on the site of the old Tom Bohnen blacksmith shop. They had the Chevrolet agency for the area for two years. Salzmann purchased the garage from the Melrose State Bank in 1927 and held it throughout the years of the economic depression. "It was a tough grind," he recalled, "but I was very careful and held my own." In 1935 he was awarded the Chevrolet agency and held it until 1954. The entire family worked in the business at one time or another, his wife and two daughters acting as bookkeepers over the years and one son as a mechanic. The garage specializes in machine work and "Connie" Salzman specializes in auto body repairing and painting. Three former employees, Raymond and Donald Maus and Gabriel Ramacher now own garages of their own.

ENGELMEYER BULK MILK COMPANY started on December 16, 1957 when Arthur Engelmeyer of St. Rosa purchased a small milk truck from James Gieske for four thousand and five hundred dollars. Beginning with thirteen customers and one truck the company hauled seven thousand pounds of milk a day. Operating chiefly in the northeast section of the area, including Millwood, Krain and Melrose townships, the firm continued to expand. At the present time it employs three drivers of three trucks and services one thousand and one hundred and thirty-seven customers. Over a hundred thousand pounds of milk are delivered every day to the Kraft plant in Melrose.

ERV'S SKELLY STATION has been owned and operated by Leonard E. Walz since 1965. Previously the station was operated as Norb's Texaco Service by Norbert Schlicht.

ESTHER'S BEAUTY SALON is owned and operated by Mrs. Esther Hinnenkamp. The shop is located in the building that was first the village harness shop and later the Hinnenkamp Plumbing Shop. Alma Heinen started a beauty salon here about 1930 which after a short time was sold to Jo Pung who, in turn, sold the shop to Mrs. Charles Froelich in 1934. After a few years the shop was sold again to Adeline Stommes until it was purchased by Mrs. Hinnenkamp in 1942. Over the years many changes have been made in hair stylng. It went from the popular spiral wave to the croquinole and the "cold wave." For many years the comb water style was popular and then the hot iron marcelling. This was followed by the finger wave to the present use of rollers. "Only one person ever fainted," said Mrs. Hinnenkamp, "since I have been working here and that incident occurred in 1971."

G & R HARDWARE is owned and operated by Gordon and Robert Peschel since February, 1965. For twenty-five years before coming to Melrose the brothers had been in the retail hardware business in Grey Eagle. The building's eastern half had been a hardware store operated by Charles Lano and the western half housed Welle Automotive Whole-sale and Supply Company. The brothers renovated the two sections, joined them to form one store and bought out Al Mareck's Gamble's store. Two years later they dropped the Gamble line and joined the Hardware Hank chain. The Peschels also own and operate the self-service laundry.

GARLAND, THE was purchased by Garland Johnson, whose wife was a daughter of the former owners, in 1958. The previous owners were Mr. and Mrs. Alex Hartmann who came to Melrose in 1935 and started a Federated Department Store in a building which had been remodeled after a fire. The Johnsons's continued to operate the store under the original name of "Hartmann's Store" until 1963. In April that year the furnace exploded and completely destroyed the interior of the building. In August the store opened again under the name of "The Garland." At that time the store dropped its line of childrens wear and shortly afterwards also eliminated the men's wear department. At the present time it is a women's clothing shop and fabrics.

GEBEKE SALES AND SERVICE AND TRANSPORT, INC. moved from Sauk Centre to Melrose in September, 1964. The present owner is Edward C. Gebeke. He is known throughout the area as a prominent and generous member of the business community. With a summer residence at Big Birch Lake he is also an ardent sportsman and conservationist, taking an active part in the ecological activities of the Birch Lake Association. One part of the firm serves as a motor truck dealer for International Harvester Company and the other part, Gebeke Transport, Inc. is a transporter of petroleum products within the state of Minnesota and parts of North Dakota. The two businesses presently employ an average of twenty-one employees.

HOMER'S LOUNGE is presently owned by Virgil Metzger. The establishment was started by Homer Lemm in 1952 with the erection of a building that was built by Raymond Borgerding on the site that was previously occupied by a bakery owned by Louis Kind. The building was constructed for the purpose of serving as the clubrooms of the American Legion on the second floor and the ground floor was intended to be used as a dry goods store. The same year the building was built it was used as such with Nick Loscheider operating the dry goods store. Later the ground floor was purchased by Homer Lemm who established a liquor business widely known as "Homer's Lounge." Metzger purchased the business from Homer Lemm in 1963 and has operated it ever since. A native of St. Cloud and a graduate of St. Thomas College, Virgil Metzger was first employed by Westinghouse Electric before moving to Melrose in September, 1963.

At this point it might be well to mention that at one time Melrose had the rather dubious distinction of having twenty-two liquor establishments. Most of them were located on the present South Fourth Avenue East Street which was more popularly known as Whiskey Street. Some of these very popular establishments were owned by Joseph Hilt, Clement Schwegman, Joseph Sandbrink, Jack Meyer, William Vogt, Anthony Terherra, Ben Schultnover, William Unger, Joseph Trisko, Peter Williams, Nicholas Koenig, Henry Schoenborn and the Forty-Nine Bar, the Hinnenkamp and Storman Bar, the Burke and Debloys Bar and the Sauer and Bursch Bar. It might be worthy of note, as will be recounted elsewhere, that Melrose never went thirsty and even during the years of prohibition the thirst never seemed to slacken.

JUNG'S STUDIO began photographic service to the Melrose area in 1954 with the coming of Richard Jung to the community. Previously the studio was owned and operated by Herbert Rydholm whose studio was located in the present Ceil's Cafe building. In 1965 Jung's Studio moved into the new building constructed and owned by LeRoy Meyer.

JACK KRAEMER LUMBER COMPANY, INC. purchased the Meyer Bros. Lumber Company on 1 April, 1967 and operates the lumber yard on the same location. Since purchasing the business the firm has built a new warehouse and sold the old lumber yard known as the Melrose Lumber Yard located near the funeral home. The Meyer brothers previously purchased the lumber company from the Borgerding Lumber Company in 1924. The present manager of the Kraemer Lumber Company is Bernard Bierschbach.

JENNIE "O" FOODS INC., came to Melrose in 1960 succeeding the Marshall Produce Company that operated the plant from 1957 to 1960. Previous to that the plant was operated by the Litchfield Produce Company from 1935 to 1957 which traded in chickens, turkeys but mostly eggs, ice cream and feed. Tragedy struck the plant shortly after the Farmers Produce Company of Willmar, the parent organization, purchased the building and equipment. On 27 October, 1960 one of the most spectacular and devastating fires ever seen in the area struck the western part of the building causing damage estimated at $250,000.00. Fortunately for the economy of Melrose Earl B. Olson, president of the Farmers Produce Company immediately announced that the damaged portion of the building would be re-built and damaged equipment replaced. In less than a year, the following September 19, the plant was opened with the latest and best processing equipment throughout the area.

The firm has been one of the mainstays of the economy of the community, employing over the years as many as two hundred and seventy-five workers. Relations between the company and the employees have continually been cordial and on at least two occasions the employees turned down the formation of a local of the United Packinghouse, Food and Allied Workers AFL-CIO. In 1966 by a vote of one hundred and fourteen to thirty-eight and again, in 1969, by a vote of one hundred and seventeen to forty-four the employees chose to remain independent of the union. Every year the company entertains the employees at a turkey dinner at Thanksgiving, Christmas and when the plant re-opens after an annual shut-down of about two months.

The first general manager was Jack Treloar who after a few months was succeeded by Bacon L. White in July, 1961. In announcing the appointment Earl Olson said, "With Mr. White at the helm of the new Melrose plant, our production should exceed one hundred and twenty-five million pounds of poultry processed in the year 1961." Almost four years later, in April, 1965 Harlan Cohrs was named manager. He previously acted as head of the packaging department and plant superintendent. Under his direction the plant produced over thirty million pounds of turkey.

In 1971 two significant events occurred for the company. The name of the firm was changed from Melrose Produce Company to Jennie "O"

Foods, Inc. and Edward Middendorf was appointed general manager. At the present time the plant processes well over thirty million pounds of turkeys a year. There are approximately two hundred thirty people employed and the weekly payroll exceeds $25,000.00 each week.

Crisis struck the city in 1957 with the closing of the Litchfield Produce Company. The company went into receivership and some one hundred and fifty employees were turned away from work. The local editor sadly noted that "Melrose hasn't had a crisis like this since the Great Northern division left for St. Cloud thirty-five years ago." Immediately the Melrose Chamber of Commerce swung into action and sought other operators who would be able to keep the egg and poultry business in the city. The Melrose Beacon correctly predicted that "it does not seem possible that the plant will remain idle too long."

KRAFT FOODS, a subsidiary of Kraftco Corporation, was established in Melrose in 1943 because of the great number of dairy farms in the area. The Kraftco Corporation was the new name given the National Dairy Products Corporation on 19 April, 1969. For many years the directors and officers of the corporation felt that the previous name no longer described either the scope or type of operation. "Instead of national," one writer observed, "it was now international, and dairy products were only a part of hundreds of items manufactured and marketed by the corporation's divisions, ranging from foods of all descriptions to chemicals and packaging supplies." Kraftco, founded in 1903 by the late James L. Kraft as a cheese company in the course of time expanded its operations into the manufacture of margerines, jellies, citrus products, gravy mixes, salad dressings and dinners. It also expanded its operations to fourteen other countries and distributed products in over a hundred other nations. National Dairy Products Corporation was formed in 1923 through the merger of Hydrox Corporation and the Rieck McJunkin Dairy Company. Kraft joined the corporation in 1930. Corporate sales in 1923 were a little more than thirteen and a half million dollars; in 1968 sales exceeded two billion and four hundred million dollars.

The first manager of the Kraft plant was E. E. Hanson who remained about ten years. He was followed by Gordon Ratke who also was manager about ten years and Robert Nelson who remained about six years. The present manager of Kraft-West is Harold Schueler who came to Melrose in 1962 and the manager of Kraft-East is Charles Lyons who came in 1967 during the planning and construction of the new plant. At the present time there are one hundred and ten employees at Kraft-West and one hundred and sixty-eight at Kraft-East. The daily milk intake exceeds a million pounds. The Kraftsman in

1968 published an extensive article about the Kraft plants in Melrose which is an appendix to this chapter.

KUHLMANN DRUG STORE has been owned and operated by Edwin G. Kuhlmann since 1951, succeeded Fred Zuercher, a life-long druggist in the city. The Rexall store covers a span of seventy-two years in Melrose, having been founded by Zuercher in 1900 and sold to Kuhlmann, the brother of Dr. L. B. Kuhlmann in 1951. Zuercher and his wife, Ann, operated the store until ill health forced him to retire at the age of seventy-eight. On the second story Zuercher operated vaudeville shows for many years and many a local swain courted his favorite girl between the vaudeville show and the drug store. Dr. August Kuhlmann, father of Edwin, suggested that Zuercher start the drug store and after it was opened the doctor located his offices in three rooms on the second floor. All of the Kuhlmann boys worked in the store at one time or another. Edwin married Ruth Kuhl in Minneapolis when he worked at the Veterans Hospital and, since the couple preferred a small town they returned to Melrose to operate the drug store.

LITE-RITE ELECTRIC SERVICE was found in 1946 by R. O. Passi. "I always wanted to go into contracting," the owner stated, "and it seemed natural for me to go into electrical contracting because of my previous experience and schooling." The firm began by building power lines, wiring farms and residences and selling appliances. After some years the company dropped the wiring and appliances division and concentrated on telephone line construction. Subsequently the company dropped the power and telephone line construction and presently is engaged in the construction of power substations, street and highway lighting and traffic signal systems.

LIZOTTE'S BARBER SHOP bought the barber shop on "Whiskey Street" in 1948 where he maintained his establishment for nine years. The other barber in the city, Edward Gruenke was located in the present Lizotte's barber shop and sold his shop to Rene Lizotte in October, 1957. Ever since Lizotte has maintained his operation in that location.

LOEHR'S SKOGMO STORE has been owned and operated since 1961 by August and Sophia Loehr. Prior to 1951 the Gamble Skogmo, Inc. operated businesses in four adjoining buildings in the present block, an auto service store, a clothing, hardware and grocery store. Throughout the years these businesses were sold to various individuals and in 1951 Richard and Ann Lundquist of Walker purchased the clothing store and operated it until 1958 when they sold it to Mr. and Mrs. G.

Hummel of Spencer, Iowa. The Hummel's operated the store for three years until they closed out in March, 1961. On 1 December that year August and Sophia Loehr opened a general family clothing store and have operated it to the present time.

LOXTERCAMP OIL COMPANY succeeded the Melrose Oil Company owned by Casper Maus, when Henry Loxtercamp purchased the business in 1935. He operated the bulk plant located close to the Great Northern rail tracks on the east side of the city and sold Texaco products to farmers in the Greenwald, Spring Hill, Meire Grove, Elrosa, St. Rosa and Melrose areas. After thirty years he sold the company to Skelly Oil Company and his twin sons, Ronald and Donald are presently employed by the firm. In the early years it was an extremely arduous job since the fuel and gas was hauled in five gallon pails since the trucks were not equipped with an automatic pumping system. This was extremely difficult during winter snowstorms. "I will never forget," Loxtercamp said, "the Armistice Day blizzard of 1940." Throughout the years the company employed eight men who were Walter Kuefler, Joseph Faber, Joseph Loxtercamp, Albert Marthaler, Hubert Welle, Norbert Schlicht, Berthold Thoenes and Lawrence Budde.

Henry Loxtercamp was also the dealer for Plymouth and DeSoto cars and was the owner of the Loxtercamp Motor Company. In 1945 he built a new showroom and garage. Three men, Olaf Becker, Frank Zitur and Louis Rau, were employed there. In 1959 he sold the garage and dealership to Raymond and Donald Maus and it is now called the Maus Motor Company. For thirty years he also was the head of the Loxtercamp Tire Company. He was the dealer in Firestone Tires and both sold and recapped these tires. He was presented with a gold watch by the president of Firestone Tire Company upon completing twenty-five years in the dealership. He is known throughout the area as one of Melrose's most aggressive and friendliest and highly respected businessmen.

MELROSE CATHOLIC DEANERY CREDIT UNION was begun in 1939 by seven members of St. Boniface parish and originally called the Melrose Catholic Parish Credit Union. Within a year the organization had grown to include fifty-two members with total assets of four hundred and fifty-five dollars. After thirty years the name of the organization was changed to the Melrose Catholic Deanery Credit Union in order to include members from the parishes of St. Rosa, Freeport, New Munich, Greenwald, Meire Grove and Spring Hill. At the present time the organization numbers over one thousand and one hundred members and has assets over eight hundred thousand dollars.

MELROSE CIGAR FACTORY was founded in 1901 by J. A. Tise in a frame building that was located on the site of the old Ford garage. The second location was the second story of a building that once stood where the Kramer Five and Dime store stands and the third location was another frame building on the spot now occupied by Meyer and Meyer Law Offices. The fourth and final location was in the building now occupied by Tise's Bar.

In the early days the cigars were sold and delivered by horse and buggy. Later, as travel became easier, the cigars were sold throughout an area extending from Detroit Lakes to New Ulm. The tobacco for the cigars was obtained from the southern states as only a small amount was grown locally. The outside wrappers were imported from Cuba and Sumatra.

In an interview taken with Charles Pallansch, a foreman of the factory, by Lawrence Tise, grandson of J. A. Tise, the factory made about twenty different brands of cigars which sold for five and ten cents. The top sellers were "Tom Stone," "Sam Richardson," and "Night Cap." The tobacco arrived at the Melrose factory in large wooden boxes approximately four feet by four feet by three feet, each box containing from two hundred and fifty to three hundred pounds. The operation started with a procedure called "casing." The tobacco was removed from large boxes in "hanks" and pulled through a water bath and put in special boxes which would retain the moisture. The next morning the operation called "stripping" began by removing the large vein running down the center of the leaf. These leaves were then placed on drying racks which were raised by pulleys to the ceiling eventually to become the filler.

The binder leaf and especially the wrapper leaf had to be treated very carefully because of the delicate nature of these fine tobaccos. The final wrapper leaf was tissue-paper thin and was handled most carefully so as not to tear it. After "stripping" the binder and wrapper leaf were put in zinc lined boxes and cured with controlled humidity so that they could be properly worked. The processes were now completed and everything was ready for the cigar maker. He would take binder material, add the proper amount of filler, roll the cigar in a rough shape and place it in a mold. This mold held twenty cigars and gave the cigar the uniform shape he desired for the type of cigar he wanted to form. The forms today, such as Panetela and Perfecto, were the same as in these early years.

After the cigar was molded it was placed on the delicate wrapper material which had been cut according to pattern by the cigar maker and rolled on a bias from the rear to the tip. The wrapper was sealed at the tip with "tragacanth," a gum obtained from herbs grown in eastern European and Asiatic areas. The cigar was clipped to square off the end that was to be lit and was ready for banding and packing in boxes. Cigar boxes have not changed much in basic shape over the years. The major difference is the boxes are now of pressed card board instead of the wood boxes used fifty years ago. The cigars were packed in box sizes of ten, twenty-five, fifty and a hundred; the number was somewhat dictated by the tax on cigars according to their sizes. Banding each cigar with its brand name and packing were done by hand.

A proficient cigar maker could make from three hundred to three hundred and fifty cigars a day. At the height of the factory's production there were approximately thirty employees of whom ten were cigar makers who were paid on a piece-work basis. Two factors contributed to the closing of the factory in the late 1920's. After the first World War cigarettes became more popular and about the same time the larger cigar factories began production by machine.

MELROSE COOPERATIVE CREAMERY ASSOCIATION has a history that reflects the progress of the dairy industry in Stearns county. It was organized in the fall of 1905 after a good number of farmers in the area realized the need to have their own marketing association. In order to secure working capital shares of stock in the association were sold throughout the area. The first creamery was a wood-frame building located on the north side of the Sauk River, on property now owned by Walter Tieman. The first officers of the organization were Matthew Thielen, president; Anthony Zirbes, secretary; Herman Thielen, treasurer; and Peter Baltes was the first buttermaker. In these early years there was no mechanical refrigeration and thus ice, usually taken from the Sauk River, was used for cooling cream and cooling the butter cooler. At this time, also, cordwood was also used for fuel. Later coal was used for fuel and in more recent years fuel oil has been employed.

Stearns county and the Melrose area has been and continues to be one of the most productive dairy sections of the country. In 1887 the county had only three creameries, namely, Kemmel and Son, Woods and Buck in Sauk Centre and J. Savercool in St. Cloud. Three cheese factories were also operated in Sauk Centre by S. Beigelman, W. R. James and Johnson and Stark. Progress was slow in these early days and we find that by 1894 there were only four creameries with but 358 patrons located in the Avon, Richmond, Sauk Centre and Melrose areas. Within two years, however, the number of creameries increased to fourteen with one thousand four hundred and sixty-five patrons. The rapid growth of the industry is reflected in the figures given for 1913 when the county boasted seventeen cooperative, fourteen independent and two central creameries with a total of two thousand, eight hundred and twenty-four patrons. In that same year the county numbered twenty-eight thousand, five hundred and sixteen cows, produced over fifteen million pounds of cream and over five million pounds of butter. These figures made Stearns County the largest producer of dairy products in the state, a title maintained for many years and rivaled by few, if any other county, today. It might also be noted that in the early years of the century Minnesota, with six hundred and fourteen cooperative creameries possessed nearly one-third of all cooperatives in the United States. The annual volume of business in 1913 exceeded twenty-one and a half million dollars in the state of Minnesota with over forty-two per cent of the farmers being patrons of cooperative creameries.

In 1920 the stockholders saw a need for a new and bigger building and during that year the present creamery building was constructed. Much of the labor in the construction of this building was donated by farmers of the community. About this time Theodore Moening started a can-milk route and began delivering a good deal of milk to the creamery with his truck. He was, perhaps the predecessor and prototype of the many milk-haulers on the highways and byways that we see today. In December, 1959 a new method of handling milk was inaugurated by Albert Niehaus with the installation of a bulk farm tank for milk storage and cooling. Henry J. Dickhaus started to pick up milk with a pick-up truck about this time and as the years passed more and more tanks have come into use. At the present time more than half of all the milk received at the creamery comes from bulk tanks. On January 1, 1970 a Grade A milk operation was initiated thus creating a new market and adding income to the patrons for their milk.

The board of directors are Herman Hellermann, Jr., president; Richard Hiltner, vice president; Urban Primus, secretary; Albert Niehaus, treasurer; Albert Welters, Albert Oevermann and Joseph Feldewerd, directors. At the present time there are five employees and Marvin Shequen, Jr. is the manager. During the past few years production has been stable, averaging about eighteen million pounds of whole milk annually.

MELROSE FEED MILL was opened in 1959 to provide a service to the farmers of the area. It was built in that year by H. H. Rothfork and Frank Maleska and is presently a privately owned company.

MELROSE MOTOR COMPANY, presently operated by LeRoy Tieman, was previously owned and operated by Casper Maus, John Enneking and Alcuin Kraemer before it was purchased by Alcuin Kraemer from John Enneking on January 1, 1957. Before moving to its present location on May 1, 1969 it was located at the corner of Main Street and Fifth Avenue East. The present owner purchased the company from Alcuin Kraemer on August 1, 1957 and, starting with three employees presently has nine people on the payroll. After purchasing the business LeRoy Tieman moved to a new location and into a new building at 423 South Second Avenue East.

MELROSE TV AND MARINE COMPANY is presently operated by Richard Van Beck. Formerly owned by Joseph Lindy the firm was first called Lindy's TV until he sold it to David Loxtercamp and Richard Van Beck in June, 1958. It was then called Melrose Radio and TV until Van Beck became the sole owner in 1964 and called the firm Melrose TV and Marine. The business was formerly located in the building where the Laundromat is now located. A new building where the firm is now located was built at 201 E. Main Street in 1959. The firm sells and services Zenith and RCA radios, stereo equipment and color television sets since 1960. In 1965 the company became the local distributor for Johnson outboard motors and snowmobiles. In 1967 an extension of twenty by fifty feet was added to the original building of twenty-four by ninety feet and in 1971 a warehouse of forty by one hundred and fifteen feet was built. The firm now employs three full-time people besides the present owner.

MELROSE IMPLEMENT COMPANY was started at the urging of the Melrose Chamber of Commerce which felt that the city needed another implement business. Accordingly, in 1945 Ben Loxtercamp founded the company and remains a partner in the business. Other partners are Alphonse Loecken, Edmund Wenker and Clarence Wenker. At the present time the company employs five full-time people, including the present three active partners.

MELROSE TELEPHONE COMPANY, ever since its beginning in the early 1890's, has always been locally owned. It was organized by a group of local business and professional men with the office located on the second story of the *Melrose Beacon* printing shop. The first manager was Mrs. Mary Zuercher, wife of Dr. Zuercher, and the first operator was her daughter, Mary Zuercher Fitzgerald. The office was later moved to a small building on West Main Street, near the present telephone building. It was purchased by William Balder about 1910 who operated it for a number of years. In turn he sold it to the Kraker brothers who incorporated the company on March 17, 1916 under the names of Anthony, Joseph and A. Kraker.

Mrs. Thomas Arvig and her son, Leonard "Tom" Arvig, purchased the utility in June, 1928. They operated the firm as partners until Mrs.

Arvig's death in 1965. The Melrose Telephone Company merged with some of the smaller companies of the surrounding communities in the course of the years. It grew from two hundred and two telephones in 1928 to over six thousand and one hundred stations at the present time. The surrounding communities served by the Company are Eden Valley, Grey Eagle, Greenwald, Kimball, Richmond, St. Martin, Watkins, Meire Grove, Spring Hill, Burtrum, Manannah, Kingston, Pearl Lake, New Munich, Roscoe, Farming and St. Nicholas.

Royale B. Arvig, "Tom's" brother, received his training in Melrose and founded the East-Ottertail Telephone Company, serving eleven thousand stations, with headquarters in Perham. Another brother, Carroll, was also trained by the Melrose Company and in 1948 purchased the Twin Valley-Ulen Telephone Company, with headquarters in Twin Valley. Carroll died in 1962 and the business is still owned by his widow, the former Bernice Tembrock of Melrose.

MELROSE THEATRE opened on September 19, 1920 under the name of the "Nickelodeon and Opera House." It featured live stage shows complete with orchestra as well as silent flicks with piano background. It was during these years the entertainment hub of the community and many future marriages were initiated on this spot. The vaudeville acts of "Olson and Johnson" were the biggest drawing cards until the advent of the talkies. The first talkie shown in Melrose, in 1928, was Al Jolson's "Jazz Singer."

With the economic crash of 1929 the Melrose theatre fell upon hard times. Within eight years its ownership passed through six different hands. In 1937 George O'Brien leased the theatre and the following year became its owner. From then until 1952 the theatre was one of the principal sources of entertainment in the Melrose community. The principal reason for its decline was the coming of television to Melrose in 1952; however, O'Brien kept the theatre in operation until his death in February 1966. The building is now used by two commercial businesses and a warehouse storage by two others.

The longest running picture in the Melrose theatre was a Lum and Abner movie in 1941 after the great blizzard that prevented any means of transportation. Lum and Abner was shown for nine consecutive days! The most popular movie with adults was "Gone with the Wind," shown on five different occasions over a period of twenty-five years. The most popular movie with the children was Walt Disney's "Snow White and the Seven Dwarfs."

MIDWAY TURKEYS, INC. started in 1956 as an independent company. A group of local businessmen pooled their financial resources with the purpose of supplying turkeys for the local processing plant, Litchfield Produce, in the hope of increasing employment in the plant. In the view of these men it seemed like a good means of making more extensive use of the sandy, largely non-productive land located along the Sauk river. By raising turkeys this group of businessmen felt that the economy of the entire area would benefit from the operation.

In 1971 the firm employed three full time employees and several others on a part-time basis. During the same year one hundred and twenty-five thousands turkeys were raised, using over three thousand tons of feed. Melrose has become one of the most intensive turkey growing areas in the state which, in turn, is the leading state in the nation as far as the number of turkeys raised. The corporation is one of the pioneers in the turkey industry in this area. The name of the firm was chosen because the farm is located on the Sauk river midway between Melrose and New Munich. The present managers of the firm are Mr. and Mrs. Erwin Feldewerd.

MINNESOTA ALL-CHANNEL CABLEVISION, INC. opened its offices in Sauk Centre in 1967 as a subsidiary of Telesis Corporation of Evansville, Indiana with Joseph W. Engle acting as assistant manager and technician. The purpose of the company is to provide more channels and better reception of television viewing to the people of the area. At the present time there are two people employed in the Melrose area for this corporation.

MINNESOTA NATURAL GAS COMPANY was organized in Melrose in 1967. Founded in 1934 to distribute natural gas in the towns of New Prague, Montgomery, LeCenter, LeSueur and St. Peter its original name was the Minnesota Valley Natural Gas Company. At the end of the first year there were forty-five miles of mains serving three hundred customers and a property investment of $150,000.00. By 1941 the company extended its services to eleven towns in the Minnesota valley area and owned one hundred and seventy-three miles of mains serving six thousand and four hundred customers and a property investment of one million dollars. Since 1954 the company has expanded into western and north central Minnesota serving fifty-eight communities. In more recent years the Brainerd, Willmar and Alexandria extensions were made.

The company serves four major types of consumers who are either home customers, retailers, institutions such as schools and hospitals and industries. At the present time the company's property investment is thirty-five million dollars, with over one thousand and eight hundred shareholders, more than sixty-three thousand customers and over two thousand one hundred miles of pipelines. The natural gas industry is the sixth largest in the country in terms of plant investment. There are over eight hundred thousands miles of mains in the country which, by comparison, is three times the average distance of the moon from the earth.

Sales manager of the Melrose office is Leo Kummet and he is assisted by two servicemen and a secretary. The office has six hundred and fifty customers in the Melrose, Albany and Freeport areas.

MUNSON FEED, INC. was founded as an independent business by Eddie Munson in 1946. After the death of Eddie Munson the business was bought by Peter F. Terres who previously was a salesman for twenty-one years. Terres managed the company one year before Munson's death. At the present time the company employs four people full time and several part-time helpers.

OAK GROVE DAIRY was founded in 1959 by Thomas Borgerding. The firm succeeded a milk route conducted by Jerry Williams who became its manager after Norbert Hiltner sold it. At first Hiltner bottled the milk and delivered it house to house. After the state legislature passed a law that all milk had to be pasteurized the paper carton came into use and replaced the bottle. About this time Hiltner started to buy milk already processed at the Oak Grove Dairy in Norwood. The present owner of the dairy continues to purchase his products from the Oak Grove Dairy in Norwood and resells them to stores and homes throughout the area.

ROSE TERRACE PARK AND SALES received its license in 1968 and began as a trailer home park by Herbert Klein. His parents, Mr. and Mrs. John Klein, operated a farm on the present location and conducted a milk route in the city. When pasteurization of milk became a law they sold the milk route. In 1965 Herbert Klein sold most of the property of the farm because of the high rate of taxes and entered into the mobile home park and sales business. In 1967 he started with the construction of fifteen lots and a public coin-operated laundry. In the following three years additions were made, the first year thirteen more lots, the second year eight and the fourth year, 1971, thirteen more lots were added and the streets were blacktopped. At the present time there are forty-nine lots, a public coin-operated laundry and a showroom for mobile home sales.

SCHAD FUNERAL HOME is operated by Bernard Schad who purchased the business in October, 1966. Previously the funeral director was Elmer Schoenecker who purchased the establishment from Harry

Meyer upon the latter's death in 1943. The funeral home has been located on its present site for many years. About 1957 an addition to the home was built and in 1970 property adjacent to the building was purchased for parking space. The funeral director has always played a prominent role in the life of the community and area. Besides performing a never ending corporal work of mercy in helping to bury the dead he is also expected to fulfill many other civic and religious obligations. Throughout the years the funeral director was always a respected and active member of the community.

SINCLAIR FREEWAY STATION presently under the management of Marson Duerr and Tom Reller was built in 1970 shortly after Interstate # I-94 was opened. It presently has seven people on the payroll.

ST. ROSA RESORT located eleven miles northeast of Melrose and two miles north of St. Rosa, is one of the few resorts on Big Birch lake. It was previously known as the Twin B Resort which was in a deteriorated condition and had ceased operations at the time Mr. and Mrs. Edward J. Worms of New Munich purchased the property. They immediately undertook an extensive renovation and repair operation and changed its name to the St. Rosa Resort. It features seven housekeeping cabins and offers many recreational facilities. Since the resort has started it has entertained tourists from every state in the union and some foreign countries.

STEARNS COOPERATIVE ELECTRIC ASSOCIATION was founded in 1936 as a result of the Roosevelt's Rural Electrification Administration Act passed in 1935. The association was established with the purpose of providing central station electrical power to people living in the rural areas of Stearns, Todd and Morrison counties. The person who spearheaded the movement was E. D. Lenzmeier, then the county agent of Stearns county. He spoke at many meetings throughout the area explaining the purpose of the act and convincing the people of the area of its value. The first general meeting was held in the city hall of Melrose on November 20, 1936 with about three hundred people in attendance. At this meeting the following men were elected to the board of directors: Bernard J. Brinkman, Henry Braun, John F. Ceynar, George Determan, Conrad Ficker, Herman G. Imdieke, J. M. Mill and Anton Ruf.

Melrose, at this time, was designated as the headquarters of the new association, both because it was centrally located and it already had a power plant from which power could be purchased. The following year the association applied for a loan from the R.E.A. for the purpose of constructing one hundred and thirty-eight miles of power lines. The loan was approved and by the following August the first member consumer was receiving service. At the present time the association serves nine thousand and eight hundred customers with two thousand and six hundred miles of line.

The first offices of the association were located in the city hall. In 1950 new headquarters were constructed on Riverside Drive and twenty years later a larger and more impressive plant was built on East Kraft Drive. The present general manager is B. W. Feierabend and the board of directors are: Joseph Kluempke, president; Al Riesner, vice president; Monroe Sletta, secretary-treasurer and Paul Bentfield, Edward Stalboerger, Chester Sanderson, Ervin Stommes and Joseph Fleischhacker, directors.

The success of organizing the cooperative cannot be credited to any one person or group. The untiring efforts of many rural people working together to start the flow of electricity in their homes and farms was the key to success. Without compensation many people traveled throughout the country-side talking to their neighbors and explaining the advantages of electricity. In some areas there was resistance to the program because people did not fully understand it; only through the efforts of neighbor talking with neighbor did the R.E.A. become a success. As a result of this neighbor-to-neighbor program the rural areas of Stearns, Todd and Morrison counties enjoy the benefits of electricity.

STOERMANN METAL FABRICATORS was purchased in 1970 by the present owner, LeRoy Stoermann, from Jerry Notch. The welding shop began in Melrose when Joseph Juen moved his business to Melrose in 1958. During the past year the firm used over seventy-five tons of iron. It makes hand railings, sanitary garbage containers, docks, boat lifts and does custom welding in homes and on the farms of the surrounding area.

STA-SO-SOFT INC. opened its doors in 1961 under the leadership of Norbert Herzog as an independent water treatment company. One of the stockholders in the corporation, Wilfred Finken was named manager and another stockholder, Florence Buttweiler was appointed secretary. In the course of years the company grew to such an extent that in 1968 it was able to purchase the Culligan Water Treatment Company at Sauk Centre, an international water treatment company with franchise dealers throughout the United States, Canada and twenty-three foreign countries. The company not only added its technical knowledge to solving many of the water problems of households and business establishments of the area but also engaged in many projects for improving the ecological balance of the area. At the present time the company employes eight people who perform services to over three thousand customers in the western part of Stearns county and a third part of Todd county.

SUNSET BEACH RESORT, one of the few resorts on the Birch Lakes, was begun in 1910 by John Buckley, Sr. John Buckley, Jr. inherited the resort property and operated the business until 1959. The resort originally catered to people from Chicago who arrived by train at Freeport and were taken on a trail that ended at the resort in horses and buggies. Many people of the area recall that there was a dance hall on the property during the prohibition years and some of these people held their wedding dance there and spent their honeymoon at the resort. The resort was purchased by Elmer J. Schieman in the autumn of 1959. In 1972 the resort will change from weekly to seasonal rentals.

John Buckley, Sr. started the resort upon the advice of his doctor who told him unless he moved from the city his life would be shortened. His settling in the country enabled him to live twenty more years of a good life.

SWANY WHITE BAKERY was started by Lawrence Schanhaar in 1923. He sold his farm near Princeton and moved to Melrose in order that his children might enjoy the advantages of a parochial school education. He was persuaded to do this by Father Joseph Willenbrink who, at the time, was pastor of the Catholic church in Princeton and later became pastor of St. Boniface church in Melrose. Schanhaar started his bakery in what is now the Welz Grocery building. Since he had no previous experience in the trade he would hire a baker for a month or two and learn the trade from one or the other and then proceeded on his own. His bakery, known as the Electric Maid Bakery, was operated by Schanhaar until 1927 when he entered into the shoe repair business. Two years later he sold the shoe shop and moved to a farm near Breckenridge. In 1929 the Freeport Roller Mills, owned and operated by Hubert and Peter Thelen, acquired ownership of the bakery and changed its name to the Swany White Bakery, the brand name of the flour that the Thelen brothers milled. During this time the bakery was operated by two brothers, Matthew and Louis Kolb, who presently own and operate a bakery in Austin.

In 1931 Lawrence Schanhaar returned to Melrose and again took over the operation of the bakery. During these years the bakery was operated as a family enterprise with Lawrence's wife, Sophia, and the four sons, Alfred, Vincent, Edward and Leo taking an active part in the operation — a practice that continues to the present day. Vincent and Edward lost their lives in World War II and Leo "Bart" returned home to take over the business because of the failing health of his father. In 1948 Lawrence purchased the former Frank Schmidt & Sons dry goods and grocery building and moved the baking equipment from the Welz building to its present location. On 1 January, 1950 Lawrence retired and sold the business to his son Leo who is the present owner.

Over the years many changes have taken place. The first ovens were fired with coke which had to be kept burning around the clock every day of the year. The present ovens are thermostatically controlled and fired with oil. At the end of a night's baking they are shut off. Earlier all loaves of bread, buns and cookies were made by hand whereas today machines take over a great deal of the manual labor. Refrigeration has also brought about a major change in the trade since many products can now be baked and frozen and thus facilitate the filling of orders in quantity.

WELZ GROCERY was established on 2 January, 1946 by Edward P. Welz. As in the case of many other returning veterans Edward "Ted" Welz purchased the store from Frank H. Schmidt and settled down to make his mark on the community. Upon the original opening of the store Joseph Schmidt, Sr. opened the front door, threw fifty dollars in cash on the floor and left in disgust. It later developed that he took this amount out in trade. "Ted" Welz and his wife have operated the store for the past twenty-five years and, as he says, "many hard times and ups and downs were experienced but we still are fortunate to make a good living and still maintain business with about twenty-five of the same customers over these pleasant years." Ted Welz is widely known and respected as a leading citizen of the community and has constantly been active in civic, religious and business activities of the area.

WESTERHAUS SPUR STATION was founded in 1932 by Henry T. Westerhaus. The gas station was built and owned by Nicholaus Finneman, St. Cloud until Westerhaus opened and rented it as a Webb Gas Station the last week of June, 1932. After two years of renting, Finneman sold the station to Westerhaus. After twenty-eight years of operation the station was sold to the son, John Henry Westerhaus, who has operated the business for the past twelve years. There were many changes over the years, such as the hard years of the drought, gas rationing in World War II, one hold-up and two break-ins.

WORMS LUMBER AND READY MIX, INC., although located in New Munich, was a vital part of the business community of Melrose throughout the past thirty years. Founded by Matthew Worms as the Math Worms Lumber Company in 1940, the father was joined by his sons, Ralph and Edmund in 1953 and are still actively engaged in the construction company. Matthew Worms originally started in the concrete products business in 1920, one of the first such enterprises in the area, and to that firm added the lumber business in 1940. During the past twenty years the firm entered into the construction business and with an average number of ten employees have built or renovated many buildings in the area. During these years the firm has built the Melrose Hospital and Pine Villa, the Red Owl Store, the offices of Meyer and Meyer, Attorneys and remodeled the Melrose *Beacon* office, Curly's Bar, Gamble Store, Garland Store, Melrose State Bank, Schad Funeral Home, Melrose Motor Company. It has also constructed new warehouses for the Melrose Utilities Company and the Meyer Lumber Company.

So businessmen came and went in the history of Melrose. Few of them accumulated a vast empire; few of them amassed a great fortune. Most of them were very much like their country cousins. They work diligently and spent many and long and hard hours at their trades. They exerted a great deal of effort, practiced an almost heroic degree of fortitude and, through thick and thin, they served the needs of the community. They did not subscribe to the philosophy of the junior Alexandre Dumas who exclaimed, "Business! It's quite simple. It's other people's money." Much more than being businessmen they were, by and large, civic and religious leaders. They constantly took an active and energetic role in promoting the commonweal of church and state and by their actions, more than their words, they lived the words George Bernard Shaw wrote in *Candida*: "We have no more right to consume happiness without producing it than to consume wealth without producing it."

The Yankee mostly disappeared from the scene by the end of World War I. He was succeeded by an enterprising, thrifty, and intelligent generation of businessmen who quite literally rose by their bootstraps from the poverty and industrious immigrant stock. From the days of the early 1920's when railroad officials threatened that grass would grow on the streets of Melrose, through the terrible years of World War II when many of the community's finest young men would be called to war and never return down to the present time when the lure of the "city" beckons many young people, Melrose has survived. More than that, it has proven to be a contradiction to the national trend. When the "flight to the city" is a national phenomenon Melrose continues to grow and attract new citizens. This is not only a tribute to the church, the school system, the sturdy rural area, but also to the businessmen who made Melrose a place of friendliness, neighborliness and helpfulness. Adley discovered his creek and Clark founded his mill — but they are gone. The Germans — Pierz' "dear Catholic Germans" founded a community — and they have the last laugh on the cynical writings of Sinclair Lewis.

APPENDIX

A GOOD TOWN NEVER DIES

Roy B. Ripley*

Impossibilities are impossible; but only thinking makes them so. What a man can imagine or conceive in his mind can be accomplished. I suppose it was this premise Harold Schueler had in mind back in December, 1965, when he penned a letter to Central Division headquarters, Chicago, in which he suggested that Kraft explore the possibilities of expanding its operations at Melrose, Minn.

Schueler, a sagacious, rather quiet man, is manager of the company's Melrose-West cheese plant. With Kraft for nearly thirty-eight years, he had made no snap judgment. The fact was he had been studying the matter for many months and, earlier, had brought it up at a division management meeting in Wausau, Wisconsin.

Schueler knew that Stearns County and the surrounding area could boast some of the most prudent dairy farmers anywhere (with six hundred pounds last year, Stearns was the highest milk producing county in Minnesota and, for that matter, one of the highest in the nation). And because of the eminently successful operation of his plant he also knew that Kraft was well established in the area and was well thought of by both businessmen and farmers.

The strength of any town, though, lies in the character of its citizens. Schueler knew these people (he had been plant manager there since 1962), thus he realized that Melrose was a good town...a good town for Kraft and, just as important, he recognized that the company could do a lot for the community and the dairymen within its operating radius.

Kraft and Melrose, which now has a population of about two thousand four hundred had come together back in 1943 when the company purchased an unoccupied building there and began manufacturing cheese. Now Schueler suggested that the town and the company grow together with Kraft adding to its present facilities or, perhaps, even building a new plant; either would mean progress because of new people and more revenue being brought into the area. By working together Kraft, Melrose and nearby dairymen...our patrons who are really the grass roots of our business...would prosper.

Schueler's ideas so impressed Central Division management that they were quickly passed on to executives at General Office. The rapidity of events which followed were extraordinary for on 6 March, 1968 just a little over two years later, Kraft started up cheese production at its sparkling, new multi-million dollar plant...Melrose-East. The new plant makes Melrose unique in that it is

* Grateful acknowledgement is made to Mr. Roy B. Ripley, editor, for permission to reprint this article from the May-June (vol. 26, no. 3), 1968 issue of **The Kraftsman.**

233

the only city or town in the nation at which Kraft has two cheese manufacturing operations.

Statistically the new plant is no Decatur, Georgia or Buena Park, California. However it is large, very modern and includes all the improvements and innovations that Kraft has developed over the years such as up-to-date cheese handling methods which take the manual labor out of moving weighty blocks, and CIP (cleaned in place) piping, a technique developed to automatically circulate water and cleaning agents through pipes, vats, pasteurizers, etc...obviously a great sanitation time saver.

Melrose-East is situated on approximately ninety acres of land, has one hundred twenty-six thousand square feet of floor space and will employ some one hundred persons when operating at full capacity, in about one year. It will manufacture specialty cheese such as Swiss and Parmesan; together with Melrose-West, the annual milk intake will be five hundred million pounds, or nearly one and one-half million pounds per day. Incidentally, although our company will not release exact figures, Melrose-East cost a small fortune. For example, two heretofore unused self cleaning separators which were installed after being tested at the Kraft plant in Milledgeville, Illinois, ran twenty-seven thousand dollars a piece...that's the price of two nice three-bedroom homes on today's market.

The method used in handling eighty pound blocks of Swiss, or the "brine system" as Central Division Chief Engineer John Ekblad calls it, is the first of its kind. After manufacture the blocks are moved mechanically by "chain falls" into brine tanks, then by conveyor into the drying tunnel and, finally, into a curing room. It's all automatic. The new plant also boasts the largest vacuum pan for whey condensation in the division...its capacity is an astounding fifty thousand pounds per hour.

Despite all of these goodies, the most amazing thing about Melrose-East is the fact that from conception to the day the plant began operation, the surveys planning, engineering, letting of contracts, construction, installation and testing of equipment...the whole shebang...took only two years. That just has to be some sort of a record.

When you consider that drawings and specifications had to be worked out and written up for every item in the building and for its operation, everything from the placement of electrical receptacles to the complicated installation of production components, the task of planning alone was monumental. Ekblad's engineers made up one hundred and fifty-one drawings and three hundred and eighty-eight pages of specifications and he said, "Never was so much done by so few in so short a time."

Land for the plant was purchased in early 1966 and grading, which included laying an asphalt road to the building site, began a few months later. Because of the comparatively short building season in Minnesota the coordination necessary to insure completion as scheduled was critical; and again Kraft engineers worked out some unique methods for doing the job.

For example, production equipment was designed and ordered a year in advance so that it was available when needed. Likewise, they pre-ordered all structural steel, a job usually handled by the contractor, in order to have it on location at the time the contractor would be ready to set it in place. "Everything was a matter of timing and this is the only job I can recall where all of it went letter-perfect," Ekblad said.

Naturally, while all this was going on, other Kraft departments were busily engaged in planning for the new plant. One of the first things that happened was naming a plant manager. The job went to Charles Lyons, a lanky, good-natured former New Ulm, Minnesota superintendent who had twenty-two years with Kraft. Charlie, his wife and their three children moved to Melrose a short time later.

Then it was a matter of recruiting qualified personnel. To train these new people the company transferred a management nucleus of old Kraft pros such as Fabian Nohner from Melrose-West, Vernon "Sonny" Arndt from New Ulm, both would take over as production foremen; Russ Lambert, a top-notcher from Stockton, Illinois, to head up the maintenance department; Roger Wiedl from Melrose-West, office manager; Charles Berigan from Milledgeville, supervisor of dairy farm specialists; and another Stockton man, Ron Flockhart, in charge of the new plant's precise quality control operation.

On 6 March when the first cheese vat was put into operation these men were already at the plant along with twenty-six new employees. In addition there were eight or ten more men, specialists in engineering, sanitation, cheese making, etc., who had arrived from General Office, Central Division headquarters and nearby plants to help this, the newest Kraft plant get underway.

Meanwhile, the company had begun its milk buildup. Already rolling into the five drive-through milk intake stalls at Melrose-East were the milk haulers. . . independent truck drivers who carry milk daily from farms within a fifty-mile-radius of the plant and are one of the main and vital links between Kraft and those upon whom we must depend. . .our patrons. Along with Berigan and his three dairy farm specialists, it is the independent milk hauler who maintains close liaison between our company and the farmer and provides the dairy help and service for which Kraft has become known over the years. Kraft's reputation has not been built on what the company was going to do; it is the farm specialist and milk hauler who put meaning into this statement.

The new Melrose plant generates its own power for refrigeration, something that a Kraft plant has never before done. The generators are gas fired which keeps smoke and air pollution at a minimum. When all this was being planned, however, the idea of gas was a particular problem in that there was no gas pipeline into Melrose.

Of course the company approached the Northern States Power Company, which in turn received approval from the Melrose City Council and when the line was finally installed it was qiute an event. Not only did it allow residents and other businesses to begin heating with gas, and cooking too, if they wished, but it marked the one-thousandth community which had been put on gas service by Northern States. Thus Kraft was instrumental in getting gas into Melrose and several other nearby towns.

The new plant is by far the most modern in Central Division. Among the things that make it so is a water conservation system. . .it's as up to date as anything you've seen. . .which is a means to two ends; it not only conserves water but also substantially reduces waste from milk solids that normally would find its way into sewage systems, according to Ekblad. Of great importance to Kraft in this same area of concern, he added, was the fact that the City of Melrose had just recently completed construction of an entire new waste disposal plant.

Other interesting aspects of the new plant are: the building, which contains nearly two hundred electric motors, is two stories with approximately one hundred fifteen thousand square feet on the first or main floor; storage or other temperature controlled rooms consist of about fifty thousand square feet and production areas total approximately thirty thousand square feet; the plant covers about three acres of land and is bounded by highway U.S. 52 and the main line of the Great Northern Railroad from which a spur line runs to two "spots" at the plant's loading dock; incidentally, there are also two truck loading ramps in addition to the bulk milk intake stations.

Melrose-East is moisture controlled; it has seven huge twenty-seven thousand pound vertical cheese vats and there is room for the possible installation of three others at some future date; the processing equipment is all stainless steel and it seems as though there are miles of stainless tubing. The new plant, along with Melrose-West, will have the ability to produce fifty million pounds of cheese annually.

When a giant like Kraft makes a substantial addition to its facilities in a town like Melrose it is natural that many good things will accrue, not only for Melrose, but for the surrounding area, and for a number of reasons.

First of all, our company has researched and developed dairy products which are advertised and sold throughout the world. Thus our seven hundred and fifty patrons in the Melrose area (in 1955 there were about forty) have an established and continually growing market for their product, which is our basic raw material, milk. What it means is assurance to the dairy farmer who wishes to remain successful and expand that Kraft will always be ready to buy from him.

Kraft's two Melrose plants will contribute heavily to the output of the company's forty-nine cheese manufacturing locations which are spread across the country from New York to California. In fact, Kraft cheese produced at Melrose will probably wind up at restaurants, institutional mass-feeding operations and on grocer's shelves in all fifty states. On the part of our customers, literally millions of them all over the world, there is a continuing and growing demand for Kraft products; thus our company has a continuing and growing need for products like those produced at Melrose. (It's an interesting fact that Kraft markets approximately four hundred and fifty different products made from milk or milk derivatives.)

For Melrose, Kraft's expansion will be like a financial shot in the arm because nearly one hundred new families will move into the town. To further this thought, **The Kraftsman** quotes from Chicago Association of Commerce and Industry estimates on what the addition of one hundred new factory workers can mean to a community.

One hundred new households mean three hundred and fifty-nine more people; ninety-seven more automobiles; seven hundred and twenty thousand dollars more in annual personal income; two hundred and twenty-nine thousand dollars more bank deposits; three more retail establishments; and sixty-five more non-manufacturing jobs. In addition, three hundred and thirty-one thousand dollars more will be spent in retail sales per year with seventy-two thousand dollars going to grocery stores, forty-seven thousand dollars to automobile dealers, twenty-five thousand dollars to restaurants, twenty-four thousand dollars to service stations, twenty-one thousand dollars to clothing and shoe stores, etc. And of course, the new people will mean more tax revenue for the city.

With or without Kraft, however, Melrose is a solid town. . .the kind of solid town that was built by average, practical people. And unlike many small communities it is not losing ground as great numbers of America's population migrate to the metropolitan areas of cities.

In a sense Melrose, the town, is much like Kraft, the company. Neither has necessarily enjoyed success because it had more men of top-flight ability, but rather because all of its people were distinguished by a small positive increment of devotion, dedication, or determination beyond that of their opposite numbers elsewhere. It is such modest differences in individual achievement that distinguish a great company or a great town from one that is indifferent.

With an eye to the future, these were the basic reasons for Kraft's expansion in Melrose. It is a good town and we know a good town never dies.

CHAPTER TEN

GOOD GRIEF,
HOW THE MONEY ROLLS IN

> Mother makes brandy from cherries;
> Pop distills whiskey and gin;
> Sister sells wine from the grapes on our vine —
> Good grief, how the money rolls in!
>
> — Author Unknown

Nations mark national holidays to keep alive the flame of patriotism in the hearts of their citizens. Churches observe holy days to develop the holiness of their members. Cities and villages throughout the country hold several commemorations and events each year as a matter of civic pride. Some events are matters of routine, such as visiting the cemeteries on Memorial Day, and others are of a more exceptional nature. Melrose in the later decades of its existence witnessed several more than ordinary events, revealing how more and more the people of the community were becoming aware of their role in the development in international, national and state affairs.

The isolationist spirit of the city, the state and the nation was reflected by the United States refusal to join the League of Nations which was formed in 1920. Two years later, a little noted fact at the time, Russia became the Union of Soviet Socialist Republics, the first communist state in the world and Benito Mussolini, founder of facism, became premier of Italy. At the same time a person by another name better known later than at this time was plotting the unsuccessful "Beer Hall Putsch." The following year his scheme failed and as he languished in prison he wrote *Mein Kampf*. Catholics throughout the world rejoiced in 1929 upon hearing of the signing of the Lateran Treaty, creating the tiny but independent Vatican City State. Little was heard of the violent persecution of the Jews that Hitler and his Nazi party was conducting during the early years of the thirties and only when his Blackshirts marched into Austria and annexed the small, picture-book country did the world become alarmed. The following year, 1939, the World War II developed into a global conflict between the Axis and Allies. Only the giddiest optimist could find any reassurance that the United States would not become involved merely because Franklin Delano Roosevelt said, "I hate war. Eleanor hates war." A few American reporters and American missionaries sent forth a cry of alarm when Japan invaded China in 1937, but their voices were not heard on the other side of the Pacific. Mao Tse-tung led the Red Army on the Long March of six thousand miles in 1934 and 1935 and most Americans shrugged it off as another kind of outlandish Chinese madness.

The 1921 issue of the *Melrose Beacon* affords a reflection of changing times and mores.

In those days people just did not die; rather, they "answered the final summons" or "responded to the call of the Grim Reaper." Conductor Fred McDorman of the Great Northern railroad went hunting and downed a one thousand eight hundred and fifty pound moose. He took the moose to Cass Lake where its age was determined by John Smith, a one hundred and thirty year old Indian. After examining the prize, the renowned Indian said, "Woof, over 100 years old, like John Smith." J. H. Stundebeck Plumbing company was advertising the delight and pleasure of having modern plumbing in the home and stated "the conveniences manifest themselves hourly." Wolves were numerous in the area during the winter of 1921 and the editor duly recorded that Anton Groetsch and Mr. Otte shot two of them. Also worthy of notice was the fact that St. Boniface church "featured a short sermon 'in English' at an early Mass." It was also observed in the columns of the weekly newspaper that a skirt which used to take a yard and a half of fifty-four inch goods to make now only took a half a yard of forty inch goods. Items from such far away places as Belgrade, St. Francis, Browerville and London, England also found their way into the columns of the paper.

In the United States people were dancing the Charleston, swallowing goldfish and enjoying a rousing good time reading F. Scott Fitzgerald and Sinclair Lewis. While marveling at a new type of journalism Henry Luce introduced with TIME during the day, they would more and more stay up half the night "listening to Pittsburg on the crystal set."

Suddenly C-R-A-S-H ! The stock market collapse initiated the Great Depression leaving sixteen million Americans unemployed. Bigotry reared its ugly head in the presidential campaign of 1928 when "the happy warrior," Alfred E. Smith, became the first Catholic to seek the presidency and received only eighty-seven out of the five hundred and thirty-one electoral votes. The Depression was compounded in the midwest states by the dust storms and drought that afflicted the rural areas of the nation. In 1932 people started singing "Happy Days are Here Again" when Franklin Delano Roosevelt became the thirty-second president and proclaimed the "New Deal." For most Americans the greatest tragedy of the period was the passage of the Volstead Act of October 28, 1919. It was a noble, national experiment that was doomed to failure even before it took the force of law.

The Women's Christian Temperance Union hailed the law as the great deliverer of all from crime and corruption. For the majority of the people of Stearns County it was a calamity. For the citizens of Melrose and the surrounding area it was an event that brought distress to many; law-breaking to some, and bootlegging to more than a few. It is the first noteworthy event to be considered in this chapter.

MARVELLOUS MINNESOTA 13

When the federal law prohibiting the sale and consumption of alcoholic beverages was passed on January 16, 1919 it was labeled the Volstead Act after the congressman from Minnesota, Andrew Volstead, who was proficient at drafting bills. No prohibitionist himself, he was a good friend of Wayne B. Wheeler, the determined and militant leader of the Anti-Saloon League. At one time the reason offered for the necessity of the bill was the conservation of the nation's grain. Closer to the truth, however, might be the fact that the lower house was weary of listening to dreary fillibusters in support of prohibition.

The law introduced into the language several new words. "Bootlegging" arose from the practice of hiding liquor inside one's boots; "moonshine" was the name given the illegal liquor because it was generally made at night; "speakeasy" was a place where one could purchase moonshine and it received its name from the custom of speaking softly when asking for a drink, a gallon or a barrel. The "feds" were agents of the United States Treasury Department whose task was to seek out the lawbreakers. By far the most popular name given the illegal liquor in the Stearns county area was "Minnesota 13."

There are several accounts on how moonshine received the name of Minnesota 13. The most popular explanation is that a new hybrid corn had been created at the University of Minnesota Agricultural School at this time. "Cookers," a term applied to those who made moonshine, soon discovered that the use of this corn, which was called Minnesota 13, made the best mash. In a short time the name of the corn was transferred to the moonshine. Another version is that the federal agents gave moonshine that name because there was a regiment of army men who fought in the Spanish-American War which was called the Minnesota Gallant 13. Another source says that it was called Minnesota 13 because county road number thirteen runs directly through an area where a great deal of moonshine was produced. Who first gave the name of Minnesota 13 to moonshine? Some say it was coined by an unknown farmer near Holdingford; others say a priest in a parish neighboring to Melrose named the brew.

Although Minnesota did not witness the extensive crime and corruption that racked such areas as Chicago, New York and the New Jersey coast, it had more than its share of arrests. Moonshiners in Minnesota were generally light offenders, although there were a few who acted as distributors to the syndicates that operated in the larger urban areas. In 1929 there were two thousand, two hundred and nineteen federal and seventy state arrests. No other of the five surrounding states had more than four hundred and three. During the twelve years the law was in effect the *Melrose Beacon* duly reported local activities. Although the publisher, C. W. Carlson, was a prohibitionist he did not reveal his own stand too strongly because most of his readers were from moderately to vehemently opposed to the law. A headline in the August 31, 1922 issue read, "Ig Lemm & Vic Gau Taken to Long Prairie and Released the Next Day" and another in the June 14th issue, "Search of Wiehoff Drink Parlor Fails to Disclose any Damaging Evidence." The local weekly reported whenever it could the presence of the treasury agents. On May 17, 1928 it announced, "Raiding Fed Agents in City" and the following September reported, "Fed Agents Pull off Big Job." The latter headline told the story of how they smashed two stills and sugar and mash on the Kraker estate. This home witnessed many raids because it was used by a few of the local moonshiners. In the basement they constructed escape hatches and underground escape routes in case of raids.

One of the better known federal agents was Angus A. E. Whitney. He would hide in the woods surrounding Birch Lake and wait until he secured enough evidence before making a raid. Many agents acted through "stool pidgeons" (another term coined these years from the fact that the informer would sit on a bar stool to gather information) who disguised themselves as farmers or railroad workers. After they gathered samples from several moonshiners they would label the bottles with the owners' names. A few days later the "feds," ten or twelve strong, would raid the place. An account of one of Whitney's raids, which resulted in tragedy, appears in the first appendix to this chapter.

Another agent, Robert Bain, acting as an undercover man, also met with his share of troubles. His story is told in the second appendix. Most agents did not like to work in the Stearns County area because of the dangers involved.

According to one prominent moonshiner about one-fourth of the homes made moonshine and almost every home made "home brew." Most people made their own stills, using copper washtubs as the base. Later an enterprising and adventurous man in Holdingford produced stills for sale to others. Because everybody followed different recipes there was a wide range in the quality of the finished product. If you were a "bourbon man" you would mix twenty pounds of corn with fifty pounds of sugar; if a "rye man" you would use twenty pounds of rye. You would cook the mash and the residue moonshine at about ninety-five degree temperature. The first distillation was one hundred proof and of an inferior quality; the second distillation was one hundred and fifty-five proof, clear as spring water and of high quality. This moonshine was often called "white lightning." Distilled water was used to reduce high proof alcohol. After the distillation process the rest of the barrel was filled with luke warm water and yeast was added. The barrel was set in a warm place to hasten fermentation, a process that took from a week to ten days.

During the early years of prohibition moonshine was difficult to purchase in the area. After the second year, however, more and more people started "cooking" and a gallon of good moonshine could be bought for four dollars. The manufacturing costs of a gallon cost only about one dollar, thus the "cooker," "the runner" and seller all made about one hundred percent profit on the transaction. The area of Melrose was one of the leading centers in the state for two reasons. A predominently German ethnic area carried with it from the "old country" a love for beer and schnapps and many of those who emigrated to the United States had learned in Germany how to make their own beer and schnapps. The second largest ethnic group, the Irish, were chiefly employed by the railroad and the love of the Irish for good whiskey is legendary. They were eager buyers of moonshine if they were not themselves engaged in the practice. The German people were also good "runners" for they had learned in Germany where many countries were no larger than some of the counties in the state how to smuggle merchandize across borders in order to escape taxes. The stories of how moonshine was smuggled are as numerous as humorous. One lady, when seeing that the federal agents were coming, lifted her long skirts and sat on the barrel all the while the agents searched the house. Another man would borrow a clerical collar from a friendly priest and drive in a car loaded with moonshine to Duluth. Another would bury the moonshine in a truckload of grain and many would have false bottoms in their automobiles. Their ingenuity was expressed by adding springs to their cars when hauling moonshine because they knew that the agents would be able to tell if the car sagged.

Bartenders, too, practiced various devices. If an agent unexpectedly appeared in one local saloon the bartender would push a button and the bottle of moonshine would drop through the floor into the basement on a pile of rocks and be smashed. The rocks were in a sand box so no evidence could be found. A strong bond of fellowship built up among all moonshiners and they kept their secrets as well as they assisted one another. When the federal agents came to the area they usually spent several days in several different towns. The "bootleggers" devised various "tip off" systems to warn friends and neighbors of the approaching agents. If desperate, they would burn down the building where the "moon was cooking," as one's son burned down the pig barn when he learned the agents were coming. Many a call traveled over the telephone party lines with code phrases such as, "Aunt Mary told me that Uncle Henry will be dropping by your place in a little while," or "John is coming over to your place to see if you can spare some corn for our pigs."

A masterpiece of understatement would be to say that prohibition was not very popular in the Melrose area. Pastors in the churches would not speak in favor of prohibition and one, a close friend of U.S. Representative Harold Knutson, was a confidant and friend of many bootleggers in the area. Many a doctor in the area prescribed alcoholic beverages "for medicinal purposes." It was even rumored that the local Legion clubrooms had more liquor than it knew what to do with because five doctors in the area were all members! Once a stranger came to Melrose and asked a local citizen where he could get "a shot of moon." Swinging his arms in all directions he replied, "Any place but the church." Many a federal agent ran for cover when a moonshiner grabbed his shotgun. He did not try to kill the agent, just hasten his departure. Local jailors and judges were also sympathetic to the "bootleggers." If they were jailed they were allowed to leave the jail every morning and go about their work and return in the evening, many times bringing with them a bottle of "white lightning." If fined they more often than not paid about ten dollars and left unpaid the rest of the fine. On April 18, 1918 the *Melrose Beacon* announced in a small front page news that the Honorable Homer L. Castle of New York would deliver a dry lecture on "Liquor Traffic." The Honorable Castle must some way or another have gotten the message for in the

June 13th issue it was reported that he did not deliver his address in favor of prohibition but rather discussed how the war could be won with the help of all good citizens.

Stearns County, however, was not as bad as some would think. The November 14th, 1929 issue of the local newspaper reported M. L. Hartney, assistant prohibition administrator, saying, "Magazine writers no longer have the right to point to Stearns County as the wettest county in Minnesota. Recent raids in that section of central Minnesota, combined with many convictions under the Jones law, effectively have cured illicit manufacturing and sale of liquor there." He also pointed out that the concentration of "dry agents" in the area during the summer of 1929 prompted many liquor vendors and manufacturers to move to the neighboring counties of Benton and Morrison. Although he claimed that previously the exportation of liquor from Stearns county "might be called a major industry," he admitted that at the present time "conditions are no worse than in other Minnesota districts." Hartney cited Winona, Ramsey, Dakota, Morrison and Benton counties to be just as bad or worse than Stearns.

Most citizens of Minnesota never believed that prohibition was "a great social and economic experiment, noble in motive," as President Hoover described it. In 1932 they showed their dislike by electing the first democratic president in eleven years and the first Farmer-Labor governor, thus breaking the Republican dominance of the state since 1909. In 1933 the United States Congress repealed the Eighteenth Amendment and the following year the Minnesota Legislature followed suit. In Melrose, Minnesota and throughout the United States beer flowed in the streets and people were once again singing, "Happy Days Are Here Again."

PLOWVILLE U.S.A. AND THE PLOWERS

Men frequently tend to forget that civilizations rise or fall upon the strength or weakness of agriculture. Archaeologists tell us that the great Mayan civilization of Mexico declined in a corresponding degree with the flight from the farm to the city. And James J. Hill created a vast empire upon a slogan: "Land without people is a wilderness; people without land is a mob." In the rapid process of urbanization and mechanization of the past forty years we tend to forget that cities and villages exist because the farm first existed. The first settlers in the area of Melrose were farmers and the village came into being to serve the needs of the rural community. Significantly the village's first major industry was Clark's mill. The city today continues to be a trading center for approximately one thousand families living on the farms in Melrose, Millwood, Oak, Getty and parts of Sauk Centre townships. The choice of Melrose as the site of national Plowville, U.S.A. - Terrarama, U.S.A. from September 14-16, 1961 was both a recognition and a tribute to the farmers who created out of the Melrose bush countryside one of the most prosperous and successful rural communities in the state and nation.

It was not always so, however. In 1859 it was realized that the new state was becoming chiefly agricultural. With great invasion of the German immigrants in the last three decades of the nineteenth century agriculture became an increasingly important economic asset to the state. "The Germans were hard-working, systematic farmers who sought out the rich river valleys," wrote Theodore Blegen.

"They built flourishing farms. But they spread into many parts of Minnesota, far from these favored valleys. They also went to towns and cities where their skill in trades made itself felt. From early days they were repelled by the Puritanism of New Englanders, and this sentiment, here as in other states, tended to draw many of them away from the Republican party, which in its earlier years was influenced by temperance sympathies."

In the early decades the farmers raised self-sustaining crops, such as potatoes, vegetables, corn and oats. By the close of the Civil War, however, "King Wheat" was in the ascendancy and would not be dethroned for the next three decades. A minister writing back to his home in the East declared, "Minnesota . . . has gone to wheat. Men work in wheat all day when it does not rain, lounge around talking about wheat when it is wet, dream about wheat at night and I fear go to meeting Sabbath Day to think about wheat." The ever-increasing production of this "liquid gold" can be seen by the Mill City becoming the flour capital of the world. Statistics tell the same story. From slightly over two million bushels in 1860 the crop increased to almost nine million bushels in 1870; to over thirty-four and a half million in 1880 and stood at over fifty-two million in 1890. Each decade more land was cleared and the acreage under cultivation rose from three hundred and forty-five thousand in 1860 to almost six million in 1890. Fifty-four percent of the acreage was planted in wheat in 1860 and reached an all time high percentage of almost seventy in 1878. Wheat, although a mainstay throughout four decades, was not the only crop raised on Minnesota farms. Figures for 1880 show that the farmers also produced twenty-three million bushels of oats, almost fifteen million bushels of corn, more than five million bushels of potatoes and about three million bushels of barley. In the decade between 1880 and 1890 the number of milking cows would increase from two hundred and seventy-five thousand to over a half million.

Wheat-raising, in the course of the decades, was being equalled and gradually surpassed by the dairy industry. Oren Gregg, a Vermont native, arrived in Minnesota in 1865 and said to himself, "My grandfather used the cow to turn the grass of the old Green Mountains into butter. Why could not I use the cow to turn the grass of the western prairie to butter?" For twenty years he preached the gospel of the dairy farm. When asked whether a farmer should go into beef or dairying, he replied: "Choose ye this day whom ye will serve. If beef than serve him, and if dairy, then serve her." When the University of Minnesota established the Farmers' Institute in 1885 Gregg served as its superintendent for more than twenty years.

Another patron saint of the dairy industry was Wendelin Grimm, who arrived in Minnesota from Germany in 1857. He brought with him a twenty pound sack of alfalfa. Year after year he planted his crop, continually experimenting with what he called his "everlasting clover." When a neighboring farmer noticed that Grimm's cattle were fat during the winter of 1863 following the failure of the corn crop, Grimm replied, "*Kein Kornschen, nur ewiger Klee.*" By 1890 almost half of all the alfalfa grown in the state came from Grimm's home county of Carver. The alfalfa crop raised in Minnesota grew from two thousand tons in 1900 to more than a million tons in 1930.

Evidence of the growing trend of diversification was shown by the formation of the dairymen's association in 1878 and the Minnesota Butter and Cheese Association in 1882. By the turn of the century dairy products in Minnesota brought a revenue of more than sixteen million dollars and in one decade increased to over thirty million dollars. Milk cows increased from the half million count in 1890 to almost two million in 1900 and, again another half million by 1910. In 1885 the state had sixty-three creameries and forty-six cheese factories. The number rapidly increased after the formation of four cooperative creameries in 1889 and 1890. Eight years later the state counted five hundred and sixty cooperative creameries and by 1918 with one thousand and four hundred cooperatives in the nation, Minnesota accounted for six hundred and seventy-one — almost fifty percent.

The amazing growth of the dairy industry is attributed to Theophilus Haecker, the "Father of Dairying in Minnesota." He founded a school of dairying at the University of Minnesota and taught there for twenty-seven years. More than two thousand young men were taught the art of being creamery operators. His students recall one of his favorite sayings: "Treat the cow kindly, boys. Remember she is a lady — and a mother."

By the end of the World War I Minnesota farmers were humming a happy tune for everything looked as if it was coming up roses. Of course, some were puzzled by the beginning of the flight to the city and Irving Berlin's ditty, "How You Gonna Keep 'em Down on the Farm?" was more than a song. It was a problem. But they could still smile for in 1919 farm crops in Minnesota were valued at over a half billion dollars. Although business boomed in the early years of the twenties perceptive farmers realized that times were getting "harder and harder." By 1930 the revenue derived from crops decreased one hundred and ninety-six million dollars. The bottom fell out in the early thirties and no one had a better right than the farmer to sing, "Brother Can You Spare a Dime?" — except he was in no mood for singing. He had to fight both the great depression as well as nature. In 1920 a bushel of wheat sold for one dollar and eighty-two cents; in 1932 his gain was a paltry thirty-two cents. In the mid-thirties came the drought, the dust storms and the grasshoppers. The lucky farmer was one able to rent land in northern Minnesota, some near Pillager and others near Pierz, where there was still enough pasture to enable the cattle to survive. The unfortunate farmer shipped his cattle and considered himself lucky if he could realize fifteen dollars for a good milk cow.

One ray of light was cast through the gloom of the great drought. In 1935 the Roosevelt administration set in motion the machinery creating the Rural Electrification Administration. Farmers at that time, however, were unable to meet the installation expenses and even five years later only one-third of the farms in Minnesota had electricity. By 1940, however, the rural economy was on the up-swing and was rejuvenated throughout the war and post-war years of the forties. By the middle of the 1950's electricity had become practically universal in Minnesota. Rural cousins kept abreast of country cousins with an ever-expanding and improving network of roads, an easy access to centers of commerce, recreation and entertainment and the mechanization and electrification of their farm buildings.

Three other factors helped in the improvement of farming techniques and farm income. With the passage of the Smith-Lever Act in 1914 the "extension service" program and the county-agent movement were set in motion. In the course of time almost every county in the state formed a farm bureau and if each did not have its own county-agent, one agent would serve as liaison man for two or more counties. In 1917 at a meeting in the county court house in St. Cloud, A. D.

Wilson, director of the extension program of the University of Minnesota explained the purpose of the farm bureau. A membership of six hundred was secured, each member paying one dollar a year dues. To this sum the county added another thousand dollars and one thousand and eight hundred dollars was appropriated from federal funds. The first Stearns county agent was P. W. Hutemer appointed to a two year term with offices in Melrose.

Another factor for improvement was the organization of the 4-H clubs in 1918. The following year 4-H clubs were organized in four county schools and numbered seventy-eight members under the direction of the principal and teachers. A great promoter of the movement was county superintendent of school, W. A. Boerger. At eighth grade graduations he would promote the work of the 4-H clubs and impress upon the minds of his listeners the importance of agricultural training and good farm management. From 1922 until 1932 the county had no agent and the extension service was dropped. There existed groups throughout the county that felt even without an agent and the extension service that the 4-H program should be continued and in 1926 these groups met and organized 4-H clubs. Funds to keep extension club leaders were raised through contributions by such groups as the St. Cloud Chamber of Commerce, service clubs throughout the county and money-making projects. Through the lean years the 4-H program survived. The arrival of a county agent in 1932 and the organization of twenty-one clubs in the county gave the movement a shot in the arm. Much credit for the survival of the Melrose 4-H club is due to Fred Welch, the club leader. "Mr. Welch," recalled Mrs. Herman Hellermann, Jr., "did not receive the credit due him for the work that he performed."

Interest in the 4-H program was at a standstill in 1933. Many people were depressed by the poverty around them and their interest in everything lagged. Others were opposed to the movement because they felt it had received too much financial assistance in past years. Even some priests advised their people to stay away from all 4-H club work. However, with the arrival of the first home agent, Noan Anderson, for the summer months of 1934 a new spirit was injected into the members and the general public. "Thrift" was the theme of the year and people were amazed to see what the boys and girls could make from what was long considered junk and left-overs. State club leader, T. A. Erickson (lovingly called "Dad" Erickson) rejuvenated the 4-H movement and introduced both rural and city youth into the clubs on a state-wide basis. For the next fifteen years the program was expanded and through the efforts of a part-time 4-H club leader in the county local clubs were increasing in membership and new clubs were being formed throughout the county.

Legislation passed in 1953 separated the farm bureau and the county extension service, thus enabling both departments to fulfill their duties more adequately. From then to the present might be called the "golden years" of the movement in Stearns county. In 1971 the county extension staff numbered five people. Francis J. Januschka, extension agent; Mrs. Barbara Jessen Klixbull, extension home economist; David Skogen, assistant extension agent; Angela Paulert, summer 4-H assistant; Jacqueline Draheim, summer 4-H assistant. There are one thousand and one hundred and ten members in fifty-three 4-H clubs throughout the county, including the five new clubs organized in 1971. The motto of the movement is: "To Make the Best Better."

The 4-H movement came alive in Melrose through the efforts of Fred Welch, county agent then living in the city. In 1929 Melrose, with one hundred and one members, was the largest club in the county and set a statewide record for membership. The following April 4-H clubs were proposed for school districts No. 73, No. 89, No. 164 and No. 187 in the Melrose district. In May a 4-H club was organized at the high school with officers being Marie Westendorf, president; Joseph Mueller, vice president; Loretta Wessel, secretary; Alphonse Herzog, treasurer. Under the leadership of Norbert Weiss the club engaged in a whirlwind of activities in 1931, ranging from sponsoring dances, eradicating common barberry bush, participating in the achievement day at St. Joseph, preparing exhibits for the Stearns county fair and enjoying a picnic on the shores of Lake Sylvia. Minutes record that the members and their parents especially enjoyed "the free ice cream donated by H. B. Otte, buttermaker at the Melrose Creamery." The club ceased functioning in 1932 due to the depression and drought.

Eight years later the club was reorganized under the adult leadership of Mrs. Mary Braegelmann and the fifteen members called themselves the Melrose Graniteers. Officers were Rose Koch, president; Armelda Eichers, secretary; Leona Braegelmann, secretary. The patriotic spirit was caught by the twenty members in 1942 and they changed the name of their club to the Melrose American Helpers.

The Adley Creek club, one of the most active in the area, was organized in 1945 under the leadership of Miss Lippert. Adult leaders of the twenty-three members were Mrs. Joseph Rolfzen and Gerhard Blenker. First officers were Stephen Petermeier, president; Clarence Enneking, secretary, JoAnn Petermeier, treasurer, Cyril Schreifels, reporter. Stephen Petermeier had the honor of giving a name to the club and he named it after Adley Creek which flowed close to the lands where many of the original members lived.

The Adley Creek club over the years actually learned things by doing them. Its members took on such projects as cooking, sewing, homemaking, gardening, dairy, livestock, rabbits, photography, health and safety. The club meets once a month and the members conduct their own meetings, learning parlimentary procedures, speaking in public through demonstrations and project reports and enjoying parties marking special occasions such as Halloween, Christmas and Valentine's Day. They compete with members of other 4-H clubs in good grooming contests, radio speaking contests, dress revues, the Morris camp and the county fair. During 4-H week the club sponsors a window display about its activities in one of the local stores. It prepares floats for such celebrations as the Harvest Festival, Butter Days, Dairy Days and Barley Days. On 4-H Sunday every year they attend church in a body and decorate the altar with flowers. In the course of its twenty-seven years it has served as an educational instrument for over three hundred members.

A third factor in improving farm conditions in the area was the rural life schools inaugurated at St. John's University in 1939 under the direction of Father Martin Schirber, O.S.B. These rural life schools continued from 1941 to 1944 and again in 1946 and 1953. Clergy, farm leaders and farmers from throughout the area attended. Agricultural leaders from state and county agencies, researchers in state agricultural schools and state and county officials conducted the courses. On many occasions St. John's was asked to organize an agricultural department by such church leaders in the field of rural life as Bishop Peter W. Bartholome and Monsignor Luigi Ligutti, executive secretary of the National Catholic Rural Life Conference. On one occasion Bishop James E. Walsh, M.M., superior general of the Maryknoll Fathers, asked for the establishment of an agricultural school where future missionaries could be trained in the skills of rural life. Although Abbot Alcuin Duetsch favored both proposals, lack of funds and personnel prevented the establishment of such agricultural programs.

One Benedictine monk, however, achieved national fame in the field of horticulture. Father John Katzner experimented with over two hundred varieties of apples, sixty of plums, thirty-five of grapes, ten of cherries. He developed and named the "Alpha grape," a cross between the area wild grapes and the Concord. He was a vice president of the Minnesota Horticultural Society in 1907 and was recognized by that society as a man who "has for years rendered splendid service to the cause of Minnesota horticulture as a plant breeder, experimenter and disseminator." Although no agriculture department ever developed at St. John's, Father Colman Barry, O.S.B., historian of the abbey, wrote in 1956:

"An agricultural experimental station has been in operation for sixteen years, and studies made on use of fertilizers, temperature and sunshine averages. Relative yields of corn, alfalfa, legumes, and hay have also been evaluated and recorded."

Many other factors contributed to make Melrose one of the leading dairy farm areas in the state. The pioneer farmers successfully passed on a heritage of industry, thrift and native intelligence to their descendants. All three gifts were tried through drought and depression, despair and deficits, but these descendants overcame obstacles with a determination that at times bordered on the heroic. Some of these descendants were Clarence Theiler, Eymard Orth and Bernard Nietfeld, to name only a few. In 1961 Theiler was named outstanding soil conservation farmer of 1961. He set aside thirty-two acres of contour strip cropping, twelve acres of contour farming and constructed two thousand and one hundred feet of diversion terrace and two acres of a grassed waterway. He became a cooperator with the district in 1959 and developed a basic soil and water conservation plan with the assistance of technicians of the Minnesota Soil Savers. In 1958 Eymard Orth won the title of "Stearns County Farmer of the Year" because of his efforts in soil conservation. He was presented a plaque given by the Minneapolis *Star* and *Tribune* at a dinner in his honor at the Melrose High School. About the same time Sylvester Rademacher was chosen as the "Outstanding Young Farmer" by the St. Cloud Junior Chamber of Commerce and represented the area in the state-wide selection. He started his farming career as a seventeen year old farm hand, later rented a farm north of Melrose and in 1952 purchased the two hundred and forty acre farm. According to the Dairy Herd Improvement Association his records show nearly a four hundred pounds butterfat average per cow while the state's average was approximately two hundred and twenty pounds. Many of his cows produced over five hundred pounds of butterfat and for this achievement he received *The Farmer* magazine's award for outstanding production.

Bernard Nietfeld, perhaps the most distinguished farmer of the area, is recognized as one of the world's great plowing champions. He was name the "Outstanding Young Farmer of the Year" by the St. Cloud Junior Chamber of Commerce in 1961 after winning the state plowing championship during Plowville, U.S.A. The next year he went on to win the United States plowing championship at Buffalo, North Dakota, after placing second in the Minnesota level land plowing contest the same year. As national champion he won a berth in the World Plowing Match held in Hoenfoss, Norway the following September. The owner of a four hundred acre farm south of Greenwald, Nietfeld also was active in the Melrose Flying Club, piloting his own Aeronca Champ.

So many lines concerning agriculture in the state, county and Melrose area are but prelude and necessary background to the only national event ever held in the community. The three-day event, under the general chairmanship of Herman Imdieke not only brought tens of thousands of visitors to Melrose but also focused the attention of the nation on central Minnesota. Such dignitaries as Donald Williams of the National Administration, Soil Conservation Service, in Washington, D.C.; then governor Elmer L. Andersen and former governor Harold Stassen; Minnesota Commissioner of Agriculture, Duane Wilson; Minnesota Attorney General, Walter F. Mondale, and Bishop Peter W. Bartholome of St. Cloud were among the speakers at various meetings and events throughout the three days. The principal speaker was Orville L. Freeman, then U.S. Secretary of Agriculture.

Site of Plowville, U.S.A. was located on five farms about four miles northeast of Melrose. The plowing contest and headquarters were located on the Norbert Nathe farm. Demonstrations in contour stripping and terracing were conducted on the Eymard Orth and Edward Mueller farms. Other host farms belonged to Steven Petermeier and Edward McCarthy. Wagon trains were available throughout the area every day to enable visitors to view conservation practices, the operation of a steam-powered saw mill and a steam-powered threshing demonstration. Air tours were also conducted so that visitors could view soil and water conservation from the air. WCCO radio conducted broadcasts each day of the event on the grounds featuring Bob DeHaven, Jim Hill and Maynard Speece. The Melrose High School and Sauk Centre High School bands presented concerts each day and ample time was allotted for viewing exhibits and demonstrations.

The banquet on September 15th featured Bishop Peter W. Bartholome as the principal speaker. His address was entitled "The Land, God's Greatest Gift to Man" and it is reprinted in the third appendix of this chapter.

LOYALTY DAY

The first large public gathering that Melrose witnessed came together on May 5, 1918. Some ten thousand people from throughout Stearns county gathered in the Legion park to hear addresses by Bishop

F. Busch and Governor J. A. A. Burnquist. "Loyalty Day," as the event was called, seemed more necessary to assure non-Germans than to remind those of German extraction of loyalty to their newly-adopted country. When war-fever was running high those who had emigrated from Germany and those who bore German names were suspect of pro-German feelings in the emotional pitch of "patriotism" during World War I. Stearns county, and especially the area surrounding Melrose, was thought to be a center of pro-German sympathizers. Nothing, however, could have been further from the truth. The people of Germanic origin could say as clearly and directly as Abbot Alexius Edelbrock, O.S.B. of St. John's Abbey:

"Though a German by birth I have lived in this country since a child and admire and love its institutions. The question of nationality should not enter into God's Church. Unquestionably Catholics should have every opportunity to practice their religion in their own language, and in mixed congregations no matter how small any particular nationality may be, those who are best acquainted with a foreign tongue should have the advantage of hearing the Gospel read and sermons preached to them in their own language.... But there is no widespread ill feeling between Catholics on account of national differences and priests and religious are respected by all irrespective of where they were born."

There was, however, a vehement anti-German feeling pervading the country, and those of Germanic origins — in spite of all logic — were suspect as being friends of "Kaiser Bill." For this reason both the city fathers and the church leaders felt it necessary to sponsor a "Loyalty Day" in Melrose not so much for the benefit of the citizenry as for the reassurance of the general public. Thus Bishop Busch and Governor Burnquist made their appearance, "two men whose stand for true American patriotism and loyalty had won for them the admiration of the entire nation." The ceremonies began at two o'clock when bands and local societies met the bishop and the governor as they descended from the *Oriental Limited* at the Great Northern railroad depot. A parade was formed and the dignitaries were escorted to the city park where Bishop Busch dedicated a new flag that was to fly over the city on a new hundred foot flag pole. The flag was a gift of the employees of the Great Northern railroad. This was no mere local event. "The entire county," reported the *Melrose Beacon,* "is cooperating in making this loyalty meeting a big success, as is shown by the fact that practically all the bands of the county have volunteered their services. "Large delegations," the paper continued, "will be present to make up the largest gathering that ever assembled in Melrose." Following the speeches delivered by the bishop and the governor there was a reception in their honor held in the Melrose Hotel "where all will be given an opportunity to meet the distinguished visitors."

The event proved to be a great success, for the next week the local editor stated in his columns, "STEARNS COUNTY IS LOYAL." The description of the flag-raising ceremony was recorded by the editor of the *St. Cloud Daily Times* in these words:

"Just before reaching the park the procession halted at a monstrous flag staff, the gift of President Hill of the Great Northern. The towering 'stick' of timber rears its majestic height a hundred feet, a splendid specimen of the Pacific coast forest from whence it was brought. For this splendid flag-staff a flag of magnificent proportions had been carried in the parade by a dozen young ladies and into its fold had been cast donations for the Red Cross. Standing by the platform at the foot of the flag-staff with the Governor of the state, at his side and surrounded by the clergy, the war veterans, and the members of the reception committee, Bishop Busch dedicated the flag by blessing it and offering a prayer that breathed the hope and the aspiration that all that is represents might triumph in the great world conflict, now being waged and that those who died in defense of this principle might have everlasting peace."

During the ceremonies that followed attorney W. J. Stephens acted as chairman. According to the local reporter "attorney Stephens laid stress on the need of unity in carrying on the work for the war at home." He then introduced Bishop Busch, whose speech, for the sake of historical record, is reprinted in the fourth appendix together with Governor Burnquist's remarks. The following week, in the "sidelights" on the meeting, the editor of the local paper recorded that "Bishop Busch has no time for Townley and made this very plain in his speech." Some of the other "sidelights" that the editor observed were also worthy of note. "An election is soon coming on," he wrote, "and candidates where here Sunday to leave their reminders." He also noted that "Belgrade is a shining spot in the county when it comes to loyalty. They have a fine band organization and are always ready and willing with their services, and bring a big following with them. Belgrade is sure on the map." The editor of the St. Cloud *Journal-Press* simply stated: "The people of Melrose are to be congratulated on having put over the top the greatest loyalty meeting of the war."

During the speech-making Governor Burnquist paid tribute to the Germans of Stearns county and the area. "Personally," he said, "I have never suspicioned this county. The manifestation here today, by your presence, shows the loyalty that is in your hearts for the great American Republic, a republic to which men and women have come to take advantage of its institutions, its environment and American democracy.

These people came here because they knew that any school they may attend, at any altar they may worship, in every hall of legislation their voices must be heard, and enjoy the rights of franchise, which we have enjoyed since the adoption of the constitution up to the present time. . . ." It was a great day of loyalty and patriotism.

Ironically, however, the same issue of the paper that announced the loyalty day celebration carried a letter from Leo Kolb dated April 17, 1918. Stationed at Philadelphia, Pennsylvania with the United States Navy he wrote to the editor of the *Melrose Beacon* as follows:

"At Chicago the Red Cross gave us candy, tobacco, and writing material. Hit Gary, Indiana after supper and next morning found us in Akron, Ohio. Toward noon we hit West Virginia and about one o'clock found us in Pittsburg. People cheered us all along the way and at Pittsburg the engine and mill whistle blew till the city sounded like a New Year's eve celebration.

At Cumberland, Maryland about 3:30 where we had 30 minutes stop and paraded the streets. Hit Harpers Ferry at supper time. Here we are at the corner of three states, Virginia, W. Virginia, Maryland and Wash. D.C. about 54 miles off. Hit Wash. D.C. after dark so didn't see much of it. . . .

We are located on what is called League Island and there are about 4000 Jackies here waiting for orders to go to sea. We get liberty every night and 48 hours week end and as Phil. is only 2 or 3 miles off, we can have a good time."

Leo Kolb was but one of four hundred young men from the Melrose area who served in their country's armed forces during World War I. Week after week in 1918 the local newspaper reported the numbers of those who answered their country's call. The case of a "draft slacker" was duly recorded in the weekly gazette and, happily, the young man, by the name of Johnson, was not from the area. "Chief of Police Gaetz," the story read,

"was instrumental last Saturday (July 20, 1918) in nabbing a draft slacker at the G.N. station when he became suspicious of the actions of a young man who was about to take No. 4 that evening, intending to go to St. Cloud. The young man was rather sassy in answering Mr. Gaetz's questions and when asked to show his registration card he admitted that he had not registered. . . .

Monday evening the man tried to make a getaway while Officer Gaetz was taking him back to his cell after taking supper at the Central Hotel. He caught the police unaware and by a quick dash was soon running through the alley toward the river. Unger's auto happened to be in front of the furniture store and the police and a number of men getting in followed him to the river dam where he was cornered and had to give himself up."

To the credit of the Melrose community many of its finest sons served with distinction in the services of their country both in the first and the second World Wars. An assistant pastor of St. Boniface parish, Reverend Sebastian Schirmers, also volunteered his services for the chaplain corps and was called up at the end of July, 1918. He was one of two priests of the Diocese of St. Cloud who served as chaplains, the other being Reverend August Preusser. The community also served the war effort at home in both world-wide conflicts. Farmers produced more; women rolled bandages for the troops; contributions to the Red Cross were more than generous. No one would be able to say, as some did unjustly, that there was a pro-German sentiment among the children of German immigrants who loyally and faithfully dedicated their time and talents to the service of their country. They were not "Dutchmen"; they were Americans and among the first to manifest their loyalty to their country. Worthy of mention is the fact that the quota of war bonds for the Melrose area in 1918 was two hundred thousand dollars and even this was over-subscribed to by almost five thousand dollars.

Leo Kolb, however, did not have much time to "have a good time." He was the first casualty of the war, having died on September 22, 1918 in the League Island Hospital "as the result of a short illness of pneumonia." In a letter to his parents, Mr. and Mrs. John Kolb, his superior officer wrote, "Your son was ever cheerful about his work, and ever ready to ease the burden on the shoulders of some fellow workman less qualified than he.... He did his duty by his country in her hour of need, as other young men are trying to do theirs." From its earliest days the citizens of Melrose have never shirked their duty to their country, many of them making the supreme sacrifice. In the fourth appendix to this chapter are listed the names of deceased members of the community who have served in either the Civil War, the Spanish American War, World War I, World War II, the Korean conflict and the Vietnam War.

CATHOLIC AID ASSOCIATION CONVENTION

The largest gathering that Melrose ever witnessed was the "great Catholic convention" of September 26-28, 1926. The highlight of the convention was a "monstrous parade" including ten divisions with bands from Cold Spring, Richmond, Roscoe, Sauk Centre, St. Joseph, St. Rosa, Little Falls, Long Prairie, Belgrade and Osakis among many other communities represented. The three-day convention, which drew over ten thousand people was the state convention of the Catholic Aid Association. The meeting was significant inasmuch as it brought together some of the most distinguished German Catholic leaders in the state. Michael A. Weiskopf of St. Paul was the grand marshal of the parade; Bishop Joseph F. Busch, Abbot Alcuin Deutsch, O.S.B. and George N. Gerlach of St. Paul, president of the association, were among the principal speakers. Local participants were Eberhart Hoehl, music director, Ignatius Lemm, chief of the parade, Theodore Hinnenkamp, secretary of the convention committee, and Henry Wessel, president of the convention committee.

The local editor called the convention "one of the greatest events this city has ever undertaken" and added, "we cannot refrain from paying a special compliment to Reverend Willenbrink of the St. Boniface parish on his able leadership and the excellent manner in which he planned for the success of the convention." Monsignor Camille Thiebaut, then chancellor of the diocese, offered the opening Mass at which Abbot Alcuin Deutsch preached the sermon. After the ten divisions of the parade passed the reviewing stand it was worthy of note that "the famous little German Band of New Ulm seated in, around and on top of an automobile, brought up the rear of the parade in a pleasing manner." The "open air" addresses were delivered in the city park and during this time "J. M. Aretz of St. Paul made an address in German and Reverend Charles Gruenwald of St. Cloud gave a splendid address in English." On Sunday evening St. Boniface parish hall was the scene of a S.R.O. crowd viewing the theatrical and musical entertainment provided by the local society. The program included such songs as *"Zillerthal, Du bist mei Freud," "Fruehling Am Rhein," "Heimathrosen"* and *"Schliess Auf"* and included a *"lustspiel in 3 acten"* entitled *"Kuriert"* starring Otto Harren and L. Hoeschen. During the *"zwischenpausen"* the New Ulm orchestra provided the entertainment. The German play, *"Kuriert"* was presented by the Freeport players and, as the local editor recorded, "the Freeport troupe being deserving of much praise on the able manner in which they rendered the play."

At the end of the convention the delegates passed several resolutions concerning youth, labor, farm questions and one that stated "an international reconciliation be effected by the Catholics throughout the world and the Mexican government." In keeping with the times and the temperment of the delegates, it is not too surprising that one resolution should deal with prohibition. This resolution, passed unanimously, read as follows:

"The federation of German Catholic societies believes in obedience to all laws of the state and nation and deplores the flagrant disregard of the prohibition laws. We believe that this defiance of the federal law is largely due to the dictatorial and unreasonable features of the Volstead law and that it should be modified so as to permit the manufacture of and sale of beverage not intoxicating in fact."

Eight years would pass before such a desire would be fulfilled. But the Germans would have their beer and they would succeed. Common sense would prevail over mass hysteria. In the end the opponents of prohibition would appear more reasonable than the defenders.

The inborn love of the German people for organizations is well known and widely accepted. The organization for a German was as important as the family for a descendant of the Irish. In the organization the German found his identity; he was at home with his brothers, a part of the group, a member of the community. Societies, both civic and religious, were part and parcel of his life and his need for such organization increased in corresponding degrees to the attacks that the *auslanders* would launch against his language, culture and way of life. This fact accounts for the strength and endurance of so many of the organizations that welded together so many of the people of the Melrose community. This fact also is a partial explanation of the fact that the Catholic Aid Association was again invited to return to Melrose in 1940 to hold its annual convention. Although not as elaborate as the earlier meeting, it was nonetheless just as important because the nation was again on the brink of war and people of Germanic origins were just as concerned about the fate of their country as people of other ethnic origins.

Fourteen years later the Catholic Aid Association of Minnesota returned to Melrose for its state-wide convention. Once again the papers spoke of a crowd of over ten thousand people, a huge parade, speeches and meetings. The convention chairman was Leo J. Beste and the honorary chairman was the pastor of St. Boniface parish, Very Reverend Lambert Haupt. The traditional German hymns were sung, such as *"Maria zu Lieben," "Dem Herzen Jesu Singe"* and *"Grosser Gott"* — and this in spite of the strong anti-German feeling abroad in the land. During the convention Joseph B. Korte discussed rural rehabilitation and J. M. Aretz reported on the activities of the Central Verein. Dr. A. A. Meyer delivered the welcoming address and that perennial speaker for all occasions, attorney W. J. Stephens, made his customary remarks. The principal guest of the convention, Bishop Joseph F. Busch of St. Cloud, praised the organization for its exceptionally large attendance.

The principal speaker at the convention was Monsignor Luigi Ligutti who "jumped into national prominence" by successfully organizing a homestead project for the destitute coal miners of northeast Iowa. In his address the social-minded monsignor outlined three ways in which prosperity could come to the individual. First, he said, the individual should be given the opportunity to achieve prosperity; secondly, one man's prosperity should not come at the expense of another man; finally, it must be a prosperity that is within the reach of every man. "The well being of humans," he said, "must be organized so that prosperity comes at the same time to society, the family, the person. It is not a just prosperity if it comes to one of these and not to the other two. Human beings who work have a natural right to prosperity, to enjoy the fruits of their toil." The children's program during this state convention heard addresses on the value of 4-H club work by William A. Boerger, the county superintendent of schools, and Joseph Kunkel.

CAPTAIN GALLAGHER DAY

If the Catholic Aid conventions of 1926 and 1940 drew the largest crowds that Melrose ever witnessed, surely the most enthusiastic crowd that ever assembled in Melrose came to pay tribute to a native son who was the captain of the "Lucky Lady II," the first airplane to circle the world non-stop in a flight of twenty-three thousand, four hundred and fifty-two miles lasting ninety-four hours. "Jimmy" Gallagher, son of Mr. and Mrs. Cornelius Gallagher, a retired engineer of the Great Northern railroad made front-page news across the nation when he and his crew landed at Carswell Air Force Base on Wednesday, March 2, 1949 after their epochmaking flight around the world. Upon landing Captain Gallagher and his crew were greeted by top officials from the government and air force. The Secretary for Air, Stuart Symington, said, "This is an epochal step in the development of air power. What it actually does is to turn our medium bombers into intercontinental bombers." Another official, whose name would figure prominently in subsequent national issues, was also on hand. He was then Lieutenant General Curtis E. LeMay, at the time chief of the Strategic Air Command, and the man who directed the fire-bombing of Japan by B-29's and the dropping of the atomic bombs on Hiroshima and Nagasaki. After congratulating Captain Gallagher he "beamed proudly" and told interviewers: "This means that we now can deliver an atomic bomb to any place in the world that requires an atomic bomb." Little did he know at the time that a subsequent generation would be opposed to that powerful atomic bomb! Captain Gallagher, however, best summarized the feelings of his crew of whom he simply said, "A lengthy snooze under Air Force 'sack duty' was better pay for their 94 hours and one minute flight than a barrage of television, radio, and newspaper glamour."

Appropriately, Captain Gallagher Day began when the Captain and three members of his around-the-world crew flew over the city in a

B-50 bomber, the "Kensman." This was the same type of aircraft as the "Lucky Lady II" which had made the historic journey. Accompanying the bomber were eleven F-82 fighter airplanes that had flown from Austin, Texas and joined Gallagher and his crew over Willmar. Three times the bomber came low over the city while the fighters buzzed the city four times. Citizens throughout the area were out to view the aerial demonstration and "were thrilled beyond words."

But whether he liked it or not, Captain Gallagher was a hero. Perhaps it was a moment when the nation needed heroes. Perhaps, too, it was the electric moment when the right man came along with the right job to instill a sense of pride and joy in a citizenry who needed so badly a national and local idol to rejuvenate its drooping spirits. Whatever it was, Captain James Gallagher filled the need at the right time and in the right place. For many years a highway sign would proclaim Melrose as the home of Captain James Gallagher, "pilot of first non-stop flight around the world." And some vivacious mothers even to the present day would recall that they succeeded in obtaining an autograph from Captain Gallagher.

Once again Melrose turned out in its finest clothing. The city and the community was welcoming home a hero, a native son who had "made good" and a son of parents who were among the finest of the Melrose citizenry. A booklet of his historic non stop flight, entitled "The Big Circle... Non-Stop" had already been published and circulated nationally. His airplane, "Lucky Lady II" was already a household word throughout the nation. His wife, Mary, was spending Mardi Gras in New Orleans at the time of the historic flight and did not have the slightest idea of the important mission that her husband was undertaking. And so Melrose prepared for the homecoming of its most famous war hero.

"Jimmy" Gallagher came home. The Stearns county court house closed on April 19th to honor him as he made his appearance in the county seat. "A giant parade and reception" was held in Melrose for the return of the twenty-eight year old air force captain.

A twenty-car caravan escorted the hero from Minneapolis to Melrose. It stopped in St. Cloud about four o'clock where it was met on the outskirts of the city by the Cathedral and Technical high school bands, Mayor Malisheski and presidents of various civic organizations. The motorcade was escorted down St. Germain Street whose sidewalks were lined with thousands of cheering citizens. From there the hero and his group drove to Melrose where he was met by the V.F.W. drill team, the Melrose high school band and the officials of the city.

With his wife and family Captain Gallagher spent a quiet evening at the home of his parents, Mr. and Mrs. Cornelius Gallagher.

The following day, Friday April 20th "a giant parade composed of approximately forty units" formed at the St. Boniface church grounds and marched to the Legion park in recognition of the local boy who became a national hero. Speakers at the park included Governor Luther Youngdahl, Colonel Ernie Miller and Brigadier General Paul P. Cullen, deputy commander of the 311th Air Division, a representative of the United States Air Force. At five o'clock a banquet was served in St. Boniface church basement in honor of the Captain, his wife, his parents and the other members of his crew. More than four hundred guests heard speeches from Frank T. Gallagher and Thomas F. Gallagher, associate justices of the Minnesota supreme court, District judge E. J. Ruegemer and the Very Reverend Matthias Hoffmann.

In his remarks Governor Youngdahl expressed the appreciation of the citizens of Minnesota to Captain Gallagher. "You are part of the world's history," he said, "Melrose is part of the world's history and, therefore, our state has been made a part of the world's history." Brigadier General Cullen said that "the Air Force and nation share with the citizens of Melrose and the members of Captain Gallagher's family the pride they have over his great achievement." The Captain expressed the appreciation of himself, his wife, his parents and his crew for the reception given in their honor and commented that "this is the most wonderful day of my life."

An invited guest unable to attend was Minnesota's senior senator, Hubert H. Humphrey. In a letter to Mr. and Mrs. Cornelius Gallagher he expressed his regrets for not being present. "It was my desire," he wrote, "to return to Minnesota and join with the hundreds of people who gathered in Melrose to pay tribute to Captain Jimmy. However, all this week the Senate has been engaged in a fight over appropriations bills and it was necessary for me to remain in Washington." The senator, however, praised Captain Gallagher's achievement on the floor of the United State Senate and his remarks are included in the fifth appendix to this chapter.

SISTER CELSA DAY

One of the last great events that Melrose witnessed occurred on May 4, 1958 when a quiet, unassuming nun was honored by the community for her distinguished, life-long dedication to the children of the community and the purposes of Catholic education. Sister Celsa at the time held the national record of teaching sixty years in the same school and fifty-eight of these years were spent teaching first-graders. No other teacher in the nation and the state had ever matched that record.

Born in Ilmtiz, Austria, she emigrated with her parents to St. Paul on May 11, 1878. She entered the Priory of the Benedictine Sisters in Saint Joseph, Minnesota and a year later, in 1898, was assigned to teach at St. Boniface school, Melrose. After teaching the third grade for one year she asked the pastor if she might be assigned to teach the first grade. The pastor, Monsignor Bernard Richter, did not feel that she was "qualified" to teach the first grade and thus denied her request. He did, however, not completely ignore her preference. Rather, he sent her to the University of Minnesota for the summer sessions of 1899 and 1900 where she majored in elementary education. Upon her return that year she became the teacher of her "beloved first-graders." There she remained the next fifty-eight years of her life.

Throughout the years Sister Celsa taught approximately two thousand and four hundred first-grade children. She proudly could recall how she was teaching the third generation of students. Many a time she would exclaim in the classroom, "I knew your grandfather and your father and you are just as lazy as they were!" But her expressions of irritation were always mixed with a deep love and reverence for the child and his ancestors. She was a teacher of exceptional ability, never content to rest on her laurels but always eager to further her own education for the benefit of her pupils. Over the years she continually kept herself abreast of the latest methods and techniques in educational circles. She attended summer school sessions at the Saint Paul Archdiocesan Teachers' College, the Saint Cloud Teachers' College, the University of Minnesota and the Dickinson, North Dakota, Teachers' College. Besides her teaching duties Sister Celsa served most of these years as the sacristan of St. Boniface parish. Never would she allow so much as a speck of dust in the sacristy and sanctuary of the church.

With a well-deserved pride she could number among her pupils eight priests and nineteen sisters, as well as of at least forty-four sets of three generations of pupils. She recalled, at the time of the celebration in her honor that she at one time taught a class consisting of seventy-two pupils. The pastor of St. Boniface parish, Monsignor Matthias Hoffmann, who knew her when he was an assistant priest of the parish in 1908, remarked, "If we have more discipline in our school it is due to the way Sister Celsa trains the children when she has them in the first grade." What is most amazing is the fact that during the year of her diamond jubilee as a teacher Sister Celsa did not miss one day of teaching.

Thus a celebration was in order. The people of Melrose turned out in loving affection on Sunday, May 4, 1958 to honor a woman who was not coming home but was "home" — and all the best that it symbolized — for many of them. Bishop Peter W. Bartholome of St. Cloud inaugurated the festivities with a pontifical high Mass in St. Boniface church that was filled to overflowing by many of Sister Celsa's former pupils. Following the Mass the ladies of St. Boniface parish served a banquet in the parish hall for the visiting religious and civic dignitaries. Sister Celsa, of course, was the guest of honor — and those who knew her well, knew very well that she was uncomfortable and embarrassed by the entire program. Many leaders of church and state attended the event and spoke words of tribute to a nun who had so faithfully performed her duties for over sixty years. During the banquet Bishop Bartholome presented Sister Celsa with the pontifical *"Benemerenti"* medal, the Vatican's equivalent of the Distinguished Service Medal. Fourth Degree Knights of Columbus from St. Cloud were present to serve as an honor guard, and among the speakers at the banquet and following the reception in the Melrose high school auditorium were Monsignor Matthias Hoffmann, Father Aloysius J. Kraemer, Father Francis J. Julig, state representative Edmund Tiemann, Sister Remberta, O.S.B. and Mother Richarda, O.S.B. Over a thousand people from the community and neighboring areas took part in the festivities.

During the civic reception in the afternoon Sister Celsa received a personal telephone call from the governor of the state who extended his personal congratulations. Toastmaster of the civic reception was Monsignor T. Leo Keaveny, diocesan superintendent of schools, who followed an introductory address by Mayor A. C. Welle, one of Sister Celsa's pupils. During the civic reception a telegram from the White house, signed by President Dwight D. Eisenhower, was read by Monsignor Hoffmann. It read as follows:

"Please give my greetings to the members and friends of St. Boniface parish joined in the celebration of the diamond teaching jubilee of Sister Celsa, O.S.B. As a distinguished elementary school teacher for sixty years, Sister Celsa has contributed much to the lives of many. Through a host of students, her grace, skill and high sense of purpose will be felt for generations to come. It is a privilege to join in honoring such a person."

Sister Celsa survived the day. She did not particularly enjoy it, for as she told this writer, she would much rather prefer to be back in the classroom teaching her beloved first graders. And that is where she was on May 5, 1958. Old age and infirmities forced her to retire. She returned to the motherhouse at St. Joseph, Minnesota and in 1958 was called to a reward she so richly deserved.

APPENDIX

THE PHITZEL BREWERY RAID

Valentine Herman and Stanley Dubois, Alvin Bohmer and Joseph Sigmuth appeared before Judge Kant shortly before midnight last night to receive sentences for conspiracy to violate the federal prohibition laws by removing beer from the Phitzel Brewery in New Munich. When they appeared, the true story of the New Munich raid was made public for the first time. It appeared that on October 25, 1923, the government seized the New Munich Brewery and placed under seal 3,640 bottles of beer and 29 cases of beer. On the morning of October 27th, Mat Phitzel, head of the brewing company telephoned the officers that someone had visited the brewery the night before and stole part of the beer. Federal prohibition officers, Angus A. E. Whitney, Morris Silvermann and Lewis F. Cole were ordered to proceed to that place. Arriving at nine o'clock in the evening they secreted themselves in a ice house near the bottling works. They remained in hiding until two o'clock in the morning at which time a Cadillac car drove past the brewery, turned around and drove away again. Very soon afterwards a large International truck arrived closely followed by a Ford truck. The men in the truck began loading up beer. The agents waited for them to get the truck well loaded but waited too long. The truck started unexpectedly and got away. The Ford truck was being loaded up and the agents decided it was time to make a capture. They rushed from their hiding place and three men fled, but Joseph Sigmuth was caught with a sack of beer bottles in his hands. He confessed and Herman, Dubois and Bohmer were arrested the next day on the strength of his statement. Following the seizure of the Ford truck and the arrest of Sigmuth, officers Whitney and Cole got into Cole's car which was concealed in the neighborhood and started to shoot at the International truck which had gotten away. They had no difficulty in following the tire tracks of the truck as the country was sandy. They followed for twenty-five miles and finally drove along side of it. Whitney jumped from the automobile onto the running board of the truck. The two vehicles were abreast. Cole drove on and drove his car across the road in front of the truck. The truck turned out and drove by him. He could see nothing of Whitney who was expected to halt the driver but he did see a flashlight turned upward in the road. He ran back and found Whitney lying by the roadside with his skull fractured. Gaining pursuit of the truck he took the injured man to the hospital in St. Cloud where he remained unconscious for days but finally recovered. The plot to rob the brewery was . . . . the soft drink parlor in Avon. According to evidence secured by the government, Stanley Dubois was the owner of the Ford truck and Valentine Herman was the owner and driver of the Cadillac car. Herman, Bohmer, Sigmuth and Dubois were taken to the Minneapolis jail the day after their arrest. Sigmuth and Bohmer made written confessions while Herman and Dubois refused to talk. Herman was placed in a cell with . . . . Thompson, a prohibition agent disguised as a common prisoner and told him the whole story. As nearly as can

263

be ascertained, Whitney was struck over the head with a truck stake when he jumped onto the running board of the International truck. The man who struck him was not one of the four men arrested but an entirely different party. It is probable that this man will be arrested within a few days. Judge Kant said that the crime of the men brought before him tonight was a foolish one but it was a first offense in all cases. He sentenced Sigmuth to paying a fine of $300; Bohmer, a fine of $650; Dubois, a fine of $1,000; and Herman, a fine of $1,000—all being ordered to be committed to Ottertail County jail until fines were paid. All expect to pay them. Herman said his business was that of County Commissioner, Stearns County; Bohmer is in the meat business in Avon; Dubois runs a restaurant and Sigmuth is a farmer.

St. Cloud Times

*   *   *   *   *   *

Melrose Beacon, Thursday, July 30, 1925

DRY AGENTS CAUSE EXCITEMENT IN TOWN; SPOTTER GETS INTO TROUBLE HERE LAST WEEK AND RAID YESTERDAY FOLLOWS.

The town was stirred during the week by activities of federal dry agents here and excitement was riled yesterday afternoon when a car of six federal men appeared for a raid. With them was Robert Bain who has been working in this vicinity as a spotter or undercover man. Bain got into trouble here last Thursday and alleges that while in the country north of here, samples of liquor he had purchased had been stolen from his car and later he and two other men with him got into a fight with three men who, he claims, came from the city and was badly beaten. Later in an attempt to round up these men on Mainstreet here, he pulled a gun but was stopped by police officer, Frank Morehouse, and was taken to the city hall where he disclosed that he was a federal agent and was immediately released. Bain then left town saying that he would return the next day to get the men but he never did appear. On their visit here yesterday, the federal men searched the backroom and basement of the Klabberich building but never found anybody in the place. Neither did they find any liquor. No other places here were searched. It was reported that federal agents had nine warrants with them but no arrests were made yesterday. The following account of the dry agents' activities here appeared in the **Minneapolis Tribune** this morning and was evidently written by a reporter of that paper who interviewed the federal men on their return to Minneapolis last evening. Minneapolis federal prohibition agents requested the sheriff of the Stearns County and St. Cloud police last Wednesday to assist in hunting for Mr. and Mrs. Ray Stranton who were missing from their farm five miles north of Melrose. On the front porch of the Stranton farm house last Friday night, the agents charge, Robert Bain, an undercover agent working out of Minneapolis, was beaten up by three men who dragged him out of his automobile as he drove along the highway. Sheriff Burns of Todd County also reported that Bain's informant, who was allowed to go free by the gang that beat Bain was missing from Long Prairie. Making a detour around Melrose in order that their approach might not be heralded throughout the countryside, two automobile loads of federal agents with Bain drove to the Stranton farm Wednesday. Mr. and Mrs. Stranton were not home. Their sixteen-year-old daughter, Mytle Stranton, was in charge. She said she didn't know where her parents were. Chief Carlson's agents are now in Melrose hunting for the three men who attacked Bain. They are believed to be residents of Melrose. Other troubles in Stearns County besides the attack on Bain engaged the action of the prohibition agents today. They were not far from New Munich where Albert Whitney, the federal agent, was beaten almost to death by a mob of beer thieves. A few months after the incident, Ollie P. Olson was shot and severely wounded by Nicholas Lahr, proprietor of a soft drink establishment in St. Cloud. More recently preceeding the attack on Bain the trouble has been of less serious but nevertheless of an exceedingly annoying matter. Reed's plan of greatest secrecy was rendered ineffective when agents arrived only to find that everyone in town appeared to know that they were coming. In prohibition enforcement circles there was a story going about that bootleggers in Stearns County offered rewards to those who beat up federal agents. Accompanied by his informer, Bain had been out working as an undercover agent buying drinks and collecting evidence when he was attacked. He had made several purchases and had samples in his car. Paying no attention to the informer the gang attacked Bain, gave him a severe beating and destroyed his samples. After the encounter Bain drove his car to Melrose. He collapsed calling for help as he alighted from his car on Main Street. A crowd gathered around him. He sent for F. M. Morehouse, constable. After some delay Morehouse arrived but questioned Bain's identity. Bain was reluctant to disclose the fact that he was an undercover agent but was finally obliged to do so and directed Morehouse to put in a long distance call for John Kraus, Bureau of Enforcement Chief. The injured prohibition agent was brought to Minneapolis Friday night. His bruises kept him in bed until Wednesday when he got up to accompany the raiding party in order to identify those who had attacked him. He also directed the agents to places where he had bought liquor while working as an under cover in Stearns County. John Kraus, Group Chief, told the story Wednesday night of how bootleggers in Stearns County had been offering rewards to those who attacked prohibition agents. Mr. Kraus said, "Our men have been in bootlegging joints and talked to fellows who had freely disclosed the whole thing." Wets were instructed how to go about knocking out an agent and were told a reward was offered by the leader in the bootlegging ring. Kraus also told about the trouble agents have had with telephone tip-offs while working in Stearns County. "Every time we start out to make a raid in the rural sections of Stearns County," he said, "we find that the farmers have been warned of our presence." The trouble in Stearns County started two years ago when Albert Whitney, prohibition agent, was struck down by beer thieves at the Phitzel Brewery in New Munich. His skull was fractured and for several weeks he lay at the point of death in the St. Raphael's Hospital in St. Cloud. Search for Whitney's assailants failed. Agents lead by H. L. Duncan, divisional chief, spent two weeks in Stearns County trying to find them. Agents were given orders to take no chances in future raids in Stearns County. St. Cloud, county seat, was the scene of the next outbreak. Nicholas Lahr, proprietor of the soft drink establishment, severely shot and wounded Ollie P. Olson, dry agent, during a raid September 18, 1924. Lahr was arrested and charged with assault with the attempt to kill, convicted and sent for seven years in the federal penitentiary. Shortly after the attack on Olson, S. B. Qvale, state prohibition director, issued "shoot to kill" orders to agents operating in Stearns County. His men were instructed to work with their hands and their gun and shoot in self-defense whenever the occasion warranted.

❖   ❖   ❖   ❖   ❖   ❖

THE LAND — GOD'S GREATEST GIFT TO MAN

✠Peter W. Bartholome, D.D.
Bishop of Saint Cloud

Plowville is a practical demonstration of the interest of people in the land. Each year it attracts national attention and, therefore, it becomes a very important event in the life of the nation for it draws to the attention of the people of the country the importance of the land in human affairs and, no doubt, inspires those who actively take part, as well as men and women of the nation who are directly or indirectly engaged in soil conservation, with a greater reverence and appreciation for the land.

The land is God's greatest material gift to mankind. Everything in human affairs depends on the land. Out of the land the body of man was fashioned and on it man depends for his continued existence in this world. By the land man lives and breathes. For its products he expends his life's energy. Industry and commerce, in all of its phases, depends on the land. The land is basic to all of the activities of the human race. Through the land man is best able to work up to the fullest development of his nature as created by God. On the land man is closest to God's creation and, therefore, is enabled with greater facility to work out his eternal destiny. At the end of his life, the body of man again returns to and becomes identified with the land. Truly, there seems to be no other relationship so intimate as that of man with the land.

The history of nations very clearly teaches us that the land, as land, is the greatest good of the state, the family and the individual. When man fell from grace the land, too, suffered and since that time the land has become an intricate and disturbing factor in the relationships of human beings. Men have vied with each other for its possession. Greed for the land has disturbed the peace of the world through history. The varied productivity of the land has unbalanced the economy of nations. The lust for wealth has brought about an inequitable distribution of the land with the resulting depletion of the fertility of the soil. Slavery, as an institution in history, was intimately bound up with the greed of men for the land.

Disturbed World

We are living in a very disturbed world at the present time, economically, politically and socially. A good deal of that disturbance is due to the inequitable distribution of the ownership of land. In all of the nations in the world at the present time that are in a state of confusion and who do not seem to be able to reach orderly government, you will find on close observation that their basic trouble is the inequity found in the ownership of the land in these countries. . .

In all of the countries south of the Rio Grande, the fundamental problem is an agricultural problem. Large land ownership has created serfdom and poverty, depletion of the fertility of the soil. This is true in all of the countries of Asia. We even found this situation, too, to great an extent in the countries immediately behind the Iron Curtain. Africa's problem is mainly a problem of the land, its ownership and its cultivation. You, no doubt, have noticed that in the past 50 years the forces of Communism have recognized this fact and whenever they wish to penetrate into any country to take over its government, their first program which enables them to succeed in these countries is a call for agrarian reform. This happened in Russia, in China, in the countries immediately behind the Iron Curtain.

Within the last few years the slogan call of Castro was agrarian reform, promising ownership of land to the poor and down-trodden. This same propaganda is being used in the countries of South America. This indicates quite clearly that the Communists are more alert to the basic problem than the free western nations as to the importance of the land and to the desire that is found in the human heart to possess a few acres for himself. The Communists have never measured up to their promises in any country. Instead of the distribution of the land to the needy people as they had promised, the State became the land holder and owner and the situation went from bad to worse. Our government is sending money in the millions and billions to these nations. It would be much better if the money were earmarked by us to develop the resources of the land in these countries so that people would have enough to eat.

In the United States of America during the past two centuries, we have found an ideal situation as far as ownership of land is concerned. The family farm which gave life and strength to our nation, which developed independence, character and free citizens has been our agricultural pattern during these years. At the present moment, however, there is a danger in our country that we are forgetting the importance of the family farm in the life of our nation. Farming is fast becoming a commercial venture. Farmers are moving off the land. There are fewer than five million farm operators in this country supplying one hundred eighty million fellow-citizens with vast unused surpluses.

Save Family Farms

Our agricultural output is out-racing the increase in population. From 1950 to 1960 the population of America went up 19%; farm production went up 27%. Another factor that is working against the family farm is the greater efficiency in production which, in turn, is due to mechanization, better education and training in farming. This seems to entice corporations and businessmen and professional men to the securing of large tracts of land in order to make profits on their investments so that we are witnessing at the present time a change of thinking as well as a change in the actual operation of a farm and its ownership. . .

Farming has, indeed, come a long way in the United States of America in its productive development. Gradually men are beginning to look upon farming more and more as a way of making a living and securing profits rather than as a way of life. In many areas it can no longer be called agriculture but, perhaps, should be called agri-business. Naturally, as the face of American farming undergoes these radical and drastic changes, one must express doubt about the wisdom of these new developments and a few questions might be asked.

Can America afford to destroy the family-sized farm? Can America afford to continue to ignore, in its legislation on a national and state level, the necessity of the family farm in the life of the nation? I answer these questions in the negative. The future of America and its strength, freedom and vitality depend in largest measure on the family-sized farm which has made this country strong and great.

As one reads the current literature on agriculture, hardly any mention is made of the family-sized farm. The thinking expressed is that the family-sized farm is doomed to oblivion. In this materialistic world in which we are living, the spiritual and moral values are spurned and the only thing that seems to count in agriculture at the present time is profits, more production, efficiency. That is even the thinking of some soil conservationists.

The land is not a commercial product. It is a living thing, a creation of God, and has qualities and properties and purposes that are not, and cannot be, evaluated in terms of dollars and cents.

Our Department of Agriculture in Washington is not thinking, for the most part, in the terms of the family-sized farm. Our agricultural legislation programs are, unfortunately, sometimes geared to the materialistic economy of the nation and the deeper values found in farming are ignored. As a result, the legislation that is evolved in most instances is destructive to the family-sized farm.

I recommend that a bureau be set up in the Department of Agriculture that will study the Christian philosophy of the land and through that thinking, which is basic to Christian civilization, laws and programs be evolved that, will foster the family-sized farm in the United States of America. I realize that this is swimming against the tide, but there must be a few voices raised that will alert us all to the dangerous trends into which agriculture is falling at the present time.

Large Land Holders

The soil bank is a glaring example of the way the government at the present time is ignoring the problem of the land and the family-sized farm. Plowville is being conducted in an area this year where more than 50% of the population is actually living on the land, where the family-sized farm is thriving and in existence. I have seen many family-sized farms of 200 acres or so that are productive, efficient, where the family is making money in a moderate degree and where a family is being raised with a dignity, independence, freedom, the spirit of sacrifice — all qualities so necessary in American life today.

Not too far away from Plowville 1961, however, larger land holding is in vogue. I drove through an area just two weeks ago where the farmers owned 500 to 1,000 or more acres. For 15 miles in this area most of the farm buildings were abandoned or, if there were people living in the house, there were no other living things around the yard. All that I saw was farm machinery in the yard exposed to the weather. The one who was driving my car said, 'Isn't this a desolate section of the diocese?" I said, "What do you mean? This is the Red River Valley. The soil is rich. The crops are good." Nevertheless, he was right.

It was a desolate 15 miles, for there were no living things, living a way of life with dignity and with freedom. . .

The great leaders of nations of the past and of today, the great leaders of industry in many instances, come from the land. A great railroad man of the Northwest, James J. Hill, who was a capitalist but who loved the land and who realized its importance in the development of a railroad, is imputed to have said that "land without people is a wilderness and people without land is a mob."

Farm Organizations

It happens at this particular time that we have in Rome a farmer as Pope. His brothers and sisters live on small farms in northern Italy. A few weeks ago he wrote a great letter to the world on the social problems of the human race in the twentieth century. In it he devoted considerable space to agriculture. Pope John is a realist. He enumerates the problems of agriculture in the world at large, some of which apply to this nation, namely, the flight to the city, the low standard of living in rural areas throughout the world, the disproportion of economic recompense for the farmer, the lack of modern conveniences in many rural areas throughout the world — not so much in the United States — the necessity of a larger outlay of capital on the part of the farmer as compared to the city worker, the inability of the distribution agencies, especially in our country, to distribute the produce of the farm, and the gradual disappearance of the family farm. These are the problems he enumerated.

The Pope goes on to say, "It is not possible to determine what the structure of farm life should be because of the diversity of the rural conditions in each political community, not to mention the immense difference obtaining between the nations of the world. But if we hold to a human and Christian concept of man and the family, we are forced to consider as an ideal that community of persons operating on internal relations and whose structure is formed according to the demands of justice and the principles stated above, and still more, enterprises of family size. With these in mind we should exert every effort to realize one or the other, as far as circumstances permit."

Pope John advocates very strongly associations formed amongst farmers to promote their material and spiritual welfare. He recommends that rural workers should feel a sense of solidarity one with another, and should unite to form cooperative and professional associations, which are necessary if they are to benefit from scientific and technical progress in methods of production. They need to organize, he says, to have a voice in political circles as well as in organs of public administration. He advocates an establishment of effective price regulations to protect the prices of farm products. He thinks that this regulation should primarily be the work of the farmer, though he will admit that supervision by public authority is necessary. He strongly recommends an equitable basis for credit for farmers, especially young farmers who are taking on the vocation of farming, so as to make it possible for them to perpetuate the family farm.

No Monopoly

Pope John firmly believes that it is necessary for farmers today to have a sense of vocation to farming, to love the soil. He goes on to say in his recent encyclical: "In the work on the farm the human personality finds numerous incentives for self-expression, for self-development, for enrichment and for growth even in regard to spiritual values. Therefore, it is a work which is conceived and lived both as a vocation and as a mission. It can be considered an answer to God's call to actuate His providential plan in history. It may also be considered as a noble undertaking to elevate oneself and others and as a contribution to human civilization."

The soil conservationists of America, in my opinion, know and understand the importance of the land in the life of a nation. They love the land. It is only when we can maintain and understand the dignity of the farmer who deals with the land and the important place that he occupies in the life of a nation that a nation remains strong.

There must never be monopoly in the ownership of land in the United States of America. If that should ever take place, the land no longer becomes an object of love but a cold exploitation. When there is monopoly in land holding, land is made to produce only for speculation while the people suffer hunger and the national economy becomes exhausted. This perversion of private, rural property is very harmful.

It is necessary, therefore, that the soil conservationists of America, the farm organizations, the Department of Agriculture, keep always in mind in their planning, in their legislation and in their programs of action the importance of the family-sized farm, not merely in the economy of a nation but in the development of independence and freedom that we Americans so highly prize.

❊   ❊   ❊   ❊   ❊   ❊

THE LOYALTY OF STEARNS COUNTY

✠ Joseph F. Busch, D.D.
Bishop of Saint Cloud

I have said before that it is always a pleasure for me to visit with the good people of Melrose, and I am very glad that today we are gathered here, not only the people of Melrose but people from all over Stearns county.

We came here this afternoon to express our sentiments of loyalty, and we begin well by dedicating the symbol of our country, the symbol of liberty, to which we now look up with joy and inspiration. Besides dedicating the flag I believe that I would best serve the present purpose by introducing to you him whom most of you came here to listen to and to see this afternoon, the representative of our great state, his excellency Governor Burnquist. This is a civic celebration and a civic meeting and his excellency always has the first place, and while you may not know very much about astronomy, you at least all know that the sun and moon cannot both shine at the same time, and therefore I do not intend to keep you waiting any longer than is absolutely necessary, but while it is not necessary for me to introduce the head of our commonwealth, it may perhaps be not out of place to introduce the good people of the county of Stearns to his excellency, our governor. It is a very pleasant task for me to present the loyalty of Stearns county, represented by so many of you here present, to his excellency, our governor.

We all know that only a few months ago some people were tempted to look upon Stearns county with somewhat of suspicion, but I stood up and said that I was satisfied that Stearns county was absolutely loyal. Some people seemed to think that because we are dominantly Catholic and mostly of German origin that we were open to suspicion, but I said no. I said just because we are more than 90 per cent Catholic and dominantly of German origin, that we were therefore more than ordinarily loyal. Let us no longer refer to these suspicions. There is no one left that would now raise suspicion about the loyalty of Stearns county. There is not any other place in the United States that has done more in proportion than the people of Stearns county, and no matter how many more sacrifices are necessary, there is no more willing portion of this state or of the United States, than here in Stearns county. We are well aware of this fact, that it is a great privilege and pleasure to give expression to these sentiments, in the presence of his excellency, our governor.

These are stirring times and it is well for us to get together to see and to feel that we are one great nation. We may read and we may argue, but from seeing and from feeling comes the sentiment that spells victory, and therefore I am very glad that his excellency has given us the rare privilege of meeting here this afternoon to listen to his words of wisdom.

There are just a few things that I would like to say. The chairman says there are some people who are afraid to express their sentiments, unless, perhaps, they might lose in popularity or be interfered with in their business. Now I am not one of these. Not because I am a very privileged character, but because I don't and I haven't got any business to lose, and just because I am so fortunately situated, I believe it is my duty, more, perhaps, than that of any others, and say right from the shoulder, the things we ought to bear in mind.

There are a great many fellows who think that the best time to go out fishing is when the water is riley. I believe that in riley water it is rather easy to catch suckers, and because the country is now disturbed, there are those who will try to profit by the unfortunate situation. When men's minds are disturbed it is very easy to cast reflections, to draw class distinctions and to raise suspicion. Let us remember that we are a great country, and what makes the country great is not its geography, it is not its resources, but what makes our country great is its government. Our great martyred president has said, "This is a government of the people, for the people, by the people." Let us remember that this should always be true. That we must consider ourselves as one great people, not as different classes of people put together. In some countries there are poor classes, there are rich classes, there are laboring classes and there are business classes, but in our country there should be no class. Just as in the human body there are different members, but they all work together for the common good of one another.

I am not a politician; I am not looking for any office; I don't care what the consequences may be for what I say: I am not out preaching politics. They should be set aside at this time. I believe that providence rules the nation and we should stand by the people who are intrusted with our government. This is no time to criticize; this is no time to raise question, but to be obedient and anticipate the wishes of our government in every way that we can. Therefore, I would say, beware of the politician; let good enough alone. They say that it is no time to trade horses when crossing a stream. So I say, let us put aside politics, and re-elect those officers who are in office at the present time, unless some of them have proven themselves disloyal. There is a heavy responsibility resting upon the shoulders of our officials, so let us stand by them and assure them that we will re-elect them, until the job they have in hand can be safely carried out. I say, let us re-elect the present governor; let us re-elect our United States Senator Nelson; let us re-elect our senators, Hilbert and Sullivan, and our representatives who are loyal, and let us beware of those who would try to raise any class questions.

They tell us there is someone around here who is soliciting the farmers to join the non-partisan league. How many of them would be willing to raise their hands, as belonging to the non-partisan league, if there are any members here present? I believe that the Stearns county farmer is too intelligent and too loyal to be led astray by a bankrupt tramp from North Dakota. This is a government of the people, for the people, by the people it is not a government of the farmers, for the farmers and by the farmers, and it is not a government of Townley, for Townley and by Townley.

I think you got my message.

* * * * * *

A Response By Governor Burnquist

THE LOYALTY THAT IS IN YOUR HEARTS

Bishop Busch, ladies and gentlemen: It gives me great pleasure to have the privilege of being here today and join with you in these exercises at this time. I have appreciated greatly what the bishop has said. I have known him for many months and I feel there is not a more patriotic citizen within the state of Minnesota than the bishop who has just spoken.

Personally, I have never suspicioned this county. The manifestation here today, by your presence, shows the loyalty that is in your hearts for the great American Republic, a republic to which men and women have come from beneath the stars of every clime to take advantage of its institutions, its environment and American democracy. These people come here because they know that any school they may attend, at any altar they may worship, in every hall of legislation their voices must be heard, and enjoy the rights of franchise, which we have enjoyed since the adoption of the constitution up to the present time, right which are great indeed as compared with the right in Prussia, where four per cent of the people, by reason of will, cast eight per cent of the vote. In this country the conditions are different. In this country the vote of the poor man is as good as the vote of the rich man, and the vote of the farmer is just as good as the vote of the wealthy man. Votes of all of them are the same and I believe that we, as a people, appreciate these rights and these opportunities, and for that reason, men who have come here, regardless of race, color, or nationality, or creed or party, are today going to stand back of the Federal Government and back of that great exponent of democracy, Woodrow Wilson, president of the United States. Prior to this war we felt that all countries were becoming democratic, but this was not true in Germany, by reason of the activities of the war lords of that nation. We find that over there one of its officials has the right to declare war, if it is a war of self-defense, and of course, as far as he is concerned, every war that he desires declared, would be a war of self-defense.

The war with Denmark in 1841 was deliberately provoked and from that country were taken the provinces of Sleswig and Holstein in order to extend the boundaries of that country, and so this war in which we are today engaged, was deliberately provoked not by the German people but by the war lords at the head of the German empire, provoked for the purpose of enlarging the boundaries of that country and deliberately provoked at a time when other nations did not desire war. England was not ready for the conflict. England had internal dissensions and did not desire war, but the German ambassador went back from England and told the German war lords. France did not want war. France drew back her armies in order to show Germany that she did not desire a conflict, but as soon as she had withdrawn her armies, the German armies moved in and took the largest iron ore properties within that country. Russia did not desire war because of internal dissensions, but the war lords of Germany wanted war, and they had finished the completion of the Kiel Canal. The war lords of Germany wanted this conflict, and now, God help us, let us unite and give them war, so they will want war no more.

❖ ❖ ❖ ❖ ❖ ❖

VETERANS OF AMERICAN WARS

Civil War Veterans
S. S. Ulmer
A. A. Whitney
Lt. Van Rensalear
S. R. Foote
Elam Morehouse
Charles Cole
W. McCadden
Frank Morehouse
William Doty
W. B. Whitney
J. J. Salfinger
Charles Lamb
Henry Didd
John Parks

Spanish-American War Veterans
William Latzka
Joseph Tise
Joseph F. Thiers

Second World War Veterans Who Died Overseas or at Sea
Leo B. Braun
Lloyd Carlson
Aloys Hollermann
George Petermeier
Francis Lent
Leo Schuman
Vincent Schanhaar
Edward Schanhaar
Clifford Fern
Juletta Niehaus

Korean Conflict
Sylvester Braun

Vietnam War
Jerome J. Schlicht

Veterans Buried in Melrose Cemeteries

St. Mary's

George Moritz
W. H. Helsper
B. Timmer
George Meyer
Alex Hinnenkamp
Andrew J. Hetzel
Henry L. Rehkamp
Louis Weitzel
Henry J. Busmann
Simon Pfau
J. H. Diedrich
Harry Morehouse
Charles Penniston
John Budde
Jacob Trossen
Joseph Kraemer
Ed J. Stalboerger
Mike Gretsch
George Vogel
Albert Fern
Walter Wampach
Jerry Tembrock
Roger Hallerman
Wilfred Litchy
Joseph Lippsmeyer
Glen Schmitz
C. P. Meyer
Eva Pearl Trisko
Herbert Wensmann
Gene Schley
Norbert Jacobs
Edward Kraemer
Donald F. Otte
Dr. A. P. Limperich
Joseph Kerfeld
Leola Tise
Frank B. Trisko

Alois Woeste
John Beste
Dr. S. J. Roelike
Henry Kuhlmann
Joseph H. Koopmeiners
Walter E. Johnson
Charles Hofmann
George A. O'Brien
George Boeckermann
Frank W. Koterba
Hubert H. Primus
Clarence Timmer
Marlin Evens
William Latzka
Carroll Arvig
John P. Goihl
Joseph Korf

Oak Hill

Ralph O. Michelsen

St. Patrick's

J. J. Ahearn
James O'Hara
Patrick Graham
Joseph Ziegler
M. Maegher
M. Cosgrove
Edward Graham
Edward Adams
Kathryn Graham
William Latzka, Jr.
Sylvester Timmer
William Latzka, Sr.
Frank A. Kilian
Edmund R. Dwyer
Michael Burke

*   *   *   *   *   *

ONE OF OUR FELLOW CITIZENS

The following remarks were made by Senator Hubert H. Humphrey on the floor of the United States Senate on May 20, 1949 and recorded in the Congressional Record of that date on pages 6665-66.

MR. HUMPHREY. Mr. President, I should like to make a few appropriate remarks with reference to a very distinguished Minnesotan who is being honored as of this date for his service to his country and for outstanding service, in particular, to the National Defense Establishment of the United States. I refer to Capt. James Gallagher, pilot of Air Force B-50 Lucky Lady II on the first nonstop round-the-world flight. He has been flying with the same bombing group since March 1944.

The city of Melrose, Minn., is his home town. Along with the official representative of the State of Minnesota, the city of Melrose is paying high tribute and honor to its distinguished member of the Air Forces for his valiant service, not only in war but also in peacetime, underlying the defense of our Nation.

I should like to place in the RECORD an editorial from the St. Cloud Daily Times, of St. Cloud, Minn., of May 16, 1949, which calls attention to the ceremonies being conducted this afternoon and this evening in Captain Gallagher's home town.

There being no objection, the editorial was ordered to be printed in the RECORD, as follows:

ROADS LEAD TO MELROSE

All roads will lead to Melrose Friday of this week when that community, together with thousands of visitors from all over the State, will say "Welcome home" to Jimmy Gallagher.

The Army plane pilot who was the first to fly nonstop around the world will find his home town ready to extend to him every honor within its power. And the honors will be in abundance, too.

Actually St. Cloud will get a preview of the celebration on Thursday. Captain Gallagher and his crew mates, escorted by Army planes, will fly over Melrose Thursday, and then land at the Minneapolis airport, since no field nearby is large enough to accommodate the huge ship. From Minneapolis the automobile procession will head for Melrose, passing through St. Cloud where a parade escort has been arranged. St. Cloud will give a warm greeting to this modern Magellan, who will go down in the history books as one of the greatest pilots of his day.

But on Friday, the festivities in Melrose will really move at top speed. The town, ablaze with decorations, will feature a parade early in the afternoon, an outdoor program, and a dinner Friday evening. It will be one of the greatest festival days in central Minnesota since another neighbor lad Charles Lindberg by name, took his tiny plane across the Atlantic to Paris.

Two great aerial feats by two great pilots - both central Minnesota boys: Lindbergh from Little Falls, 30 miles north of St. Cloud; Gallagher from Melrose, 30 miles west of St. Cloud.

A committee of Melrose men is working on final preparations for the notable event, Robert Meyer, himself a Navy fighter pilot, is one of the Gallagher committee, along with John Lang, Ted Kennedy, Walter Carlson, and, of course, many others. They are doing an outstanding job, and are getting the cooperation of thousands of folks from all over Minnesota.

Two big dates then this week - the first welcome to Captain Jimmy, Thursday, as he passes through St. Cloud en route to Melrose. Then the big homecoming festival at Melrose Friday. These will be notable occasions for us all.

MR. HUMPHREY. Mr. President, I wish to take a few moments of the time of the Senate to make a statement in regard to Captain Gallagher.

On March 2, 1949, Captain Gallagher and crew brought their plane to the ground at Carswell Air Force Base, Fort Worth, Tex., after 94 hours and 1 minute aloft on a history-making 23,452-mile flight around the world.

Captain Gallagher was born September 17, 1920, at Melrose, Minn., where he attended public school. He attended the Minneapolis Business College a year and a half before coming to Washington, D.C., in February 1941 for a civilian assignment in the office of the Surgeon General. In May, 1942 he enlisted as an aviation cadet and was called to Maxwell Field, Montgomery, Ala., in October of that year for preflight training.

He received primary training at Lakeland, Fla., basic training at Macon, Ga., and advanced training at Valdosta, Ga., before being commissioned a second lieutenant July 28, 1943. He received B-17 transition training at Hendricks Field, Sebring, Fla.; following which he was transferred to Great Bend, Kans., in October, 1943, to enter the original B-29 program. He went to India in March, 1944, with the Four Hundred and Forty-fourth Bomb Group, and flew as a B-29 copilot in 15 missions against enemy targets in Japan, Singapore, and Manchuria. He participated in the first B-29 raid on the Japanese homeland June 15, 1944, when the Air Force attacked Yawata, Japan's steel center.

In May 1945, Captain Gallagher moved with the group to the Marianas, where he took part in 20 more missions against Japan. He returned to the United States in October, 1945, with the Four Hundred and Forty-fourth Bomb Group, and was stationed at Merced, Calif., until May, 1946, when the group was transferred to its present station at Davis-Monthan AFB, Tucson, Ariz., and subsequently redesignated the Forty-third Bomb Group.

As assistant group operations officer for the Forty-third, Captain Gallagher organized the standardization board prescribing instructor training for his base. Besides serving as an airplane commander, he also has been group intelligence officer. He has flown B-50's regularly since January 1, 1949. His awards include the Distinguished Flying Cross, the Air Medal with three clusters, six battle stars, and three unit citations.

Mr. President, those of us who come from the State of Minnesota are honored by having Capt. James Gallagher as one of our fellow citizens.

We pay tribute to his great service, and we join his wife and daughter and his mother and his father in celebrating his splendid service to his country.

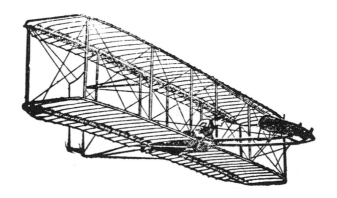

CHAPTER ELEVEN

WE LOST OUR HEARTS
BUT NOT OUR SOULS

> I've been working on the railroad,
> All the live-long day.
> I've been working on the railroad,
> Just to pass the time away.
>
> — American folk ballad

Cities, like people, have their share of crisis. Melrose met its greatest crisis in September, 1923. A brief notice in the local newspaper told of the imminent catastrophe:

"Effective next Sunday, September 9th, St. Cloud will become the operation headquarters of the local division of the Great Northern and the Melrose Yards will be eliminated from all train schedules . . . .

The present change will affect about 200 families in the city who will sooner or later have to move to St. Cloud or other terminal points. Many of these own their own homes in the city and they are at the present time finding it difficult to dispose of their property without suffering a heavy loss, and for this reason many will continue their residence here."

So brief a notice, consisting of no more than six inches of type, recorded calamity beyond measure for the city and the community. An official of the railroad predicted that "grass will grow on main street in Melrose," indicating ill will between the railroad and the local employees. Some say the transfer of the division headquarters back to St. Cloud, after twenty-seven years in Melrose, was caused by the economic situation arising from faster and newer trains. Others say it was management's revenge against a restless labor force. Whatever the reason for the move, the loss of the Great Northern division headquarters was a lethal blow to the development and the economy of Melrose.

In spite of the objections of citizens from Melrose, Albany, Avon, Collegeville and other stops along the route, the railroad won its battle.

In the end, however, the railroad lost the war. The automobile and truck had come into their own. The times were changing and the railroad, like it or not, was identified with a previous era. The "iron horse" was being replaced by the "horseless carriage" and other means of transportation. It was not, however, just methods of travel that were changing. People were changing and as a later song would proclaim "the times they are a-changin." The world and the nation were developing at breakneck speed.

Although a generation would pass between the economic depression that hit Melrose, the nation and the world, in the pages of history it was no more than the twinkling of an eye between the economic disaster that befell Melrose in 1923 and 1945 when the United States created a new era by setting off the first atomic bomb at Los Alamos, New Mexico. In the same year, to the nation's shame, World War II ended with the dropping of the atomic bomb on Hiroshima and Nagasaki. A new world was born. Traditional values crumbled like clay in the potter's hand. New names made the headlines, strange names like Batista and Castro, Eisenhower and DeGaulle, Pearson and Duvalier. Headlines brought to our attention such unknown, far-away places as Fulton, Missouri, where Churchill gave his famous "iron curtain" speech and the Bay of Pigs where the Cuban exiles' invasion ended in disaster. We read about such people as Sukarno who was elected president of an unknown new country by the name of Indonesia in 1950 and heard about a battle at Dienbienphu in 1954 where the French surrendered control over Indo-China only to leave the United States with a Vietnam problem twenty years later. Gandhi was assassinated in 1948 by a Hindu fanatic and the world mourned the death of a great pacifist who won by the gospel of peace the independence of his country. Events happened at such lightening speed that no one man or community could keep track of them. Thus we entered the "computer age" where the machine would extend the limits of man's intelligence.

"Uncle Miltie" became a household symbol, as more and more people were watching television and fewer and fewer were visiting the local theatre. Big league baseball and football came into its own with the advent of television, putting an end to the "sandlot" teams and causing unnumbered hours of distress to the nation's housewives who became week-end widows as husbands glued their eyes to the idiot box on a Saturday and Sunday afternoon. The nation experienced the "silent fifties" when the younger generation were content to follow the "grandfather image" of Dwight D. Eisenhower. The same nation was alarmed by the youth revolution that took place during the "sexy sixties" with promiscuity, dope and rebellion the hallmark of the college campus and the city street. Tragedies shattered the nation. The assassination of President John F. Kennedy in 1963, the assassination of Senator Robert Kennedy and Dr. Martin Luther King, Jr. in 1968 brought a sometimes proud and sometimes haughty nation to a sense of national shame and humility. The historic flight of Neil Armstrong, Edwin Aldrin, Jr. and Michael Collins to the moon, and the famous moon-walk restored some pride and prestige but the nation remained uncertain about its future and citizens were still disturbed by problems of the city, ecology, war and the quality of life.

In Minnesota people were first enthralled by Floyd B. Olson who breathed life into the Democratic-Farmer Labor party and were saddened by his untimely death in 1936. Four years later Minnesotans marvelled at the genius of the youngest governor in its history, Harold E. Stassen. He was called by some the "finest politican that Minnesota ever produced" and has been, over the years, a perennial candidate for the presidency on the Republican ticket. Melrose, too, had more than its share of distinguished men who served their state and community well. To cite but four worthy of recognition there was Dr. P. A. Hilbert, the city's first mayor who served in the state legislature; Ignatius and Homer Lemm, both father and son, who served in the state's house of representatives; Edmund Tieman, who also served in the state's house of representatives.

During these years the value of the dollar depreciated considerably and, although statistics would report a great amount was made by both farmer and merchant, the purchasing value of the dollar decreased more and more as the years passed by. Using the year 1857 as a base of one dollar equalling one dollar the Federal Reserve Board estimated that in 1890 one dollar would have been worth three dollars and twenty-six cents; in 1910 the same dollar would have been worth two dollars and fifty-nine cents and its value in 1972 would be worth seventy cents.

During the years of World War II the local newspaper provided helpful hints to the merchants of the area. One item reminded grocers that they "can do much to prevent hoarding of canned goods by limiting one can of each particular food to each customer." In 1943 local creameries were instructed "to be prepared to set aside 30% of their total butter production for military purposes." Louis Limperich, feature writer of the *Mel-Hi-Script*, concluded his column with the words, "Bye-Bye: Buy Bonds." The local paper also noted that a woman in Fairmont received one thousand, one hundred and fifty-eight letters from her husband stationed overseas within the period of one year. State war manpower commissioner Dreng Bjornaraa expressed "great pride" in the fact that over six thousand Minnesotans had directly or indirectly taken part in the development of the atomic bombs that flattened Nagasaki and Hiroshima. A popular fashion during these war years was a wool-rayon dinner dress designed to keep the wearer warm "while shivering in her fuel-rationed home."

Long before the telegraph, telephone, radio and television, even before the establishment of the weekly newspaper, Melrose kept in touch with the outside world chiefly through the United States postal system. The post office in Melrose was established August 17, 1859, a year following the establishment of the community, and the first postmaster was Robert Wheeler. The following year he was succeeded by Moses Adley and in 1861 W. M. Adley became postmaster for five months. He was followed by Moses Martin who retained the position for a year. August Lindbergh was postmaster from 1863 to 1865 and was then followed by M. A. Taylor. In 1867 S. R. Foot was named postmaster and he was followed by D. B. McDonald in 1870. August Lindbergh returned as postmaster in 1879 and retained the position until 1887 when he was succeeded by H. B. Edelbrock. J. E. Campbell was appointed in 1889, succeeded by Nicholaus Koenig in 1893, John Kolb in 1897.

With John Kolb a degree of stability came to the post office. Appointed by President McKinley and re-appointed twice by President Theodore Roosevelt, he held the office for sixteen years. He was succeeded by Joseph H. Seal on May 27, 1913. His wife, the former Linda Lindbergh, acted as the assistant postmaster until his sudden death at the age of sixty-eight in 1926. Mrs. Seal was appointed acting postmaster for a few months until Carl W. Carlson assumed the position on March 1, 1927. Mrs. Seal remained assistant postmaster during the eight years of Carlson's administration and was a beloved member of the community. Carlson was succeeded by Jake Egerman in 1935 and he remained postmaster until his retirement in 1957. For several months Al Thelen served as acting postmaster until he was commissioned on August 18, 1958. During 1971, according to Thelen, the Melrose post office processed and dispatched six hundred and thirty-three thousand pieces of letter mail; about ten thousand pieces of bulk mail, an estimated three thousand and five hundred parcel post packages and the gross receipts were $63,877.90.

Every city has its boosters and in most cities and villages the Chamber of Commerce keeps the wheels of industry and commerce spinning. The Melrose Chamber of Commerce has been doing this since its organization on June 24, 1938. Its first co-chairmen were Frank Schmidt and Martin Wander, secretary-treasurer was H. C. Stalboerger and members of the board of directors were William Peifer, John L.

Meyer, Alexander Hartmann, John Enneking, U. C. Schlicht, C. P. Meyer, Arnold Schwegmann, J. H. Welle, John V. Free and H. F. Loosbrock. At one of its first meetings the Chamber of Commerce discussed the possibility and the urgency of converting the vacant brewery building into a business establishment. In August of the same year the organization sponsored a rural electrification celebration and on September 26-27 sponsored the first Harvest Festival, an annual event that has attracted thousands of visitors to Melrose each year. The first festival consisted of band concerts, race contests, a boxing tournament, an amatuer contest, a community songfest, two dances and a baseball game between the Minneapolis Millers and Melrose.

In 1939 the Chamber of Commerce invited farmers to attend its meetings and also voted to close all business places on Sundays. The following year it sponsored the first Santa Claus day which has since become an annual event. In 1941 it sponsored a free dance in the new Litchfield Produce building and awarded script money on the weekend drawings. During this year the organization considered starting a zoo in the Melrose park, having two lions as a beginning. The resolution was tabled, however, because "it would smell too bad." Hiltner and Lamb built the Melrose locker plant this year. The following year, under the sponsorship of the Chamber of Commerce, the Boy Scouts were organized in Melrose with Reverend Vincent Huebsch serving as the first scoutmaster.

A group closely associated with the Chamber of Commerce was also organized in 1938. Forty young men in the area organized the "Melby's 40". Members had to be single and when one was married he no longer qualified for membership in the group. They assisted the Chamber of Commerce in many activities, such as putting up Christmas decorations and sponsoring trips to Minneapolis baseball games.

Closely associated with the activities of the Chamber of Commerce was the Junior Chamber of Commerce which was organized on St. Patrick's day, 1969. Louis Norngren, president of the Sauk Centre Jaycees, extended the chapter of the Melrose chapter at its first meeting. The first officers were James Ricklick, president; William Kluempke, first vice president; Thomas Kolb, second vice president; David Fox, secretary; Daniel VonBank, treasurer. Other charter members of the organization were: Anthony Bechtold, Donald Loxtercamp, Harry Hoelscher, Mark Meyer, David Linehan, Reverend Robert Schmainda, Daniel Praska, Marvin Notch, Joseph Timmins, Robert Nelson, Richard Kuhlmann, Patrick McCauley, Charles Gebeke, Al Revermann, George Traeger, Michael Roose, Kenneth Thomas, Charles Berrigan and Herbert Welle. From the original twenty-four members the group has grown to number thirty members. Subsequent presidents have been David Fox, Richard Kuhlmann and William Bethke.

The first project of the Jaycees, directed by David Linehan, converted St. Mary's parking lot into two fenced-in tennis courts and three baskets for outdoor basketball. In 1969 Melrose witnessed its first tennis tournament. With the senior Chamber of Commerce the Jaycees sponsored a project of erecting grandstands in the city park and the Sunday afternoon Donkey softball game. The group also sponsored the first Miss Melrose Queen Pageant with Debra Caspers as the first winner. Among the many other notable projects sponsored by the Jaycees were the Legion Park project and the "Welcome to Melrose" booklet published in cooperation with the area businessmen. During its first year the organization's activities involved a budget of expenditures totaling $6,000. and in its second year, $2,000. One of its most "smashing" fund-raising activities was a smelt fry that netted $1.18.

The purpose of the Junior Chamber of Commerce is summed up by the last two lines of the Jaycee Creed: "That earth's great treasure lies in the human personality: And that service to humanity is the best work of life."

Every group of men who are defined as "social animals" needs a government for the preservation of the commonweal. When Stearns county was organized in 1855 it was divided into three districts for election purposes. On May 19, 1858 the county was divided into eleven townships which were St. Cloud, St. Joseph, Winnebago, Clearwater, Marysville, St. Domingo, Sauk Centre, Lake Henry, Two Islands, Richmond and Hanover. In subsequent years the original townships were subdivided into the present number of thirty-seven. At a meeting in the home of August Lindbergh on January 1, 1867 the township of Melrose was created, being taken from the original township of Sauk Centre. Joseph Niehaus, became clerk of the township at the age of twenty-six, an office he held faithfully for fifty-four years. In 1956 he resigned from the post and had the unusual distinction of swearing in his own son, Anthony, as his successor. Township clerks who succeeded August Lindbergh were Frank Weisser, George Rehkamp, Fred Rehkamp, Joseph Niehaus, Sr. and his son Joseph who came to the office in 1902. The office of township clerk, accordingly, has been held by three generations of the Niehaus family for the past seventy years.

Thoughout the years the city of Melrose has been fortunate in having fine civic-minded men to serve as mayor. Strikingly, the first two mayors were doctors of medicine; the first was Dr. P. A. Hilbert and the second, Dr. J. E. Campbell. Other mayors over the years have been Henry W. Goehrs (1917-1920), Andrew Kolb (1920-23), Dr. A.

A. Meyer (1923-1933), Andrew Kolb (1933-1939), Dr. A. A. Meyer (1939-1947), P. J. Welz (1947-1951), A. C. Welle (1951-1959), Louis A. Kunkel (1959-1963), A. C. Welle (1963-1965), Jerry Notch (1965-1970). Upon Notch's resignation on October 1, 1970 Charles Lyons was appointed and is serving as the present mayor. From 1920 to 1947 only two men served as mayor, Dr. Meyer and Andrew Kolb. Ambrose Welle was the first native son of Melrose to serve as its mayor.

Over the years the city and the county continued to grow in population. In 1920 the population of the city of Melrose was two thousand five hundred and twenty-nine; in 1930, one thousand eight hundred and one; (indicating the migration from the city when Great Northern car shops moved in 1923); in 1940, two thousand and fifteen; in 1950, two thousand one hundred and six; in 1960, two thousand one hundred and thirty-five; in 1970, two thousand two hundred and seventy-three. Over the past four decades the population of Stearns county has steadily increased from sixty-seven thousand two hundred in 1940 to ninety-five thousand and four hundred in 1970, an increase of twenty-eight thousand and two hundred people. Population figures for the Melrose area published in 1965 by the Stearns County Planning Commission reveal that Melrose township had three thousand and sixty people; Getty, five hundred and forty; Sauk Centre, four thousand seven hundred and fifty; Oak, one thousand five hundred and eighty; Millwood, seven hundred. A disturbing figure, as far as the economic, social and religious development of the area is the one that shows a decline of three hundred and sixty-two farms in the five years between 1964 and 1969.

The people of Melrose were proud of their community as an incident in 1872 testified. A bill introduced in the state legislature testified this fact. The bill proposed the creation of a new county called Franklin with Sauk Centre as the proposed county seat. It provided that twelve townships from Stearns, including Getty, Melrose and the adjacent ones, and eight townships from southern Todd county. When put to the vote of the people in all the Stearns townships it was defeated by a majority of one thousand six hundred and sixty-three out of the two thousand and one hundred and sixty-nine votes. Melrose township voted nine for and fifty-six against; Getty township twenty-five for and thirty-one against; Oak township none for and sixty-three against; Millwood township none for and forty-nine against.

Cities also need officers to enforce the laws of the land. The first constable of Melrose was Frank M. Morehouse, Sr. who served in that capacity for thirteen years beginning in 1893. He was succeeded by his son, Frank M. Morehouse, Jr. who served from 1906 until his retirement in 1955. When he began his duties he worked twelve hours a day, seven days a week, for forty-five dollars a month. He was a kindly officer and respected by all. Another father and son who served the area well were Ignatius and Homer F. Lemm. Ignatius Lemm was elected state senator in 1926 and served in the state legislature four years. Homer F. Lemm, succeeded his father in 1950, marking a span of twenty-four years between the election of father and son. Another son who succeeded his father in public office was Donald Primus. His father, Anton, was fire chief for seventeen years and previous to that had served on the force for twenty years.

The first hospital in Melrose was operated by Mary Pfeffer (now Mrs. Joseph Stundebeck) in her home. Miss Pfeffer was a registered nurse and because the doctors in practice in the community had no facility in which to do surgery and take care of acutely ill people, on February 14, 1916, she opened a five bed hospital in her home at 1072 Second Street West. Prior to the opening of her hospital, the doctors transported operating tables and supplies to the patient's home and did surgery in the homes. The only transportation they had was horse and buggy, and in winter a sled was substituted for the buggy. She continued to operate her hospital until 1921 when Dr. A. A. Meyer, a practicing physician in the community, established a hospital on Riverside Avenue, the present City Office Building. This too was a large home, originally built by the Henry Borgerding family and converted to hospital use. Various additions and remodelings took place over the years, and in 1956 when the facility was sold to the City, it consisted of twenty-two licensed beds.

On July 1, 1956, the City of Melrose officially became owners of the hospital, and because of licensing standards and requirements, had to consider building a new facility if they wished to continue having a hospital. A special election was held in fall of 1956. The citizens of Melrose authorized a general obligation bond issue of $350,000. for the purpose of constructing a new hospital. Construction started in Spring, 1958, and the facility was dedicated on April 6, 1959, and the first patients received on April 9, 1959. The new hospital consisted of thirty-four beds. Later it became apparent that there was a need for nursing home facilities in the area, and revenue bonds, pledging the earnings of the hospital and proposed nursing home, were sold for the construction of a forty-five bed wing addition to the hospital, which became known as Pine Villa. This was completed on December 1, 1961, with first patients being received on that date. With the advent of Medicare in 1966, it was necessary to make certain structural changes and add certain services, and in 1968 a plan for a twenty-three bed addition to Pine Villa, with remodeling of the existing hospital was implemented.

This project was completed on November 1, 1969. The total complex now consists of thirty-four hospital beds and sixty-eight nursing home beds.

The City of Melrose is the owner and operator and a governing board consisting of five citizens of the City of Melrose, are responsible for the operation. The Board is appointed by the City Council.

The original Board members appointed in 1956 were: Father Francis Julig, M. J. Shay, Mrs. Clara Raeker, August Loehr, and R. O. Passi. Father Julig and M. J. Shay are deceased, Mr. Loehr is the only original member still on the Board.

Present Board members are: August Loehr, chairman; Joseph Hollermann, vice chairman; Mrs. Pauline Angelbeck, secretary-treasurer; Edmund C. Tieman and Rene Lizotte directors. Miss Julia Westendorf is the present Administrator of Melrose Hospital and Pine Villa.

The Melrose Riverside Airport, Inc. began in the year 1952 when a strip of land was purchased from the owner, the Joseph Schmidt, Sr. family. The strip was one hundred and fifty feet wide and four thousand and five hundred feet long and located north of the railroad tracks and south of the old highway number fifty-two. The original founders and stockholders were Walter E. Carlson, Joseph Lindy, Donald Molitor and Richard Martin. All were flying enthusiasts and owned their own aircraft. With the help of friends the founders built four hangers, installed a gas pump, tie-downs, runway markers and other equipment. The sod airstrip was prepared by Ralph Job, a Freeport farmer and flying enthusiast. He used his own farm machinery to level the ground, to prepare seed beds and seeded the same. Before the end of that first year Richard Martin left the community. He sold his stock to Ray O. Passi, who did not fly but liked to ride.

Over the years and after many hours of flying, the original owners disengaged themselves from flying. Joseph Lindy left Melrose and sold his share of stock to Thomas Arvig. The stockholders at this time are Carlson, Molitor, Passi and Arvig. The airport has been maintained and the taxes paid throughout the years by the stockholders. Presently there is no airplane stationed there and its land is used chiefly by snowmobilers. The owners suffered a severe blow when that portion of the land lying in the city limits was assessed almost four thousand dollars for the adjoining road improvement. At this writing the tax is delinquent and the future of the airport shaky and unknown.

According to a comprehensive planning study conducted by the firm of Hodne and Stageberg, Partners, there is reason for optimism by the citizens of Melrose and the surrounding area for the coming generation. The report states:

"Population growth during the next 20 years is estimated to be about 350 persons, a moderate increase, as population continues to gravitate to the larger metropolitan centers where work and leisure opportunities are more plentiful. However, Melrose's considerable industrial base coupled with high producing agricultural land will enable the City to "hold its own" economically with population growth kept to manageable increases."

This writer prefers to share the hopeful optimism expressed by former mayor, A. C. Welle when he wrote, "I have always believed the distinguishing characteristic of any community is its people, and herein lies our greatest asset."

Sister Dignata, O.S.B. with an early music group of St. Boniface parish.

Below: Beloved teacher for many years at St. Boniface school, Sister Ursula, O.S.B.

Above: The St. Boniface ladies choir, appearing in a recital, with the director, Sister William, O.S.B., the pastor, Monsignor Hoffmann, and the assistant pastor, Father Ervin Braun.

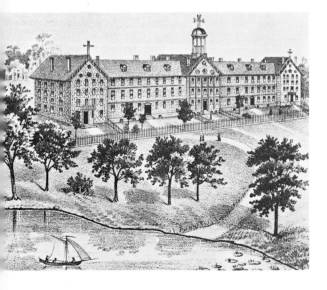

St. John's College as it appeared in ANDREAS ATLAS in 1874.

St. John's University, Collegeville, as it appeared in 1904.

The first St. Patrick's church built in 1872 and dedicated by Rt. Rev. Abbot Rupert Seidenbush the following year.

The Methodist Episcopal church of Melrose, built in 1876.

St. Patrick's church and parish house as it appeared at the turn of the century.

First Mass invitation of Father Frederick Hinnenkamp in 1907.

Below: First Mass portrait of Monsignor Benedict Petermeier.

Above: First Mass portrait of Father (later Bishop) Henry Soenneker. Shown left to right are: Wilfred Wessel, Anna Mae Niehaus (Mrs. Lawrence Wiechman), Norbert Hellerman, Hildegarde Wessel and Rita Pohlman (Sister M. Paula, O.S.F.)

Right: First Mass portrait of Father Norbert Hinnenkamp with his brides.

The rectory of St. Boniface parish.

Below: The home of Mrs. Nettie Meyer.

Right: The Fred Zuercher home.

Below: The home of John L. Meyer.

The former home of Herman Hollermann.

The former George Rehkamp home.

The Melrose Hospital.

Entrance to Melrose from Interstate number 94.

The new "foot bridge" constructed in 1967.

Badge worn on Captain Gallagher Day.

Captain and Mrs. Gallagher with popular radio commentator Cedric Adams and Monsignor Matthias Hoffmann.

One of the many business establishments that serves the community, Melrose Implement Company.

Another thriving business in Melrose, the G & R Hardware Company.

Stearns Electric Association lighted up the community.

Empire Memorials, Inc., erected this modern granite manufacturing plant in 1952.

Two views of Melrose today.

2 THE MEL
AND
THE ROSE

AUTHOR'S NOTE

The second part of this book may raise several questions in the mind of the reader. Why is religion in the back of the book? Why is it receiving such brief treatment in comparison with the first part of the book? Why does the author stop at the year 1958? These good questions deserve a good answer. I shall try.

The section on religion is placed at the end of the book for a practical printing and pastoral reasons. It is the intention of the pastor of St. Mary's parish to print several hundred copies of this section in pamphlet form to give to new members in the parish and to sell to visitors of the parish. It is to be hoped that when this is done a full description of the interior of the church will be added to these pages.

From the very beginning of the planning of this book it was the general consensus of the members of the committee that the story of the church in Melrose could not be told apart from the life, activities and interests of the people. We did not feel it necessary to repeat what already appeared in the first section of this book since everything and every activity about life should be sacred. It was not our intention, nor was it our wish, that the role of God's people should be played down in the story of God's Church in Melrose. We presumed that the first part of the book will bear out that conviction.

We decided to stop at the year 1958 for two good reasons. This book is a centennial book of two parishes, St. Patrick's and St. Boniface's, joined in bonds of common love and faith to form another distinct parish, St. Mary's. It was not our intention to write the history of St. Mary's parish. Secondly, this is a historical story of what happened in the past. As we mentioned elsewhere this story does not have an ending, but keeps unfolding generation after generation, in man's search for the spirit that makes him human and holy. We are too close to the events of the past fifteen years to be able to write about them in their true perspective. The year 1958 — a hundred years between the Adley's settlement in Melrose and the year St. Mary's parish was established seemed the logical point to interrupt our story. We hope another generation will be able to write the golden jubilee of St. Mary's parish in 2008.

We sincerely hope that these comments will answer the questions that arise in the mind of the reader. We even more sincerely hope that the following pages will give the reader a greater love and pride for the Church.

FOREWORD

TO THE REVEREND CLERGY, THE CHRISTIAN COMMUNITY
AND FRIENDS OF MELROSE

It was with great joy that I learned from Father Lang that Melrose is going to celebrate a Homecoming-Centennial this year. I rejoice with you for it is widely known that Melrose is one of our strong Christian and civic communities in central Minneosta. You are all to be congratulated in undertaking this celebration that is as much a remembrance of the past as a promise of the future.

Those of us who read the signs of the times would like to think that both Church and State have a sound and secure future in the rural life and rural community such as exists in the area of Melrose. We see in the agricultural development of the area, the business economy of the city, the strong religious life of the community many indications of future growth and development. We see also evidence of a movement of population from the big cities to the smaller towns happily reversing an earlier trend. We hope that this will bring growth to Melrose and at the same time strengthen smaller communities in the area. We urge area solidarity and cooperation.

As a spiritual shepherd we also see the strengthening and fostering of solid religious values in communities such as Melrose. Time after time in these pages such religious values are cited and explained. We can only hope and pray that such values will continue to be part and parcel of the social fabric of the Melrose community and all the Christian and religious minded people who with faith and generosity have contributed to its spiritual strength.

Finally, I extend congratulations to the Chamber of Commerce, the officials of the school district, Father Raymond Lang and all who have cooperated in making this centennial homecoming the opportunity to open the door to the future through reviewing the past.

Sincerely in Christ,
Most Rev. George H. Speltz, D.D.
Bishop of St. Cloud

INTRODUCTION

TO THE PEOPLE OF MELROSE, FRIENDS, ALL:

It is with a modest sense of achievement that I introduce the following pages of this book to the reader. I know that the committee has worked diligently for the past nine months but I also know that three-quarters of a year is hardly sufficient to produce a perfect product. The author, the committee, and myself, however, feel that we have done the best we can and believe this product is a fitting tribute to the life and living of the good people of Melrose.

I would be negligent if I did not express my deep appreciation to the author and the committee for the countless hours of work and research that went into the production of this centennial history, not only of the community but of the parishes. It is, I believe, a work that will be referred to for countless decades to come. Future generations will look upon this book with pride and satisfaction. No doubt some omissions have been made, and no one knows this better than the author and his collaborators: that will always be the case as long as we are on this side of eternity. We will fail more by omission than commission.

This centennial-homecoming that we are marking is, I trust, an occasion to manifest the harmonious relationship that exists, at least in Melrose, between Church and State. It is a joint venture on the part of the civic and religious community. "Collaboration" and "cooperation" have been key words in our present society. We sincerely hope that this celebration will be a manifestation of these words in the practical realm of working together.

I wish, finally, to express my own deep appreciation to the numerous men and women who have worked together on the many committees to make our Homecoming-Centennial a success. It is my wish and prayer that this occasion will bind all of us more closely together in a community of worship, and work. The past memories of our faithful pioneers will inspire us with hope and courage to meet the challenge of the next one hundred years.

Faithfully Yours in Christ,
Raymond H. Lang
Pastor, St. Mary's Parish

CHAPTER ONE

THE CHURCH IS PEOPLE

"The foundation (abbey) should be a center from which
we will be of service to the people of Minnesota."

When the Adley's came to Melrose in 1858 the Catholic Church
had seldom been in such low repute and disarray as it was during the
middle decades of the nineteenth century. Pope Pius IX, who began
his reign as a reforming pope and surrounded himself with liberal
social thinkers, in 1848 had to flee Rome's Quirinal palace disguised as
a priest because of the threats made upon his life. Three years after
his death in 1878 the mobs of Rome hurled mud and stones at his body
as it was being transferred to the basilica of St. Lawrence outside the
Walls. Many French intellectuals, nobility and clerics were openly
opposed to the Church and through their journals and salons vented,
sometimes vehemently, their hatred of the Church. As someone remarked
about this period, "France, the eldest daughter of the Church, had
some very strange sons. Germany was beginning to pass anti-religious
laws and by the time of the *Kulturkampf* in 1873 the persecution was
full-blown. Ireland, too, the most loyal of all nations to the Church,
was suffering not only persecution through the penal laws imposed by
English force but also the confiscation of the peasants' lands and the
greatest famine ever witnessed for many centuries in Europe. English
Catholics were still being persecuted through many laws on the books
and, even worse, ridiculed and scoffed at as being second-class citizens
and benighted, ignorant people. The factors of hunger, persecution,
bigotry and penury swelled the ranks of Irish and German immigrants
throughout the last four decades of the nineteenth century. They sought
new opportunities and a new way of life "in the land of the free and
the home of the brave."

Unfortunately their adopted country was neither as free nor as brave as they dreamed it would be. Life was not, perhaps, as harsh as their native countries but it was a hard one. The German and Irish immigrants who had suffered under the oppression of the state well understood a principle enunciated by Bishop John England in 1825 when he wrote, "I am convinced that a total separation from the temporal government, is the most natural and safest state for the church in any place...." While they appreciated such a position they soon found themselves as oppressed and scorned as the minority people in the United States today. They were the victims of three militant and strident bigot groups — The Nativist Movement, the Know-Nothing Party and the American Protective Association. Each group had two major objectives. First, keep America for Americans, meaning no more foreign immigrants. Secondly, keep America Protestant, meaning no more Roman papists allowed. Many an Irishman could recall passing a business place with this sign in the window: HELP WANTED — IRISH NEED NOT APPLY. And many a German could recall the epitaph hurled with scorn, "You dumb Dutchman." In response to such bigotry that created false accusations against the Church, the pope and Catholic clergy and people, two men performed a magnificent role. One, the dean of the American bishops, Cardinal James Gibbons of Baltimore, stated:

"For myself, as a citizen of the United States, without closing my eyes to our defects as a nation, I proclaim, with a deep sense of pride and gratitude, and in this great capital of Christendom (Rome), that I belong to a country where the civil government holds over us the aegis of protection without interfering in the legitimate exercise of our sublime mission as ministers of the Gospel of Jesus Christ."

The second, a lay convert, was Orestes Brownson, who through his books, essays and articles, rightly deserves to be called one of the greatest publicists of the Catholic church in United States.

There were other forms of prejudice against Catholics during these decades, more subtle, perhaps, but also more de-humanizing. Chief among these were the social and economic segregation. The Catholic immigrants worked long and hard hours, building railroads, ditching canals, serving as the most menial laborers in factories, stores and homes. They knew they were social out-casts and thus formed their "shanty towns" in the cities, such as Boston, New York and Baltimore. In the countryside they tried to form their own villages and communities to find their strength in numbers. The Irish immigrant had one advantage the German did not; he could speak the language — even if spoken with a brogue. This disadvantage caused many land offices, banks and businesses to take advantage of the German immigrant. The Irish immigrant fought back with the only means available; he threw his hat into the political arena first as a ward heeler, then as a councilman, then as mayor and up the political ladder to such as extent that a Catholic, Alfred E. Smith could be nominated for president in 1928 and John Fitzgerald Kennedy elected in 1960 as president of the United States. The German immigrant, however, could not enter the political arena because of the language factor; thus he formed institutions and organizations to preserve his culture, his religion and his dignity by largely remaining with his relative and *lands'mann*. In both cases not willingness but necessity created the "Catholic ghetto."

These observations can as well be applied to the German Lutherans who came about the same time as their Catholic brothers, and to the Scandinavian Lutherans who arrived several decades later. They tended to form ghettos for similar reasons, largely in the Midwest. Willmar Thorkelson, the religion editor of the Minneapolis *Star*, has noted in a booklet concerning Lutherans in the United States:

"Lutherans come to this country for a wide variety of reasons. For many it was to improve their economic lot. For others it was to escape military service or to find anonymity and adventure. For still others the reasons were religious — to find greater freedom of worship than they had in their homelands.

Wherever they settled, the Lutheran immigrants brought with them their Bibles and hymnals in their native languages and the traditions they had learned. Sometimes pastors came with them; sometimes religious worship was lay-conducted."

At first the Scandinavian immigrants would form a congregation which later became a member of a synod. Most of these synods reflected the national origins of the member churches, such as the German-Lutheran, Swedish-Lutheran, Danish-Lutheran and Norwegian-Lutheran among others. Not only language and cultural background, however, distinguished one synod from another but also theological positions. Some synods tended to be more conservative and others more liberal concerning the doctrinal content of their faith. Leaders of the synods began to realize the harm this fragmentation was doing to all the synods. So mergers began in the Lutheran synods in about the turn of the century. "An effect of the many organic unions," wrote Willmar Thorkelson,

"that took place in the late 19th century and in this century was to bring almost 95 per cent of the 9 million Lutherans of North America into three large bodies. The other five per cent are divided among 10 bodies."

The three large church groups are The Lutheran Church in America, The Lutheran Church — Missouri Synod and The American Lutheran Church.

St. Paul's Lutheran Church in Melrose is a member church of the Missouri Synod. With two million and eight hundred thousand members this synod is the second largest and fastest growing Lutheran church in North America. Led by Pastor Martin Stephan approximately seven hundred Germans from Saxony sailed for the United States in 1838, calling upon God to "preserve them in their integrity and purity for themselves and their children." The Missouri Synod was organized in Chicago in 1847 and consisted of twelve congregations and twenty-two ministers. The Synod from its beginning was active in areas of education, social welfare reform and missionary activities. Few adults in the United States have, either knowingly or unknowingly, not heard The Lutheran Hour and its famous preacher, Dr. Oswald Hoffmann. The program is heard over one thousand radio stations and broadcasted in thirty-six languages. Despite its name, The Missouri Synod while strongest in Illinois, has over a hundred thousand members in Minnesota.

St. Paul's Lutheran Church in Melrose finds its origins in the days when circuit missionary pastors served vast areas by riding horseback or oxcart and meeting in the homes of the people they served. One of the first permanent missionaries had his headquarters at St. Cloud. His name was the Reverend H. Vetter and he served the area from 1873 to 1876. He was succeeded by the Reverend Carl Mende, a missionary at large from 1876 to 1880. He was the first Lutheran missionary to serve in Melrose on a regular occasional basis. The Reverend J. Von Brant, with residence in Farming township, served the Lutheran people of Melrose on a regular missionary basis for the next fourteen years. In 1893 the Reverend W. F. Hitzmann aided in having the Reverend Theodore Krumsieg installed in 1894 to serve St. Paul's Church. During this year St. Paul's Church was organized and in 1897 joined the Missouri Synod.

The Melrose congregation built its first church in 1900 during the tenure of the Reverend Otto Richter who served as the first resident pastor from 1897 to 1902. Four resident pastors succeeded him throughout the next twenty-seven years. They were the Reverends L. Krueger (1902-1915); Theodore Schubkegel (1915-1917); C. A. Dashmer (1918-1920); Paul Gierke (1920-1929). Between 1917 and 1918 the Reverend J. A. Stein, pastor in Sauk Centre, served the Melrose congregation.

After the Reverend Paul Gierke's pastorate the following pastors from surrounding parishes served St. Paul's Church: A. Schwartz (1929-

1931); R. G. Troeger from Grey Eagle (1931-1944); W. A. Schultz from Grey Eagle (1944-1945); E. Roth from Farming township (1945-1953); Henry Sporleder from Sauk Centre (1953-1959); E. C. Larson from Sauk Centre (1959-1963); G. B. Eschenbacher from Sauk Centre (1963-1968). During the tenure of Pastor Wilmer Schultz the old parsonage was sold and the church building was moved to face south on part of the same lot with a basement and other improvements being added.

With the help of the Minnesota North District — Missouri Synod the parish approved and completed the building of a new parsonage in 1968. Again the parish acquired the services of a resident pastor in the person of the Reverend Allan M. Hastings. After serving a short time Pastor Hastings was succeeded by the Reverend Kurt H. Mueller in 1970.

St. Paul's parish has enjoyed the services of an active Ladies' Aid Society for many years. In 1945 it became affiliated with the National and State Lutheran Women's Missionary League of the Missouri Synod. This affiliation has greatly assisted the parish in supplying aid for local improvements and assisting in the missionary work of the church.

In the earlier decades of its history Melrose also had three other Protestant Churches. The first and oldest was organized in 1876 with only five members. This congregation began construction of a church building the same year under the direction of the Reverend L. Wright. The church building was located on Riverside Avenue one block west of City Hall and was known as the Trinity Methodist Episcopal Church. A notice in the 1910 issue of the *Melrose Beacon* reveals that Pastor F. L. Kirk conducted "Public Worship" at ten-thirty in the morning and eight o'clock in the evening on Sundays. Sunday school began at eleven-forty-five on Sunday morning and a "Prayer Hour" was held at eight o'clock Wednesday evening.

The Protestant Episcopal Church was organized in August, 1879. A little church was constructed the following year. Twice a month the Reverend Dr. Hamilton came from Sauk Centre to conduct services for the fledgling congregaton. The fourth church was the Presbyterian Church. It was organized in 1899 under the direction of the Reverend Findley. With residence in Duluth, he was pastor at large of the St. Cloud Presbytery.

The first church to appear in Melrose was the Catholic Church. Since this church has continually had the largest number of adherents and since more documentary evidence is available, the writer trusts that the reader will not feel offended if more space is alloted the history of the Catholic Church in Melrose community.

When the Adley's were grubbing out their homestead in 1858 a French shepherd girl during the same year said she saw a vision of a beautiful lady. The girl was Bernadette Soubirous and the beautiful lady said to her, "I am the Immaculate Conception." Four years previously Pope Pius IX had defined the doctrine as a dogma of faith. Two years previously the recently arrived Benedictine Fathers organized a parish in St. Cloud and entitled it St. Mary's in honor of the Immaculate Conception. A century later, in 1958 a parish in Melrose became the twenty-eighth parish in the Diocese of St. Cloud to be named St. Mary. In the course of those hundred years, however, much laughter and sorrow, sin and grace, life and death came to the thousands of people who would reply when asked, "I belong to St. Patrick's parish," or "I belong to St. Boniface parish." In either case the answer would be given with varying degrees of justifiable pride. This then is not so much a record of buildings as it is of people, for the Church Universal, the Church in the United States, the Church of the Diocese of St. Cloud and the Church in Melrose ultimately exists only to bring the People of God to the glory of God's Life Eternal. This is a record of the attempt of thousands of men and women, clergy and religious, parents and friends, to fulfill the final purpose of the Church.

The stirrings of Catholicism in the present area of Minnesota originated with the arrival of the "Proto-Pastor of Minnesota," Father Lucien Galtier. He was sent to minister to the needs of the Catholic people who had settled about Fort Snelling. Four months after his ordination he was "commissioned" by his superior, Bishop Mathias Loras of Dubuque, Iowa, who was the chief shepherd of an area that included all of the present state of Iowa, all of the state of Minnesota and the two Dakotas as his field of labor. When his parishioners were removed as squatters from the area around Mendota and moved down the river Father Gaultier followed them. On a high cliff overlooking the Mississippi River he built a log chapel eighteen by twenty feet in size and dedicated it to St. Paul the Apostle. Catholicism in the new territory had planted its roots.

After four years Father Galtier was moved to serve other parishes in Iowa and Wisconsin, and was replaced by his classmate, Father Augustine Ravoux, who had been a missionary among the Sioux tribes in the western area of central Minnesota and western South Dakota. From 1844 until 1851 he served as "the Lone Sentinel of Rome." On July 19, 1850 Father Joseph Cretin was appointed first Bishop of St. Paul. The following year "a gift from God" came to him in the person of Father Francis Xavier Pierz, a man who later would be called "the Father of the Diocese of St. Cloud." He served not only his beloved

Indians in Northern Minnesota but also ministered to the spiritual needs of the ever-increasing numbers of Catholic immigrants whom he encouraged by his numerous writings to come to Minnesota. He was delighted and relieved when the Benedictine Fathers appeared on the banks of the Mississippi near St. Cloud on May 20, 1856. He was now free to return to his Indian missions and leave the Benedictines to serve the numerous German immigrants who were pouring into the Sauk river valley area. The growing numbers and more demanding spiritual needs caused Bishop Thomas Grace as early as 1861 to observe that "the whole of the Sauk Valley is rapidly filling up with German immigrants, mostly Catholics, and at intervals of every few miles churches will be required, and the great fertility of the soil will quickly enable the people to build them." Fourteen years later, on February 12, 1875 Rome established the Vicariate Apostolic of Northern Minnesota with Abbot Rupert Seidenbusch, O.S.B. as its first bishop. The Benedictine monks made "the first permanent religious impact on the region from 1856 to 1866." Through hardships and sufferings unbelievable they established a strong and active Catholic way of life among the pioneers and created parishes of such vital and sacramental life that they and the people they served were the envy of many of their contemporary and subsequent priests. Describing these hardy monks Father Colman Barry wrote:

"It was a period of small steps: visits to private homes, erecting mission stations, buying acres for the first log church, erection by priest and people of their hard-won house of God, bartering in wood or produce, and finally the taking up of residence by the missionary to sow the seed of the gospel. Where the noble Indian missionary, Father Pierz, had passed through the forest and over the lakes in search of souls, the Benedictines now brought the first stable Catholicism to the area and made deep inroads on the religious isolation of the region."

A drive through Stearns county today attests to the heroic work of accomplishment by these fearless, zealous sons of St. Benedict.

Exhausted by the burden of his office and a victim of declining health and age, Bishop Seidenbusch resigned his office on October 30, 1888. The Diocese of St. Cloud was created on September 16 the following year along with four sister dioceses of Winona, Duluth, Jamestown and Sioux Falls. St. Paul was elevated to the rank of a metropolitan Archdiocese. The first Bishop of St. Cloud was Otto Zardetti who, coming from Sioux Falls to St. Cloud, ushered in a new and difficult era that would have lasting effects on the diocese and on Melrose. One of the priests Bishop Zardetti brought from South Dakota was Bernard J. Richter. He also would leave a permanent mark on Melrose.

A brilliant, colorful and rigorous man, Bishop Zardetti is one of the intriguing prelates in the history of the Catholic Church in the United States. He was faced with three problems: First, to create a sense of diocesan unity and loyalty; secondly, to establish a diocesan organization; thirdly, to effect a diocesan identity. Five years later he was transferred to the Archdiocese of Bucharest in Rumania. This time he left behind Bernard Richter which would prove to be a great boon for Melrose. His successor was Bishop Martin Marty, O.S.B. who was previously Vicar Apostolic of South Dakota. Marty served first as a missionary priest and beginning in 1876 as a vicar apostolic on the plains of both Dakotas. By the time of his arrival in St. Cloud he was already a man worn-out from his labors. He arrived in St. Cloud on March 25, 1895 and died while conferring the sacrament of Confirmation at St. Wendelin's parish, Luxemburg sixteen months later, on September 19, 1896. On July 28, 1897 the pastor of St. Agnes church in St. Paul, Father James Trobec was appointed the third bishop of St. Cloud. A quiet, kind, gracious man he was beloved by all who knew him. Upon his appointment the diocese and the city of Melrose were prepared to enter upon a new era.

ST. PATRICK'S CHURCH

The founding local parishes of the Church throughout its history generally followed a similar pattern. Missionaries were sent to neighboring cities and villages by Christ Himself "to preach the good news" and thus the disciples went out two by two. Paul and Barnabas were commissioned by the church of Antioch and similarly many thousands of missionaries throughout the centuries "were sent forth" in fulfillment of the Savior's command: "Go and teach all nations." So Patrick went to Ireland, Boniface to Germany, Cyril and Methodius to the Slavic nations, Ansgar to Scandinavia, Francis Xavier to India, Matteo Ricci to China and the heroic band of Jesuits to North America. We now call them the North American Martyrs. In the nineteenth century Abbot Boniface Wimmer, O.S.B. sent forth five monks who were commissioned joyfully by Bishop Joseph Cretin in 1856 to minister to the needs of the German immigrants in the Sauk River valley. From their humble monastery first on the banks of the Mississippi and later, from the Indianbush which we now call Collegeville, the monks fanned out in all directions to be the spiritual servants of a good and loving God.

A glance at the map of Stearns county reveals the firm foundation they laid with the help of their good and generous people. St. Joseph, Richmond and New Munich were among the sub-stations they used as bases from which to fan out and literally cover almost every mile in serving God's people and in planting on firm ground the cross of Christ. The few Catholic families that had homesteaded near Adley's settlement were overjoyed to learn that a good Benedictine father was stopping at Oak settlement (New Munich) from time to time as early as 1861. Often they walked the five miles to seek spiritual strength and consolation from the ministry of a priest. Among these were some of the earliest pioneers of Melrose, the William Chambers, the Samuel Brown, Sr. and the Patrick Graham, Sr. families. They considered themselves fortunate to be a part of a parish, however primitive it may have been and however infrequently the priest could come. One of these pioneer missionaries wrote how it was possible to attend numerous mission stations:

"The secret of attending each of these many places once a month lay in the fact that we celebrated Sunday wherever we held services . . . . Our calendar was prepared two months in advance in order that the larger congregations might have services on Sunday at least twice a month."

Five years passed before the venerable and veteran missionary, Father Francis Pierz, journeyed through Melrose. On a July evening, 1866 he and his companion stopped at the log cabin residence of William Chambers. Traveling from one of the Indian camps to St. Paul he asked for the hospitality of the house. Recalling this event fifty years later Catherine Hannon wrote:

"On seeing the priest the gratitude and joy of Mr. Chambers' heart found expression in these words, as he fell upon his knees, "Glory be to God, a priest!" Father Pierz expressed his intention . . . of celebrating Holy Mass in the morning. News was hurriedly sent to the few nearest settlers who were profoundedly (sic) for the opportunity of hearing mass and receiving the sacraments."

In such a humble manner Christ in the Blessed Sacrament came to the Melrose community, humbly and quietly, as He came into this world on that first Christmas night.

The following year Father Augustine Burns, O.S.B. came to Melrose to administer to the few Catholic families scattered throughout the area. A native of Tipperary, Ireland he was ordained a priest of the Diocese of Pittsburgh and served as a missionary in western Pennsylvania for sixteen years. There he became acquainted with the Benedictine monks of St. Vincent's Abbey and grew in admiration of their way of life. He entered that community and after his profession as a monk volunteered to become a member of the new abbey in Minnesota. Since most of the monks at St. John's could speak very little English, Father Augustine was in great demand in those areas populated predominantly by English-speaking Catholics. He was a familiar figure in such areas as Melrose, Sauk Centre and Rooney's Settlement (Padua). The doors of the Chambers', Brown's and Graham's homes were always open to him and these three homes served as the first "churches" in Melrose. So conditions remained until 1872.

That year thirteen Catholic families met and organized the first Catholic parish in Melrose. Besides the names already mentioned some of the other chartered families of the parish were Thomas Grolian, Michael Hannon, Matthew Hanrehan, George Moening, B. Flahaven, Michael Burke and J. Flahaven, J. Dwyer, J. F. Crossen and Joseph Moritz. The group of men constructed a modest wooden cabin for a church, the best they could build with limited numbers and means. The timber and rough lumber was procured from nearby homesteads, with the men themselves doing all the work. Finishing lumber, seats and other equipment were purchased in St. Cloud and hauled to Melrose by ox teams. Abbot Rupert Seidenbush, O.S.B. blessed the building at the end of the summer and one can only imagine the pride in the hearts of these pioneers to know that at last they had their own church. Their joy was increased when Father Augustine took up residence in Melrose to live among them.

The rectory at this time was a modest nearby house. The wisdom of this decision was proven a few months later when Father Augustine was transferred and mass was once again offered on an irregular basis. The small number of families and their own economic needs made it impossible at the time to build a rectory. For two years St. Patrick's was served by the priests stationed at Richmond. With the coming of Father Burkhard Bauernschubert, O.S.B. in November, 1874 as the first resident pastor of Meire Grove, St. Patrick's parish was placed under the charge of St. John's parish in Meire Grove.

Anyone who reads the surnames of the founding families of the parish can immediately see why the parish was placed under the patronage of St. Patrick. The priest who first served the parish came from Tipperary and at least ten of the original thirteen families had surnames that proclaimed if not they, at least their ancestors, had come, from the Isle of Saints and Scholars. The children of St. Patrick transplanted to Melrose received joyful news in 1880. Father Clement B. Gamache was coming to them as a resident pastor with charge of Sauk Centre and Rooney's Settlement. With the coming of the railroad in 1872 more and more Irish arrived in Melrose, bringing their deep reverence for the

Church and "the good Father," (The early Irish immigrants would never simply say "father;" it was always prefixed by "good," just as a loyal supporter of the Confederacy always prefixed "Yankee" by the adjective "damn").

Most of the immigrants from famine-ridden Ireland were desperate men and women when they arrived in the United States — everything to win and nothing to lose. One authority estimated that the population of Ireland was decimated by some two million people during 1845 and 1850; one million by starvation and the other million by immigration (mostly to the United States). It is recorded that Father Gamache counted two hundred and fifty members in St. Patrick's parish by the time he left St. Patrick's in 1884. During the two years and four months he served St. Patrick's he baptized nineteen children in Melrose out of the total thirty-four he baptized in the surrounding areas of Birchdale (Ward Spring), Sauk Centre, Lake Henry, Rooney's Settlement (Padua) and Westport. Among the names of the children baptized in Melrose were: Meagher, Sexton, Mooney, Eagan, Graham, Lent and Killeen. Looking at the baptismal register for the year 1900 (by this time the railroad division headquarters was firmly established), of the eight baptisms performed there were three Morehouse's and a Wilkinson, Burke, McCafferty, Graham and Donohue.

The Irish had put their mark on the city if not the surrounding area. Most of them were singing what they did in fact, "I've Been Working on the Railroad." Many of them lived on the north side of the river and because of that the foot bridge was built to save time coming and going to and from work. This would eliminate the longer trek by way of the mill bridge. Their loyalty to their language, their families and their parish in time would provoke more than gentlemanly discussions with their German co-religionists who were pouring into the surrounding area in increasing numbers each year.

Upon the arrival of Father Gamache the parish set to work building a rectory for the parish at a cost of $2,000. In later years the rectory would serve as a convent for the teaching Sisters. Before their arrival, however, through inability to make payments on the debt the parish lost the rectory. Undoubtedly the loss of the rectory caused consternation if not a display of Irish temper for on May 12, 1885 Bishop Seidenbush wrote a letter as follows:

"Mr. Edwin Clark
Melrose —
    Please let me know whether you would be willing to return the priest's house to the Church provided the congregation would pay you your claims etc. . . . . It would be a great favor to ourselves if you will

kindly consent to give time for redemption and satisfy the Irish there. Please answer.

s/ Bishop Seidenbush"

Clark was a busy man and replied to the bishop's request the very next day. He wrote:

"Rt. Rev. Rupert Seidenbush
St. Cloud, Minn.
Dear Sir:

I have yours of yesterday at hand and in reply wish to say that I am perfectly willing to deed back the property referred to in payment of the cost of the same to me with expenses and within a reasonable time.

Yours truly,
Edwin Clark"

Because the parish was small in comparison to faster growing parishes throughout the area it was served by the priests of St. Boniface parish. From 1895 until 1910 the assistant pastor of St. Boniface parish served also as pastor of St. Patrick's parish. Those who served St. Patrick's as pastor during these years were: Father Richard Zoller (1895-1898), Father Herman Klein (1898-1899), Father James Walcher (1899-1902), Father Vincent Weigand (1903-1904), Father Francis Zitur (1904-1905), Father George Rauch (1905-1906), Father Matthias Hoffmann (1908-1909), Father James Walcher (1909-1911), Father Francis Welp (1911-1914), Father J. A. Killian (1914-1929), Father Matthias Hoffmann (1923-1932), Father James Walcher (1932-1933), Father Peter A. Lorsung (1933-1938), Father Francis Julig (1938-1958).

Even the most casual reader recognizes the difficulties the parish experienced from the time of Father Gamache's departure until 1895 when the assistant pastor of St. Boniface parish was appointed. The railroad employee received such small wages that he had little if anything left to give to the church after meeting the needs of his wife and family. The Benedictine fathers served the parish as best they could but due to the shortage of priests they had to spread their ministerial service over such a broad area that no one knew better than themselves that only a modicum of parish life could be expected in the two, three and even four communities they served. The growth of St. Boniface parish overshadowed St. Patrick's growth. The faster the former grew the more religious jealousy filled the people of St. Patrick's. One can imagine the joy these people experienced when they heard the news that they would again have a pastor, even though he would also serve as assistant pastor of St. Boniface's parish. They welcomed their first pastor since Father Gamache's departure most heartily. A young priest and a zealous priest, Father Richard Zoller, was the first assistant pastor under Monsignor Bernard Richter, both coming to Melrose to assume parochial leadership after the departure of the Benedictine monks. It marked a turning point in the history of St. Patrick's parish.

ST. BONIFACE CHURCH

As more and more German-speaking people moved into the area, and they were predominantly rural people, they became more and more dissatisfied with the religious situation. They were tempermentally different from the Irish; the former more serious and solemn, the latter more lighthearted and gay. Socially the conflicts and differences were accentuated because the former were chiefly farmers and the latter chiefly city people. Economically the farmer has down through the centuries felt that the shopkeeper was making too much money from the produce he brought to town and, conversely, the merchant was suspicious that the farmer was receiving more recompense for his goods than his labor deserved. The tensions and suspicions and ultimate conflicts were no mere local exception. Wherever Irish and German Catholics were brought together incidents by the thousands happened in parishes throughout the nation — to the shame of the antagonists and the glee of many bigots living among them. The ire of the Irish was aroused by the attitude of the German because, as one writer remarked, the German emigrant thought "there is no better or higher culture than German, and the practice of religion by a German must be the best in the world."

This tension mounted throughout the last two decades of the nineteenth century and sooner or later spread to the religious, the clergy and the bishops. "The German Catholics settled together in colonies wherever possible," wrote Colman J. Barry

"often by their own choice, more often under the direction of a zealous German priest or missionary. They desired to have churches of their own in which their traditional religious observances and customs would be carried out, where they could hear sermons in their mother tongue, go to confession as they had learned to confess from early childhood, and take an active part in parish life through their beloved societies. They wanted the order and discipline of parish life as they had known it before coming to the United States."

They did not see much *ordnung* manifested at St. Patrick's, nor did they quite understand why the Irish had so few traditions and customs such as the Germans had brought with them. For almost three hundred years Catholicism had been outlawed in Ireland and the practice of it was against the law. It was of no use trying to explain what a "hedgerow priest" was for the German could not understand it. It would take many decades to rid traces of nationalism from the Catholic Church in the United States. Two world wars, the two threats of communism and secularism and the desire to be an American were needed to sound nationalism's death knell.

When grandfather tells of the days when the men of St. Patrick's would lock and bar the door of the church to prevent a German from entering, he was not exaggerating. It was a fact, one bitter fact from among countless that could be told. If a German grandfather also would tell of the time he hit an Irishman over the head with a candlestick from the church — because he donated it and wanted to move it to St. Boniface's along with himself and his family — he is also telling the truth. If an Irish grandmother would tell of her complaints about the aloofness of a German grandmother, little did the former realize that the latter was aloof simply because she could not understand the English language. If the German grandmother would complain because she could not understand the sermons her counterpart would say she should learn English — not realizing the long, hard and difficult day the German grandmother put in as the wife of a pioneering farmer.

Less than six years after the establishment of St. Patrick's parish fourteen German families petitioned to have their own parish. Their request was granted. Father Paul Rettenmeier, O.S.B., was assigned as pastor to the fledgling congregation. Born in Germany and ordained in 1875 he was a priest only three years when assigned; remained only two years; was transferred to Arlington, Minnesota and died in May, 1895 at the young age of forty-three. His successor, Father Meinrod Leuthard, O.S.B., was also a young priest who was much beloved in life and long remembered in death for the heroic acts of charity he performed. When he arrived a small pox epidemic hit Melrose. Day and night he was found at the bedside of victims, praying with, and for the dying. He himself contracted the disease and died in Melrose. He is the only Benedictine priest buried in the old St. Boniface cemetery.

Father William Eversmann, O.S.B. succeeded Father Leuthard the same year and remained for ten years. During that decade, as more and more German immigrants settled in the surrounding area, the parish size increased considerably. This forced building an addition to the wood frame church; building a convent for the Sisters; a school for the children and a rectory for the pastor. The convent and school cost $4,000 and the rectory, $1,800. The parish was passing from childhood to adolesence and nothing manifested the transformation more than the coming of the Benedictine sisters in 1882. Little did Father William realize at the time "the tempest in a teapot" his invitation to the Sisters would have in a few brief years. Nonetheless, Mother Scholastica, O.S.B.

in October agreed to send sisters. The story of their coming and its effect not only upon Melrose and Stearns county but also throughout the state is told in the appendix to this chapter. "The Melrose Conflict," as Sister Nora Leuthmer, O.S.B. recounts it is a small section of her magnificent unpublished doctoral thesis concerning the Catholic schools in the Diocese of St. Cloud.

Father William, a kindly, out-going man, did more than become involved unwillingly in a school controversy. He was father confessor, spiritual director, economic consultant and temporal mentor to the families of the parish and the increasing number of new arrivals each year. He cultivated their already deep devotion for *Kinder, Kuche, Kirch* and succeeded in instilling a sense of deep loyalty for their adopted country. By the time he left the parish in 1881 the number of families had increased to one hundred and fifty. He was succeeded by Father Lawrence Steinkogler, O.S.B. in 1891 who remained as pastor until June, 1894 when he was transferred to St. Mary's church at Red Lake Falls.

For twenty-six years, the first generation of Catholicism in Melrose, the People of God were served by Benedictine monks from St. John's Abbey. As that courageous band of three priests and two lay brothers departed from their home in St. Vincent's Abbey, the great Benedictine pioneer in the United States, Abbot Boniface Wimmer, O.S.B. wrote: "The foundation should be a center from which we will be of service to both the civilized and uncivilized people of Minnesota." Seldom had a mortal man prophesied so accurately.

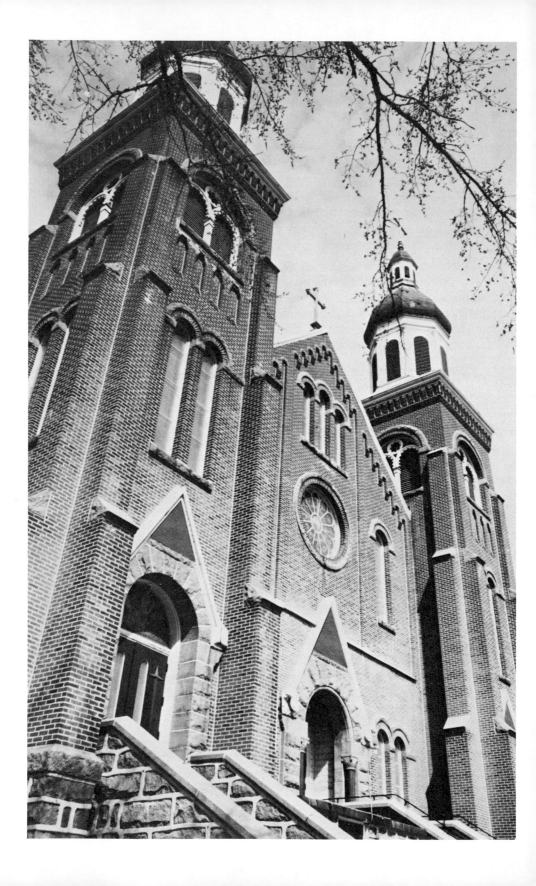

APPENDIX

THE MELROSE CONFLICT

Father Cogan's founding and operation of a new school for American boys in the later nineteenth century, accompanied by acclamations and denunciations from different parties divided according to national loyalties, was a prelude to a quarrel of considerable proportion in the town of Melrose. This seemingly insignificant and quiet railroad town became the focal point of state-wide attention in 1887. A skirmish which was part of the language problem developed. This language problem blossomed into the Americanism issue during the following decade and had national and international complications.

The first settlers of Melrose were Moses Adley, Robert and E. C. Wheeler, and Warren Adley, all of whom came from the state of Maine. The township was organized in 1866. The supervisors were W. Chambers, Charles W. Taylor, and Charles G. Lamb, Augustus Lindberg was clerk. For seven years, the Melrose village was the terminus of the St. Paul and Pacific, later the St. Paul, Minneapolis and Manitoba Railroad. This branch was pushed through to form a junction with the main line at Barnesville in 1878.

The first school in the village, District No. 48, was built in 1868 and was replaced by a new and larger building twelve years later. This was a graded school with two departments each having fifty-three pupils in 1880. The village of Melrose was incorporated by an act approved on March 3, 1881. That year St. Patrick's, the first Catholic parish, had more than forty families. The Irish had begun the parish with a log church built in 1868. By 1878, thirteen German Catholic families had settled in the village. These withdrew from the Irish parish and built their own church to seat 150. The village had a Protestant Episcopal church which was organized in 1879, and a Methodist Episcopal church building which was constructed in 1876. In June of 1887, Donald McDonald published the first issue of the Melrose **Record**.

There were six general stores, three hotels, a drugstore, and a flour mill in the flourishing village. The settlers who operated the business enterprises were predominantly men who had migrated from the New England states. The earliest Germans were from Rhine, Prussia, and were interested in farming. There were two active societies in 1881: the Melrose Lodge, A. F. and A. M. No. 145, instituted in February that year with fourteen members; and the Melrose Lodge, I.O. of G.T. No. 100, which was organized in 1876 with thirty charter members. By 1881, it had nearly doubled its membership.

This vigorous and heterogeneous population was motivated by a civic pride. These "Americans" regarded the German Catholic as foreigner and his manner of doing things confirmed their opinion. Opposition to the increasing number of foreigners was aroused and this feeling was spurred on by the national emotion against the incoming "hordes." The German-American, on the other hand, was taking a stand and beginning to demand consideration in a church governed by Irish bishops. In 1886, the Abbeln Memorial was taken to Rome. By it, representative German clergy asked the Pope to consider the German people and give them the right to their own parishes, an equal status with the Irish, and an episcopate that would administer the church affairs for them in an understanding manner. This Memorial pointed out:

> In all this controversy, besides a difference of language, we must
> not by any means make light of the difference and discrepancy of the

305

Catholic customs as they are to be found among the Germans and Irish. The Irish, on account of the oppression and persecution which they suffered in their own land, love simplicity in divine service, and in all the practices of religion, and do not care much for pomp and splendor. But the Germans. . .love the beauty of the church edifice and the pomp of ceremonies, belfries and bells, organs and sacred music, processions, feast days, sodalities, and the most solemn celebrations of First Communions and weddings. These and other like things, although not essential to the Catholic faith and life, foster piety and are so dear and sacred to the faithful that not without great danger could they be taken away from them.

The Stearns County countryside gives evidence of these traditions which were inculcated and nurtured in the young with a zeal that was often misinterpreted by the Irish and the "American." True to custom, the Germans of the new St. Boniface parish in Melrose, in 1879, celebrated the blessing of the new church on June 5 with the "pomp of ceremonies." They had 1,800 visitors, an impressive procession, and great festivity. The debt was paid on the eve of the celebration. With equal enthusiasm this handful of Germans went about the task of establishing the school, for they were convinced "that the destructive influence of the public schools" was in great part the basis of a loss of the faith. Father Wapelhorst had given the German position on parochial schools in the **Pastoral Blatt.** All other causes, Wapelhorst said, would mostly disappear of themselves if, with properly regulated care of the souls, the children were brought up according to the spirit of the Church in good Catholic schools.

In May of 1882, the school was nearly completed. It was a school-convent building 24 by 40 feet. The first floor had classrooms, kitchen and dining room. The second floor had two bedrooms, a general living room for the sisters, and an office used by Father William during the school day. This school, according to the **Nordstern,** was roomy and functional, a tribute to the pastor and his parish. The Benedictine sisters ot St. Joseph, on October 29, agreed to staff it. On January 5, there were fifty-six pupils under the instruction of Sister Seraphica Kennedy and Sister Opportuna Blemmel.

According to their manner of settlement, the Germans would cluster around a parish center and then encourage other fellow countrymen to join them. In a few years they would build up a strong community, a homogeneous colony where they could observe their religion and conduct their societies and traditional social life in characteristic European fashion. These customs were annoying to the "American" in Melrose, as elsewhere, in those late 80's.

After the school was built, pupils were withdrawn from the public school. Additional families arrived and in ten years the school population had reached 200. With German "sparsamkeit" these settlers immediately began accumulating funds for the construction of a new and more impressive church building. By 1887, the German Catholics were well implanted in business as well as farming. They were said to be "in preponderance." Meanwhile, the attacks by some national Catholic leaders on the "godless" public schools, the multiplication of parochial schools after the decrees of the Third Plenary Council at Baltimore, and the resistance by Catholics to "double taxation" contributed to a strengthening of a nativist group in the midwest.

The American Protective Association, under Henry Bowers, had a following in Minnesota. It revived the campaign of the Know-Nothing Party against the increasing power of the Roman Catholic Church in schools and public institutions, and was antagonized by the revival of the Church's demands for public school funds. Its influence was more local than national and produced a crop of secret anti-Catholic societies which aimed to keep Catholics out of public office. It rallied to the defense of the public school system, and urged a limitation on immigration and naturalization. Circumstances in Melrose were ripe for a coalescence with such a nativist group. Polarization began as early as 1878, intensified during the next few years, and in August, 1887, the Germans and Americans clashed.

In the year 1878 when the Germans began their own parish and the area expressed partisanship over Cogan's endeavor, Chambers wrote to the editor of the Melrose **Record** that they, the Americans, were getting tired of the "gentlemen" from the St. John's college, "for they want to confiscate our St. Patrick's church...the same as they want to run all the schools in the county. These very gentlemen stop emigration from coming into this diocese." Feelings against this German-dominated school system in Stearns County and in the diocese had heightened to the point of an outbreak. Father William Eversmann took the action which ignited this pent-up resentment.

The **Nordstern** of August 4 announced that the Germans in Melrose took the opportunity, on election day, to express their interests through a vote. They elected Joseph Kraker to the public school board and "took power out of the hand of the Americans and placed it into one who had their interests." They also voted for a school year shortened to five months. This angered the Americans. The writer of the article lauded the Germans for looking after their own interests, "since the Americans had heretofore managed well for themselves." He described the situation as quite a contest. Two school meetings had been held, one on July 16, and a special meeting on July 30. "If there was heat prior to the annual meeting, there surely was heat after the agitation between meetings.

"Many citizens" reported the American view to the **Pioneer Press.** They said the German Catholics "turned out en masse and voted five months of public school for the ensuing year and a tax of $200." The decision angered the Americans who called a special meeting to extend the term from five to nine months and to raise an additional $400 school tax. They were defeated by a vote of 112 to 121. They declared they would not let the matter rest, but would have special school meetings every ten days for the next year "before we will surrender the rights belonging to the republic in which we live." They continued:

> Our schools are the grandest of our institutions. We can never afford to see them trampled beneath the feet of their enemies, as ignorance is the father of all vice...The idea of the wealthiest common school district of Stearns County having only five months of school in a year and voting a paltry sum of $200 school tax!...We are thoroughly roused, and the indignation we feel is of a consuming kind. We despise the motives, whatever they may be, which would make a transaction possible in the nineteenth century...

Apparently the Germans were saving for a church construction fund. They were reluctant to contribute their money through taxes to the public school, which like "a dry milk cow in pasture" brought no return to them. By shortening the school year and cutting down the tax, they could save for their own purposes.

A group known as Friends of the Public Schools was formed within days and a battle was fought in the newspapers of St. Paul, St. Cloud and of all the communities in central Minnesota in which a paper was published. A group of St. Cloud citizens wrote to the **Pioneer Press** about the conditions in their town:

> The Catholic clergy take active part in the fight, and it is thought to be the beginning of a contest in this country against the public schools. In this city two large parochial schools have been built at considerable expense, and the Catholic children are to be withdrawn entirely from the public schools, and the same plan is to be pursued throughout the country wherever the common schools are not completely under Catholic authority. It is feared that the consequent taxing of Catholics to support both school systems may result in an open conflict on the question.

The Melrose situation had become an open conflict which raged for three months. A compromise was reached there; but because the real issue was not solved it went underground for a decade only to surface again in Avon. Melrose was the location which provided the first organized effort to stop the so-called Catholic control and clergy domination of public education in central Minnesota, specifically Stearns County, where the Catholic Church was thought truly to be the enemy "trampling" the "grandest of our institutions under its feet." According to report, the "consistent appeals that Father William made from the pulpit and other contacts" were responsible for the unfavorable election results in Melrose. Father William enlisted the support of the merchants and bankers for his cause. The **Pioneer Press** reported:

It is more than probable that this is an isolated case of misdirected sectarian zeal on the part of a village priest not well up in the ways of this country; but the issue he has made at Melrose is one which challenges the attention of the people of the whole commonwealth. This attempt to suppress or cripple the public schools in places where there is a local majority opposed to them will not be tolerated, and the sooner it is abandoned the better for all concerned.

Herman Kraker replaced August Lindberg on the board. Lindberg explained that the election did not arouse the people. He had resigned with no intent to run again, so Kraker had no opposition. But he objected to the accusation by the editor of the **Nordstern** that by this election the Germans had taken the blade of "corruption" out of the hands of the Americans and placed their interests in the right hands. The school's management was without fault. "Our last nine months' school cost the district only $679. The state apportionment and one-mill tax paid the rest, $326; the total being $1,005.

On the day this message reached the people the **Journal Press** announced another meeting to be held on August 13 in order to raise the tax and vote for a nine and one-half month school year. The announcement declared: "This school question is a matter of vital importance to the citizens of Melrose, but will apply equally to every school district in Stearns County as well as in the entire state of Minnesota."

The **Northwestern Chronicle** printed an article conveying the impression that the Germans were reasonable in the means they had used to express their opinion; namely, the ballot. Extremism increased in momentum. The St. Paul **Globe** attacked the clergy who used ecclesiastical position and power to "overthrow a system that is peculiarly dear to the American heart." A few days later the **Pioneer Press** under the major headline, "The Power of the Pope," informed the people that Rev. Samuel Smith dealt with Roman Church matters and the public-parochial school difficulty in Melrose in an address entitled the "Paw of the Bear." The text was taken from the words of David before he slaughtered Goliath, "The Lord who gave me strength against the paw of the lion will deliver me from this Philistine." The full address was printed, and the paper continued to run articles in defense of the public schools almost daily.

Because the entire Stearns County school system was implicated in the attacks, L. J. Rocholl, the county superintendent, addressed a notice to the people of the county in answer to "certain false statements as to the manner in which the schools of this county are conducted. In reply I would say that all the schools under my supervision are being conducted in accordance with the laws of this state. Any violation of the same will be reported by me to my superior, which is the limit of my personal responsibility."

This action brought Rocholl personally into the situation, and he was accused of having been a Catholic teacher who himself taught German and religion in the public school in which he held a position. Furthermore, he became a central figure in the Avon school fight in 1896. The **Nordstern** got further into the fray with the report that the Germans had sought a compromise and proposed a seven-month year which had been rejected by the Americans.

This compromise apparently was accepted but not much publicized; or, if it was, it was overshadowed by a news story on "An Impending Conflict," which had subheadings: the History of the Struggle for the Stearns County Public Schools, Catholic Catechism Taught During Lawful School Hours by Benedictine Monks and Sisters, A Burning Question in Which the Whole State must Sooner or Later take Part. It ran as a September 19 special in the **Pioneer Press,** and explained "How the Great Benedictine Order Controls the Public Schools in Stearns County." Melrose, the article claimed, was not a new question in Stearns County which, in addition to being the most Catholic, "is, moreover the governmental seat of the great Benedictine Order for the Western United States." This religious order, it was stated, also controls the diocese through Bishop Seidenbusch, "also an O.S.B." "Furthermore, the author remarked, the Mother Superior resides in St. Joseph and her sway over the Sisters reaches to the Pacific coast." He spoke of the extensive lands and buildings in the hands of the church, tax free. Two localities besides Melrose were mentioned as examples of schools taught by the Sisters; namely, Lake Henry and St. Martin. Both were now having troubles. ;He said, "In St. Martin it was voted at the regular school meeting this fall. . .to have nine months school, and the necessary funds were appropriated. It was then voted that during three months of this term the school would be conducted as a public school, and for the remaining six months by the Sisters."

Two other significant complaints were aired. The German Teachers' Institute had been conducted by the county superintendent the previous month (August), had been attended only by Germans, and had used only the German language. The second complaint concerned the situation in the city of St. Cloud to which reference has been made. It was reported:

> In St. Cloud the question was solved in 1875 by the Catholics quietly securing through the efforts of Ex-Lieut. Gov. Gilman, then representative from that district, the passage of a bill establishing an independent school district in the northern and western part of the city, populated wholly by Germans. . .Since that time the church has regulated the school calendar and it has arranged for the convenience of the priests to teach in the schools. . .This summer two new schools were built $4,000 and $15,000. The Catholics will have to attend these and it is proposed that the independent district be again restored to the main district from which it was taken. . .By absorbing the public schools and controlling them it has avoided the double taxation problem. . .And so the church holds sway in Stearns county.

The **Nordstern** claimed that this article was written by Mitchell, the editor of the **Journal Press** in St. Cloud. The **St. Cloud Times,** in a defense of the Catholic in St. Cloud, called it a "fantasm of a Mitchellian brian." Editorial battles continued.

Bishop John Ireland in St. Paul was interviewed about the Melrose public-parochial school conflict. He claimed that his knowledge of the situation was entirely from the newspaper and he regarded the whole affair 'as merely a tempest in a teapot.' "What are the facts in the case?" he asked. Then he defended the Catholic citizen's right to vote. He doubted the statement made in the **Pioneer Press,** and that three-fourths of the schools teach catechism during the lawful school hours. He remarked that outside the hours the Catholics have as much right to instruct in their religion as any other group. He indicated that the state superintendent, Kichle, had no knowledge about the claims in the schools as they were described in that article.

Two significant events followed immediately: Kiehle was asked to investigate the situation in Stearns County, and a meeting was held in St. Cloud on the evening of September 20 to select delegates to go to the Melrose school convention. An article identified as a St. Cloud Special to the **Globe** entitled "The Olive Branch of Peace" says:

> The convention is called to affect a compromise, if possible, between two warring factions of the public and Catholic schools. . .;The following delegates were elected: C. S. Mitchell, E. H. Atwood, George C. Woller, C. W. Cooper, O. W. Baldwin, J. E. Wing, G. W. Stewart, W. A. Mitchell, O. F. Carver, and D. W. Bruckart.

The "mass meeting" was held and the newspaper reported that resolutions were adopted "declaring vigorously against sectarianism in the public schools." The people organized and agreed on "radical plans for future action" in Stearns County schools. They protested against improper influences in the operation of their public schools, and resolved that the essential principles of the constitution are to be upheld in regard to the public schools."

A trustee of the school district, William Clark, Sr., thought the Americans held this mass meeting over a dead issue. The Germans had already held a special meeting and extended the term for five to seven months. Little did he realize that a few years later the constitutionality of the sectarian activity in the Avon school would be tested in a lawsuit which was planned with a little more sophistication than Melrose's "tempest in the teapot."

The final episode in the conflict was the release of a report from State Superintendent Kiehle on December 6. The State Institute Conductor, W. F.

Rochelan, under instructions from Kiehle, had made unannounced visits to representative Stearns County schools, especially those against which complaints had been made. He disclosed that the county had 141 districts with a population of 30,000, sixty-five percent of which were exclusively German and Catholic. The language of the home was German, of course, and the first appearance of the English was the introduction of English words in colloquial German, "making a language neither English nor good German."

He did not find any evidence which indicated opposition to the public schools. Sixty-five percent of the schools had school for six months or more, the average for the county was 6.5 months. Wages for the male teachers averaged $44 per month and for females $33, three dollars above the average for males and females in the state.

Richmond school had one teacher with 107 pupils enrolled and an attendance of ninety-five. The teaching excelled even with so large a number of pupils "indicating that the teacher makes a great deal of difference in the quality of education." He then described the qualifications of this teacher, Lucas Gertken, the man who was so active in the German Teacher Association of Stearns County.

Kiehle summarized the general characteristics of other schools which were visited as due to lack of organization and system: No program of work was found in any school visited; and, in many, "an ignorance of the ordinary appliances and methods that we are accustomed to see." He said that in some schools the German language had a prominence not allowed by law, and not in the interests of the children if they are to become intelligent American citizens. But this situation was understandable to Kiehle, and it did not seem to cause him a great concern. His closing remarks were:

> I feel warranted in the conclusion that the local controversy at Melrose, which involved personal, national, and religious elements has led to some wrong judgments concerning the condition of things in the county. Doubtless the facts of a foreign people with a foreign language, very many of whom are illiterate in their own tongue, and of a religious faith whose clergy strongly favor parochial schools, tell heavily against the efficiency of the public school system in that county. As a result, schools are neglected, the qualifications of the teachers are made of secondary importance, and the improvement of the children is very unsatisfactory. But there is no disloyal feeling or antipathy to the school prevalent. The people are growing more and more interested and many are desirous of gaining all the advantages for their children that the state offers, and at the same time will remain loyal to their religion. At the late institute held in St. Cloud nearly all the teachers were Catholics, including several Sisters from the Benedictine convent, who, in appreciative attention and interest, took high rank in the institute.

The American faction could not let the episode close with Kiehle's report. They retaliated with the following statement:

> The friends of the public schools at Melrose met and adopted a resolution: Resolved, that the school controversy as it existed in Melrose was not of a personal, national or religious character on the part of the friends of the public schools but altogether and solely on the part of its enemies; that the comments of Prof. Kiehle on our public schools of Stearns County shows that he is not correctly informed as to the facts in regard to the important matters complained of; that the friends of the public schools of Melrose have no feeling of enmity towards those who are opposed to our public schools here or elsewhere, but would welcome them all to a hearty cooperation in the best interests of our school system, inasmuch as we hold that the proper education of the masses is the bulwark of personal, civil and religious liberties; that we submit to the fair and candid judgment of the public whether an examination of the matter complained of in our public schools, where only one side is represented, is not a fraud; that we depreciate the fact of the existing opposition to our public schools here and elsewhere as a great public calamity, and particularly so because the opposition is of a somewhat national and so-called religious character.

St. Boniface Church.

St. Patrick Church

Above: Interior of St. Patrick Church.

Right: Interior of St. Boniface Church.

Below: St. Boniface convent.

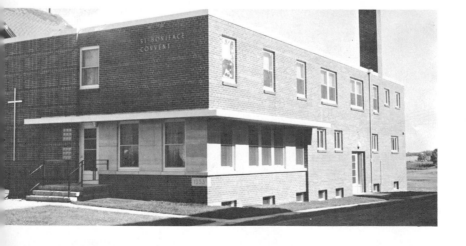

The old St. Boniface school.

Below: The new St. Boniface school.

The old St. Boniface parish hall.

The old St. Boniface school, destroyed by fire in 1910.

Grades four and five of St. Boniface school at the turn of the century with their teacher, Sister Millieanna, O.S.B.

Sister Ada, O.S.B. with her class in 1912.

Music class of St. Boniface school in 1910.

Father Schirmers and the members of St. Boniface dramatics society about 1915. They are seated left to right: Fred Schultenover, Rose Meyer, Father Schirmers, Olivia Peter; standing left to right: Nettie Rehkamp, Brownie Hoffman, Jake Wolter, Frank Schmidt, Leo Michaels, Nick Kraick and Gertrude Waldorf.

The gravestone of William J. Hannan, one of the early pioneers in Melrose.

St. Patrick's cemetery.

St. Boniface cemetery with school, rectory and church in the background.

PASTORS OF THE MELROSE PARISHES

*Father
Augustine Burns, O.S.B.*

*Father
Paul Rettenmaier, O.S.B.*

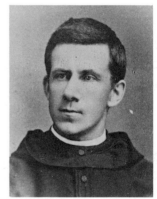

*Father
Meinrad Leuthard, O.S.B.*

*Father
William Eversmann, O.S.B.*

*Father
Francis Welp*

*Father
James Walcher*

Father
Joseph Kilian

Monsignor
Peter A. Lorsung

Monsignor
Bernard Richter

Father
Joseph Willenbrink

Father
Lambert Haupt

The investiture of
Monsignor Matthias
Hoffman (center), with
Bishop Peter W.
Bartholome and Abbot
Baldwin Dworschak,
O.S.B.

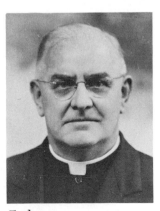

Father
Sebastian Schirmers

Monsignor
Matthias Hoffmann

Father
Francis Julig

The sixtieth anniversary banquet of the Women's Catholic Order
of Foresters, St. Philomena Court number 631, on May 16, 1965.

Fathers of sons who are priests were honored at a dinner sponsored
by the Melrose Knights of Columbus in November, 1959.

*Two recipients of the
Bishop's Medal of Merit in
1964 posed with Bishop
Bartholome and Father Julig.
They are Mrs. Teresa Meyer
and Mr. Henry Loxtercamp.*

CHAPTER TWO

A GLEAM IN THE BISHOP'S EYE

. . . the condition of the diocese is now satisfactorily
and permanently settled. The secular clergy can no more
complain. They have now a good number of good missions.

— Bishop Otto Zardetti

They say that Pope St. Pius X died of a broken heart on the eve
of World War I. His successor, Pope Benedict XV, offered a fourteen
point peace plan to the warring nations, but his pleas fell on deaf ears.
His successor, in turn, pleaded and begged for peace as he watched
the nations stock-piling armaments. But to no avail. Pope Pius XII,
called "the Pope of Peace" let not a day go by throughout the holocaust
of World War II without praying for peace, preaching peace and
urging peace upon men of war. "Peace" was the watchword of the
Vatican; "War" was the business of the world.

In the United States a new spirit was abroad in the Church's
schools and seminaries, rectories and parishes, convents and chanceries.
New institutions were being created such as the Christian Family Movement, the Liturgical Movement, the National Catholic War Council
(later, the National Catholic Welfare Conference and still later, the
United States Catholic Conference). Old organizations were rejuvenated,
such as the Knights of Columbus, the National Councils of Catholic
Men and Women, the Central Verein. New experiments were tried,
such as the Grail Movement, the National Catholic Rural Life Conference, the Newman Apostolate and the Catholic Worker. The social
teachings of the Popes was coming through and as a result a generation
of priests under such leaders as Monsignor John A. Ryan, Father Frank
Cronin, Monsignor Charles Owen Rice and Monsignor George G.
Higgins were being formed.

But the Catholic Church in the United States faced hard times as well. One great light went out in 1918 when Catholic people mourned the death of Archbishop John Ireland. His long-time friend and associate, James Cardinal Gibbons of Baltimore, only a few years before his own death said:

"The last Prelate who has descended below the horizon of the tomb was the Venerable Patriarch of the West, the great Apostle of temperance, the sturdy Patriot who had endeared himself to the American people, without distinction of race or religion, the man who had contributed perhaps more than any other to demonstrate the harmony that exists between the Constitution of the Church and the Constitution of the United States. Needless to say, I am speaking of John Ireland, the Lion of the fold of Juda."

The Church proved to be a church of the poor, for her people were poor, her priests went without salaries and her mortgagor was ever at a door of a church looking for payment of interest, if not capital, on the parish debt. The Church in the United States joined her sister churches in Europe in prayers that God might spare His people from another world war. Church leaders warned of the evil of communism and the growing communist menace in the United States. In spite of the joys and the sorrows of the past the Church knew, with some fear and trepidation, that the atomic bomb was not the end of an era — but the end of a world. The atomic age was born and the Church, as well as nations and institutions and the man on the street, was caught completely off guard.

The world was restless in those post-World War I days and the Church was restless. The Church was helpless and saddened by the religious persecution in Russia. The Church in Germany was silent in the face of the growing Nazi evil. The Church in France was a cast-a-way by the new generation of fun-lovers and intellectuals who gathered on the west bank of the river Seine. There, too, the Church stood helpless as every perceptive viewer realized that the Church was losing the workingman. By the time of World War II, Henri Perrin brought the attention of his fellow citizens to the reality in a book entitled, *France Pagan?* And the prophetic Archbishop of Paris, Emmanual Cardinal Suhard, tried to supply some answers in his historic pastoral, *Growth or Decline? The Church Today.* Ireland had been bathed in blood in search of independence from England and came out the winner with a new nation called Eire. And that empire, England, upon which "the sun never sets" became more civilized in granting fuller freedom and greater respect to those people called "the Roman Catholics;" this as the empire was melting in her hand like a gob of ice cream. Later the Kingston Trio would sing a little ditty entitled, "They're Rioting in Africa" which captured the facts of the preceeding decades. Colonialism was breathing its dying gasp — and it died so quickly that some of the readers of these lines might not even remember the vast colonial empires of the European powers. (You may get an insight into the system if you catch the movie "Gunga Din" on the late, late show). Unfortunately too many of the Church's missionaries who went to serve the native people ended up, instead, by serving some home office or foreign ministry.

Minnesota during these years took pride in three leaders of the Church who did honor to the Catholic people and shone as brightly as the north star. The first was an exceptional leader, Archbishop John Ireland; the second, a distinguished scholar, Archbishop Austin Dowling; the third, a holy man, Archbishop John Gregory Murray. Well they guided the destinies of the Catholic people and clergy for so much of what we cherish and possess today in our parish churches was sown by the leadership, scholarship and holiness of these three metropolitans of the Province of St. Paul. Their mark was left on almost every Catholic institution and organization throughout the state. Although not directly a part of our narrative, they were men concerned and committed to the spiritual welfare of all the people of the state.

We have already mentioned the first three Bishops of the Diocese of St. Cloud. One more bishop appears on the scene in the course of this chapter. Born in Red Wing of a distinguished Catholic family Joseph F. Busch and his two brothers entered the priesthood. He attended the University of Innsbruck in Austria and was ordained in 1889 — the same year the Diocese of St. Cloud was established. He served as a priest of the Archdiocese of St. Paul on its Mission Band and through that experience came to be familiar with many problems of priests and people. In 1910 he was appointed Bishop of Lead, South Dakota. Immediately and vigorously he defended the miners who were suffering deplorable and de-humanizing conditions. This did not please, to say the least, the owners of the mines. The story of the struggle between the bishop and the mining companies is one that someday should be told. (Louis Budenz, a cub reporter on a New York paper later told this writer that the admiration he had for the Bishop and the social teaching of the Catholic Church turned him away from communism; led him to take instructions from the then Monsignor Fulton J. Sheen and become a Catholic.) Bishop Busch was installed by Archbishop Ireland on March 19, 1915 as fourth bishop of St. Cloud. Upon his death in May, 1953 he was the oldest bishop in the United States, having been a bishop forty-four years. No single church leader, perhaps, ever witnessed so many changes in the Church, in his diocese and the parishes and institutions of the diocese over so many years as did Bishop Busch. (The only exception this writer knows of is Archbishop Patrick Mannix of Melbourne, Australia.) But Bishop Busch's troubles of subsequent years were not the problems that faced Bishop Otto Zardetti in 1889. In the eyes of the latter, Melrose was part of one of Bishop Zardetti's biggest problems.

Upon assuming his obligations as the first Bishop of St. Cloud, Otto Zardetti knew his first duty was to create a diocese which in fact until then was a diocese on paper. In his summary report on the conditions of the diocese which he left to his successor he wrote:

"On coming here I found the diocese existing by name and *de jure*, but otherwise yet the confusion of a vicariate existed. The diocese was nearly in the power of the Benedictines. There were but fifteen secular priests in the poorest missions . . . . From the beginning I strove to build up a diocesan clergy, to educate young men and to provide the secular clergy with missions so that I could hope to attract a new generation of priests and destroy the prevalent impression that the St. Cloud diocese was but a dominance of the Benedictines. Already when Abbot Bernard took up the administration he by my request gave over to the secular clergy the following missions: Holdingford - St. Anna - St. Stephen - Belle River - Perham - St. Nicholas - Lake Henry - Spring Hill - Kraintown - Kimball Prairie - Alexandria.

The missions, however, being poor, most of them only stations and yet nearly all regular and perfect parishes in their possession, so that I was greatly embarrassed when obliged to make changes, that the secular clergy justly complained, etc., I resolved to take steps toward securing some good missions to the secular clergy. In a memorial to Rome of forty pages I stated the condition of affairs, asked for at least six perfect parishes out of ten they had, went personally to Rome pleading my cause. Although my claims were found just by the authorities, still they after asking information from St. John's hesitated to do anything."

Bishop Zardetti changed his mind after asking for fourteen parishes and requested that only six well-established parishes in Stearns county be assigned to the care of the diocese. Both Bishop Zardetti and Abbot Bernard Lockinar, O.S.B. went to Rome to plead their respective causes. The Cardinal Prefect of Propaganda listened to both sides and then appointed Archbishop Ireland to effect a compromise. The Bishop was eager to knit together a diocese and the Abbot was just as eager to preserve the good order of the monastery. In June, 1893 the Cardinal Prefect in Rome informed the Bishop and the Abbot that the abbey would continue to serve Richmond, Cold Spring, St. Martin, Farming, Meire Grove, New Munich, Freeport, Albany, St. Joseph and St. Mary in St. Cloud. The Cardinal Prefect at the same time informed the Bishop that the diocese would have the care of six former Benedictine parishes: Luxemburg, Millerville, St. Augusta, Pierz, Rush Lake and Melrose. After the decision was made Bishop Zardetti wrote:

"The Rt. Rev. Abbot . . . was always fair and just. Thus the condition of the diocese is now satisfactorily and permanently settled. The secular clergy can no more complain. They have now a good number of good missions. Small and new ones will grow and multiply. All counties except Stearns are free from the religious."

One of the first actions Bishop Zardetti took was to appoint an old friend from his South Dakota days as pastor of one of the "good missions." A year to the month later Father Bernard J. Richter arrived in Melrose as the first diocesan priest to be pastor of St. Boniface parish. The appointment signaled not only a new era in the life of the diocese but also a new era in the life of the parish. Father Richter spent the next twenty-seven years of his life in Melrose until his death on December 18, 1921. No pastor to this day has accomplished in the two Melrose parishes as much as Father Richter. He was, the right man, for the right job, at the right time. If for no other reason than sending Father Richter to Melrose the people of the community should be grateful to Bishop Zardetti.

Father Richter was born near Muenster, Westphalia, Germany on September 23, 1863. That fact that many of his parishoners in Melrose were also Westphalian was a decided advantage in his, and their favor. After completing his studies at the University of Muenster he emigrated to the United States, completed his studies for the priesthood at St. Francis Seminary, Milwaukee and was ordained a priest on June 24, 1887. He joined the Vicariate of Dakota Territory as a missionary and was appointed pastor of White Lake, South Dakota. His ability was recognized by Father Zardetti, then the vicar general of the vicariate, and when the latter was appointed Bishop of St. Cloud, Father Zardetti asked Father Richter to join him. Immediately he was named pastor of Holy Angels Pro-Cathedral and on June 7, 1894 appointed pastor of St. Boniface parish.

Father Richter as pastor of St. Boniface found himself an assistant pastor to help him. The assistant pastor, Father Richard Zoller, (1894-1898) served as the pastor of St. Patrick's parish. The former kept more than busy studying the problems that needed the most attention; the latter kept busy pulling together the loose strings that appear in a parish without a pastor. Father Zoller strove mightily to form a community out of what was merely a congregation when he arrived. For the next fifteen years this arrangement continued with one man serving as both pastor of St. Patrick's and assistant pastor of St. Boniface. The pastors of St. Patrick's parish during these years were: Father Herman Klein (1898-1899), Father James Walcher (1899-1902), Father Vincent Weigand (1903-1904), Father Francis Zitur (1904-1905), Father George Rauch (1905-1906), Father Matthias Hoffmann (1908-1909).

St. Patrick's parish had grown stronger during those fifteen years. The city's growth in population and the stable economic progress that followed the depression of 1893 gave a stability that St. Patrick's parish had never previously experienced. In 1910 Father James Walcher became full-time pastor of St. Patrick's parish and, again, there was rejoicing and pride among the "gandy-dancers" — the railroad employees. In a community of two thousand people St. Patrick's parish continued to grow if not flourish. In 1905 a sacristy was added to the side of the wood frame church and in 1908 a tower was added, a gift of J. Rauch of Vancouver, British Columbia. In 1909 Father Francis Welp succeeded Father Walcher (of whom it was said at this time, and again when he returned as pastor in 1932, wanted to close the parish.)

1910 was a busy year for the people of St. Patrick's. They undertook the building of a new rectory for their first resident pastor who had no other duties but to provide for the material and spiritual needs of the people of St. Patrick's parish. Gladly they built the house with most of the work being supplied by the men of the parish. At the same time they increased the lean-to on the sacristy so that daily Masses might be offered there and thus save fuel during the long winter months. Neither rectory nor addition to the sacristy satisfied them. There were rumors that a new church should be built. There were rumors that St. Patrick's should have its own school. These rumors became reality with the appointment of Father J. A. Kilian in 1914.

What Father Richter was to St. Boniface parish, Father Kilian was to St. Patrick's. Both were builders. Both were loved by the people they served so zealously, the former chiefly by "desk work" the latter chiefly by "personal contact." Both, too, loved the city and country elements of Melrose and took great pride in being citizens of Melrose. Under the leadership of Father Kilian, St. Patrick's parish proceeded to build a cement block building faced with stucco. The basement and first floors were used as classrooms for the school and the second floor was used as a church. The structure cost $26,000. The people were delighted both with having their own school and their own new church. Two items in the church were highly prized by the parishoners. One was an alleged reliquary containing a piece of the garment worn by St. Patrick. The other was an 1871 painting of St. Patrick casting the snakes out of Ireland.

Another event of importance occurred in 1922 when the parish of eighty-five families marked the golden jubilee of its existence. The little church (that is, the first church which was still being used as a parish hall) "took on a festal appearance," wrote Catherine Hannon, "with its freshly cleaned walls and altar, and other added improvements." The solemn jubilee Mass was celebrated by Father Welp, celebrant, assisted by Father John Kral, subdeacon, and Father Sebastian Schirmers, subdeacon. Among the visiting priests a position of honor was given Abbot Alcuin Deutsch, O.S.B. of St. John's Abbey who was also the homilist during the Mass. Announcing the jubilee in the pages of the *Melrose Beacon*, Father Kilian noted, "To accommodate a great many, it has been decided to charge only fifty cents for this delicious dinner, and for the children in the grades who will have their own tables, only thirty-five cents."

Few parishes in the diocese, perhaps, suffered as severely as St. Patrick's did when the division headquarters of the Great Northern railroad was removed in 1923. The employees were given the opportunity to move with the railroad and many of them did. It was estimated that fifty families moved away from Melrose in 1923 and 1924. For all practical purposes this decimated the ranks of the people of St. Patrick's. It was a blow to their morale which had been raised so high during the previous year of the golden jubilee. There were rumors that the parish would also close. But the people, following their pastor's lead, did not lose hope. Those that remained in Melrose found other jobs and held the parish together. It became a tightly knit group and with more pride than the material resources warranted, they kept alive both church and school.

Six years later they were hit even harder by the "great crash" of 1929. For the most part they were city, not rural, people. The economic squeeze was on and again many men lost their jobs. Those who were shopkeepers or tradesmen barely eked out a living. The school that they worked for and sacrificed for was forced to close. There simply was no operational money. If that was not enough trouble, they soon discovered that trouble frequently comes in the double. Father Kilian who frequently went without his own salary for the benefit of the parish was transferred. They lost a pastor of whom one of his parishoners wrote, "During these years he has labored unceasingly and generously for the parishoners and the welfare of the parish in general. Owing to his untiring efforts and optimistic spirit which surmounts all difficulties, the school was built and equipped and the enrollment grown large."

A former assistant pastor of St. Boniface who had served as pastor of St. Patrick's for one year in 1908 returned as pastor. Father Matthias Hoffmann was well known to many of the people of the parish and they welcomed him. He served during the lean years of the depression and consequently was unable to engage in any major material project. He had a hobby of making Christmas cribs and small household shrines, a hobby he continued throughout his life. Not a few churches in the diocese are adorned with the cribs he made and many households in Melrose proudly claim to this day one of his cribs or shrines. He loved St. Patrick's very much and the people of St. Patrick's loved him. When this writer served as his assistant pastor Father Hoffmann more than once remarked that the happiest days of his priesthood were spent as pastor of St. Patrick's parish. Difficult as it was to understand then it is understandable now. Those who suffer and endure hardship together form a bond of unity and friendship that is understandable only to themselves.

When Father Hoffman was appointed pastor of Sacred Heart parish, Urbank, he was succeeded by Father James Walcher, who previously served as pastor from 1899 to 1902. He was not too enthusiastically received because the older members of the parish recalled his efforts at closing the parish. He was received, however, though coldly yet graciously in a manner known and practiced so well by the sons of St. Patrick.

After one year he was transferred and Father Peter Lorsung succeeded him. He was warm, open-hearted and made friends easily. He took an especial interest in young people and worked closely with the faculty and administration of the schools. He stretched what little income there was to make as many necessary improvements as he could with the help of the men and women of the parish. With regret the people of St. Patrick's received the news that he was to be transferred to Sacred Heart parish in Sauk Rapids.

Father Francis Julig succeeded Father Lorsung in 1938. What Father Kilian did to rejuvenate the parish between 1914 and 1929 Father Julig did even more in the twenty years he served the people of St. Patrick's. In recalling his memory more than one of his brother priests remarked, "He was the finest priest I have ever known." Both he and Father Lorsung were from the same parish in Millerville. There, however, the comparison stops. Father Julig was short in stature with an inclination to be stout (a struggle against which he waged all his life). Father Julig was mild, soft-spoken, gentle and kind. His love for children is already legendary and his impatience with any type of rowdiness always upset him for it cut directly across the grain of his own gentleness.

He was an avid outdoorsman and when the hunting seasons opened he would be tramping the hills near Birch Lake seeking squirrels, marching through corn fields near Meire Grove chasing out pheasants or sitting in a duck blind near St. Rosa waiting for the quacking of the ducks. He was also a bee-keeper and was proud of the honey they produced. He waited for the afternoons when he and his good friend, Father Henry Soenneker would come from the seminary, to check out their hives together.

He was a brother to all priests and St. Patrick's rectory was a haven of friendship and fellowship to the priests of the diocese and the abbey who would "take five to say hello to Frank". He was almost scrupulous in fulfilling his obligations to be a good neighbor to the priests and people of the surrounding parishes. More than one assistant pastor learned from the silent example of Father Julig of what a priest should be like in a one-priest parish.

ST BONIFACE PARISH

No grass grew under Father Richter's feet. Immediately he realized that the wood frame church that Father William O.S.B. had already added to was inadequate for the one hundred and fifty families of the parish. He realized also that the convent-school was also inadequate because the parish was growing so rapidly that almost one new family arrived each week. The rectory was already appearing more like a tumbled-down shack than a priest's house. He realized as the weeks grew into months that more land would be necessary in order to carry out the dream that was taking shape in his imagination. Finally, and above all, that the glory of God was not enhanced by buildings that more resembled car shops and warehouses than schools and churches. Needed were buildings in which the sacraments could be administered worthily to the People of God. He launched a two-pronged attack, one material and the other spiritual. He would plan first a new church and then a rectory, convent and school.

And again he was faced with the age-old dilemma. One only builds dream castles out of thin air, not churches, homes and schools. He was aware fully of the fact that the parishoners of St. Boniface's were still suffering from the economic panic of '93 and would continue for some time to come be economically depressed. He began with the spiritual problem by first striving to win the confidence of the people. He tried as best he could to carry out Bishop Zardetti's program of making the members of the parish aware of the new Diocese of St. Cloud, now governed by a bishop, and not appendices to the Abbey, governed by the abbot. This was no easy task, for the people loved the Benedictine monks who had served them "through thick and thin" for the past sixteen years when the parish was established. In doing so he quite naturally met some opposition but as time passed the parishoners realized his objectives and as the building program was taking shape they readily transferred their affections to the diocese and the parish.

Throughout the years of his pastorate he was aided in his work by able assistants. Two of them, Father Sebastian Schirmers and Father Matthias Hoffmann at later dates would return as pastors of St. Boniface parish. The other eight were Fathers Herman Klein, James Walcher, Vincent Weigand, Francis Zitur, George Rauch, Eugene Scheuer, John Bussmann and Adelbert Wagner. Most of them grew to love St. Boniface parish and kept that love with them throughout their priestly life. By the same token the parishoners of St. Boniface loved them and never forgot them. When a former assistant returned for any occasion he was always warmly greeted by the people of the parish.

By the time the parish was ready to begin construction of the church the people had already set aside $20,000. In 1897 the basement of the church was built at a cost of $5,000. A good deal of the work was volunteered by the men of the parish. The huge granite blocks, set neatly side by side as a column of marching soldiers, were carried from the sheds of the Melrose Granite Company after they were cut there by many stonemasons of the parish. Farmers of the parish volunteered their horses and teams and arms and backs to assist the stonemasons in settting the three foot by one foot blocks in place. Even the boys and young men assisted by acting as hod carriers and assistants to the stonemasons. The women of the parish, as they always do, provided the sustenance of life. In March of the following year the contract for the new edifice was let to E. C. Richmond, a leading contractor of Melrose. On May 1 the cornerstone was laid with great solemnity and celebration. Bishop James Trobec, present for the solemn high Mass delivered his sermon, first in German and then in English.

Within a year the church was completed, measuring one hundred eighty feet by seventy feet with towers reaching over one hundred feet into the sky. It was then, and continues to be, the largest church in the Diocese of St. Cloud.

The architect used the same basic plan in the construction of St. Boniface church as he did when he built St. Michael's church in Spring Hill. The striking difference between the two churches is the towers. Whereas St. Michael's has two Gothic towers, St. Boniface was built with two onion-bulb-like towers. Father Richter had traveled extensively in Bavaria and Austria in his younger days and came to like the domes that surmounted the Catholic churches in those countries.

In early June, 1899 Bishop James Trobec returned to Melrose to dedicate the church formally. Ten priests of the area were on hand as well as hundreds of parishoners and well wishers. A writer in the *Melrose Beacon* recorded the event and ended with the simple sentence that proclaimed more than words could express, "The congregation has increased to 230 families and Father Richter went to work with a will, and the result is that on June 7th of this year was dedicated one of the finest churches in the diocese, costing more than $50,000." Allowing for editorial license, there was five thousand dollars more than the sum quoted. Another writer wrote, "It is indeed a magnificent structure and stands as a monument to the untiring perseverance of Reverend Father Richter and his co-workers."

The one hundred and fifty families of the parish who were present when Father Richter arrived had grown to two hundred and thirty families in five years. This was an average of sixteen families a year or more than three new families a month. The old church was transformed into a school of six rooms making more room in the convent for the teaching Sisters. From the handful of girls that enrolled in the Sisters' school in 1882 the number of pupils had increased to almost four hundred.

The same year as the dedication the high altar, the side altars, and the pulpit were also installed, all hand-carved by the finest craftsmen in Germany. Two years later the stations of the Cross were installed at a cost of $1,600 and the Christmas crib was purchased at the same time for $500. Bishop Trobec returned in 1903 for the blessing of five new bells that were purchased at a cost of $250. The following year the parish bought a new pipe organ costing $4,000 and in 1906 it was noted that "a water motor was put in as power with which to run the new pipe organ."

At this point it might be well to examine a rumor that had been circulated at the time of the completion of the church building and has been many times since then. The writer first heard it twenty-one years ago when serving as an assistant pastor of St. Boniface. The story goes like this: Bishop Otto Zardetti did not like the Benedictine fathers nor did he like to be surrounded by them in the See city of St. Cloud. He wanted to move the See city of the diocese away from St. Cloud and thus called in Father Richter, sent him to Melrose with the order to build a parish complex that would be suitable to be named a cathedral parish. Thus the Diocese would be moved from St. Cloud to Melrose upon his petitioning the Holy See.

It is a good story and contains all the ingredients of a good novel. Twenty-one years ago I asked Father Matthias Hoffmann about its veracity. He neither affirmed it nor denied it but said he had never heard Father Richter even so much as mention it in all the years he knew him. Its credibility is further questioned by the very reasons Bishop Zardetti advanced for having six parishes in Stearns county. Finally, in all the documents this writer has researched there is not even so much as a hint about such an intention. That St. Boniface church was built according to the proportions of a cathedral and that the strong strain of Catholicism that was so evident in the building of the church could well have made some think that it *should* be a cathedral. But there is a world of difference between the "if" and the "is."

The pastor was now in a whirlwind and the marvel of his activities would astound most pastors and parishoners today. Within five years he had led his people to engage in the most ambitious building program ever undertaken to that date in the history of the diocese and both the pastor and people knew that there were three major projects yet to be undertaken. The most amazing fact of all was that he unfolded these plans to the parishoners of whom the majority were willing and eager to continue this program of material expansion. With the magnificent new church the priests and people were able to give greater honor and glory to God in a more dignified and worthy manner.

No sooner had the church been built and embellished than pastor and people were planning the new parish house. At the first sign of Spring, work was begun. In 1902 the parish had purchased two lots south of the new church as the most appropriate place for the rectory. The building was erected at a cost of $15,000, with Anthony J. Blix, St. Cloud as the architect and Henry Stockling of the same city, general contractor. The heating contract was awarded to John J. Kraker of Melrose and the plumbing contract to Joseph Renner of Alexandria. The heating unit was located in the basement which had ten foot high ceilings. The foundation of the basement was made of granite with *coursed range wood* above grade in order to match the foundation of the church. The rectory, measuring forty-two by sixty feet, was built of solid brick walls, faced with red sand mould brick on the outside and gray granite trimmings. A writer in the *Melrose Beacon* described the rectory as "modern in every respect and easily the finest parish house in the entire St. Cloud diocese."

Once again priest and people set out on a new project for enhancing the parish plant. The rectory was completed in the autumn of 1907 and before the snows had scarcely melted construction began on the new convent. The Sisters who had given so much to the parish and had served without discontent or disillusion were still living in the original tattered and torn convent-school built in 1878. The school children were being taught in the old church renovated into a school. Directly to the east on the site of the present convent, the pastor and people set to work building a convent. In its day it was elegant and all that a Sister's house should be. Forty-five years later, however, it had served its purpose well but was showing the signs of old age. In the 1950's the Sisters joked about the assistant pastor who would come to their chapel to offer Mass one day a week. "I know when you are coming, Father," one said. "I can hear you before I see you." When asked why, she replied, "The stairway creaks with age." By late autumn the convent was completed and the Sisters moved into their new home.

For the past decade St. Boniface had been engaged in a continual and, surely to some, a weary building program. Father Richter, his assistant pastor and the Sisters all felt the same way. It was time to pause, catch one's breath and figuratively return to the desert to refurbish the spiritual life of the parish and individuals. There was need, of course, for a new school — but that could wait. But wait it did not.

Disaster — or perhaps a blessing in disguise — struck St. Mary's parish the night of January 5, 1910. The disaster was that the school burned to the ground as quickly as a moth is cremated when he flies into a fire. The blessing was that the building was empty and no one was injured. Another blessing was necessity again proved to be the mother not of invention in this case but of initiative. After a few days of shuffling and borrowing and a great assist from the Melrose public school district, classes for the St. Boniface school were resumed in the basement of the church.

Back to the drawing boards went the pastor, the lay committee, the Sisters and once again the sterling spirit of the people of St. Boniface parish rose to the call of duty. No doubt it was Father Richter who demanded that the new school must be the best in the area. With an expenditure of $45,000 it proved to be just that. The architect and contractor, with suggestions from the priests, the lay committee and the Sisters, incorporated into its construction and furnishings the latest and the best in school design. Many of the members of the parish recalled the struggle and sacrifice they endured to preserve their school and they were now determined to have the best. When completed the spacious and ornate structure was prepared to accommodate 450 pupils. Once again pastor and people experienced a great joy in bringing to completion another milestone in the life of the parish when the sparkling new school opened its doors in 1913. Two of the all-time great teachers who served the children so exceptionally well in St. Boniface School together would represent a total of 105 years teaching in the same school. They were

Sister Celsa, O.S.B. who taught for sixty years and Sister Ada Nordick, O.S.B. who taught for forty-five years.

St. Boniface choir was for many years the pride and joy of the parish, for it represented the innate love of the German people for music as well as their pride in lavish ceremonials. One of the early choir members, Mary Borget Tise, recalled that she joined the choir in 1899 at the age of fifteen and sang in the choir for four years, but then was forced to retire at that time because married women were not allowed to be choir members. She recalled that during these years Frank Weiser was both organist and director and was assisted by John Kraker at times as organist. Other members of the choir were Frank Mohs, who on occasion also acted as director, Matthew Nathe, Alexander Wolders, John Vogel, Christine Kramer Moritz, Jennie Weiser Capser, Mary Albers Blossingham, Minnie Lampert Wood, Lena Kolb Ochs, Regina Wampach Rosicki and Anna Grine. All of these early members of the choir are deceased with the exception of Mary Tise.

In succeeding decades the choir continued to flourish under the exceptional direction of Sister Dignata, O.S.B. who served as director for many years. During many of these years Mr. Schiltz served as organist and members of the Wolter and Meyer families were the mainstays of the choir. The excellence of St. Boniface senior choir was recognized throughout the diocese. Another prominent member of the choir during this time was Dr. Harold Roelike.

Another era in the history of the parish choir occured in August, 1951 with the coming of Sister William, O.S.B. The mixed choir was dissolved and Sister William organized a ladies' choir, acting as both organist and director. Four years later the mixed choir was introduced, with twelve men volunteering to join the choir. Throughout the years the members of the choir have always manifested a comradeship and generosity seldom seen in other organizations.

Once again priest and people thought they would enjoy a well-deserved respite from their labors. Once again they were summoned to action. This, however, was not a task to be overcome but a labor of love. While the new school was in the process of being built the pastor and his people received the news in 1912 that Father Richter had been elevated to the rank of a prelate with the title of Right Reverend Monsignor. His labors, as well as his pastoral zeal had not escaped the attention of Bishop Trobec and at the latter's request Pope Pius X conferred this honor upon him. He accepted it then, as so many have done since that time, with the observation that this honor was more for his people than himself. Secretly, however, he enjoyed every moment of wearing the sacred purple.

World War I came and Monsignor Richter, although born in Westphalia, Germany was as patriotic as any other American. He urged his people to be active in supporting the American cause and took an active part in promoting every activity that promoted the war effort. In 1917 his assistant, Father Sebastian Schirmers volunteered to serve in the United States Army after serving the parish for five years. The headline in the local newspaper proclaimed, "Monstrous Gathering Honors Rev. S. Schirmers Sunday Eve." In his opening remarks Monsignor Richter said the gathering had a twofold purpose; first, to honor Father Schirmers and secondly to serve as a loyalty meeting. In his address he also mentioned that there were fifty-six young men from the parish serving under the colors of their country. Father John Bussmann shortly thereafter became the assistant pastor of St. Boniface parish.

The years were running short for the "patriarch of Melrose." He was fifty-eight years old in 1921 and although not old as is normally reckoned both his huge girth and many years of hard labor had taken their toll. For several years he had been ailing with heart trouble and after several serious attacks he managed to rally his forces and return to his daily round of duties. On December 18, 1921, however, there was no fight left. At nine o'clock in the evening he committed his soul to God and left for his people one of the finest, if not *the* finest parish plant and spirit in the Diocese of St. Cloud. The writer of his obituary stated:

"Among his parishioners Monsignor Richter's ability as a priest was held in high regard. He commanded the love and devotion of all and they willingly and faithfully followed his leadership in building up the church and in behalf of the spiritual welfare of its members. As their spiritual guide, his memory will long remain a cherished treasure."

For three months Father Adelbert Wagner and Father Joseph Snyers, O.S.B. acted as administrators of the parish. In February, 1922 the new pastor appointed was Father Joseph Willenbrink. He, too, was a contrast to his predecessor. Tall and lean, quiet and unassuming, almost shy at times, he was the type of a man whom the parishoners did not expect as a successor to Monsignor Richter. With the Monsignor, however, he shared two important qualities. He was a good administrator and had a deep pastoral concern for his people. He was also the first native-born American to become pastor of St. Boniface parish. Born in Richmond on April 24, 1879 of parents who were among the earliest settlers of Stearns county, he received his primary education in Richmond. After completing his theological studies at St. John's Seminary he was ordained a priest on June 15, 1910. For sixteen months he served as secretary to Bishop Trobec and chaplain at the State Reformatory. From 1912 to 1919 he was pastor in Princeton; two years was pastor in Perham and for a brief period was rector of the Pro-cathedral in St. Cloud. He arrived in Melrose in February, 1922.

The people of St. Boniface parish and the entire community soon realized the kind of man the new pastor was. He took an active part in civic affairs so much so that the editor of the weekly paper at the time of the pastor's death wrote, "Melrose has lost its best citizen and full realization of this great loss can come only in the memory, which will long remain, of this fine, noble man." Never a strong man physically, he continually fought the battle against illness. After serving as pastor for eleven years he was taken to the St. Cloud Hospital with a severe case of pneumonia from which he did not recover. He died on November 17, 1933.

His love for young people and desire to see them enjoy themselves in wholesome recreation prompted him to build the St. Boniface Recreation Hall in 1926. The hall provided a center for parish socials, theatrical productions and a bowling alley. He also saw to the purchase of land adjoining the school and turned it into a large playground for the youngsters of the city. The present St. Boniface school is located on part of that land. The assistant pastors who served with him were: Fathers John Bussman, Paul Kunkel, Joseph Block, Rev. Nicholai, James Kunz, Aloys Kraemer and Adolph Schmidt. Father Schmidt made his home with Father Willenbrink in Perham and was received into the Catholic Church on October 22, 1921. Throughout the years of his seminary training he stayed with Father Willenbrink until the latter's death.

Change was once more a part of the history of St. Boniface parish. Bishop Busch decided to appoint Father Kraemer and Father Schmidt administrators of the parish, a position they held until Father Lambert Haupt was named pastor in 1935. This appointment together with Father Julig's appointment signaled a new chapter in the history of the two parishes of Melrose.

APPENDIX

VITAL STATISTICS OF THE CATHOLIC PARISHES

The first recorded baptism in St. Patrick's parish was Marla Brun on January 1, 1872. The first decade of the parish's existence witnessed fifty-four baptisms. The year 1953 witnessed the largest number of forty-three baptisms. Throughout the years of the parish's existence there was a total of one thousand, two hundred and thirty-two baptisms recorded.

The first recorded marriage in St. Patrick's parish occured on January 24, 1881 between James Dolley and Margaret Shea in the presence of Father Clement Gamache. The most marriages recorded in a given year was fourteen and this occurred in 1948, 1955 and 1956. The total number of marriages performed in the life of the parish was two hundred and forty-six.

The parish existed for twenty-eight years before the first death was recorded and that was Jacob Barrett in 1900. The highest number of deaths recorded was twelve and this took place in 1936 and again in 1956. The total number of recorded deaths was two hundred and seventy-eight.

The first recorded baptism of the four thousand, five hundred and ninety-nine performed in St. Boniface parish was Catherine Borgerding on January 14, 1876 by Father Antony Casper, O.S.B. The great wave of German immigration is reflected in the large number of baptisms performed during the closing decade of the last and the opening decade of the present centuries. Between 1890 and 1900 there were six hundred and fifty-eight baptisms; during the following decade there were eight hundred and five baptisms. The combined total of one thousand, four hundred and sixty-three baptisms during this twenty year period represents more than thirty percent of all the children baptised throughout the eighty-two year history of the parish. The "baby boom" peaked in 1923 with eighty-eight baptisms, the highest number for a given year.

St. Boniface parish also witnessed its share of marriages, with one thousand, one hundred and thirty-four being entered in the record books. The first couple married were Patrick Graham and Ellen Brown on October 9, 1876 with Father Antony Casper, O.S.B., as the witness. The post-war years of World Wars One and Two are reflected by the twenty-nine and twenty-eight marriages in 1920 and 1921 and the thirty-five and thirty-three marriages in 1946 and 1947. No year in the life of the parish witnessed more marriages than the last mentioned.

Throughout the life of St. Boniface parish death also claimed one thousand, four hundred and thirty-seven members. The terrible influenza epidemic of 1918 is reflected in the thirty-six funerals recorded during that year — the highest number of deaths recorded for any year except for the thirty-seven tallied in 1945, reflecting the number of casulties of World War Two.

Since the two parishes were joined in 1958 there have been one thousand, and fifty-five baptisms, with one hundred and nine taking place in 1962; three hundred and ten marriages, with thirty-three occurring in 1961; and four hundred and two deaths, with forty-five recorded in 1963.

VOCATIONS TO THE PRIESTHOOD FROM ST. PATRICK'S PARISH

Reverend Arthur Hoppe
Reverend Henry Miller, O.S.C.

Reverend Joseph Miller

VOCATIONS TO THE PRIESTHOOD FROM ST. BONIFACE'S PARISH

Most Rev. Henry J. Soenneker, D.D.
Reverend Monsignor Joseph Och
Reverend Joseph Wessendorf
Reverend Frederick Hinnenkamp
Reverend Monsignor George Rauch
Reverend James Walcher
Reverend Joseph Wolter
Reverend Benedict Petermeier
Reverend John Westekemper
Reverend Robert Nathe
Reverend Norbert Hinnenkamp
Reverend Adolph Schmidt

Reverend Lawrence Bohnen, S.V.D.
Reverend Oscar Schoenberg, O.S.C.
Reverend Robert Schulzetenberg
Reverend Bernard Mischke, O.S.C.
Reverend Thomas Meyer
Reverend John Braun
Reverend Virgil Braun
Reverend John Igers, O.S.C.
Reverend Ralph Broker
Reverend Monsignor Francis Zitur
Reverend Monsignor Joseph Woeste

VOCATIONS TO THE SISTERHOODS FROM ST. PATRICK'S PARISH

Benedictine Sisters

Sister Viola Schlicht, O.S.B.
Sister Joel Stalboerger, O.S.B.
Sister Leola Kennedy, O.S.B.
Sister Patrice Donohue, O.S.B.
Sister Josella Schlicht, O.S.B.

Franciscan Sisters

Sister M. Joseph Rauch, O.S.F.
Sister M. Aloysius Petermeier, O.S.F.
Sister M. Valeria Soenneker, O.S.F.
Sister M. Elizabeth Soenneker, O.S.F.
Sister M. Agnes Soenneker, O.S.F.
Sister M. Zita Zitur, O.S.F.

Sister M. Julitta Westendorf, O.S.F.
Sister M. Dominica Stadtherr, O.S.F.
Sister M. Helen Niehaus, O.S.F.
Sister M. Venard Niehaus, O.S.F.
Sister M. Inez Niehaus, O.S.F.
Sister M. Cecile Meyer, O.S.F.
Sister M. Consolata Weisser, O.S.F.
Sister M. Paula Pohlmann, O.S.F.
Sister M. Janet Kunkel, O.S.F.
Sister M. Bernadette Meyer, O.S.F.
Sister M. Rita Kraemer, O.S.F.
Sister M. Jean Marie Kunkel, O.S.F.
Sister M. Lorraine Olmscheid, O.S.F.
Sister M. Margaret Marthaler, O.S.F.
Sister M. Elizabeth Ohmann, O.S.F.

VOCATIONS TO THE SISTERHOODS FROM ST. BONIFACE'S PARISH

Benedictine Sisters

Sister Chrysette Primus, O.S.B.
Sister Colette Primus, O.S.B.
Sister Dominica Borgerding, O.S.B.
Sister Edna (Priscilla) Otte, O.S.B.
Sister Jane (Jeron) Igers, O.S.B.
Sister Louise (Godfrey)
    Enneking, O.S.B.
Sister Lucia Zinniel, O.S.B.
Sister Lynnette Primus, O.S.B.
Sister Marilyn (Kennan) Athmann,
    O.S.B.

Sister Oranda Primus, O.S.B.
Sister Pacifica Beste, O.S.B.
Sister Prudentia Taylor, O.S.B.
Sister Remberta Westkaemper, O.S.B.
Sister Ulmara Woeste, O.S.B.
Sister Anna (Lou Ann) Moening,
    O.S.B.
Sister Ephrem Hollermann, O.S.B.
Sister Kayleen Nohner, O.S.B.
Sister Shirley Nohner, O.S.B.

FORMER ASSISTANT PASTORS OF ST. BONIFACE PARISH

The Reverend Fathers:
  George Rauch
  Matthias Hoffmann
  Eugene Scheuer
  Sebastian Schirmers
  John Bussmann
  Adalbert Wagner
  Joseph Snyers, O.S.C.
  Paul Kunkel
  Joseph Bloch
  Res. Nicholai
  James Kunz

Aloys Kraemer
Adolph Schmidt
Claude Schwinghammer
Vincent Huebsch
Edward Ramacher
William Kloeckner
Harold Kost
Frank Ebner
Vincent Yzermans
Irvin Braun
Edwin Kraemer

FORMER HOUSEKEEPERS OF ST. PATRICK'S PARISH

Gertrude Nickolaus
Mrs. Anna Kilian
Olivia Weisser
Margaret Moeller

Teresa Vernevald
Monica Woeste
Mrs. Kelley
Mrs. Nettie Meyer

FORMER HOUSEKEEPERS OF ST. BONIFACE'S PARISH

Mrs. Otto Kuklinski
Susan Bohner
Teresa Vernevald
Mary Kettler
Angeline Willenbring
Helen Blonigan
Vica Stilling
Olivia Peters
Margaret Moeller

Lena Moeller
Agnes Duevel
Irene Casey
Agnes Borgerding
Marian Lux
Margaret Worms
Margaret Hemmisch
Alvina Stilling

HOUSEKEEPERS FROM THE MELROSE AREA

Agnes Duevel
Sally Jacobs
Adeline Klein
Alma Kramer
Loretta Schwieters
Bertha Sonnen

Catherine Sonnen
Alvina Stilling
Vica Stilling
Monica Woeste
Freida Tinkev

RETIRED HOUSEKEEPERS FROM THE MELROSE AREA

Catherine Ahrens
Margaret Hemmisch
Catherine Kuhlmann
Nettie Meyer
Othielda Primus

Olivia Peters
Anna Rauch
Nettie Timmers
Olivia Weisser

DECEASED HOUSEKEEPERS FROM THE MELROSE AREA

Susan Bohnen
Sophia Hiltner
Mary Hinnenkamp
Mary Kettler

Clara Schulzetenberg
Pauline Stilling
Margaret Worms

CHAPTER THREE

ONE SMALL STEP FORWARD AT A TIME

One would have to had lived through the drought and the dust storms of the mid-1930's to know what effect they had on a man. It was not the sickly feeling in the stomach at seeing your own crops wither and die before your eyes. Nor was it the dizziness in the mind caused by not knowing where the next penny was coming from to put bread on the table for your family. Nor was it the nervous feeling you got when you had to pass by the doors of the bank or the doors of your many creditors. It was, rather, the crushing of the spirit, pulverizing it like tiny kernels of corn into a powder and blowing away the spirit of man like the winds blew away the top soil of the earth.

That was one experience. Another was the receipt of a letter or a telegram or a phone call in the middle of the night. Goose pimples would break out on the mother and father for fear that their son must go to war and, even worse, might never return from war. Rationing and retread tires and curtailment of electrical power one could tolerate. But the absence of a son or daughter from the home and the gnawing fear that he or she might never return eroded the spirit.

The giddiness of the 1950's was also a debilitating experience. The war was over; money was plentiful and for millions of people it was the call to "eat, drink and be merry" — and that is exactly what they did. But a life of pleasure, an entire pattern of human existence built upon one "good time" after another forming a circle of pleasure for pleasure's sake was not what God intended. Nor was it good for man as man. Pleasure stiffled the spirit in man and man cannot live without a spirit.

Depression and dust storms, war and conscription, pleasure and a "good time" all combined to rob man of his spirit. This was not only the problem in far away Paris or London or New York but also the problem in Stearns county and Melrose. Man needed to restore a sense

331

of spiritual values. Man needed the nourishment of a sound spiritual life to recall himself to his proper role in life. Man needed to find his soul which through suffering and hardship, pleasure and hedonism, he was on the brink of losing.

This was, in the late 1930's, and to a certain extent remains, man's central problem: To find his spirit, to find his place in God's universe, or as they say today, to find his own identity. This was the central problem that faced the pastor of St. Patrick's parish from 1938 to 1958. This was the same problem facing the three pastors of St. Boniface for the same twenty year period. Even at the conclusion of this narrative the problem will not be solved for it is the perennial problem of men seeking themselves in God and in their fellow-men. In this sense, this narrative is a very poor story for every story should have an ending, either sad or glad. But this story cannot end here and now for this problem will be with mankind until the end of the world.

One major change took place in the Diocese of St. Cloud during this period.

Priests, religious and people throughout the diocese greeted with joy the appointment of Father Peter Bartholome, pastor of St. John's church, Rochester, as the coadjutor bishop of the Diocese of St. Cloud. Bishop Bartholome came to the diocese in 1942 not only to assist the aging Bishop Busch but also to bring a new vigor and strength to the religious life of the area. Upon Bishop Busch's death in 1954 Bishop Bartholome automatically succeeded to the See of St. Cloud. Bishop Bartholome brought with him to St. Cloud three major objectives. First, he wished to see a parochial school in as many of the parishes as possible, for from his reading and experience he knew very well the advantages of a Catholic education. Secondly, son of the soil that he was, he maintained an interest in rural life throughout his episcopacy and was a frequent speaker at national and state rural life conventions. Finally, he was a zealous advocate of family life. Seldom would he speak publicly without some reference to family life. Under his leadership the Marriage Preparation Course was inaugurated and married couples' retreats became an annual event in most parishes. Bishop Bartholome was coadjutor bishop and ordinary of the diocese throughout this entire period of our narrative.

ST. PATRICK'S PARISH

In 1938 Father Francis Julig came to St. Patrick's after being "loaned" as an assistant pastor at St. Michael's church, St. Michael, in the archdiocese of St. Paul. At the time St. Patrick's was a poor struggling parish with only a handful of parishioners. In his own quiet, unobtrusive manner he set out to instill a spirit into the members of the parish. Many of them were still suffering from the effects of the depression. Some of them looked with jaundiced eyes at the splendid plant that had been built at St. Boniface's. A few of them were indifferent in the fulfillment of their religious duties. The children of the parish who were not enrolled in St. Boniface's school were receiving very poor and intermittent religious instructions. There was very little money in the parish treasury. The rectory and the cement block-stuccoed church-school-auditorium combination were badly in need of repair.

The people welcomed him and as time passed grew to love him because of his truly priestly heart and zeal. They responded to his appeals for assistance. The parish first rejuvenated the existing C.C.D. religious instruction program. Women of the parish volunteered to help. Classes were held on a release-time basis. Within two years all the children of the parish who were not enrolled at St. Boniface were, practically speaking, enrolled in St. Patrick's C.C.D. religious instruction program. That program was kept alive and active for the next twenty years.

A parish cannot properly function with only the pastor, for a parish is made for people. In these early years Father Julig set his mind to the rejuvenation of parish organizations and societies as well as national organizations. The Men's Club and the Christian Mothers became active, decision-making bodies of the parish. The pastor urged his people to join such city-wide organizations as the Knights of Columbus, The Columbian Squires and the Daughters of Isabella.

The church in the basement of St. Patrick's building was completely redecorated as well as the rest of the building. The first floor was used as classrooms and small meeting rooms and the third floor was rented as a meeting place for such organizations as the Veterans of Foreign Wars, the Daughters of Isabella and others. As time passed the rivalry between Germans and Irish diminished, as well as the discontent between city people and rural people. Many attribute this lessening and eradication of tensions between these groups as the result of Father Julig's manner. His people learned more from how he acted than from what he said. As time passed the parish grew as more and more new industry located in Melrose. The love of the people for their pastor was demonstrated when in 1950 they took up a collection in order to send him to Rome for the Holy Year.

No sooner had he returned than talk began about building a new St. Patrick's church. The parish was debt-free and had a little money in reserve. Father Julig gained a new lease on life. The spiritual life of the parish was well in order. The parish spirit was strong and faithful. The education of children, the meetings of societies, the physical condition of the existing plant all seemed to be in order. The people were becoming more and more eager to have their own new church and were generous in their contributions. An architect was called in to provide some preliminary sketches. These were approved by the pastor, trustees and the building committee. The architect returned with his plans. All was going well.

Father Julig took the plans to Bishop Bartholome for approval. The bishop hedged; he did not know whether or not it was wise to build at this time. He postponed giving approval. Time passed. Both pastor and people were becoming anxious. Once again Father Julig went to see the bishop. This time the bishop dropped a bomb that nearly crushed Father Julig. He did not think there should be two churches in Melrose but only one. He thought Father Julig would be ideally suited to be the pastor of the two parishes combined into one. The name of the new parish would be St. Mary's. This writer recalls going to lunch with Father Julig the day he received the change in plans. I do not know what we ordered for lunch that day. I do know that neither of us ate very much.

ST. BONIFACE PARISH

When Father Lambert J. Haupt assumed the pastorate of St. Boniface parish he faced that same problems that later Father Julig did in 1938. Father Haupt's, however, were different on two scores. First, he came to Melrose in 1935 at the height of the depression and the drought; secondly, with a parish numbering almost four times the size of St. Patrick's his problems were that much the greater. Three assistant pastors served with Father Haupt at various times during the seven years of his pastorate in Melrose. They were Fathers Adolph Schmidt, Claude Schwinghammer and Vincent Huebsch.

Throughout these seven years no major improvements were made for two reasons. First, the parish plant was in good repair and secondly, these were the hard years for everyone. The parish hall built during Father Willenbrink's time proved to be a social hub of the community and good use was made of its facilities. Although money was scarce, people had to learn how to make good times for themselves. This they did. "Karten-spielen" was the great pass time for older people, as was baseball for the younger set.

After seven years Father Haupt assumed the pastorate of Our Lady Help of Christians parish in St. Augusta. His successor was a man well known to the community. Twenty-five years earlier St. Boniface parish had a "monstrous gathering" in his honor before he assumed duties in the chaplains' corps of the United States Army. Father Sebastian J. Schirmers was well loved by the people of Melrose. Judging from records and interviews, he was the best loved pastor the parish ever had. And he loved people. He enjoyed visiting with people and they enjoyed visiting with him. Throughout the diocese he was recognized as one of the best and most-in-demand preachers and speakers. The people of St. Boniface also knew this and would come to hear him faithfully. One of his more eloquent sermons is published in the appendix to this chapter. Four priests served as his assistant during his term of office. They were Fathers Vincent Huebsch, Edward Ramacher, William Kloeckner and Harold Kost.

Father Schirmers, however, by the time he returned to Melrose was not a well man. World War I had taken its toll of him and in honesty he told himself that the burden of St. Boniface's was too much for him. The local editor wrote as follows about Father Schirmers' leaving:

"The members of the St. Boniface parish were surprised and moved with deep regret Sunday to learn from their pastor, Very Rev. S. J. Schirmers, that he is to leave them. He goes to Urbank on July 24 to become pastor of the Sacred Heart parish there. . . .

"Father Schirmers has had four very active and strenuous years in serving his parish since he came to Melrose from Perham in August, 1942. To him it was a surprise and disappointment to learn recently that the state of his health did not permit that he continue his pastorate of the large St. Boniface church."

A man well known to the people of Melrose made his third return to Melrose in the course of his thirty-five years as a priest. Father Matthias Hoffmann served first as assistant pastor under Monsignor Richter from 1908 to 1909; as pastor of St. Patrick's parish from 1929-1932 and in August, 1942 became pastor of St. Boniface parish. A native of Trier, Germany (and he was always proud of the fact) he emigrated to the United States, took his theological studies at St. John's Seminary and was ordained to the priesthood April 2, 1907. He was overjoyed to return to Melrose, as most priests have a soft spot in their hearts for the parish to which they are first assigned, so it was with Father Hoffmann.

When appointed pastor of St. Boniface parish Father Hoffmann also was given charge of the mission, St. Bernard's parish, at Ward Springs. Located on the southern shores of Little Birch Lake, Ward Springs at one time had the possibilities of developing into a good size community because it was one of the stops on the Soo Line railroad.

As a matter of fact, in its earlier days the community boasted a hotel, an elevator, a general store and a saloon, a small livestock yards for shipping and a lumberyard. It was also a popular summer resort area for people from Melrose and Sauk Centre. The community even boasted a horse-drawn taxi service. When J. W. Ward, depot agent in Sauk Centre, discovered the beauty of the lake and the woods he took a more than usual interest in the place that was then called Birch Lake City. He purchased some land and encouraged his acquaintances to do so. Three springs on his property were believed to have certain medicinal properties. Ward bottled this water and sold it. Thinking the community would grow Ward approached the Todd county surveyor and asked that the land, which he would donate, be surveyed. At that time he also requested that the name of the town be changed from Birch Lake City to Ward Springs. The community around Kraker's store felt it best to become a part of Ward Springs and thus the name of the community about a mile southwest of the three springs came to be called Ward Springs. The village, however, did not grow but in the course of years, rather, declined. Father Hoffmann however assumed the responsibility for it and from time to time would offer Mass for the small group of families who attended St. Bernard's church.

Only in latter life did he admit how disappointed he was, for so many faces and places had changed since 1908 and 1929. He covered his disappointment by a gruff attitude and approach to people and those who pierced that wall found behind it the most gentle of souls. Children were frightened by him, but he was even more frightened by children. He loved them very much and could not understand why they were afraid of him. Those of the older generation who knew him well understood and knew that he was the same good, zealous priest that they knew ten and thirty-five years ago. One of his habits that made his priestly soul shine forth was visiting the sick. As long as he was able he would call upon some one, or two or three sick people every day.

His delights were priestly delights. Nothing would please him more than a good visit with a priest friend and neighbor. Those occasions demanded a good cigar and a glass of Mosel wine. His delights were pastoral delights. The four greatest delights of the years in Melrose were the visit of the Pilgrim statue of Fatima; the episcopal consecration of a son of the parish, Henry J. Soenneker; the building of a convent for the Sisters and his own investiture as a domestic prelate with the title of Right Reverend Monsignor. He had lesser joys as well, such as attending receptions of those whose marriage he witnessed in the parish; of walking to the cemetery on a Sunday evening and reciting the Rosary with parishoners standing around. His dogs provided great personal enjoyment (he preferred Black Labradors!).

The Pilgrim statue of Our Lady of Fatima arrived in Melrose on Saturday, September 16, 1950, accompanied by Monsignor William McGrath and Father Stringer of Ontario, Canada. It was placed in St. Boniface church until about seven o'clock and then moved in procession to the Melrose park for a holy hour of prayers, recitation of the Rosary and Benediction of the Blessed Sacrament. Delegations from all the parishes in the deanery were present. The following day prayers, recitation of the Rosary and Holy Mass were conducted for the city and the deanery. The Fatima shrine that is located south of the present rectory, and cared for by the senior citizens, is a result and a reminder of this religious experience in Melrose.

Father Hoffmann was a priest always seeking vocations to the religious and priestly life. Although generous in many things, he was most generous in contributing to the education of priests and sisters. His joy knew no bounds when he heard the news that a son of the parish had been named a bishop. Henry J. Soenneker had only a few months previously been named a Monsignor on the occasion of his silver anniversary of ordination. He chose St. Boniface to be the church in which that ceremony would be held. Father Hoffmann again was delighted when the new Bishop of Owensboro asked to offer his first pontifical Mass in St. Mary's church. For many years the new bishop assisted Father Hoffmann with Christmas and Easter services. Father Hoffmann considered the bishop a priestly son.

The wise Sisters in St. Boniface school appreciated Father Hoffmann very much for they knew that he always held the best interests of the Sisters and children uppermost in his mind. Those who did not see through his sometimes rough and casual manner were truly afraid of him. One of the things he wanted to do most before he retired was to secure a suitable home for the Sisters. That joy was his in 1956 when construction on the new convent began with himself turning the first shovel of dirt. That joy was consummated the following September 27 when Bishop Bartholome blessed the convent. The same evening the Bishop conferred the sacrament of Confirmation on fifty-one children of the parish. It did not escape Father Hoffmann's roving eyes to notice a Henry Soenneker in the class, a young man named after his uncle, the Bishop.

There are few priests who wanted to be a monsignor more than Matthias Hoffmann. He went, one day before Christmas to the Bishop. He recounted all that he had done in the fourteen years since he served as pastor of St. Boniface and felt that the Most Reverend Bishop did not appreciate his labors. On the contrary, the Bishop did appreciate his work and from his drawer drew out the document from Rome. It informed Father Hoffmann that he had been elevated as a domestic prelate with the title of Right Reverend Monsignor. That afternoon the new Monsignor drove home a more humble man. He was invested with the purple the following January 25, 1955. The new honor and title gave him a new lease on life. Three years later, on May 24, 1957 he celebrated the golden jubilee of ordination to the priesthood. Shortly after he took a three month trip to Europe to visit relatives and friends and view the places in which he lived as a boy. He returned home, a bit weary, but more overjoyed than ever.

Monsignor Hoffmann did not fail to have his share of troubles. His one overriding ambition was to build a new rectory for the parish. The people were against it and in no soft speech let him know exactly how they stood. The plans were already drawn up by the architect and the Monsignor felt until the end that the new rectory would shortly become a reality. When the Bishop did not approve it, the Monsignor bowed obediently and set the plans aside. (To this day no one has ever found the plans for that would-be rectory.) He also had differences with some members of the parish because of the recreation hall — a building that held many fond memories for two generations of the people. He had been advised by engineers that the building was no longer safe for occupancy and so it was closed. Accordingly, he wanted it torn down and dismantled. Again a good number of the parishioners opposed him for, in their minds they thought with a little repair work the hall could be saved. Monsignor Hoffmann stood his ground and the building was never used again, never repaired, but eventually demolished.

In 1958 Monsignor Hoffmann retired. He moved into the rectory of St. Patrick's parish and was aided by his faithful housekeeper, Miss Alvina Stilling. He took great interest in visiting and being visited by people. He also was proud of his garden and, of course, his ever faithful dog.

APPENDIX

THE MOST BEAUTIFUL FLAG

Sebastian J. Schirmers

We are assembled to dedicate a Service Flag; to bless it; a blessing intended for those whom it represents.

It is a memorial erected by love and gratitude, and it directs our thoughts to our dear ones in the Service, our prayers for their safety and protection, for blessings from above for a victorious return to their homes, to a life of peace and happiness.

It is a Flag. Flags are standards representing a country, a state, a community or even a family. The most glorious of all is the standard of the Cross, which at the end of the world shall appear in the heavens, the victorious sign of the Redeemer, which sixteen centuries ago appeared to Constantine with the promise of victory, "in hoc signo vinces" which three centuries before stood on Calvary in ignominy. Its glory was brought by sacrifice.

The most beautiful Flag is naturally Our Own, the Stars and Stripes which embodies part of the family flag of George Washington. Our Service Flag Is prepared in the National Colors. What a blessing to be a citizen of a truly great and good country. "It is sweet and honorable" says the Roman senator "To die for one's country." Life may be given only for a most worthy and important cause; how many have given it for their homeland or are prepared to give it!

Our country was discovered by sacrifice; fearless of the treacherous vastness of the unexplored waters Columbus sets sail for new worlds to be won for the cross, in danger even from mutiny by his own mariners. Pioneers braved everything, colonists sanctified our country by their blood to make it free; Unionists and Confederates fought a bitter strife, an internal strife, to determine if it should continue One or Divided. For a better world, twenty-five years ago, the fathers of this generation, the fathers of the stars now on this Service Flag, fought and died, and NOW a younger generation equally valiant and loyal is giving ALL, that the universe may not be overrun by brute violence and treachery, but may again become a place where peace-loving men can live peaceful lives.

Men in the service are often referred to as numbers: (as the Savior said that a general before entering upon war will first number his men to see if he may engage the enemy) so are also patients in large hospitals; but each number is a living being, a sufferer from pain, from sleepless nights subject to any kind of treatment prescribed; a number is ordered to the operating room, but a human being appears, a man, a woman, a child recovering or dying. A NUMBER is ordered to a submarine, to a bomber, to a tank, to a pill-box — a number is picked up on "bloody ground" — or someone wore that number! Where is he now? In an improvised hospital, maimed, blind, stunned, torn in limb, or is he buried beneath the debris! A warm heart beat under that number, a heart that prayed to God, a heart that thought of home thousands of miles away, apparently cheerful, so that it should not bring pain and worry to the heart of a loving wife, a mother or semi-orphaned child, who fortunately cannot understand the hardships that number had to undergo, who cannot realize the labor, the privations, fatigue, hunger and thirst, fear and strife, pain and wounds, often worse than death itself.

A sad number wearily spending the days in enemy captivity — days too long to be measured — hard, unnatural to a free born American, seemingly unending. Laborers buried in a mine, awaiting rescue, experience such hours. Yet these numbers fought for their country, they vowed all, they gave all and should come back safe.

These numbers are taken from our state, from our community, yes from our very homes. They are not abstract but real and alive. A mother's Rosary is engaged in asking the Virgin's blessing upon one; for another an aged father offers his toil and labor; a loving sister, a kind brother, a dear relative calls on the Saints of God to protect and bring home safe a third one; innocent children talk to Jesus about a father, missed, oh so much; a true sweetheart continues resignedly her hard employment hoping for better days; a faithful and loving wife carries on in loneliness, torn by the uncertainty of her husband's fate, weary of the responsibilities of management of home and children in health and sickness; loyal and true she turns to her Heavenly Mother and to her God for strength and guidance. "Oh, Peace must come soon!" "NUMBERS on that Service Flag," we want to assure you that we are loyal and true to you. You are not NUMBERS to us, you are flesh and blood from Melrose! In spirit we see you present everywhere; your Church here calls together all your loved ones, and oh, how faithfully and unceasingly do they gather here, at Holy Mass, and Communion, at other services, pouring forth prayers for your well being, for your speedy and victorious return.

You Men and Women in the Service: Today we dedicate this flag to you; by it we keep you ever present before us; by it we place you all under the powerful protection of Mary. We count 218 Blue Stars alive, active, most of them fighting. Several are prisoners of war; oh, Virgin Mary support them, their lot is heavy! We also see Three Gold Stars: Lt. Leo Braun, Ensign Juletta Niehaus, T-Sgt. Aloysious Hollermann. Their sacrifice was accepted. We plant a Gold Star. God has better things to offer them. "Greater love than this no man hath, that a man lay down his life for his friends." They did, animated by the spirit of the Master, who gave His life for us. They were human, they had plans for earth, they hoped to live and carry them out; life could have given them much more than it did; but real life is eternal in heaven. In deep reverence we remember them, we pray for them, may God reward them, immortal is the crown of Heavenly Glory.

THE PAST IS PRELUDE
TO THE FUTURE

Remember O Most Holy Mary,
That never was it known
That anyone who fled to thy protection,
Was left unaided.

Memorare — St. Bernard.

On Sunday, August 9, 1958 the following letters were read from the pulpits in St. Boniface and St. Patrick's parish. They deserve to be recorded for posterity.

August 9, 1958

To the People of St. Boniface Parish in Melrose:

About a year and a half ago I announced the dissolution of St. Patrick's Parish of Melrose as a parish. With the resignation of your pastor, the Right Reverend Monsignor Matthias Hoffmann, as pastor of St. Boniface Parish, we are now realizing this change. Father Francis Julig, the pastor of St. Patrick's Parish, has been appointed pastor of St. Boniface Parish. The appointment will take effect on August 18, 1958. Your pastor will retire to the old St. Patrick's rectory to spend his remaining days in your midst.

It is my intention during the next few weeks to dissolve the legal corporations of St. Boniface and St. Patrick's and to form a new corporation, and the new parish will be dedicated to Our Blessed Lady. It will be called St. Mary's Parish of Melrose under the title of Her Immaculate Conception. The twentieth century is the century of Our Blessed Lady. She is becoming increasingly recognized throughout the entire world, and naming the new parish of Melrose in Her honor is only giving due recognition to the unique position that She occupies in the world at the present time. I am sure that She will bring many blessings to your families.

We intend to use old St. Patrick's Church for weekday Masses during the school year so as to give the high school children and the teachers an opportunity of daily Mass and Communion. I ask all of you to cooperate fully with Father Julig in the work that he will be doing during the years ahead.

Asking God to bless you, I am

Sincerely yours in Christ,
Peter W. Bartholome, D.D.,
Bishop of St. Cloud

August 9, 1958

To the People of St. Patrick's Parish in Melrose:

About a year and half ago I announced to you at the time of Confirmation that St. Patrick's Parish would be dissolved as a parish. Your pastor, Father Julig, has been appointed to St. Boniface Parish.

It is our intention to continue using the church of St. Patrick during the school year for weekday Masses for the convenience of the high school children and the teachers in the Melrose public school. There will be no Sunday Masses in St. Patrick's Church at any time after August 17. Monsignor Hoffmann, who has resigned St. Boniface Parish, shall take up residence in the St. Patrick's parish house. He will have the Privilege of a Private Chapel in his house.

It is my intenton to dissolve the legal corporations of both parishes and to form a new corporation and to dedicate the new parish in honor of Our Blessed Lady and call it St. Mary's under the title of Her Immaculate Conception. Many blessings will come to all the people because the parish is dedicated in honor of Our Blessed Lady, Who is coming into Her own during this twentieth century all over the world. This change of title will only be another recognition of the unique position She occupies in the world.

These changes have been deemed necessary in order to bring about greater unity in the Catholic life of the community of Melrose and the additional consideration of the shortage of priests has also urged me to make this change.

Asking God to bless you, I am

Sincerely yours in Christ,
Peter W. Bartholome, D.D.,
Bishop of St. Cloud

ACKNOWLEDGEMENTS

This book could not have been written in so brief a period of time without the collaboration of numerous people. Although it is impossible to mention all who have assisted, the author would be remiss in his obligation not to mention the following:

1. Mr. Russell Friedley and the staff of the Minnesota Historical Society for assistance and direction:

2. Mr. Jesse Lovelace, Mr. Joseph Leach and Mr. Lawrence Van-Havermaet for writing, researching and supplying materials for the first chapter:

3. The members of the community of Melrose for supplying information concerning the geneological trees of their families:

4. Mrs. Russell Lambert and Mrs. Herman Hellermann, Jr. for contacting organizations and individuals and supplying information concerning the organizations and industries and events of the city and surrounding community:

5. Mr. Norbert Weiss for writing and researching most of the material concerning the schools of Melrose:

6. Mr. Peter Jung for writing and researching a good deal of the material concerning athletics in Melrose:

7. Mr. Henry Moser for writing and researching the material concerning the Melrose State Bank and the merchants and businessmen of Melrose for supplying the information concerning business in Melrose:

8. Mr. Gerald A. Klasen for researching and supplying the information concerning prohibition and Mrs. Herman Hellermann for researching and supplying the information concerning the 4-H Clubs:

9. Reverend Raymond Lang and Reverend Ralph Keller for their assistance in the chapters concerning the churches:

10. Mr. Walter Carlson for use of the bound copies of the *Melrose Beacon*:

11. Mrs. John Goihl for assisting with typing, transcriptions and other necessary office tasks and Mrs. Lucille Vincent for keeping body and soul together:

12. Miss Nell Sullivan who assisted the author both spiritually and materially throughout a good deal of the writing of this book:

13. Mr. Richard Jung, Mr. James Schiely and Mrs. Gerald A. Klasen who acted as photographers; to the Minnesota Historical Society who supplied photographs; and to the numerous individuals who offered photographs for this volume:

14. Provost W. A. Drummond of Melrose, Scotland for supplying information and photographs:

15. Sister Clara Antony, O.S.B. of St. Benedict's Priory and Sister Maurice Bellefeuille, O.S.F. for supplying information concerning the Benedictine and Franciscan Sisters from the Melrose parishes:
16. Miss Alvina Stilling who supplied a "gold mine" of information in the pages of scrapbooks that she had kept throughout the years:
17. Mrs. Marson Duerr who typed the manuscript for the printer and was assisted by Miss Ruth Wiechmann and Mrs. Vernon Klasen:
18. Reverend Wilfred Illies for reading the manuscript and offering suggestions and opened his home often as a haven of refuge for a weary writer:
19. Mr. Alfons A. Yzermans, Mr. Louis C. Yzermans, Mrs. Eugene DeWitt, Mrs. Frank Fehrmann, Jr., Mrs. Raymond Langevin, members of my family, for putting up with the author and tolerating his absences and omissions during the time of writing this volume.
20. Reverend Robert Harren for supplying information from the St. Cloud Diocesan Chancery and Miss Rosemary Borgert for supplying information and photographs from the *St. Cloud Visitor*:

V. A. Y.

Mr. Norbert Weiss expresses his appreciation to the following for the assistance they provided in writing the chapter on the schools of Melrose:

> August Eveslage
> John Provinzino
> Walter Carlson
> Mrs. Nora Eveslage
> Mrs. Alma Pappenfus
> Mrs. Irma Yaeger
> Mr. and Mrs. Raymond Borgerding
> Mr. and Mrs. Anthony Niehaus
> Mrs. Joseph Tise
> Mr. Henry Petermeier
> Mr. Ben Eveslage
> Mr. John Kemper
> Mr. George Kolb
> Mr. and Mrs. Anthony Sunderman
> James Winter
> Joseph Niehaus
> Sister Inez, O.S.F. and Sister Venard, O.S.F.
> Mr. and Mrs. Joseph Zirbes
> Roman Hellermann

Herman Hellermann, Sr.
Carl Ohmann
Mrs. Herman Hellermann, Jr.
Olaf Becker
Mark Rieland
Mrs. P. W. Huntemer

SOURCES

It was not my intention to write a doctoral thesis but merely a narrative that would recount the story of Melrose. For that reason we eliminated all reference to sources in the text. There were, however, many written, oral and published sources upon which we relied for every statement made and these can be easily verified if any reader would like to delve more deeply into a specific subject.

1. *Oral Sources.* These consisted chiefly of interviews with people, most of these taped, who remembered what happened in years gone by. Norbert Weiss conducted many hours of interviews on the subject of the schools; Henry Moser, numerous hours on the subject of the banks; Gerald Klasen, many hours on the subject of prohibition; Vincent Yzermans, many hours on the subjects of rural life, industry, business and church affairs; Mrs. Russell Lambert, many hours on the subjects of organizations and societies and many more hours checking data received. Much of the history of St. Boniface and St. Patrick churches was supplied the author by Monsignor Mathias Hoffmann twenty-two years ago in conversations. After many of these conversations the author made notes and from these notes he drew heavily in chapter two of the second section.

2. *Written Sources.* These chiefly consisted of the parish records in both parishes, annual statements of business establishments, minutes of the meetings of organizations and personal letters loaned to the author by individuals.

3. *Published Sources.*

Ahern, Patrick H., ed., CATHOLIC HERITAGE, Diamond Jubilee Observance of the Province of St. Paul. The Most Reverend Archbishop and Bishops of the Province of St. Paul, St. Paul, Minnesota, 1964.

Barry, Colman J., THE CATHOLIC CHURCH AND GERMAN AMERICANS, Bruce Publishing Company, Milwaukee, 1953.

_____, WORSHIP AND WORK, The Centennial History of St. John's Abbey, St. John's University Press, Collegeville, Minnesota, 1956.

Bergeron, Ernest J., A HISTORY OF THE MELROSE BEACON AND ITS EDITORIAL POLICY, Unpublished Thesis, 1964.

Blecker, Paulin, DEEP ROOTS, One Hundred Years of Catholic Life in Meire Grove, Sentinel Publishing Company, St. Cloud, Minnesota, 1958.

_____, ONE HUNDRED YEARS IN CHRIST, Immaculate Conception Parish: New Munich: 1857-1957, Sentinel Publishing Company, St. Cloud, Minnesota, 1957.

Blegen, Theodore C., MINNESOTA: A HISTORY OF THE STATE, University of Minnesota Press, Minneapolis, Minnesota, 1963.

Ellis, John Tracy, ed., DOCUMENTS OF AMERICAN CATHOLIC HISTORY, Bruce Publishing Company, Milwaukee, 1962.

_____, PERSPECTIVES IN AMERICAN CATHOLICISM, Helicon Press, Baltimore, 1963.

Folwell, William Watts, A HISTORY OF MINNESOTA, 4 vols., The Minnesota Historical Society, St. Paul, Minnesota, 1956.

Luetmer, Sister Nora, O.S.B., THE HISTORY OF CATHOLIC EDUCATION IN THE PRESENT DIOCESE OF ST. CLOUD, MINNESOTA, 1855-1965, Unpublished Thesis, 1970.

McDonald, Sister M. Grace, O.S.B., WITH LAMPS BURNING, St. Benedict's Priory Press, St. Joseph, Minnesota, 1957.

Massmann, John, GERMAN IMMIGRATION TO MINNESOTA, 1850-1890, Unpublished Thesis, 1966.

Mitchell, William Bell, HISTORY OF STEARNS COUNTY MINNESOTA, 2 vols., H. C. Cooper, Jr. & Co., Chicago, 1915.

Morison, Samuel Eliot, THE OXFORD HISTORY OF THE AMERICAN PEOPLE, Oxford University Press, New York, 1965.

Nolan, Hugh J., ed., PASTORAL LETTERS OF THE AMERICAN HIERARCHY, 1792-1970, Our Sunday Visitor, Inc., Huntington, Indiana, 1971.

Thorkelson, Willmar, LUTHERANS IN THE U.S.A., Augsburg Publishing House, Minneapolis, Minnesota, 1969.

Reardon, James Michael, THE CATHOLIC CHURCH IN THE DIOCESE OF ST. PAUL, North Central Publishing Company, St. Paul, Minnesota, 1952.

Yzermans, Vincent A., ed., CATHOLIC ORIGINS OF MINNESOTA, Minnesota Fourth Degree Knights of Columbus, St. Paul, Minnesota, 1961.

PHOTO CREDITS

We express sincere appreciation to the following individuals and societies for their kind permission to reproduce the drawings, illustrations, and photographs which appear in this volume. Acknowledgement is made in the order of first appearance in each illustration section.

Section I: Joseph Leach; Minnesota Historical Society.

Section II: James Schley; Melrose Camera Club; Minnesota Historical Society; Melrose *Beacon;* Hermann Hinnenkamp; Mrs. Thomas Arvig.

Section III: Melrose *Beacon;* Mrs. Thomas Arvig; Minnesota Historical Society; Mrs. Bertha Hofmann; R. C. Borgerding; Frances Tiemann; Mrs. Herman Hellermann Jr.; Oswald Botz; Ed Salzmann; Ernie Winter; Munson Feed Company; Jung's Studio; Henry Loxtercamp.

Section IV: Joseph Rolfzen; Henry Petermeier; George Moening; Sophia Loehr; Leo Schnanhaar; Mrs. Thomas Arvig; Frank Hinnenkamp; Alvina Stilling; Herman Hellermann Jr.; Ursuala Welle; Joseph Wielenberg; Mrs. Joseph Soenneker; Henry Hollermann.

Section V: Collection of Norbert Weiss; Jung's Studio; U. O. Welle; Raymond Borgerding; Frank Hinnenkamp; Mrs. Thomas Arvig; Alvina Stilling; Myron Hall.

Section VI: Melrose *Beacon;* Mrs. Thomas Arvig; Ben Hinnenkamp Jr.; Herman Hellermann Jr.; Minnesota Historical Society; St. Cloud *Visitor;* Kenneth Herzing; Jung's Studio; Joseph Rolfzen; Frank Wielenberg; Richard VanBeck; Ted Welz.

Section VII: Nora Eveslage; Mrs. C. P. Meyer; Alvina Stilling; Minnesota Historical Society; Herman Hellermann Jr.; Mrs. Richard VanBeck; James Schley; *The Kraftsman;* Jung's Studio.

Section VIII: James Schley; St. Cloud *Visitor;* Jung's Studio; Mrs. R. Borgerding; M. Rauch; George Moening; Frank Hinnenkamp; R. C. Borgerding; St. John's Abbey Archives; Herman Hellermann Jr.; Alvina Stilling.